"I WANT TO GO HOME."

Eleven-year-old Eddie Werner tried to struggle as Sam Manzie dragged him to the upstairs bedroom. "Let me go. Let me go," he cried, but it was already too late. Manzie had decided to kill him.

"Get on the floor facedown and close your eyes." Manzie grabbed his alarm clock and ripped it out of the wall. Taking the cord, he stretched it against Eddie's neck.

Eddie began to scream, fighting as the heavier teenager strangled him. Manzie pulled tighter and harder at the cord until the kicks and screams stopped.

Forty minutes later, his rage and energy spent, Manzie finally stopped pulling at the cord around his victim's neck. He kicked Eddie to make sure he was dead. He kicked him a second time, then got a camera to take a picture.

BOOK YOUR PLACE ON OUR WEBSITE AND MAKE THE READING CONNECTION!

We've created a customized website just for our very special readers, where you can get the inside scoop on everything that's going on with Zebra, Pinnacle and Kensington books.

When you come online, you'll have the exciting opportunity to:

- View covers of upcoming books
- Read sample chapters
- Learn about our future publishing schedule (listed by publication month *and author*)
- Find out when your favorite authors will be visiting a city near you
- Search for and order backlist books from our online catalog
- Check out author bios and background information
- Send e-mail to your favorite authors
- Meet the Kensington staff online
- Join us in weekly chats with authors, readers and other guests
- Get writing guidelines
- AND MUCH MORE!

**Visit our website at
http://www.kensingtonbooks.com**

INNOCENT VICTIMS

Brian J. Karem

PINNACLE BOOKS
Kensington Publishing Corp.
http://www.kensingtonbooks.com

Some names have been changed to protect the privacy of individuals connected to this story.

For Pam, Zachary, Brennan, and Wyatt, with love

One

"Has Anyone Seen My Son?"

Monday, September 29, 1997, early evening

For Valerie and Ed Werner, hope was a fragile thing that could be torn asunder by the ringing of either the telephone or their front doorbell. For the last two days, Valerie had openly wept, fidgeted and worried about her oldest son, Eddie. Her husband, Ed, after whom their son had been named, had been her partner in pain as both had tried to find their missing child. There was just one question on their mind that night: where was Eddie?

Outside, in the cool September breeze that caressed mid-New Jersey, searchers and rescue workers were struggling to find an answer to that question.

On September 27, Saturday, eleven-year-old Eddie Werner had taken off on a walking tour of his neighborhood to sell wrapping paper and candy for a school project. Eddie's modest goal was to sell enough to buy a walkie-talkie set he had his heart set on.

After Eddie took off on his quest for sales, a few neighbors reported seeing him and even buying candy from him. But sometime that afternoon he seemed to have disappeared into thin air; no one had seen him since about 5:00 P.M. It had been a nice, bright Saturday, and Eddie had left the house well before sunset. Nothing had seemed out of place in the quiet neighborhood. It was unsettling to its residents that a child could simply vanish without a trace. It didn't seem possible.

Valerie Werner had gone to work as an associate at the nearby Wal-Mart that day and remembered trying to call home to talk to her husband. "I guess it was busy because Ed was calling the police and calling neighbors. I lost it when Ed called me at work and told me Eddie hadn't come home. I knew something was wrong. The cops tried to say that they would find him and he could've just been at a friend's house. I actually remember arguing with a cop. Eddie would never do anything like that. It wasn't him," Valerie said.

That Saturday night, first his parents, then neighbors and eventually police joined in the search for Eddie. Valerie Werner remembered wandering through the woods near her home looking in vain for her lost son. "I was very edgy. We walked through the woods and came out at Wood Lane," right near the home of Nick and Dolores Manzie, two nearby neighbors whom Valerie didn't know. "I just looked around for my son and I was sort of out of it. It was all a blur."

During the next two days, the search grew to hundreds of volunteers who, with the aid of maps, systematically combed through several square miles of surrounding brush, woods and even in the backyards of homes for the small boy.

Inside the Werner home, the fear was palpable. Both Valerie and Ed were holding out hope that their son was OK, but the longer Eddie stayed missing, the harder it was to keep that hope alive. Each time the phone rang, they prayed it was news about their son, but they also feared that it would be news about him. Each time the doorbell rang, the same hope and fear raced through them.

"It was maddening," Ed Werner said later. "I didn't know how we could function under that pressure."

Valerie Werner had been close to the breaking limit since Eddie had disappeared. She was seen wandering through her neighborhood with a photo of her son, querying anyone who happened by: "Have you seen my son?" Then she would hold up the picture. Some neighbors thought she was a broken woman. A few cried as they thought about their own children.

Compounding their concern were the police officers who seemed to be everywhere. They even began to suspect Ed Werner might have done something to his son. There were no clues to suspect him, but investigators know a parent intent on harm sometimes will show their child a good day before they assault or kill them. Ed had said the day he spent with Eddie prior to the boy's disappearance was among the best he'd ever had with his son.

"I remember I came home and just fell down in the bed exhausted," Ed Werner said after the first day of searching. "I couldn't go anymore. That's when the cops came in and they started questioning me. I guess they figured I'd crack if I was so tired."

He didn't mind the questions, Werner explained, and he understood that he himself might be a suspect. He sat up in the bed and tried to think. All he wanted to do was help. All he wanted was to find his son.

The cops continued to question him. "You're big Ed. He's little Ed," one of the cops said. "You're one and the same. Tell us where he is. You have to know."

Ed Werner wanted to help, but he knew they were trying to coerce a confession out of him. The painful thing for Ed Werner was not knowing where his son Eddie was. Maybe as a father he *did* know something. Maybe he *could* find his son. He racked his brain trying to think and then agreed to take the police around to Eddie's favorite hangouts. The cops may have suspected Ed Werner had harmed his own son and were trying to coerce him into giving that fact up. They may have even thought that when Ed Werner agreed to take them around to Eddie's hangouts he would take them to his son's body. But Ed Werner took their questions in a completely different direction. "I never got offended. I didn't think that way," Ed Werner said. "I just took it. I wanted to find my son."

Meanwhile, the volunteer searchers went about their business. After two days of unsuccessful searching, the volunteers themselves began to lose heart. By nightfall Monday, it was becoming increasingly obvious to them that the search for Eddie Werner was becoming the search for the recovery of Eddie's body. A team of "cadaver" dogs were put into action.

About that time, Valerie Werner lay down to sleep. She had been heavily sedated again, beside herself with worry and grief. The last thing she remembered as she crawled under the covers was the sound of a helicopter taking off to aid in the search.

Moments later, it seemed, the dogs, trained to hit on decomposing flesh, began running around and barking loudly. It seemed as if they had found something not too far from the Werner home.

"They haven't hit on something already?" one of the searchers asked.

"No," someone else said. "Can't be. We've already searched that area."

At the makeshift food stand that had been set up to serve searchers hot chocolate and other snacks, the incredulous feeling spread. "We all thought it was going to be a long, drawn-out process," one of the workers later said. "In fact, we kind of hoped it would be. No one wanted those damn dogs to find anything."

In a wooded lot behind a home on Wood Lane, mere steps from where Valerie and Ed had looked for their son the previous Saturday night, the dogs continued their loud barking. Without a doubt, they'd hit on something. It could've been a dead squirrel or dog, or anything else, but as rescue workers approached the dogs, it became apparent it was no small animal upon which the dogs had stumbled.

At first it was hard to believe it was Eddie. The area had been thoroughly searched the first night the boy had turned up missing—and not just by Eddie's parents. Dozens of volunteers had walked through the very patch of woods to where the dogs had traveled.

The rescue workers looked again. Next to a small stream the dogs had found the remains of a child. It was a boy approximately eleven years old. He had a footprint on his back and was obviously dead.

The search for Eddie Werner was over.

Valerie Werner, asleep at the time, had no idea what was going on. Neither did Ed Werner, who was trying to keep a stiff upper lip for a house filled with friends and relatives. He was walking through his house in a daze trying to entertain, worry and keep up with the latest news. Werner made sure the television set was constantly on.

Someone suggested they stop watching television and put on a videotape. Thinking back on it, Ed Werner believed his relatives already had heard that little Eddie had been found dead and wanted to keep him from finding out about the grisly events by seeing it mentioned on television. At the time, he didn't think too much about his relatives' actions. Someone mentioned putting on a good comedy. "I thought it would take my mind off of my worries and I tried to talk myself into thinking the police would find my boy—healthy—soon," Werner said.

The two police detectives who had been working the case since Eddie had been reported missing knocked on the door. With them was an older officer whom Ed Werner didn't recognize.

"Do you know anything?" he asked the police as he opened the door. Looking in the front door, the cops could see the Werners had a packed house, but what they had to say didn't need to be said in front of a crowd. They asked if they could talk to him in the backyard, away from everyone else. Werner obliged. When they found a quiet spot, one of the cops cleared his throat.

There was simply no easy way for the cop to say what he had to tell Ed Werner. He hesitated, and Werner could see in the man's eyes the news was not good. It was almost an anticlimax as the cops told Ed Werner they had found the body of a little boy that matched Eddie's description. Werner responded with a scream that could be heard throughout the house. A look of horror, disgust, terror and overwhelming loss was stamped on his face; just from this reaction, the cops knew that the father had nothing to do with his son's death.

They had suspected as much when Eddie was found, but had to see it in Ed's face to be sure. It wasn't anything they looked forward to or wanted to see, but they had to nonetheless. The policemen tried to console him, explaining that nothing had been confirmed yet. The body hadn't been identified. They were trying to give the father something to hang his hope on, but Werner was grim. "Sure," he said, "like there's another boy out there missing who fits Eddie's description."

The older cop pulled up a chair and asked Werner to join him. The man had been silent up to that point and his sudden declaration hit Ed Werner strangely. Numb, full of rage and fear, Werner obeyed and listened. The cop told Werner he knew exactly what he was going through because the cop, too, had lost a son. Ed Werner had just joined the club of parents who'd lost children, and the cop tried to explain bluntly, though politely, what he could expect.

"Can I get you anything?" the cop asked.

Ed Werner sat in his backyard and took a breath. His son was gone. He had to tell his wife. He had to tell his family. He had to prepare a funeral for an eleven-year-old boy. Werner didn't want to think about how he would break this news to his wife and his other children. He didn't want to think about the coming days filled with funerals, television reporters and an investigation.

He turned and looked at the cop sitting there, calmly evaluating him.

"Yeah. You can get me a glass of scotch," Werner said.

After he had a few moments to himself, under the watchful eyes of the police, who were now worried about *his* well-being, Ed Werner emerged from his exile in the backyard and joined his family in the house. As he walked inside, he could see the compassion on the faces of his family. They knew what had happened, probably before Ed did, but nobody wanted to talk. Someone had even turned off the television set; the room was eerily quiet.

"I felt like I was just swimming through my own living room," Ed said. "Or drowning." He swooned and sat down, trying to clear his head. He can't remember much of what was said to him that night, can't remember what any one person did for him specifically. Someone had thought to hunt up a priest. Someone else, probably his own brother, Werner said in retrospect, went with the cops to identify the body. His family was there for him that night, as were his friends, but Ed Werner was too numb and too shaken to do much. He walked into his bedroom and looked at his sleeping wife. He couldn't bring himself to wake her, so he sat at the foot of the bed the rest of the night.

As the first light of dawn broke through their bedroom window, Valerie Werner awoke. "I can't believe Eddie's still missing," she said to her husband, who just sat there quietly.

"Why can't they find him?" she wondered out loud. It was the opening Ed needed to screw up his courage.

"They did find him" was all he could say. It was a flat, lifeless statement and Valerie knew exactly what it meant. Her oldest child was dead. She became hysterical and Ed was powerless to stop her. Moments later, as an ambulance rushed his wife to the hospital, Ed Werner stopped to think. His son was dead and his wife was in hysterics. Friends and family members had to watch his other children while he watched the paramedics fight to fit his wife with an oxygen mask. Three days ago, his biggest beef with his son had been over where Eddie had parked his bicycle.

Now that was gone. So were all the good times, so were Eddie's hopes for any kind of a future. The young boy had been robbed of everything he'd ever had and everything he ever was going to obtain. Ed just wanted to know who had done such a thing to his son and why. Later he said that the answers to those questions were more disturbingly horrifying than the questions themselves.

Two

Ready to Snap

The local police were looking at a messy business. An innocent preteen boy—Eddie Werner—had been found dead less than a mile from his house. He had disappeared on a cloudless, somewhat balmy afternoon. No one had heard a scream. No one had seen anything. There were few clues, other than some of the physical evidence found with the body, and no one could think of anyone that would want to kill the child. There were no other unsolved crimes in the area, no hint of danger in the neighborhood, nothing to look at and no one to interview. "It was as if he'd simply been plucked off the face of the earth," Ed Werner said. "We couldn't imagine why or how it had happened."

Investigators, searching for answers, considered several possibilities: Eddie's death could have been at the hands of a traveling serial killer, a friend of the family, a family member or someone completely unknown. They even considered that it may have been a random killing.

Police had quickly eliminated Ed as a suspect after Eddie was found and they were able to gauge Werner's reaction to the news. With little else to go on, reconstructing Eddie's final day on earth became a priority. Police tried to determine who had seen the boy last and when. Hopefully, it was thought, such a reconstruction would bring them some answers. From their efforts, the police were able to determine fairly accurately what Eddie had done on his last day.

Saturday, September 27, 1997, early morning

That morning Ed Werner, a mid thirties, trim, sandy-haired, slightly balding attorney in Jackson Township, New Jersey, casually walked over to his car, opened up the door and got ready to leave his home on an errand. As he eased himself behind the wheel of the car and stuck the key in the ignition, he told police he had glanced over his shoulder, then put the car in reverse, and backed out of his driveway.

He heard an unmistakable crunch and felt a jolt to the car. He said he knew almost immediately what had happened. He had backed over his eleven-year-old son's bike. Eddie was generally a happy child, but Werner said his son wasn't happy about what happened to his bicycle—its rim was mangled. Moments later when Eddie was ushered outside and heard about the accident from his father, he became visibly upset, but he didn't stay mad long. Like most sons, he idolized his father, and when Ed senior convinced his son that they could fix the bike, Eddie relaxed.

After an exchange of words, some of them conciliatory and some of them reprimanding, Ed Werner looked at the bike and at his son and knew he couldn't stay angry too long, either. He knew of Eddie's bad habit of dropping the bike wherever the boy felt like, so Werner said he partially blamed himself for not looking closer as he pulled the car out.

The father sighed, smiled at his son, then summoned him over to the twisted bicycle frame. He quietly admonished Eddie for forgetting the bike. "I didn't want to get too angry with him, but he did have a bad habit of leaving his bike out," Ed Werner later said. "We had to take it to the bike shop to get it fixed."

By the time the bike was loaded in the family car, the need to reprimand Eddie had subsided. Werner looked again at his son. He loved him and thought he'd been a little rough on his firstborn. After the pair drove to a nearby shop and dropped the bike off to get it fixed, both father and son decided to make up by driving out to a farm market, where they purchased a couple of pecan pies for that evening's dinner. Then they stopped off at a little Italian restaurant in New Egypt, New Jersey. Werner had a meatball sub and said his son had a big plate of sausage and peppers. "I knew he wouldn't be able to finish it, but he was happy when we took it home in a doggy bag. He thought he was going to eat it that night for dinner," Ed later said with a smile. He remembered that day as one of the best he ever had with his son.

"It was just a leisurely day," the father recalled. "You know, just a father and son out enjoying themselves. It was one of the nicest times we ever had together."

Eddie, a good-natured boy, was a sixth grader at Christa McAuliffe Middle School. Born on Christ-

mas Day, 1985, he was regarded by both his father
and mother as their ongoing Christmas present. He
suffered from a mild case of Tourette's syndrome
and wasn't very athletic. When he was very young,
Werner said, his son did exceptionally well in preschool and kindergarten, but in the first grade he
became difficult in class. His parents, devout Catholics, then took him out of parochial school, and after
therapy, doctors, and a prescription for Ritalin, reen-
rolled him in public school, where he'd really blos-
somed. Little Eddie liked to read and was a very good
conversationalist, sometimes talking to his parents
about books as complex as *The Count of Monte Cristo*
and *A Tale of Two Cities*. He was also a bit of a cutup,
a ham and perhaps even a bit of an actor. His mother
had recently used him as a model in a series of ad-
vertisements that would run in the local Wal-Mart
circulars during the coming Christmas holiday. "He
really looked good in those ads," his mother said.
"He was a cute little boy and I loved him dearly."

The apple of both his father's and his mother's
eye, Eddie was captivating, precocious, bright and
warm. As he spent his last afternoon talking with his
dad, Eddie had his father captivated again.

The pair reached home after lunch and Ed
Werner asked his son if he would join him in taking
one of the pies they'd bought to a neighbor who'd
recently given the Werners tickets to a New York Jets
football game. "Come on, let's go together," Ed had
said, but his son begged off. He had other ideas.
Eddie had planned a day of fund-raising for school—
selling candy and wrapping paper door to door. Eddie loved to get outside and meet people, so he was
looking forward to making an afternoon of his sales
efforts. The walkie-talkie set turned out to be the
only motivation Eddie needed to work so hard.

"He was really an outgoing child," his father said. "Very sociable and very bright."

Ed Werner waved as Eddie took off down the street. Together with another friend, Eddie worked the neighborhood like a veteran politician, knocking on doors, peddling the candy and wrapping paper, striking up conversations and enjoying himself the entire time. It was a bright day, one of those early fall days that feel warm and cool at the same time, and the two boys had no trouble amusing themselves as they spent the afternoon raising money. By mid-afternoon Eddie's friend was tired and decided to go home, leaving Eddie to venture on by himself. That, essentially, was where Eddie's story ended.

Police surmised that just a few hours later, he was dead. Although a few residents in the area had seen him walking through the neighborhood, no one had seen what had happened to him. The case was very vexing. There were no clues, no witnesses and no motive.

It was logical to suspect that a serial killer or some other random act of violence might have claimed the little boy. Kidnapping also remained a possibility, although a remote one. Police were stymied until they received a call from a nearby township and began working with police officers George Noble of the Monmouth County Prosecutor's Office and Guy Arancio of Howell Township.

With their help, the police in Jackson Township had a suspect: Fifteen-year-old Samuel "Sam" Manzie was a tall, gangly and troubled neighborhood child. He had a history of violence.

Police had first questioned Manzie during the search for Eddie. In a routine attempt to gather information, they had knocked on the Manzies' front door. Nick Manzie, Sam's father, answered and was eager to help out the police. He had been gone during the afternoon that Eddie had disappeared, but he told police that Sam had been home.

"So did anyone see Eddie?" the policeman asked the elder Manzie.

"Yeah, I think my son did," Nick said earnestly and quietly, wanting to help out the search. "I'll go get him. I think he can help you."

Moments later Nick Manzie returned to the door apologetically and said his son didn't want to talk to any cops. "He's being a little ornery," he told the police. "Why don't you come back in about a half hour?"

The police shrugged and left, vowing to return in thirty minutes. A short time later, Sam Manzie walked outside to sit on a bench on his front porch. He lit up a cigarette and tried to relax. When the cops returned, they found the teenage boy very defensive. "Hey, why are you cops hassling me?" he asked. Taken aback, the police carefully questioned the youth, noting his anger and his defensiveness.

"The boy gave us a lot of attitude from the very beginning," said an investigator who preferred anonymity. "But at the time, we didn't know why. It just seemed very suspicious."

After Eddie's body was found, the police got a tip from Guy Arancio. "If you want to look at someone who could've done this murder, you need to definitely look at Sam Manzie" was the advice from Noble and Arancio. Police investigating Eddie's death took the information seriously.

"We were looking at all kinds of possibilities," said Sergeant Rick Ferrarelli of the Jackson Township Police Department. "But at the time, there weren't many promising leads. We knew we had to take a good look at Sam Manzie."

Police working the case pored over what they could find of Sam Manzie's past, and were encouraged enough with the background check to want to continue further. Police had been called to Manzie's home on occasion and both of the parents had complained to police that their son was violent and potentially dangerous. The boy had also been involved in a police investigation to some extent, although it was not immediately known by the homicide investigators what the investigation was or to what extent Sam Manzie was involved. The bottom line was Sam Manzie looked to be as viable a suspect as the police had.

There was just one problem: Sam Manzie was a minor. While there appeared to be strong circumstantial evidence that he *could* have been involved in Eddie Werner's death, there was no hard evidence and no way the police could approach him without one or both of his parents being present. Police decided to bring him in and figure out a way to handle the problematic matter of questioning him.

They approached the Manzie home, cautiously and carefully. They wanted to speak to Sam Manzie, they told his parents, and they wanted him to come to the police department for questioning in the death of Eddie Werner.

Dolores Manzie, Sam's mother, was at first in shock. Much had been said about the young Eddie Werner in the press and it seemed difficult for her to grasp what role her son had played in Eddie's demise. But she didn't play the role of the overprotective mother who couldn't believe her son had anything to do with the crime. Sam Manzie asked his mother to accompany him to the police department and she did. The police took her aside and told her what they had in mind and what they wanted to question her son about. She nodded and volunteered to talk to her son herself.

"Do you want me to ask him?" she asked the cops, surprising them with not only her candor but her cooperation. They were looking at her son as a suspect in a killing and she seemed willing to help the police. She told the police she thought it was her responsibility to do so.

Dolores Manzie took Sam aside. Nervous, upset and fearful, she didn't mince words with her son. "Did you do this thing, Sammy? Did you harm this little boy? Did you hurt this little boy? I have to know. Look me in the eye and tell me."

Sam Manzie didn't lie. "I wasn't hurting that little boy," he told his mother. "I was killing [my psychiatrist], killing him over and over."

Sam then told Dolores and eventually the police all of the details. He even told his mother that he'd taken a picture of Eddie and kept some of Eddie's things, including the money from the sale of the candy bars and wrapping paper in his dresser drawers.

Stunned, Dolores Manzie went home, found the money wrapped around the photograph and handed it over to police. Sam also told his mother that he had dumped some of Eddie's clothes at Shoreline Behavioral Clinic, a facility Sam Manzie had been attending on an outpatient basis. She told the police and they retrieved what they could. The police were finally able to fill in the blanks with Manzie's confession; they now knew what had happened to Eddie the day he died. According to Manzie, shortly after Eddie decided to venture out on his own to knock on doors, he found his way to Iowa Court, where Sam Manzie lived.

The fact that Eddie had decided to strike out on his own after his friend decided to go home probably didn't cause him much concern, nor at that time would it have been a cause for concern for most parents. Eddie was just mere blocks from home. It was his own neighborhood; a twelve- to fourteen-year-old conglomeration of tall trees, siding, brick and paved driveways that seems ubiquitous in that area of the New Jersey suburban countryside. Carved out of the woods, it is in many ways a typical American suburban landscape, and in that way, it lulled many of its denizens into a false sense of security.

Eleven-year-old Eddie Werner stood just four feet eight inches tall and weighed about seventy pounds. He felt no trepidation as he left his friend that afternoon and struck out on his own.

As he approached Iowa Court, a woman living on that cul-de-sac remembered seeing Eddie, dressed in a black shirt, black jeans and sneakers, walking up and knocking on doors, eventually making his way to her.

"He was just a cute little boy. Full of smiles," she said. "He was very friendly and very outgoing."

His first stop on Iowa Court was the Manzies' house. He was greeted by fifteen-year-old Sam who stood around six feet tall and weighed close to 150 pounds. Manzie towered over the eleven-year-old, but seemed bored and distant. He didn't care what little Eddie was selling. He didn't want any. When asked if his parents wanted anything, Sam shrugged his shoulders. Sam Manzie's father, Nick, seemed to work all the time at a trucking company to pay for the family's suburban lifestyle. His mother was around the house all but one weekend a month when she worked. However, Sam Manzie didn't feel close to either his father or his mother. Sam only felt close to one other human being on the planet and that person wasn't with him that weekend. Sam was all alone. His older sister was visiting friends, and his father was helping his mother on her monthly job of working for a gambling tour bus that visited Atlantic City.

"I don't want anything," Sam Manzie said to little Eddie, who returned the scowl with a smile. After all, there were plenty of other houses in the neighborhood. Eddie walked off with apparently little concern for the teenager who had declined to purchase anything from him.

Sam Manzie didn't go back into the house. Instead, he watched Eddie intently. He especially liked the way the eleven-year-old was dressed—all in black. It was dark; it was appealing; to Sam Manzie, it was inviting. The way the boy dressed reminded Manzie of a close friend.

"I can have him," Manzie thought to himself. "I could have that kid."

Since summer camp almost three years earlier, Sam Manzie had fantasized about having sex with a younger boy. Lately, because of events even Sam's parents were unaware of, the dark desire had become a twisted obsession.

Sam Manzie was ready to snap.

"Hey, wait a minute, kid," Sam called out after the boy had left for another house on the cul-de-sac. "I changed my mind. Come on back."

Out in the middle of the street, Eddie Werner stopped and dutifully walked back to the taller teen. Manzie felt a rush come over him.

"Hey, kid, why don't you come inside?" Manzie asked.

Manzie later said Eddie didn't want to, so he tried a different tactic.

"I forgot my glasses," Sam, who doesn't wear glasses, said. "Come on inside and I'll get them."

According to Manzie, Eddie reluctantly decided to follow him inside the white two-story home.

He wouldn't walk out alive.

Perhaps Eddie Werner knew that the moment he walked inside, but it was already too late by then. Manzie immediately locked the door and smiled at Eddie, who responded, according to Manzie, by bursting into tears. "Let me go. Let me go," he cried. But Sam Manzie didn't let him go. He didn't want to. "I knew right then and there, when I locked the door, I was going to kill him," Manzie later told a doctor. He wanted this. In a way, he liked the struggle, so Manzie grabbed the younger boy by the arm and half-dragged half-carried him upstairs into his bedroom.

Once inside the bedroom, Manzie tried to settle the child down. He first put on a recording by the Smashing Pumpkins and tried to talk to Eddie. But Eddie acted deathly afraid of Sam and wasn't listening. Like a cat toying with his prey, the prosecution later argued, Sam Manzie tried to seduce and cajole Eddie Werner. He used the Smashing Pumpkins music, the computer, the video games and the CDs. But nothing was calming Eddie, who was still too young to grasp Sam's mind-set or the music of the Smashing Pumpkins. He was an eleven-year-old boy trying to sell candy and wrapping paper for school. He liked to read and tease his siblings. He liked the outdoors and his parents. He wanted to ride his bicycle and have fun on playgrounds. He didn't know or think about sex.

"I'll do anything you want," Eddie cried. Manzie

didn't like the crying. He had enough of that and picked Eddie up and put him on his bed. Then he stripped off Eddie's clothes while the young boy continued to cry.

Manzie's rage was building to a crescendo now. The rush he had felt earlier was coming on stronger and stronger. He could no longer contain himself. When he got Eddie's clothes off, Manzie began trying to preform oral sex on the pre-pubescent boy. But Eddie wasn't excited. He was afraid and completely helpless. Only half the weight of Sam Manzie and much, much smaller, he couldn't stop whatever it was the teenager wanted to do. He couldn't strike back. All he could do was cry and moan pitifully and beg for mercy.

"I want to go home. . . ."

But dark-haired, dark-mannered and dark-thinking Sam Manzie wasn't about to let Eddie go home. He had other, more sinister and deadly plans.

"Get on the floor facedown and close your eyes," Manzie commanded.

Still crying, Eddie obeyed.

Manzie searched around for a Sega Genesis game cord. He'd once seen a movie where someone had been strangled with such a device. But in his blood lust and the rush of the moment, Manzie couldn't find it. Instead, he grabbed his alarm clock and ripped it out of the wall. Then, taking the cord from it, he stretched it tight against Eddie's neck.

Eddie began trying to scream again. He fought with every ounce of fiber in his seventy-pound frame, but he couldn't keep Manzie from strangling him. Soon Eddie couldn't breathe and began to black out, but Manzie didn't let up. He pulled tighter and harder, and after a few minutes, the kicks and the screams from Eddie slowed and then stopped. When

Eddie ceased to even twitch, Manzie still didn't let go. For more than forty minutes, he pulled at little Eddie's neck with the cord from his alarm clock. When he finally let go, after he'd spent his rage and energy and couldn't strangle the dead, discolored child anymore, only then did Manzie drop the cord and look at his victim. Then he kicked Eddie to make sure the boy was really dead. He walked around the boy and then walked back and kicked him again.

Manzie could scarcely believe he had really killed Eddie and was almost convinced it hadn't been real. He felt the odd rush again and walked over to a closet to get the family's Polaroid camera. He had to take a picture just to remind himself that what had happened was a real event and not some twisted fantasy.

Manzie sat on his bed and thought for a few moments. His parents would soon be home and he couldn't leave Eddie lying in a heap on his bedroom floor.

He said later he had to figure out what he could do. He didn't feel guilty or remorseful, nor did he think of Eddie's parents, the young boy's three siblings or even of his own parents who would be horrified if they knew what their only son had just done in their home.

Sam Manzie was concerned at that point only with hiding the evidence, young Eddie's body. He looked around the house for some way to get rid of the child.

He didn't want to wrap him up in blankets, didn't want to dispose of him in a garbage can and could think of nowhere to hide him. It all started feeling like a dream again. Finally Manzie grabbed a suitcase and took it up to his room. There he carefully folded Eddie into the suitcase and hid it in his room. Later he dragged the suitcase downstairs and into the dining area of the house. He opened up the sliding glass door and hid the suitcase on the back wooden deck not far from the swimming pool.

He could be reasonably sure the dead body of the innocent boy would not be found there. His parents would come home, tired after a day of working. They wouldn't go outside looking for anything and they certainly wouldn't suspect anything. That would give him some time, and under the cover of darkness that night, he could do something with the body.

Sam Manzie was just fifteen years old. He couldn't drive. He couldn't buy alcohol or in some states cigarettes legally. He'd never made love with a girl, didn't own property, hadn't finished high school. Like Eddie Werner, until that day he had his entire life ahead of him. But as of September 27, 1997, like that of his victim, Eddie Werner, Sam Manzie's life was effectively over. The biggest difference was that Manzie chose the path and Eddie was forced to walk it.

Manzie retired to his room and waited for his parents to come home. When they did, his father, Nick, pulled into the garage and began unpacking the car. It took him about twenty minutes. Meanwhile, Sam's mother, Dolores, went upstairs and knocked on Sam's closed door.

"Are you OK, Sam?" she asked.

"Yes," he replied.

"Are you hungry?" she asked through the closed door.

"No."

"Do you want anything?" she cautiously asked.

"I'm tired," he replied.

He stayed in his bedroom until his parents went to sleep for the night. While his parents slept, Sam Manzie dressed, walked downstairs and out the sliding glass doors in the dining room. Under the cool night sky, silhouetted by the moon, Manzie picked up the suitcase containing Eddie's remains. He couldn't go far with them—he wasn't that strong. By that time, there were also searchers going through the neighborhood trying to find Eddie. Some of them remembered seeing the lanky teen with the suitcase and later wondered, "What if?" But no one stopped him as he walked across the street and toward a house he knew to be empty; the neighbors who lived there were away on vacation. It was late and his luck held, and within a few minutes, he found himself, undetected, standing in a copse not far behind the neighbor's house.

Manzie looked around. There was no one out now and it was eerily quiet. He trudged deeper into the woods, toting the dead child in the suitcase. When he was finally far enough so he couldn't be seen, he opened the suitcase. Eddie Werner was dead and unmoving. Manzie had to blink to make sure it was all real and stuck his finger in Eddie's mouth. He had to make sure just one more time.

The small stream nearby was perfect for his purposes. Manzie dragged the body to the stream and unceremoniously dumped Eddie there in an area volunteers had already searched. Before anyone else could see, or stop him, Manzie hurried home.

The police who took Sam Manzie's confession were moved to tears and anger. It all seemed so cold-blooded, so diabolical, that nothing could top the murder of little Eddie Werner. But the case involving Eddie Werner and Sam Manzie was just beginning, and the twists and turns to come would at times overshadow the gruesome murder—much to the chagrin of the Manzies and to the horror of the Werners. Nothing in the case, as it turned out, was as it appeared to be on the surface. The twists in the road started as soon as the police announced they had a suspect in custody for killing little Eddie Werner.

Three

The Patience of Job

Sam Manzie was the only son born to his parents, and like the younger Eddie Werner, he was also loved deeply by his father and mother. Sam also shared other traits with his young victim; both were independent minded, strong willed and had emotional troubles—though Sam's were far more severe than Eddie's, and that's where the similarities ended.

While Eddie had a mild case of Tourette's syndrome, Sam's emotional troubles were far more difficult to categorize. They took on dark and treacherous tones and had built over the years to the point that he was uncontrollable. His parents, his doctors, clergy and anyone else who tried to intervene had little success.

"We've tried to figure out where this all started," Nick Manzie later said. "And we honestly don't know." Though they didn't know the wellspring of Sam's violence, in retrospect Nick and Dolores Manzie say they did recognize a few harbingers of the disaster—though at the time they didn't seem as such.

Sam Manzie was born in 1982, and one of his earliest memories perhaps foreshadowed his own violence. For many of us, our earliest memories from childhood are of fragmentary moments of idyllic pleasure. It is a memory of our mother's face, the front door to a house we lived in or perhaps the smell of a meal on a table. For others, our first memories are of events more melancholy: witnessing our mother or father cry, or perhaps it is of some news event on the television. There are as many different first-memory events as people on the planet, but perhaps none so unique and perhaps telling as Sam Manzie's. His first memory in his life is of someone putting a bag or a sack over his head in a day-care center.

That haunting memory stayed with him throughout childhood and he never felt safe anywhere. He wasn't sure his own parents could protect him, and yet he wasn't quite sure why. But the feelings of safety and comfort that come from being in a family were not emotions that Sam Manzie carried with him. When Sam was six, his father, a soft-spoken, dark-haired man with a salt-and-pepper beard, took a large carving knife from Sam's school backpack. "I remember asking Sam why he had it there and Sammy couldn't tell me," his father said. The boy didn't seem to know and neither did his father.

But Nick Manzie did see the episode as a cause for concern and it ultimately led him to employing a therapist for his son. In fact, Sam was and had been in therapy at the time he killed Eddie. But it hadn't been enough, and what caused Sam Manzie to explode was a question that tortured his father from the moment he realized his son was guilty.

It tortured his mother from the moment she suspected her son of committing the crime, from the time she found a "trophy" photograph of the dead child to the time she coerced a confession from Sam and turned him over to the police. It haunts both parents to this day.

Indeed, it was a question that haunted most of the people who worked on or knew of the case in that suburban New Jersey area. It made headlines across the country and became fodder for scores of television shows like *Oprah* and *20/20*.

At the heart of the matter for most everyone was the question of why Sam Manzie killed Eddie. Reporters' questions, the stories on television and in the newspaper seemed to focus, more than anything else, on why one child would kill another. There was also a lot of questioning as to blame, with Manzie's parents catching a lot of chiding and criticism. "I know I wasn't always the best parent," Nick Manzie said much later. "But I always tried to be there for my son. He was much brighter than I was, but I never ignored him. I never walked away from his life."

In hindsight, after the case and all its sordid details came to the public's attention, Nick and Dolores Manzie were vindicated by many of the facts that came to light. They had acted promptly, they had tried to find help for their son and they never made excuses for him. It made those who watched the case closely even more perplexed. There wasn't a convenient scapegoat, which caused Sam's parents and even Sam himself to wonder what had happened to him.

"I don't even know if Sam can answer that question," Nick Manzie later said. "And I know that I can't. We always wondered about the day-care episode, but there were other things that happened when he was younger, that looking back on [them] make me wonder."

As early as eight years old, Sam later told psychiatrists, he wanted to be a woman. By the age of eleven, he believed he was a child molester. By the time Sam Manzie had reached his twelfth birthday, he began to believe that there was more to his first memory in life than just a vague remembrance of a sack being put over his head. He began to believe he had been molested by the day-care worker who had done it. It was roughly during this time of awakening that Sam Manzie started having fantasies, both of violence and sex with older men and younger boys.

He was confused and angered by these fantasies, and frightened. These were not the fantasies and idle thoughts of a normal Catholic boy, he told himself, and certainly not the thoughts his devout Catholic father would understand. A man taken to novenas and prayer could view Sam Manzie's twisted desires as demonic and unnatural, and Sam wasn't sure himself the source of his desires.

Sam Manzie became extremely adept at hiding his feelings and shielding his growing infatuations from his father and mother. All his parents saw was an increasingly cold and distant son. Not understanding the source of this distance only seemed to compound the problem.

"I couldn't reach him," Nick Manzie said of his son. "He began to see me as the enemy and I began to lose touch with him. He hated me. I never even found out about some of his fantasies until later."

"He was always closemouthed about his feelings," Dolores Manzie said. "It wasn't until much later, after so much had happened, that we knew for sure what was going on." Though Sam's parents didn't know what was bugging their son, they still tried to be there for him. "I would've done anything for him and tried my level best to do it," Nick said often to the press during the ordeal after Sam was arrested for murdering Eddie Werner. "I just didn't know what to do."

The Manzies, like many professional couples, found themselves moving several times when Sam was younger as Nick pursued better employment. The family finally settled in Jackson Township with Sam and his older sister in 1987, buying a house in a brand-new subdivision. The residents were mostly of the white-collar professional stock. A few boats dotted the neighborhood as did swimming pools and screened-in porches. Real estate agents referred to the neighborhood as "quiet." While living there posed the problem of multi-hour commutes to work for Nick Manzie, it was thought the suburban life-style would be beneficial for raising two children. Nick didn't mind the sacrifice if it would be good for his kids. He even took extra money he had saved and had a pool and deck built for his children in their backyard. The Manzies loved the neighborhood, and as a family they painted and decorated and grew up along with the others who lived nearby. It seemed for many years, as the Manzies had hoped, an idyllic place to live.

When Sam was of school age he enrolled at the Holy Family School in Lakewood for grammar school. When he was in the first grade, a school psychological evaluation noted that Sam "presents himself as a sad little boy who fights a lot." Dolores Manzie, a thin woman with an aquiline nose, doesn't remember the fights, but does remember Sam and his odd lack of communication. He continued in grammar school with a bright scholastic record while having a few disciplinary problems that his parents said were not serious. However, his growing emotional distress at home and in social settings, including school, were beginning to be very serious. By the time Sam was thirteen years old, Nick said his son confided that he wanted to kill himself "because nobody understands me." One of the problems that Sam Manzie thought for sure no one would understand was that as an eighth grader he found himself frequenting a boys' bathroom at school in the slim hope of having a sexual encounter with a fourth grader with whom he had become infatuated.

Manzie later told a psychologist that it was around that time in 1995 that he sexually molested a three-year-old he was baby-sitting and forced the child to drink cleaning fluid. He told another psychologist that he wanted "to kill a little boy." Manzie was only thirteen at the time. He couldn't understand his violent tendencies and felt horrendously and increasingly isolated from his family. He felt they could never understand him.

In contrast to those horrifying fantasies, in school Sam Manzie seemed to find an outlet and excelled. By the time he was ready in 1996 to start Christ Brothers Academy High School in Lincroft, he had an excellent scholastic record and told his father he wanted to be a historian.

Just weeks before the school year began, Sam seemed to hit a new low in his problematic relationship with his parents. Both Nick and Dolores noticed a precipitous decline in Sam's attitude. Where he was standoffish before, he had become completely distant. He spent hours alone in his room and rarely went outside. Where he had few friends, he suddenly seemed to have none. There was no one in his life but his family and he was holding them at arm's length. When he did interact with his family, it usually ended up in a violent shouting match.

A few years prior to the summer of 1996, Nick Manzie had been involved in a painful and near fatal car wreck. When he came back to work at the trucking company, a temporary worker came up to him and reassured him that he had survived because God had a plan for him. Manzie took it as a sign, but didn't know what the Lord had in mind. He just knew because of his painful injuries he couldn't do yard work for a while. So Nick had been paying a service $25 a week to cut and trim his lawn.

In the summer of 1996, Nick decided to keep it in the family and give the money to Sam, provided Sam do the job expediently and thoroughly. At first Sam had no problems with it. He was earning money he could pour into the family computer, which had made its way into Sam's room. He could buy CDs or anything else he wanted with the money he was earning. But, by midsummer, Sam Manzie decided he wasn't getting paid enough money. One day while cutting the lawn, he decided to stage a labor strike.

"I want thirty dollars or I'm not going to finish the front yard," he told his father.

Nick looked out on the lawn. Sam had cut it in such a haphazard manner that unless his father caved in to his labor demands, Sam had guaranteed the lawn would look horrible. Nick was still recovering from the back injury sustained in the car crash and it was unlikely he would cut the yard. Sam seemed to have the upper hand.

But Nick Manzie wasn't in management at the trucking firm for nothing. He knew how to break a strike and he demanded Sam finish his current job and negotiate future payments after the fact. Sam refused. Instead, he ran to his father screaming.

"Fuck you. Fuck you," Sam shouted.

Fuck me? No, fuck you, Nick said to himself. And when Sam ran upstairs and slammed the door in his father's face, Nick—in a rare display—kicked open the door, raised his voice and made his son finish his assigned duties.

In many households, this wouldn't have been a point of high drama and father and son would quickly make up with one another. But it was another incident that further served to drive a wedge between the distant and moody teenager and his father. Soon Sam began to throw things at his father, torture the family pets, start fires in his room and knock holes in the walls of his bedroom. While the argument about cutting the grass wasn't directly responsible for it, Sam Manzie did come to believe that it was his father who was wrong for disciplining him. As Sam grew physically to tower over his own father, at times Nick even seemed fearful of his violent son.

One day Nick had seen a breakthrough. While they were shopping in a mall, Sam questioned his father about his upcoming confirmation, a sacrament of passage in the Catholic church. His father explained the meaning of it and why Catholics chose a "confirmation" name—usually a saint or someone from the Bible who represents a character trait or illustrates a virtue the young Catholic admires or desires in his own life.

Sam asked about Job and Nick explained the phrase the "Patience of Job" and how one must suffer sometimes and had to have faith. One sometimes must walk through fire for one's faith, the elder Manzie said to his son.

Sam smiled. "I want to have that name for my confirmation name," he told his father.

Nick Manzie had connected at some deep level of

which he was only vaguely aware. His son had smiled at him. They were at peace for the first time in a long time. But it didn't last long and for many reasons. Sam's fantasies, horrid as they were, kept him separate from his family, and having few friends to confide in taxed him heavily. At a time when children desperately need to fit in and have a peer group of friends with whom to socialize, Sam Manzie had no one. He was exceedingly lonely. His parents tried to fill the gaps in his life, but few preteens or teenagers want to hang out with Mom and Dad exclusively—if at all.

Recognizing that problem, Nick and Dolores got Sam a summer pass to the nearby Six Flags Great Adventure Amusement Park. Perhaps, they hoped, the pass would enable Sam to go to the amusement park and mix with kids his own age. They allowed Sam to keep the family computer in his room and got him a second telephone line. They tried to instill discipline, love and respect. In turn, Sam Manzie manipulated his parents to his own ends. The trouble was, Sam wasn't even sure as to what ends he was manipulating them. He wanted his way all the time. "And when he got in moods like that, it was his way was the only way," his mother later told reporters. "He was extremely stubborn and violent." And above it all, he remained very lonely.

It was at that point in time that Sam Manzie found what he believed was his salvation; a life in cyberspace. More than anything during the last year prior to Eddie Werner's murder, the Internet came to dominate Sam Manzie's life. He designed and edited his own Web page, published his essays on-line, posted his picture there and even tried his hand at commerce by offering bootleg copies of his favorite music group to those who surfed his Web site.

Sam Manzie joined the virtual world on the Internet before he was a teenager, and it was his time there, especially in chat rooms, that brought some of his more despicable acts into focus. When Sam first got on the Internet, he cruised through different chat rooms, but as he became increasingly curious about his own sexuality, he settled into a gay chat room.

The world of Sam Manzie became a darkened room in which a confused and lonely teenage boy sits typing away at his computer. His family is asleep. As the boy types away on the computer, he thinks of them. They seem so normal and the boy sees himself as a monster. No one feels the way he does. He's not even sure how he feels about himself. He only knows that he sees the world differently. He sees it in colors of pain and in the isolation that he himself has imposed on his life. In his pain and in his isolation, he spirals away, down a hole, afraid of the future, confused about life; he is despondent, depressed and dejected.

Girls don't seem to like him. He isn't good at sports. He's a nerd and people make fun of him. He aches to be liked and be in a group of people who recognize him as the nice, funny guy he thinks he can be, but no one gives him a second look. More despair. If girls don't like him and he doesn't seem attracted to them, maybe he's gay. More pain. More despair. He must not be normal. He thinks himself a freak.

Then one night while typing on his computer, he finds a chat room where there are other people who seem to think the way he does. It's a lifeline to him more real than the real world and more satisfying than any experience of his life. He's accepted. He's not alone and there are others who feel as confused and as desperate as he does. In many ways, he thinks the chat room has saved his life.

The Internet was a far better world for Sam Manzie than the real world where he was referred to as "Manzie Pansy" by his schoolmates and occasionally faced their wrath for being, as his mother described him, "a bit of a nerd."

Since halfway through kindergarten, Sam Manzie had been, according to the information he provided on his Web site, attending private Catholic schools. He wasn't baptized, however, until he was seven and was confirmed in the seventh grade. Rigid adherence to the Catholic faith was countered by his growing dissatisfaction with the Catholic church and his underlying questions of his sexuality. "My current theory on God," he wrote on his Web site, was similar to that of one of his favorite musical artists: "I don't care if he exists and if he does, I don't think he cares if I care that he exists."

At Christian Brothers Academy, Sam Manzie said he had to adhere to a strict dress code of a tie and a shirt designed for a tie; no flannel shirts were allowed. He wore long pants, solid colors, no jeans or corduroy pants. He was also forced to wear dress shoes, with no sneakers or boots of any kind.

It was a school that focused on scholastic achievement and on one level it appealed to the bright, conservative young man that Sam Manzie was becoming. Like his father, Sam had become a fan of Rush Limbaugh and the conservative movement. In March 1997, that part of him found his voice as he wrote an essay discussing the benefits of Christian Brothers Academy remaining an all-boys school:

> First of all, it must be understood that our opinion doesn't matter and that CBA will be an all boys school for a long time to come no matter what we say. Even the state has no say in this since CBA is a private institution which does not receive public funds.
>
> For three hundreds years it has been a tradition for the Lasallian educational institutions to teach males only. The few exceptions to this is when the Christ Brothers took over a school that was already co-ed or when a Christ Brothers school was suffering financially so bad that they had to let girls in to remain opened. One might say about the all boys tradition that it should stop since society accepts more and more the rights of women in modern times. This is a liberalist idea and since I am a conservative, naturally, I do not agree with it. The liberals might call me sexist, but they should take a long look at one of the major reasons that people who share their opinion want girls in CBA: They want to have something to stare at during those long, boring 41 minute periods. I say that this reason for wanting girls to go to CBA is more sexist than not allowing them into CBA in the first place.

Manzie goes on to say that without girls, social pressures are relieved and that you don't have "to worry about looking good to impress anyone." The absence of girls "makes participating in class more comfortable; there is less worry about getting an answer wrong." He also goes on to say that without girls, the boys in school will concentrate more on academic studies.

Manzie posted this essay on his Web site, as he did other essays, including an attempt at parody and humor where he tried to logically decide who would win a fight between the cartoon characters Beavis and Butt-head. Although Butt-head constantly picked on Beavis, Manzie concluded the weaker Beavis "will burst into a paroxysm of violence against Butt-head," and thus would win a fight.

Finally Sam Manzie added a very poignant essay on his Web site. "True Friendships Are Forever" is its title and it won first place in the Catholic Daughters of America Contest.

A true friend is hard to find, but once you have found one, the friendship can last forever. There are certain qualities that true friends have. A true friend helps you out when you are in trouble, sticks by you through hard times, and is someone you can count on to tell you the truth. A true friend wouldn't just say what they think you want to hear and wouldn't get mad at you if he/she disagrees with you. A true friend will stick by you, even when the popular crowd doesn't. Anything else is being a crowd pleaser, someone who values their own popularity more than the friendship. Also, a true friend is someone you can trust to talk to and share secrets without fear that they will become public knowledge.

Even if someone has all these qualities, it may not be a true friendship, because true friendships go both ways. All of the qualities that your friend gives to you should be given back, otherwise one is taking advantage of the other and it wouldn't be a true friendship. True friendships are a very great and valuable thing to have, and if both friends work together, the friendship can last a long time.

All of this information was available to the world in cyberspace, where Sam Manzie felt most comfortable. His daily routine at his rigid school, while appealing in some regards, was causing him enormous pain. His parents not only didn't understand him but couldn't communicate with him; of course, much of that was because Sam wasn't honest with them. He kept his desires, fantasies and relationships hidden from his family. When they tried to find out what was going on in his life, Sam would punch a hole in the wall or set something on fire. As a consequence, he was angry most of the time, and that spilled over into his Internet life where he felt comfortable; people were a step removed from his life by virtue of being at computers all over the country and not actually sitting in a room with him.

He could say the most outlandish things, think the most outlandish things and pretend to do those things on-line and there was nothing anyone could do to stop him. Sam Manzie began to think that if he got angry there was no recriminations for that anger. The feelings of power he got on-line from venting his anger would eventually come tumbling back into the real world, where his frustrations had begun, with disastrous results.

Manzie also developed an interest in a young girl on cyberspace since they both liked the Smashing Pumpkins rock group. He posted her picture on his Web site and told the world they had "become very close." He'd never met her and she lived thousands of miles away in Arizona, but for Sam, she was his girlfriend.

His interest in the Smashing Pumpkins apparently branched out to include selling bootleg copies of the band's recordings and quoting them extensively on his Web site. Sam was "in love with my sadness," he wrote, quoting a lyric, and felt the Pumpkins were relating to him in an extremely personal way. Sam Manzie was not the first to take rock lyrics so close to the heart and miss the point; Charles Manson managed to do that with John Lennon and Paul McCartney lyrics, but through the Smashing Pumpkins lyrics, Sam Manzie found a voice for venting his own frustrations. About "Muzzle," by the Smashing Pumpkins, Manzie wrote that "almost every line from this song has special meaning for me," and quoted the line "I fear that I am ordinary just like everyone."

Other real-life ventures that found their way into Manzie's Internet life included laser tag. He wrote on his Web page how much he enjoyed dressing up all in black and hiding so people couldn't see him. Then he would fire at them as they walked past him. "I always love shooting people over and over and watching them get real confused trying to figure out where the shots are coming from," he said.

In retrospect, perhaps there is plenty in Manzie's Web page that could tip someone off that he had a growing desire for violence, but at the time he certainly didn't see it, nor did his parents who rarely cruised through the Internet, nor apparently did any teacher, psychiatrist, doctor or therapist who saw Sam ever pick up on it.

But those who met him in cyberspace began to know, understand and even fear Sam Manzie because Sam's crueler nature eventually became evident to those who communicated with him in the chat rooms. Some are still scared of him even though he's now behind bars. One boy about Manzie's age even had his Internet account manipulated by Manzie, who had become an accomplished hacker. Manzie's motive was jealousy, because the other boy had become increasingly more friendly with an older man Manzie had met on-line and with whom Manzie had become infatuated. He'd met the man while cruising through the chat room of virtual friends who had become an extended family to him. The man's name was Stephen Simmons and he was a pedophile.

"America Online has been a godsend for the gay community," said Stephen Simmons. "Kids who thought they were so alone and didn't have anyone else to talk with could find other kids who had the same thoughts and the same desires."

But the chat room was also a godsend to pedophiles, and Sam Manzie was about to find out why.

Four

The Chicken Hawk

Psychologists and psychiatrists refer to them as chicken hawks. That is a name they often call themselves, but it doesn't do justice to what they say they really are. They claim they are lovers of young boys in a totality that the larger population cannot understand. It isn't just sexually, although that is how the rest of the world sees it. It is much, much more. They are pedophiles.

Stephen Simmons has said he is openly gay and openly a pedophile, and he has no shame in claiming either. Born overseas, Simmons doesn't remember much of his native England. When he was very young, he and his family moved to the New York City borough of Brooklyn. Consequently, his accent is much more indicative of the citizens of Brooklyn than of the countryside of Great Britain.

At an early age, Simmons said, he knew he both wanted to be an actor and liked boys. Even as he grew past boyhood, into young adulthood, and then middle age, he continued to like young teen boys.

"My problem, you see, is that I got stuck," he said. "I got stuck emotionally being attracted to teenagers. As I got older, I just never grew out of it. I was attracted to teenagers when I was a teenager and before that, and I've been attracted to them ever since."

Simmons said while many heterosexuals don't understand or condone his activities, he has never tried to hurt anyone. In fact, he continues to maintain that he is just trying to spare gay teens the frustration and hurt he himself felt when he was growing up. Simmons also said he wants to help gay teens get more in touch with their feelings and "open up" about their gay yearnings. That, too, he has claimed, comes from his own life experiences.

Although Simmons claimed that he knew he was gay at an early age, he didn't—in retrospect—know what that meant. He said he never felt guilty for his feelings. He just knew he was always attracted to the cute boys in his class and to older women. He said he has had affairs with older women, but he prefers the company of young boys and has for many years. His attraction, he said, is not just sexual, although he readily admitted that is part of it. He usually just liked to help out gay teens who felt they had nowhere else to turn.

Simmons said he doesn't know what caused him to get "stuck." He doesn't blame his childhood for it, though, he said, his childhood was less than exemplary. He remembered his father as a drunk who occasionally was prone to violent rages. His mother doted on him and showed much sympathy, kindness and nurturing. He said his mother is still there for him today. "I worry about my mother," Simmons said. "She's getting older and I want to make sure she's taken care of. God knows she always did her best to try and take care of me."

Simmons's other fond memories of growing up in the late 1950s and early 1960s are of playing stickball with Curtis Sliwa, New York radio personality and founder of "The Guardian Angels." He remembered his mother teaching him to care for those on "life's periphery," those less fortunate than himself. During the turbulent 1960s, with the renaissance of "free love" and the joy of getting in touch with oneself that seemed to permeate the narcissism of that era, Simmons said he was enabled to get in touch with his feelings. Ultimately, for Simmons, that meant getting in touch with the fact that he was attracted to members of his own gender. He "came out" and tried to lead an openly gay lifestyle.

It was much harder, however, to admit to his desires for younger boys, and harder still to be open about those desires. At times he tried to control them and at other times gave in to them. In order to be close to the young boys whom he liked so much, Simmons said he coached pre-high-school football. With the advent of the Internet, he met the young boys on-line frequently—where it was much safer—and occasionally paid their phone bills. When it suited him, he liked to have sex with them. Sam Manzie wasn't the first boy he developed an on-line attraction to nor, probably, was he the last. Simmons, though, always believed he was doing the right thing by Manzie, always believed he was Manzie's friend and always believed he could help him.

Call it naïveté or manipulation, or anything else, but Simmons never saw himself as doing harm to the boys with whom he associated. He said he honestly wanted to help them get in touch with their own feelings so they wouldn't have to go through the painful process of rejection, loneliness and isolation that he said he went through as a gay teen. To Simmons, it was always "No harm, no foul," and he always thought he was doing right.

On the Internet, Simmons constantly offered his opinion to others, cajoled, caressed and tried to help those boys he found who seemed troubled. Simmons, an outgoing, dramatic man given to flights of self-importance, has more than a passing resemblance to the late actor Zero Mostel. He smiles easily and talks softly and likes to laugh and joke. Although not particularly good-looking, he said of himself, that he does have a disarming and friendly air about him. That quality served him well as he met boys on-line. "It is amazing that when I used a phony screen name and acted like a fourteen-year-old, the come-on lines and pressure [I saw] adults used on kids. I learned very early to treat them [gay teens] with respect," Simmons said. "Many adults didn't."

The outside world didn't see Simmons's activities as benevolently as Simmons did. He'd been arrested in the past and charged with crimes related to children. He'd also moved several times, but by 1996, he had settled down on Long Island and had become involved with a fifty-nine-year-old man in what Simmons called a steady relationship. He also had taken a job in a T-shirt business run out of his employer's home. His boss described him as not being very energetic and "often lazy" about his work.

Simmons was not lazy about his self-styled mentoring program for gay teens. At home he found himself spending time on-line cruising some of the very same spots Sam Manzie frequented. Teens in those rooms said he saw himself as a big brother and a protector—but he also apparently didn't like people to question his authority.

"Steve couldn't stand to be challenged," one teen said. "He started a lot of rumors concerning me and my friends, that we were posers and we were cops."

Simmons said he wasn't sure of the identity of some of the teenagers on-line. He thought they were in fact posing as teens and were really adults. "It happens, unfortunately," said Simmons, who also admitted *he* occasionally posed as a teen on-line.

Others said when Simmons got on-line he was like a cyberspace Pied Piper. "When Steve was on-line, we all pretended to be in a great big living room; it was Steve's living room and it had a hot tub and television and a sofa. It was fun," a teen member of Simmons's virtual living room said. Some teens flocked to Simmons, while others said they were disgusted by him. But even Simmons's detractors said it was often fun for them to visit Simmons's on-line living room; there they found a sense of belonging they could not get in the real world. Many of these scarred, scared and socially maladjusted teens found themselves in a gay on-line fraternity. No one was going to smack them, they wouldn't be picked on for being gay and they didn't have to worry about school bullies beating them up. They literally and figuratively could let their hair down. Many of them also took their clothes off and sat in front of their computer masturbating as they connected with their gay friends on-line. In a world consumed with worry about safe sex, this turned out to be the safest sex. Most of it was all inside the individual participant's head. It became a narcotic to which many teens and adults became addicted and to which some still are. "You see, something happens on-line," one of the teens explained. "[the internet] opens this anonymous door where you can meet people and openly deal in fantasy. You break down barriers that are probably good to have and then you wake up in the real world confused. And if you act [in real life] like you do on-line, you're in trouble."

Some of the trouble in Simmons's virtual living room was generated because it was run like one big gay party. "He'd type in stuff like '<okay that's it, off with your pants and in the hot tub>,' or he'd type '<unzippin yer jeans>,' or he'd pretend he'd be sitting next to you on the couch and say '<puttin my hand on yer thigh and rubbin up>,' all of it was very suggestive and if you're sitting in front of your computer in the middle of the night naked, then it's like some guy is jacking you off."

Sam Manzie stumbled into this on-line gay fraternity sometime while he was still in the eighth grade and met Simmons there during the summer of 1996. "I remember meeting Sam on-line," Simmons said. "His screen name changed at least once a day. All of his names seem to have Coke or Coca-Cola in them because he loved Coca-Cola. If you called him and got his answering system, you'd hear 'It's the real thing' for twenty seconds before he spoke. Within a week of talking to him on-line, he gave me his phone number and I called him. This was highly unusual. Getting a kid to give info like phone numbers, last names or addresses is next to impossible."

Sam Manzie later told investigators that he met Simmons, who was living in Holbrook, New York, at the time, in an America Online chat room "for gay teen males and pedophiles, because I knew I was bisexual. . . ."

"We talked about experiences he had and I had him call me," Sam Manzie later said.

When Simmons made that call and first talked with Manzie, there was nearly an immediate and mutual infatuation. Simmons thought Manzie sounded

intelligent and Manzie though Simmons sounded
kind and friendly. Simmons asked questions about
Manzie's growing curiosity about homosexuality, and
Manzie asked Simmons questions that only an older
homosexual could answer. In a short amount of
time, Steve Simmons and Sam Manzie became the
best of friends—on-line.

In late July 1996, Manzie was barely a teenager and
Simmons was forty-two. Though young, Manzie was
learning fast. Through Simmons, he was able to find
out the most intimate details about his homosexual
friend and was able to consort with homosexual men
and gay boys his own age without recriminations. His
parents didn't even know what he was doing. Sam
Manzie had become free to explore anything and everything he wanted about Simmons and the rest of
his friends in those gay chat rooms.

They spent most of their time on-line getting acquainted, finding out each other's desires, looking
for what they had in common and trying to establish
a friendship. But the talk also revolved around sex,
and soon the two were scheming to meet each other.
Simmons said Sam Manzie was the first gay teen he
ever met face to face after having talked to him on-
line. "I don't usually do that sort of thing," Simmons
said. But, just a few weeks after meeting on-line, they
decided to schedule a date.

Nick Manzie was going to go shopping at the Freehold Raceway Mall on August 10, 1996. Sam decided
to come along, and Nick warmed to the possibility.
"I thought it was another attempt for Sammy to reach
out to me and I wanted to be there for him." But Sam
had other ideas. He had a long-standing desire to
have an affair with an older man, and on that August
day, he took steps to make sure it would happen—using his father as an unwitting accomplice.

The Manzie men went to the Raceway Mall with two completely different agendas. Nick planned to buy a CD and a fragrance candle. Sam said he wanted to tag along with his father, then maybe spend some time by himself there. Nick agreed. Sam hinted that he might want to see a movie.

They walked into the mall looking much like any other father and son: Nick Manzie was focused on finding the store he wanted; Sam Manzie was blissfully unaware of his father as he walked around with a pair of headphones on, listening to music. But things weren't as they seemed. Sam was dressed as he was and wearing the headphones as a subtle sign of recognition for Simmons, who was waiting for him in the mall.

Simmons recognized Sam Manzie immediately as the boy walked into the mall with his father. He felt a glimmer of excitement as he did so, and Sam felt the same odd sensation and couldn't wait until his father left him. Sam, Simmons said, was a lonely child who needed a friend. Like a lion waiting in the high weeds, police later claimed, Simmons saw the wounded animal, Sam, and didn't hesitate to pounce. "We hadn't known each other two weeks when he asked to meet me," Simmons said. "Sammy made all the plans, and to be honest, he made me feel good. I looked forward to it."

Nick Manzie had no idea what was going on. He bought his fragrance candle and when his son said he would stay to see a movie, Nick said good-bye and agreed to pick up Sam later. He expected to get a telephone call from his son after the movie, a few hours later, but that didn't come.

Dolores Manzie had arranged for her son to carry a pager in order to maintain some sort of control over his solitary excursions, but she only used it to page Sam when she planned on picking him up—whether it be from Six Flags Amusement Park or from the mall or the movie theater.

That Saturday, Dolores Manzie paged her son after a few hours, intent on picking him up from the mall. Sam didn't answer the page. That's when Nick and Dolores began to get worried. They called the mall security office "and got no positive results," Nick Manzie said. "That's when I hopped in the car to look for him."

The Manzies' first thoughts were of doom, so Nick arrived at the mall in a panic. He opened up the car door and walked nervously inside. He met with security officers, but even as the officers began looking, he split off and began his own frantic search through the stores, restaurants and the parking lot. Ten minutes later, they had nothing. Fifteen minutes later, there was still nothing. Nick and Dolores Manzie could feel the fear rising. Dolores began to imagine the worst.

"I didn't know if he was dead or hurt. I was beside myself," Dolores Manzie said. It was the first time, though not the last, that her son would stress her almost to the point of breaking.

They remembered that Sam said he might see a movie, so the Manzies headed to the movie theater. People were everywhere and at first both parents thought and half-hoped that Sam was still inside, blissfully unaware of the time and sitting through more than one showing of a movie. It wouldn't be too unlike him to forget everyone else in the world, but as it turned out, Sam Manzie wasn't in the movie theater.

"I went up and down every aisle," Nick Manzie later testified. "I searched everywhere. I couldn't find my son, and my wife was ready to break." The

Manzies then called the police, who met them at the mall. They filled out a missing person report and continued their search.

"Don't worry, we'll do everything we can," the police assured the Manzies. But Dolores wasn't so sure that would help. She got into the family car with her husband and drove home. She looked over at Nick on a couple of occasions, afraid to talk, as if verbalizing her fears would somehow make them real. Nick, too, didn't want to think about it. He knew his son had some money on him, perhaps someone had robbed him. "I kept thinking, Was he dead? Was he alive? Who wants to think like that?" Nick Manzie said.

Meanwhile, according to subsequent police reports, Sam Manzie and Steve Simmons were exploring their mutual attractions in ways not sanctioned by the Bible. While Nick and Dolores Manzie were busily searching up and down the aisles of a local movie theater, calling the police and imagining their son dead at the hands of some robber or thief, Sam Manzie was with Steve Simmons at his Long Island home.

"We went to a movie," Simmons said. "During the movie, Sammy and I touched each other's penis over our clothing. After the movie, we walked to a wooded area behind the theater, where we kissed each other and I felt his butt."

This happened at the Freehold Mall, where Manzie's parents had dropped him off that afternoon. "Sammy asked me to take him home to my house on Long Island. I said no, but he insisted. He said he would run away or commit suicide. I agreed to take him to my house and said I would do it if he agreed to have sex with me. I said that because I thought he would chicken out. He didn't chicken out, so I took him to my house," Simmons said.

In the woods under the moonlight and within sight of the bright parking lot lights of the Freehold Raceway Mall, according to their statements to police, Simmons told Manzie he would take him to Long Island only if the fourteen-year-old boy, just out of grammar school, would agree to have sex with a man three times his age. It thrilled and delighted Manzie, who had fantasies about older men and liked the clandestine aspect to the relationship. So he went.

"Ever since I was about twelve years old, I had this fantasy about meeting an old guy who would take me to his house to have sex with me and to spend the night with him," Sam Manzie said in his subsequent police statement. "This seemed like the perfect opportunity to fulfill that fantasy, so I asked Steve to take me to his house on Long Island. At first he didn't want to do that because I was fourteen years old at the time and my parents would be worried about me. I insisted, so he agreed on the condition that I didn't back out of having sex with him."

Sam Manzie remembered Simmons's home as multilevel with a garage attached. He also remembered the house as being extremely neat, and noticed that inside one of the bedrooms there were several paintings and one of the largest was of a naked man. Once inside this home, Manzie and Simmons saw that Simmons's fifty-nine-year-old lover was making himself dinner. After cautious and polite introductions were made all around, Simmons and his new boy toy retired to the garage where there was a hot tub.

Manzie and Simmons eagerly undressed and splashed their way into the tub's confines. Simmons, who later claimed to police he only agreed to have sex with Sam as a way of frightening him from coming to his Long Island home, then eagerly and happily kept his word. They had sex.

Nick and Dolores Manzie were still searching and fearing their son was dead. Simmons never called the Manzies and apparently Sam was also disinclined to let his parents know he was okay. He hadn't spoken to either parent about his homosexual tendencies, so it seemed problematic at that point to call them and let them know where he was. There wasn't much information Manzie wanted his mother and father to have. He later told police the specifics of the sexual encounter, but he certainly wasn't going to make a call and tell his parents the graphic information.

Manzie and Simmons both told police they then went to Steve Simmons's bedroom and then into his adjoining bathroom to take a shower together before going to his bed.

When they got there, they found Simmons's smiling lover lying aroused in bed, wearing a pair of shorts. He wanted to join in and began, along with Simmons, to kiss Manzie on his chest. But Manzie wasn't impressed by the pale white flesh of the fifty-nine-year-old. He wanted Simmons and Simmons alone. He told police he agreed to try a threesome, but found he just couldn't consummate and moved closer to Simmons.

This had, for Manzie, the desired effect of chasing away the unwanted lover. But it also caused problems for Simmons, who had to leave the room to talk to his lover. Simmons was confronted with the dilemma of telling his steady lover that the boy he brought home was only for himself. It wasn't an easy thing to do, and Manzie said Simmons and his steady lover argued for several minutes before the older man stormed out of the house.

For Simmons's lover, it was a horrible letdown. He left the house knowing what would happen without him. For Simmons, it was just a problem that could be dealt with later. He didn't want to anger his steady, but he had a willing teenager lying in bed, waiting for him. Manzie cared little about the ruckus he'd started. He didn't give the older man a second thought as Simmons came back to bed eager to enjoy their physical intimacy.

About this, Manzie's parents had given up for the night, scared they'd never see their son again. Dolores Manzie remembered a night of pain and anxiety. A fitful sleep awaited her at home as she tossed and turned. Nick Manzie couldn't get the sight of Sam and the money out of his mind. He was sure Sam had been the victim of robbery, mayhem, thievery or murder. They feared the worst and dreaded getting up the next morning. Each phone call brought hope and despair. It was a nightmare that the Manzies both relived later when Eddie Werner turned up missing.

"Absolutely, I felt like I knew what the Werners were going through the days before they found out," Nick Manzie later said. "I can't say I understand what they went through after they found out [he was dead] and it's hard to accept sometimes what my own son did to them. But before they found out, I knew what that was like. It was a nightmare."

The nightmare ended being not what they feared, but what they didn't know had happened. "Just before I ejaculated the second time, Steve wanted me to come in his mouth, so I did," Sam Manzie told police later. Then, "We both fell asleep."

The next morning, Simmons woke his new conquest and helped him get dressed. Sam Manzie later told police that Simmons also fed him breakfast. Where was the fifty-nine-year-old? Manzie never said and didn't seem to care. While angry at the moment, Simmons's live-in lover never even seemed to bat an eyebrow at his steady lover having sex with a teenage boy. Sam Manzie, in his own right, never seemed to mind being the gay-teen equivalent of a home wrecker, either.

He just got dressed that next morning and bathed, and after eating a healthy breakfast, he gladly rode back to New Jersey in Simmons's car. There he was unceremoniously deposited near the mall where they'd met the night before.

"I know what he did was wrong, but it was an enjoyable experience," Sam Manzie told police nonchalantly.

Early Sunday afternoon, August 11, the phone rang at the Manzies' home. It wasn't the police. It was Sam. He was alive, well and safe at a Barnes and Noble bookstore across the street from the mall where Nick had last seen him.

The words stung and overjoyed Dolores. He was safe. But she wanted to know where her son had been the previous night. Nick, upon hearing the news, felt a flood of emotion. His son was alive. "Call the police," he said to his wife as he headed out the door. He was going to get his son.

On the drive over to the bookstore, Nick Manzie was again overwhelmed by his emotions. "I was glad he was OK, but I really couldn't believe it. I kept wondering what had happened to him and where he had been," Nick said.

As he pulled up to the Barnes and Noble, he saw a Freehold police car. Inside of it, he saw his son. Any concern or anger at his son's disappearance evaporated at the joy of seeing Sam safe and in the police car. To Nick, and later to Dolores, Sam appeared "well groomed," clean, washed, almost immaculate.

Nick Manzie approached the car, full of smiles and with his arms out.

"God, I'm glad to see you, son," he said as he tried to hug Sam.

But Sam Manzie pushed his father away. "He had a look of hate in his eyes that I'd see for a whole year after," Nick Manzie later testified. The father was hurt, concerned and immediately suspicious. He had no idea what happened to his son. At first Sam wouldn't tell his parents anything about what happened the night he disappeared. Nick was flustered and frustrated, but Dolores tried a softer approach. Finally that night after she'd put Sam to bed, she tried, softly, to quiz him on what had happened.

Sam said he'd spent the night in the woods. Later he confessed to his mother that he was there to meet another boy, but the boy didn't show up.

"Are you gay, Sam?" his mother asked.

"No, Mom. I'm bisexual," he said.

"For a year, I prayed my son wasn't gay," Nick Manzie later told reporters. "I would say a rosary going to work every morning. I guess I was praying for the wrong thing."

Dolores Manzie didn't pray for her son to be a heterosexual. "I didn't care if my son walked around in high heels all day long," she later said. "I just wanted to know why he was so violent." She also wanted to know what happened to her son on August 10, 1996.

The Manzies didn't have a clue, but doubted Sam had told the truth. "If he'd spent the night in the woods, why was he so clean when he returned home?" Dolores remembered asking herself. Nick, too, thought something was fishy, but as the days wore on, the concerns were shuffled to the back burner as Sam's violence escalated, subsided and escalated again. Inevitably, school started in the fall. The event of August 10 came to be seen by Nick and Dolores Manzie as just another in a long string of problems with their son. It wasn't immediately seen as the catalyst for destruction that it came to be.

Sam Manzie's strong desire to consummate a relationship with a pedophile directly led to the worst angst a parent can imagine. In retrospect, Manzie never thought about what his parents would do if he disappeared for a night. He didn't think about them calling the police or searching through a crowded mall. Nor did he envision the panic that set in with Dolores and Nick.

Nick said later he had no idea what Sam's plans were that day and he was crushed when he found out. "Did I miss something?" he asked himself often. "Was I that out of touch with my son's life?" He had struggled to know Sam, but his son, bright and conniving when he wanted to be, had managed to manipulate his trusting parents into helping him consummate his teenage lust for an older man. In retrospect, there wasn't much for Nick to miss. Sam was hardly comfortable enough to introduce Simmons to his father. "Hi, Dad, I'd like you to meet my forty-two-year-old boyfriend" was not high on Sam's list of things to do. So he did the opposite. He lied to his parents and hid everything from them.

When Sam Manzie told his mother and father the following day that he had spent the night in the woods, and after he eventually conceded to his mom he was supposed to meet another boy there, what he ultimately was hiding from them was the fact that

Steve Simmons, a man convicted before for his dalliances with minors, had picked him up from the mall and eventually taken him home to Long Island. Manzie was hiding that they had had sex and that the next day Simmons had dropped him off at the bookstore from where he had called his parents.

For months his parents had no idea what had happened, although they were worried about it and had questioned the story about sleeping in the woods. Still, Nick and Dolores Manzie couldn't get much out of their son and he continued to retreat more and more into his Internet world. Neighbors said he rarely, if ever, came out of the house. "I know his dad bought him a basketball goal, but I don't think I ever saw Sam take one shot," a neighbor said. "He was strange."

Sam Manzie met a girl through the Internet and began corresponding with her regularly. By Christmas 1996, Manzie had a real-life girlfriend as well, and Nick's prayers about Sam's sexuality seemed to be answered. By Valentine's Day, Sam was even asking his father's advice while shopping for a present for his girlfriend. "It was another moment for the two of us. His anger toward me subsided, although briefly, and it was a moment I cherish," Nick Manzie said. "He actually wanted my advice on something. He wanted to know what to get this girl."

But, soon enough, that relationship ended while Sam's relationship with Simmons flourished.

Five

The Slippery Slope

Sam started ninth grade at Christ Brothers Academy in the fall of 1996, with his parents still unsure as to what really happened in August and why their son, the good scholar, was so violent. The violence briefly subsided while at the same time Sam Manzie withdrew more and more from everyone in his life. It was a mixed blessing. Nick and Dolores Manzie breathed a sigh of relief as Sam's anger waned, but they were also disturbed at how lonely he seemed to be and how withdrawn he had become. Their concern compounded when they discovered they couldn't do anything about it.

"We began to seriously consider therapy again. We were concerned about how we would pay for it, and if insurance would cover it, but we knew we had to do something," Nick Manzie said. "We had periods where he was just completely isolated and then at times he was getting out of control to the point where there was nothing we could do for him."

Something else was also getting out of control at that time: the Manzies' phone bill. September 1996 saw an immediate and dramatic rise in the phone bill as Sam became interested in the Internet and calling his new Internet friends. Particularly suspect was a telephone number that appeared "literally dozens of times" on their bill; it was a Long Island, New York, phone number. Neither Nick nor Dolores knew anyone there, nor had any business contacts there, so at first they thought the number was a mistake on their bill. Then Dolores Manzie thought again about the phone calls. She had no reason to suspect Sam of anything, but still with mother's intuition, she thought all was not well. She approached her moody son and asked him what the deal was with the telephone calls to Long Island. But Sam wasn't feeling close enough or trusting enough of his mother to tell her he was conversing with, let alone having an affair with, a pedophile. "He told me that it [the phone calls] was just another kid his age and they just talk on the phone," Dolores Manzie told investigators. "So I had proceeded to tell him that he could not call this person anymore because it was too expensive."

Dolores Manzie didn't stop there. She didn't feel comfortable with Sam's response, so she asked her husband to call the phone number and find out who it belonged to. Nick first called the number from home and got an answering machine which said, "Hi, this is Steve and Steve, and leave a message and we'll return your call."

That got Nick Manzie curious, but not concerned yet. It could have been a business; it could have been a dozen other things; it could have been nothing. The next day, Manzie tried the phone number again while he was at work. When a man answered the phone, Nick asked him to identify himself. The man said his name was Steve. It was Stephen Simmons.

"I said, 'Hi, Steve. I'm Nick Manzie, Sam Manzie's father,' " Nick said. "I asked him why he was in communication with my son so often and that his phone number appeared on my telephone bill a lot."

Simmons wasn't about to confess his relationship with Sam Manzie, so he told a half-truth to Nick. He said Sam was "a very bright boy who was helping me out on my computer. If you want me to stop accepting phone calls from him, I will." Nick Manzie said that would please him very much as a parent and Simmons agreed.

After hanging up with Simmons, Nick called Dolores at home. "She said that I should have threatened the 'motherfucker.' Then I told her that I really felt it was over because this individual knows I have his number and he sounded scared on the phone. . . ."

Neither of the Manzies at that point knew anything about the budding physical nature of Sam and Simmons's relationship. Had Nick known, he said, his conversation with Simmons might have been less cordial. Whatever the case, the phone calls did stop and Nick and Dolores Manzie breathed a sigh of relief as the school year started and Sam began high school. But just a few months later, the phone calls showed up on the Manzies' phone bill again. About the same time, Sam began missing a lot of school because of his attitude and a bout of mononucleosis. Racked with religious guilt over his affair with an older man, frustrated with hiding his secret life from his parents, teased by his schoolmates and feeling lonely and bitter, Sam Manzie had already begun his emotional descent down a slippery slope. Sam again reached out to Simmons, the one kind ear, the one true friend he thought he had.

When the phone calls showed up a second time, it was Dolores Manzie who called Simmons. She wasn't too kind to him. "I said I was Sam's mom and I knew he had talked to Sam on the telephone and through the computer, and I told him that if he didn't stop having contact with my son I was going to call the police and hire a lawyer because I knew he was an older man. Then I hung up," Dolores said.

Apparently, however, Dolores's phone call to Simmons was too late. Sam had already met with the pedophile in person yet again. The second time fourteen-year-old Sam Manzie met with Simmons they rendezvoused at an amusement park and then retired to a local motel, where Simmons had made a reservation. According to statements they both made to police, they engaged in oral sex and masturbated each other. Simmons also brought along a drug he called "Special K," a tranquilizer for pet cats, Simmons claimed—and they both partook of it.

It was then, Sam Manzie explained, that Simmons pulled out a Polaroid camera and took some pictures of him, some nude and some clothed. "I think in one of them I was masturbating," Manzie said. This time the lovers didn't spend the night together. They couldn't chance it. Simmons drove Manzie back to the amusement park, where his parents picked him up—none the wiser.

Manzie and Simmons met again at Great Adventure later that year and they went to a hotel near the Freehold Raceway Mall for a sexual encounter like the previous one. Simmons denied the anal sexual aspect of this meeting and later accused the police of making up details. Manzie later seemed ambivalent on the point. He never testified in the case against Simmons, and prosecutors were content to just use Manzie's statement to police in seeking a conviction against Simmons.

It is the rather graphic description offered by Sam Manzie in the police statement that Simmons said proved the statement had been made up. "Anyone who has never had anal sex always says it hurt at first, but then I enjoyed it," Simmons offered as an explanation.

At some point during this time frame, Sam Manzie said that Simmons dropped a small bombshell on him. According to Manzie, Simmons had a ten-year-old son, who lived with the boy's mother, and occasionally Simmons would fondle his own son. As proof, Manzie said, Simmons offered him a photograph of his son and mentioned that maybe Sam, Simmons and Simmons's son could get together for a threesome.

According to Manzie, not only had he been invited to have a sexual threesome with two older men, but had been encouraged by Simmons to do the very thing that Manzie confided to his therapists that he had fantasies about—molesting a small child. In every way possible, the police later said, Simmons was feeding Manzie's violent sexual tendencies.

Simmons originally claimed he was only trying to reach Sam on another level because the teenager had begun to tell him about violent fantasies involving young boys. According to Simmons, he was either trying to put Sam off, or help Sam see the error of his ways. But Manzie denied that to the police. Simmons soon admitted the story was a lie, but he did show Manzie a bag of dildos, including one large and one small, and suggested that perhaps he and Sam could use them to their satisfaction. Politely, but emphatically, Sam Manzie said he turned down his lover on that score also.

Manzie however, didn't turn down yet another visit with Simmons. Police documented one additional meeting between the two. For Manzie's parents, it was frightening because the pedophile didn't meet their son at an amusement park or a hotel or some other remote location. In October or November 1996, Simmons visited Sam at the Manzies' home. It was a rainy, dreary day and Sam's parents were away for the weekend in Connecticut. Sam's older sister was in town, but had decided to spend the night at a friend's house. That left Sam home alone and he didn't hesitate to invite Simmons, who didn't hesitate to come over. Again Sam Manzie said the pair engaged in numerous homosexual activities. The next morning, Manzie gave Simmons a computer modem before Simmons left.

Simmons remembered the encounter differently. According to him, Sam did nothing but play on the computer all night. "He wanted to show me he was in control and he got very childish," Simmons said. "So I just went downstairs and slept on the sofa." There was no sex, according to Simmons in their last encounter, but a hint of the violence in Sam showed itself. Simmons wanted to have nothing to do with it. "You could see that if he didn't get his way he could be very angry and become very violent. He wanted to push people away, but didn't really want to be alone. He was very good at manipulating people."

Around this time, Sam Manzie began confiding in Simmons. Simmons said some of it was scary, even to him. "He bragged about his pornography . . . not only child pornography but bestiality, sex between

men and boys, basically disgusting stuff," Simmons
said. It was during this time that Manzie began to
elaborate about his rape fantasies involving little
boys, and he told Simmons about setting fires and
described how he'd tortured animals. "I only saw a
small part of that. I saw what he did to the family
dog," Simmons explained. According to Simmons,
Manzie threw the family pet down a flight of stairs
during Simmons's visit to the Manzie house in late
fall 1996.

Simmons did very little about Manzie's growing
infatuation with violence. He didn't contact authorities nor did he talk to the teenager's parents. Simmons said he tried to help Sam out himself, but
Simmons didn't seem to have the background to do
much more than listen. Evidently, that wasn't
enough. It became obvious that Manzie, while comfortable with Simmons, wasn't finding much solace
or help. Soon he began talking to Simmons about
suicide. Simmons said the troubled teen talked
about suicide often and he told the *New York Times*
that Manzie called him in the middle of the night
once and asked, "What's the easiest way to die?
Should I drink Drano?"

Sam Manzie wasn't doing well in school, either.
He was still a bright student, but had increasingly
become known as "Manzie Pansy," apparently in reference to his budding homosexuality. Other students saw him as aloof and arrogant, and claimed
he tried to cultivate a reputation as a misunderstood
loner. Specifically, he was accused of emulating
Holden Caufield from *The Catcher in the Rye.* Classmates claimed Sam Manzie saw himself as a type of
character who was smarter and more worldly than
his contemporaries and Manzie thought he just
couldn't fit in because of that. "I remember one time

he told me I was just a stupid little kid," a fellow student said of Manzie. "The thing was, I was two weeks older than Sammy! He always acted like he had this 'big secret' or knew more than the rest of us. He made it hard on himself at school."

By January 1997, Dolores Manzie said, her fourteen-year-old son was losing weight, and wasn't going to school. He dropped out of school in spring 1997, although he came back later to take the exams. Unknown to his parents, Sam had solicited sex from one of his teachers that early spring by writing the teacher a letter and offering the teacher oral sex. Sam Manzie was told he needed counseling and his parents were told he had to have a psychological evaluation before he could return to Christ Brothers Academy. Nick and Dolores Manzie said they weren't told why.

Sam Manzie turned to the computer. More than anything else, it was his lifeline, his friend and his salvation, or so he thought. But other teens who knew him from his on-line excursions said Manzie was becoming increasingly difficult in cyberspace as well. "He was always asking everyone if they liked him. He did it all the time," said one cyber-friend. "I liked Sam, but I knew what Steve Simmons was all about, and after a while so did a lot of others."

That fight would bring out the worst in Sam Manzie. Sam's cyber-friends had originally met in a private chat room now banned, called "Boys." About thirty or forty of the most frequent visitors to the chat room founded their own super-private chat room. "We became suspicious of anyone with a different screen name," one said. "Sam was hard to pin down because he changed his screen names every day, it seemed like. He needed reassurance all the time that people liked him. He would talk about how he didn't have any friends at home. They didn't understand him and how he pretty much spent all of his time by himself." The one exception, of course, was Steve Simmons. "Steve could do no wrong," the cyber-friend said. "Sam became convinced that Simmons had hung the moon. And the problem was, it really split all of us up. The room became divided into those who thought Steve was great and those of us who thought Steve was pathetic."

That became the source of Manzie's greatest anxiety. He loved Simmons and there were a group of young boys in the chat room who shared his feelings. But another group, whose numbers began to swell, came to realize that Simmons was occasionally interested in more than cybersex —he actually wanted to meet the teens face to face. Simmons became "a sleazeball waiting for a vulnerable child."

Sam Manzie was the perfect vulnerable child, according to those who knew him. They said after a while Manzie dropped his pandering act and entered the chat rooms "like a bitchy tyrant" and that he thought he was above most of the teens in the room. "We were having cybersex," said one. "He acted like he had the real thing all the time, and then when he met Simmons, they talked on-line about getting together." During this time, his friends say, Manzie changed from looking for acceptance among his peers on-line to being openly combative with such aggressive rantings as "<bitch slapin u>" and "<slammin the door in yer face>" and ran to less vitriolic and quite affectionate comments regarding Simmons. This all occurred after Simmons and Manzie began seeing each other, a move Manzie may have thought was unique because Simmons said he often didn't meet kids that he talked to on-line. It was an experience others claim was more frequent for Simmons than he admitted.

They said Simmons tried to make physical contact with many of them and even traveled to Florida to meet one boy, who said Simmons "disgusted me." Simmons acknowledged that he met the boy in Florida, but said it was he, not the boy, who didn't want to have sex. "I'm not always looking around to have sex with young boys. After all, I had a lover at the time who was fifty-nine years old." As for taking advantage of Sam Manzie, Simmons disagreed with that notion as well. "Here it is years later and Sammy is in prison for murder and I'm still standing by him. Isn't it obvious I care for him?"

The on-line chat room soon disintegrated into chaos with Sam Manzie carrying the banner for Simmons and striking out on-line against those who opposed his friend. There are indications, however, that Manzie wearied of his role and may have questioned his own motives in spending time with Steve Simmons. There was a falling out between the two in cyberspace that led to them no longer seeing each other. Simmons maintained that he wanted to quit having a physical relationship with Sam. "I became more like a surrogate father," Simmons said of his relationship with Sam. Nick Manzie later accused Simmons of "grooming" Sam into being a pedophile by pretending to listen to him. Debby Mahoney, who works with children who have been exploited by pedophiles, not only agreed but said what Simmons does is "manufacture more pedophiles" through coercion and manipulation. "Often these children who are molested by the adults come to see them as their only friend. They, in turn, grow up and display the very behavior they were taught by the pedophile."

Dr. Nathaniel Pallone of Rutgers University, a clinical psychologist who followed the Manzie case intensely, said it was more than that. "Sam Manzie was a boy without social skills. He didn't know how to approach a girl, and didn't know how to talk to one. Simmons took advantage of that. Many pedophiles are out there just looking for maladjusted kids like Sam Manzie."

Whatever was going on, apparently Sam Manzie began to feel guilty and was concerned about the situation himself. By spring 1997, he even acted on his concerns. Using the Internet as he had to solicit an affair with an older man, Manzie then used the Internet to find some help. In March 1997, Manzie reached out to the Cyber Angels, a nonprofit group affiliated with Curtis Sliwa's Guardian Angels. Based in California, it helps out children and protects them from pedophiles on the Internet. He sent an e-mail as "Sam82," one of Sam's screen nicknames. His letter to the Cyber Angels said that he was a boy who was having sex with a man and he knew it was wrong. The man, Sam82 said, was also having sex with other boys. The Cyber Angels forwarded the information to Debby Mahoney, the founder of Safeguarding Our Children, another Internet group that helps children. She read the e-mail and was touched. She'd left her job of eighteen years to voluntarily help patrol the Internet after her own son had been abused by a pedophile for close to two years. Sam82 got to her and she felt she had to do something, so she called the FBI. Two weeks later, she called them back to find out what was going on. "They told me that they couldn't tell me anything because it would compromise an ongoing investigation." Debby felt relieved. Someone would help Sam82 before things got out of hand. She felt the FBI had told her that much when they classified her call to them as an "ongoing case."

It was standard FBI public relations blarney that agents use with any call to the Bureau. It has a legitimate reason for existence; loose lips do sink ships and letting any information out about an ongoing investigation can lead to the wrong people finding out about it. Unfortunately, the FBI standard public relations speech also can cover up for a nonexistent investigation and it's a convenient way to dismiss cranks, kooks and busybodies. Debby Mahoney had no way of knowing that, and the FBI certainly wouldn't volunteer that information. As of March 1997, therefore, Debby thought there was still some hope for Sam82, whoever he was.

It was during this time that Sam Manzie's parents said that his rage became overwhelming. Not knowing everything going on with Sam, both Nick and Dolores wondered if the Internet alone could be responsible for his behavior. A quick tour through the gay chat rooms shows a life many of us would find offensive. There are member-initiated chat rooms on AOL that divide the gay community into lesbians and male homosexuals. It further subdivides the community into young girls looking for other young girls, young girls looking for older women, young boys looking for young boys, young boys looking for older men, men looking for men and women looking for women. These chat rooms are further divided by geographic location and sexual desire. There is, for example, one room called "Bears4Bears," which is a chat room for very hairy men who want to talk to and meet other very hairy men. If that gives someone pause, what goes on inside those chat rooms can be downright frightening to the uninitiated.

The chat rooms themselves often consist of men

and boys concealing their real identity as they seek out conversations with those they believe they can trust. One of the quickest ways to gain that trust is for the boys to send pictures of themselves via e-mail to those with whom they are conversing.

Consequently, the first few moments in a chat room where young boys wish to talk to older men can be laced with the "ping" of an instant message and the shout of "You've Got Mail." Sometimes the photographs sent are as innocuous as a school picture. Many times they are not. Child pornography is rampant in these chat rooms and most often it is distributed by the children themselves. This pornography is not limited to graphic photos of naked children, but often includes pictures of children in sexually explicit poses and acts of sexual activity with older men, younger boys, dogs and other animals. It is not for the squeamish and it is mind numbing how frequently the pornography is gleefully passed around.

"Did you see me? Aren't I hot?" typed one boy as he e-mailed a photograph of himself naked with another teen to an adult on-line. There may be twenty or more people in one chat room, and usually if the chatter and the on-line profiles are any indication, between a dozen and eighteen of these voices belong to young teenage boys. The rest are adults, some pedophiles, some not. Lou claims he is no pedophile but rather an older gay man who wants to help younger gay teens accept and deal with who they are. Think of it as an informal gay "Big Brother" program, at least that's what Lou claims.

"Some of these kids have a hard time accepting who they are," Lou said. "When they find the courage to come out, then they suffer the horrible consequences and pressures from home. Some are thrown out of their homes and end up on the street selling themselves to make ends meet."

Lou says he spends time not only on-line counseling gay teens, but does it face to face and over the telephone. "You have to understand that for a gay teen it has been a long process for themselves to recognize they are gay. They start out, often, telling themselves they are just 'curious' and then they claim to be bisexual, and then later on they admit they are gay. It's very difficult for them. They feel isolated and lonely and they consider themselves 'damaged goods' in today's society. They believe there's something wrong that they can't change. Many of these kids on-line are despondent and many talk about suicide."

Lou knew Simmons and said Simmons tried to counsel gay teens as well, but Lou differed in his approach and often had arguments with Simmons on-line about the best way to deal with a gay teen. "For one thing, I'm *not* trying to get a boy into bed," Lou said. "I just want to help them accept themselves for who they are." Simmons, Lou said, occasionally let himself get carried away and consequently began and nurtured closer relationships with the teens than Lou felt were warranted.

Unfortunately, an informal support group for gay teens is a perfect place for a pedophile predator to hang out, and Lou said there were several who would cruise through the gay chat rooms, although he did not classify Simmons as predatory. "Steve wanted to help out kids, but he was also attracted to them. I don't think he ever made the first move on a kid, but he let his sexual feelings get mixed up with his job of helping these kids out."

One of the kids Simmons wanted to help was Sam Manzie, and in many ways, Manzie fit the profile of a troubled gay teen—at least according to Lou and other adults who frequent gay chat rooms. Manzie was depressed, despondent, lonely and first began calling himself "curious," then bisexual, and finally admitted he might be gay. After the incident on August 10 with Simmons, Sam Manzie told his mother he "may be gay" and that he was "bisexual." He also collected a lot of pornography and had had it long before he ever met Simmons. Sam's father found a binder full of bizarre pornography and had a hard time dealing with it. As a longtime, devout Catholic, Nick Manzie found this pornographic material both macabre and frightening. It appeared to him like something straight out of a vision from the Apocalypse in Revelation. Nick Manzie hid the pornography in his garage, telling his wife to keep it there. He wanted to find the right time to talk to Sam about it. He never did.

Meanwhile, Sam Manzie progressed from photographs of bestiality and pornography to an interest in violence. Lou said Sam's penchant for violence was unusual for a gay teen. "Usually they only want to kill themselves," Lou said. "Rare is it that they want to kill someone else."

As the informal private gay party Manzie attended daily in cyberspace began to bust up into those who supported Steve Simmons and those who didn't, Manzie's rage increased. It was compounded by his disconnection in the real world from everyone in his life. Frustrated and angry, he began to lash out. His parents had no idea what the cause was; they could only see the results. His cyber-friends saw it, too. They didn't get to see Manzie throwing things or punching holes in walls, they just watched as he tortured other teens on-line, hacking into their computer files and disrupting their AOL service.

One of those teens who knew Manzie said he was both bright and frightening. "Sammy was a really funny kid sometimes. He had a really cutting sense of humor. But you could see he was cruel and he wouldn't hesitate to say things to hurt you," he said. "I knew one kid in particular he was jealous of because that kid had talked to Steve Spstsg (one of Simmons's screen names). Sam didn't exactly threaten to hurt him, but it was always an implied threat. It was like, 'You know there are things I could do to you' and stuff like that. I just got the impression that Sam was very lonely and very scared that he'd lose Steve to someone else. It was sad really."

There is little doubt, according to those who knew Sam and Simmons from the chat rooms, that fourteen-year-old Sam Manzie had a serious crush on the forty-two-year-old Simmons after they met on-line in 1996. Some of the teens in the chat room said Manzie even appeared to have fallen in love with Simmons. He certainly was showing signs of jealousy to others who displayed affection to Simmons. For Manzie, Simmons became the embodiment of the friend Manzie had written about in his award-winning school essay. Simmons was the only true friend Manzie said he ever had. Manzie in turn, wanted to be a true friend to his pedophile lover.

After Nick and Dolores Manzie got an inkling of what was going on from their telephone bills and had Simmons cease communicating with their son, it seemed to throw Sam Manzie into a tailspin. By summer 1997, he was hurt, lonely and increasingly violent. His venture to find help on the Internet apparently hadn't worked, either, and he was feeling ambivalent about it anyway. After all, Simmons had never said an unkind word to him. In his pain, Manzie tried again to reach out to Simmons by sending his gay lover a picture of himself.

The picture was an innocuous photo, but the results of sending the letter were for Manzie, and ultimately Simmons, catastrophic. The letter and photo were addressed to Simmons at his place of employment. But since Manzie had also included the name of the company on the letter, Simmons's boss ended up with the letter before Simmons did. Joe Ferraro, at that time, was running his T-shirt business out of his own home, and when a letter came for his business in care of Steve Simmons, Ferraro became curious. He knew about Simmons's sexual orientation and had wanted to fire him for a while, but he thought firing him for a "lousy work ethic" would never stick. Ferraro was sure he'd be sued for discrimination.

He'd bided his time and when he saw the envelope from Sam Manzie, he felt compelled to open it. By doing so, he opened a Pandora's box for Sam's parents, whom Ferraro contacted shortly afterward.

"The envelope looked like it had a kid's handwriting," Ferraro later said in court. "I was concerned, so I called the Manzies and told them I had received this picture and I was worried."

According to Dolores Manzie's subsequent statement to the police, Ferraro told her, "I must warn you that if you don't know who Steve Simmons is, he's a gay man and makes believe he's an adolescent on the computer with teenage boys."

Ferraro also told Dolores Manzie that he was concerned about opening himself up to legal recrimination by receiving pictures of adolescent boys like Sam at his T-shirt shop where Simmons worked. Ferraro told Dolores Manzie that Simmons was "a shady character" and that he had been looking for a rea-

son to fire him. Ferraro said Simmons didn't have
the best work ethic, and the picture was the "icing
on the cake." Ferraro planned to call his attorney
to make sure he could fire Simmons without worrying about Simmons suing him for discrimination because of Simmons's sexual orientation.

Ferraro kept in touch with the Manzies over the
next few weeks, and also contacted the FBI. Although agents had no way of knowing that Steve Simmons was the same man Sam82 had talked to the
Cyber Angels about, it was the second time the federal government was called into what eventually
came to be a molestation and a murder case. Ferraro
became upset because an FBI agent told him there
wasn't much that could be done about Simmons receiving an innocent-looking picture of a fully
clothed Sam Manzie, even though Manzie was a juvenile and Simmons a pedophile.

At that time, the Manzies were still not aware of
their son's search for help, or of the physical nature
of his relationship with Simmons, or just about anything else in Sam's life. They only thing they knew
for certain was that the family violence had returned
and gotten worse. Both parents were angry, but they
knew, or suspected, they'd only scratched the surface. They decided to confront Sam and hopefully
get him to come clean about his relationship with
Simmons. But the strategy didn't work. Sam didn't
act shocked when confronted by his mother. He simply told her that it was all a big misunderstanding.
Sam Manzie claimed that Simmons was just helping
him out on the Internet. He didn't have a scanner
and wanted Simmons to scan the picture into the
computer and e-mail it back to him so Sam could
post it on his Web site.

Dolores and Nick Manzie were openly skeptical

and no longer were convinced of the veracity of their son's claims. Sam was spending his credibility very quickly with those who loved him most. Nick and Dolores Manzie both became concerned that their son was protecting a pedophile and lying to them about it. They also both knew they had to find help for their son; he was rapidly taxing them to the point that they could no longer cope. Events in their life, however, postponed an immediate visit to the doctor when Nick's mother, with whom Sam had been close, died on June 1, 1997. With the death of his grandmother, it seemed that Sam retreated into his room and away from his family even more.

He had gone back to the Internet as a way to find solace. Dolores Manzie said that Sam was a "bit of a nerd," and by 1997 he spent almost all his free time on the computer. He shunned sports and other activities of teenagers his age. He got a pasty white complexion as he spent most of his time indoors and his social skills with others were dissolving.

By that summer of 1997, Nick and Dolores Manzie were close to their own individual breaking points. Nick was stressed with his long drives to and from work, worrying about his son, his job, his wife and his daughter. He was also increasingly beside himself trying to find a way to reach his son. He alternately wondered if he was paying too much attention to his son, or not enough. He debated whether he had disciplined Sam too often or not often enough. He worried about his wife's grief and despair being so close to the problem all the time and he wondered if his daughter was suffering from a lack of attention because of Sam's many problems.

For Dolores, her pain was perhaps more acute. Nick had long drives into work every morning where he decompressed, said his rosary and thought about

the endless cycle of depression and despair, rolling
it over constantly in his mind and searching for an
answer. Dolores, being at home more often, did not
get as much time to think about the pain. She was
living in close proximity to Sam's daily rage and anger with little respite. As Sam's chief caregiver and
disciplinarian, Dolores's life was increasingly fragile
and tenuous.

At that point in time, Nick Manzie said, Sam was
so full of rage, for reasons his parents couldn't
fathom, that when either Nick or Dolores walked
upstairs in their suburban New Jersey home to tell
their son it was time for dinner, they would be
greeted with a seemingly unending string of cuss
words or worse.

"Sometimes we'd walk upstairs and he'd just
throw things at us," Nick Manzie later told reporters.
Nick wanted to get angry but realized that would
not solve the problem. Increasingly, it seemed like
nothing would. Finally, during a summer rage when
Sam threw a television remote control at Nick, he'd
had enough and called 911. The police took Sam
Manzie to the Psychiatric Emergency Screening Service at Kimball Medical Center, a private hospital in
Lakewood. Perhaps, Nick thought at the time, someone else could step in and help. Instead, they sent
Sam home that night.

The Manzies could take no more. The combination of violence, the lack of school, too much time
on the Internet, Ferraro's earth-shattering phone
call and Sam's inability to connect with anyone other
than through a computer compelled the Manzies to
reach out for help. They got Sam in touch with a
psychiatrist, who told them that their son was clini-
cally depressed and that he "was beyond his help,"
Nick said. The psychiatrist recommended Shoreline

Behavior Health Care Center in Tom's River. There Sam Manzie was again diagnosed with depression and prescribed Paxil and began outpatient therapy. Five days a week for five-and-a-half hours a day, he would go to therapy instead of school, or as Sam called it, "day care" for troubled teens.

Sam Manzie may not have liked it, but his mother said she began to see some "good days." Unfortunately, the bad days became much more violent. Sam started fires, he threw things. He put holes in walls all throughout the home. The holes alone cost Nick and Dolores Manzie several thousand dollars to repair. "It was embarrassing when we had the contractors come to the house," Dolores recalled. "They looked at those holes and I told them, 'Don't even ask.' What could I say to them?"

At the same time, there seemed to be no way to get through to Sam to make him understand *how* he was emotionally taxing his entire family. "It was like he had all the answers to life and we were just there to provide his material needs," Dolores Manzie said. That fall Sam didn't immediately go back to school and he wasn't going back to Christ Brothers Academy anyway. That further frustrated his parents. "I saw this very intelligent kid falling into a hole and making nothing of his life," Dolores said, adding that by the third week of September the Manzies finally got Sam into Monsignor Donovan High School.

Just a few weeks before that, however, the other shoe had dropped. Nick and Dolores Manzie had received a telephone call from Shoreline. A nurse told them, "Your son is possibly gay and he's been with somebody. It's an older man."

That was it for the Manzies. They called Simmons. They called Simmons's boss. They redoubled their efforts to find out why their son had sent a photograph to Simmons, whom they were convinced had sexually abused their son. Finally they decided to call the police in August.

It was at this time that Simmons, under the moniker of "Spstg," and Sam Manzie, under his moniker of "XSpaceboy1," wrote each other for one last time on AOL via immediate messaging:

> Spstg: We can't talk any more Sammy. Sorry.
> XSpaceboy1: What's wrong with on-line occasionally?
> Spstg: Supposedly your parents are threatening my boss now and I may lose my job.
> XSpaceboy1: They didn't tell me about that.
> Spstg: I know. Seems all your problems are my fault. It's not your doing or mine. It's just parents I guess.
> XSpaceboy1: Okay . . . and the whole thing with sending it [the photo] to your work was so that you wouldn't get in trouble.
> Spstg: I know and you know, but everyone seems to think it was a scheme for something.
> Xspaceboy1: I hope you don't lose your job.
> Spstg: Maybe you can talk to your parents and tell them we only talk here sometime, but that will get them angry too.

They continued writing:

> Spstg: Not that anything illegal was done.
> XSpaceboy1: Shit.
> Spstg: It's a big mess over nothing.
> Spstg: Your mom said fire me or she will press charges against the company.

Spstg: Silly.
Spstg: Just remember we never met and just talked on phone and here.
XSpaceboy1: Yes.
Spstg: That's all and there is nothing legal that can be done.
XSpaceboy1: Right.

Having established a mutual lie to protect their affair, Simmons then went on to tell Manzie that everything would be fine. Sam, Simmons said, didn't deserve the hassle and he had turned out OK.

Spstsg: Look for me from time to time. Okay love and take care. . . .

On August 28, 1997, Officers George Noble and Guy Arancio began investigating.

A month later, Eddie Werner was dead. The Manzies, the Werners and many people in New Jersey came to believe the timing was not a coincidence.

Six

False Hope

In life there are few sins and few crimes that will bring upon the sinner and the lawbreaker the emotional zeal a police officer will bring to a child molestation case. The most hardened cops, able it seems to cope with any manner of horrendous act adults will put each other through, can be seen to melt into a puddle of tears while investigating the hell many children must endure by the hands of unscrupulous adults. "The children are the most vulnerable and therefore most in need of protection by the law" is the mentality most police bring to cases involving children.

In prison a convicted child abuser can expect the worst physical and emotional treatment from his or her fellow inmates. The life expectancy inside the prison walls is not long for convicted molesters unless the institution takes care to protect them. Cops have been known to refer to pedophiles and molesters being assaulted and killed in prison as being victims of "a self-cleaning oven." In a nutshell, life doesn't go easy for the pedophile in the system and so they try to avoid it at all costs. That is the power the gay teen has over his pedophile lover. A wrong move by the adult, or the wrong move by an emotionally disturbed gay teen, and headlines usually ensue.

Making a case against a pedophile is also a great way for a prosecutor to be seen in a favorable light in his community. It is cut and dried. In a world of political correctness, there is no group that will spring forward to defend the pedophile. There is no one who will come forward publicly to support a pedophile. There simply is no political downside to arresting a pedophile. For a prosecutor to get any kind of backlash for going after a child molester, there must be a serious breach of protocol or of the Bill of Rights for anyone to come to the aid of the accused molester. Even then it is rare. Who, after all, are the few who want to publicly defend a child molester?

Thus, in late August and early September 1997, Nick and Dolores Manzie had cause to hope that things would get better soon. Sam was being seen by doctors, and the police were involved.

Officer Guy Arancio of the Howell Township Police Department and Officer George Noble of the Monmouth County Prosecutor's Office are typical police officers; or they've been described by their coworkers as "regular guys." Both men are dark haired and of reasonably good humor. Arancio, a big, strapping man with a strong handshake and perpetual smile, looks like a bouncer at many of the strip clubs that dot the suburban New Jersey area where he works. Noble, a slighter man, looks like he manages those same clubs.

In court, their demeanor was elevated to another degree by attorney Howard Golden, who represented Steve Simmons after 1998. Golden managed to cast them as overzealous, strident investigators who may or may not have bent a few laws in order to get Simmons into court. The Manzies told reporters similar stories of arm-twisting and browbeating; in the end, they said they felt as abused by the police as their son was by Simmons.

As the case unfolded at the end of August 1997, there was no hint of the strife to come. Although neither Arancio nor Noble was especially eager to investigate Manzie's claim—after all, most cops know that child molestation cases rank right up there as among the most emotionally difficult to handle— they were not shying away from their duties and both thought the Manzies were up to the challenge.

" 'In the beginning, I was sure this was something Sam wanted to do as part of the healing process,' " officer Noble said Dolores Manzie had told him at the time. "I just want you to know that I love you and support you," Dolores told Sam. At first it seemed the Manzies had everything to gain by co-operating with the authorities. The Manzies, once they became aware of their son's affair with Steve Simmons, reasoned that helping Sam come to grips with the abuse could not only ease his pain, but their own. She was "on a mission for justice," Noble said of Dolores Manzie to the *New York Times*. At the start, Noble said the whole family was "on board" for what they had to do to get Simmons arrested, tried and convicted.

It also looked like Sam Manzie was making strides to break away from the influence Simmons had over him. He had publicly fought with Simmons on-line, and he had taken up with a new girlfriend. With the help of his girlfriend, Sam Manzie penned a letter demanding that Simmons stay out of his life.

"The victim's mother, Dolores Manzie, stated she, her husband, as well as her son, wished to have this matter investigated thoroughly and as expeditiously as possible and that they wanted Stephen P. Simmons brought to justice and to be punished for what he had done," Noble subsequently wrote in his report. That was on August 28, 1997.

Around 7:00 P.M. that night, Dolores Manzie and her son made the trek to the Monmouth County Prosecutor's Office in Freehold, New Jersey, to give an official statement to the police. Dolores was nervous and Sam ambivalent. He especially wanted to keep most of what had happened with Simmons from his parents. Nick Manzie said his son made the police promise that the information Sam provided would remain confidential.

With that promise secured, Nick said Sam opened up and gave the police an eleven-page statement, which read like a horror story. The police investigators, who have remained extremely closemouthed about their investigation, did tell their comrades on the force that they were "floored" by what Sam Manzie told them in a calm, "almost cavalier" manner. He sat before Arancio and Noble and recited with all the emotion of a man reading a phone book the most frightening sexual events one could imagine between a teenager and a man three times his age. Sam Manzie outlined all the intricate details of the August 10, 1996, meeting with Simmons and the other sexual adventures the pair had together.

Manzie told them about some of the fallout of the affair: missed school, trouble at home, trouble with most everyone in his life. When Noble asked Sam Manzie if Simmons had ever expressed any concern about taking him away from his parents on August 10, Sam piped right up: "I told him that they would be worried but that I didn't care."

The next day, Noble and Arancio showed up at the Manzie home in Jackson Township. Although Arancio worked for the Howell Township Police Department, he had been assigned the case because of jurisdictional consideration; Manzie alleged one of the places he met with Simmons was at a hotel in Howell.

On Friday, August 29, 1997, the two investigators showed up at the Manzie home and confiscated the Polaroid pictures Sam Manzie said Simmons had taken of him at a hotel. Some of them showed Manzie dressed, and several showed him naked below the waist in what a court reporter later termed, "shocking and lewd poses." Dolores Manzie and her son, after turning over the photos, calmly turned over Sam's computer hard drive, a printout of a conversation between Sam and Simmons that occurred on-line and other "computer components."

Dolores Manzie was nervous about the first meeting and yet very hopeful. She gladly helped the police collect any evidence they wanted. "I welcomed them into my home and tried to make them feel comfortable. I kept thinking to myself, we're finally going to get some help."

When, after collecting the evidence, the police said they wanted Dolores Manzie to allow Sam to go on a ride with them, she readily agreed. She trusted them completely. She had handed over evidence and she even handed over her son. The police said they wanted Sam to ride with them and point out the different places where he and Simmons had met and consummated their affair. Sam Manzie agreed and Dolores shrugged her shoulders as she did, too. Although there is some indication that Dolores didn't know exactly what would be involved on the trip or other subsequent trips the police took with her son, she was eager for what she perceived to be help.

Down the deeply wooded and sparsely traveled countryside, Sam Manzie took the police toward Great Adventure Amusement Park. During their leisurely drive, Manzie sat in the back of the unmarked police car, numb and calm. He later said he wasn't entirely convinced he was doing the right thing. His mother thought he was; she told him she supported him. Manzie, however, still wasn't sure, though he did hope cooperating with the police would quell his violent urges and help him to solve his problems. He was isolated, alone and increasingly desperate. Grasping at straws, he had decided to do whatever the police and his parents thought was right. They were adults; they had to know. There was something about the policemen, though, that Manzie didn't particularly like. They were rough around the edges, and while they acted polite to him, he couldn't get the fact out of his mind that they were going to arrest Steve Simmons. Manzie had been mad at Simmons, but with the two policemen driving him around the New Jersey countryside, his desire to get even with Simmons was becoming far too real. In cyberspace there were no consequences; everything was ephemeral. The real world, Manzie was finding out, was nothing like his fantasies and he was having a difficult time coping with that fact.

He directed Arancio and Noble to a small convenience store near the amusement park. It was there, he said, that Simmons stopped and bought him a soda and some food. The detectives dutifully climbed out of the car and took pictures of the place. For what reason Manzie didn't exactly know at the time. It all seemed so ominous and official. He showed the cops the entranceway to the amusement park, where again they snapped pictures. The photos were innocuous: a street sign, a convenience store, the entrance to the amusement park, a park bench. The police hoped to use the photos to paint a picture of abuse and coercion. In court they appeared to many like ordinary tourist shots, telling little about the case.

The detectives had better luck when Sam Manzie directed them to a Days Inn located in Freehold Township. The unmarked car pulled slowly into the motel and Manzie, from the backseat, pointed out a room in which he said he'd met Steve Simmons; room number 118. The police pulled the big unmarked car to a stop and left Manzie as they went inside. For what seemed like hours, he sat in the car and stared out at the motel room, the passing traffic and people passing by.

Later he questioned if he'd done the right thing. He hadn't spoken with Simmons in weeks, there had been the horrible fights in the chat room and school was getting ready to start. Just more pressure, that's all. Just a little more pressure.

Arancio and Noble weren't actually inside very long, but they found a manager and secured credit card, parking and telephone receipts that showed without a doubt that someone named Stephen P. Simmons had checked into the Days Inn on the day Manzie said he'd been with Simmons at the motel. It was corroborative evidence that would be essential to making a case. The detectives had cause to smile; things were going well for them. "Phone records also indicate several calls were made from the room to both Holbrook, New York, as well as at least one phone call placed to a phone number at the victim's home residence," Noble wrote in his report.

For five hours, the detectives kept Manzie, who seemed quiet to them, as they checked out his stories of sexual assault that occurred in motels and hotels near the Freehold area. When Manzie got home, his mother remembered smiling, a big broad smile, the first in many months for her. There seemed to be some hope after all. The long nightmare was finally, she prayed, coming to an end. The evidence gathered and the information retrieved made her seem "elated at the progress that was able to be made in such a short period of time with their cooperation," Noble later reported. Sam Manzie, too, seemed happy at the progress, at least according to Noble, and the investigators thought they were on to something. They had a cooperative victim, a cooperative family and corroborative evidence of a particularly foul crime against a minor. It seemed like smooth sailing.

The icing on the cake came when the two investigators returned to their office and Detective Arancio conducted a computer search of Steve Simmons. He "advised me that this subject did, in fact, have a rather lengthy criminal record and had, in fact, been arrested in the past for sexual offenses including endangering the welfare of children and sodomy," Noble reported.

On Tuesday, September 2, 1997, Dolores Manzie showed up at the police department to give her statement. Her housework and family concerns kept her from arriving until close to 5:00 P.M., but when she finally got there, she volunteered an eight-page statement, which outlined what would become part of the backbone of the case against Simmons. The detectives were encouraged with the amount of evidence Dolores brought to the table; telephone records, bills and conversations with Simmons all helped the investigators to think they were moving swiftly toward the completion of the case.

Dolores Manzie's details also brought home to the detectives the suffering the family was going through, and more than ever it cemented their need to arrest Simmons. There is no doubt that Noble and Arancio meant well and no doubt they could tell the depths of Dolores's despair. When they questioned her about Sam's disappearance the previous August, she told them how she and her husband had searched for Sam and the horrible revelation that her only son had spent the night with Simmons. The clincher—she'd only found out the truth about August 10, 1996, a week before she gave her statement. For a year, she hadn't known, had only speculated and could only guess. The next questions from the police hit that point hard.

"What exactly did Sam tell you and your husband as to where he was the two days he was missing?" the detectives asked.

"He said he was in the mall and was supposed to meet a kid in the mall, a kid his age who he said didn't show up and he was upset about it. After the mall closed, he said he went to the movies and then in the woods to stay for the night," Dolores Manzie said.

"Did you and your husband believe this story at that time?"

"It was very questionable. After Sam had been picked up by the police at the Barnes and Noble bookstore, the police had called me and told me that they did not believe his story because he did not have a speck of dirt on him; he looked like he had just gotten out of the shower. The police stated that they felt he had been with somebody; they didn't know with who, or what was going on. They said to give him a few days and question him as to the truth and to let them know if something developed. We kept questioning him, but he stuck to the story to the end."

By the time Dolores Manzie gave her statement to police, she was close to the edge herself. Unloading all of the fear and problems she'd had with Sam onto the police felt like a weight lifting from her shoulders. She told the detectives of the porno stash that Nick had found, which belonged to her son, but also informed them that it would be a few days before Nick could give a statement as he was out of town on business. Two days later, Dolores Manzie dropped off the black binder containing the loose-leaf pages of pornography that Sam Manzie had collected.

Apparently, few warning bells went off as the detectives looked through the sometimes violent and often salacious and perverted material. While it was obvious, in retrospect, that Sam Manzie was not only a victim of Simmons, but of his own warped psyche, the investigators did not discuss with the Manzies Sam's mental condition and the prospect of mental illness. At the time, they knew they were dealing with an intelligent, physically and in some respects emotionally mature minor who had an ongoing affair with a pedophile and had a collection of the most macabre pornography imaginable. On the other hand, Sam Manzie was also very emotionally immature, having few friends and social contacts. He was still on medication and still in therapy. It should have raised some warning flags, but apparently didn't. The police could only see the focus of their investigation: a sick, perverted pedophile who preyed on the young and helpless.

On September 5, 1997, the two investigators greatly expanded the scope of the investigation, contacting the Freehold Township Police Department, the state police and the Suffolk County, New York, Police Department as they continued to go after Simmons. Freehold deferred jurisdiction as they were suffering from a manpower shortage, the New Jersey State Police Department agreed to analyze Sam Manzie's hard drive for evidence and the Suffolk County New York Police Department requested that Sam Manzie take a little drive up their way at a convenient time in the future to help them out in their investigation. It wasn't the best move. Manzie, already skittish, wasn't eager to talk to more cops.

Later that day, Arancio and Noble contacted America Online Inc., in Dulles, Virginia, and notified them of the ongoing criminal investigation into Steve Simmons and requested they put a hold on the account "of the target of this investigation."

By September 15, Nick Manzie had returned home from his business trip and arrived to give the police his statement. It was as lengthy as his wife's and provided the police with further corroboration and insight into both Sam and Simmons. Nick remembered it all too well. He told the police what he knew, and then was surprised, he said, when the police took the interview off the record for a moment. "They took like a time-out and told me they couldn't tell me what Sam had said in his statement [from August 28], but they told me I would find some very interesting information in it and I should secure it at a later date after the case went to court."

Nick Manzie shook his head. He didn't know what the police knew about his son. He seemed to be completely out of the loop when it came to his child's life. It was right where Sam Manzie wanted him, and the worst place for a father to be. "I felt very help-less," Nick said upon being tipped off by the cops as to the extent of his son's molestation by Simmons.

Meanwhile, armed with all the information they had collected from the Manzies, the police decided it was time to take the investigation up a notch. For days they'd considered how they could get direct evidence of Simmons's involvement with Sam Manzie. The logical decision was to record a telephone conversation between Manzie and Simmons and see if Simmons gave up anything that would and could be used later against him in a court of law.

This was not an easy decision for the police. They were dealing with a troubled juvenile, and the allegations against Simmons were of a very crude nature. There had been trouble in the home and trouble with the young victim. But, in weighing all of the variables of the case, the police believed the best way to get solid, incriminating evidence against Steve Simmons was to have Sam Manzie make a simple phone call.

As everything else in the case, the phone call wasn't all that simple.

Seven

The Telephone Call

Sam Manzie was unstable. His parents knew it. The police knew it and so did the social workers he visited on a regular basis. Still, the police pressed on with the idea of having Manzie call Steve Simmons, his pedophile lover.

"This is going to be a textbook example of how not to do things on the part of a prosecutor who is so anxious to rack up the conviction of a cyberspace chicken hawk that he hounds the victim to the breaking point," Dr. Nathaniel Pallone, a clinical psychologist and criminologist at Rutgers, told newspaper reporters when the timing of the telephone call came to light.

Dr. Fred Berlin, a psychiatrist who founded the sexual disorders clinic at Johns Hopkins University, told the *New York Times* that adults' punitive impulses can end up hurting the children abused by child molesters. "We have to be more aware of the possibility that he has fond feelings toward this guy most people want to send to jail for thirty years," the doctor said.

Whether or not the local police considered any of this at the time they decided to call Simmons is unclear, but a July 22, 1999, *Asbury Park Press* editorial made it clear that the local community thought the police should have considered Sam Manzie's feelings a little more:

> The best that can be said for the way law enforcement handled its attempt to bring Stephen P. Simmons, a low-life pervert of the first degree, to justice is that serious mistakes were made. A less charitable assessment would have to conclude that heads should roll in the Monmouth County Prosecutor's Office and at a Long Island police department.

Sam Manzie wasn't exactly eager to make the telephone call when the police asked him to do it. He'd had only sporadic conversations with Simmons since their falling-out in the chat room, and he wasn't even convinced Simmons would take his call. But by September 17, detectives say Manzie was eager to help them out. Arancio and Noble got permission from their superiors and then put into play a plan to run a "sting" operation on Simmons. So, on September 17, 1997, as little Eddie Werner worried about his bicycle, played with his friends and thought about the beginning of the school year, Sam Manzie was hosting a parade of police and law enforcement officials in his suburban New Jersey home.

According to the official report, on that day, Detective Marty Temple of the New Jersey State Police was assigned to assist in the Sam Manzie/Steve Simmons case. Assistant Prosecutor Marc Fliedner, who eventually took the case to court, was briefed, as was Lieutenant John Cernak of the Sex Crimes Unit. Monmouth County prosecutor John Kaye and Ocean County prosecutor E. David Millard both authorized a request for a wiretap on Manzie's phone and the request was also OK'd by William Lucia, Chief of Detectives of the Monmouth County Prosecutor's Office.

The cops were very specific about what they wanted and needed. They seemed all business. Sam Manzie was intimidated, though, and concerned about whether or not any of the cops cared about him. He didn't know, but he was determined to get on top of things. He had one simple request: he had to be given "the leeway to run the conversation, as he felt he knew how to best handle the conversation wherein Mr. Simmons would not become suspicious of what was transpiring," Noble noted. Manzie said he wanted to do that because he hadn't spoken to Simmons in weeks in accordance with his parents' wishes. If the wrong thing was said, he was sure Simmons would get wind of what was actually going on.

On September 17, 1997, at 8:40 P.M., Technician Steve Padula of the Monmouth County Prosecutor's Office helped Sam Manzie call Steve Simmons and record the telephone call. Simmons had no idea what was up and started the conversation saying, "My God. I was thinking about you today."

"Really?" replied Sam.

"Yeah."

"That's cool."

Manzie talked to Simmons that night about a lot of things, hinting around that Simmons had a drug problem, which Simmons denied, and talking about a girl Manzie had met and with whom he had some interest. Simmons called Manzie a "silly boy" for giving his new love interest his computer password and said doing so showed how insecure Manzie still was. Neither one of them, though, mentioned that having a girlfriend might mean that Manzie had heterosexual feelings for girls. Manzie may have had several reasons for not discussing it, but Simmons clearly had personal reasons for not wanting that issue aired; he was a pedophile who enjoyed Manzie's company.

They then began talking about Simmons's love life and how Simmons couldn't trust a man he'd been dating. Simmons also told Manzie about a teenager named Oscar, who was of legal age and had a drug problem. Simmons claimed he was trying to help the kid to work through the problem; although Simmons also admitted he was sexually interested in the teen.

Manzie talked a little about counseling and how he was attending a psychiatric program for depression and isolation. "Well, we know you suffer both of those problems. I mean, this—this you've been in for, for six weeks you been in a program and that's all they've come up with. They could have called me, I could have told them more," Simmons offered.

Simmons's observation, although interesting anecdotally, was also very telling, Dr. Pallone and other court observers later noted. Had Simmons cared as much as he claimed, they argued, he should have made Manzie's psychiatrists and counselors aware of the teenager's problems. Simmons himself later said he harbored some guilt for not doing so. "I'm not an evil person," Simmons said in court. "I'm as capable as anyone else of making mistakes," he later added.

The conversation began with Manzie being very distant. He was, after all, making the telephone call to trap Simmons into making statements that could be used in court against him. Occasionally Manzie would look at the police furtively as he spoke with Simmons. They would smile or make no remark at all. They were all business and the business at hand was trapping Simmons.

"It was a huge, colossal mistake," said Dr. Pallone, who was often quoted by the *New York Times* and the *Asbury Park Press* about the case. "If the prosecution wanted to help out the Manzies, all they had to do was to pay a visit to Simmons and let them know exactly what was going on and tell him if he ever had contact with Sam Manzie again they would prosecute him. But the prosecution wasn't interested in what was right for the Manzies. Instead, they got involved in this *Mission: Impossible* fantasy of under-cover and headlines. It was all about grabbing head-lines. They put too much pressure on Sam."

Simmons had no way of knowing what was going on at the other end of the telephone line, but was tuned in enough to Sam to know there was some-thing wrong as they spoke on the telephone that night. He said Sam sounded "so down" and very tired. But Manzie was having a crisis of conscience at that very moment. It began when Simmons said, "Sammy"; he replied, "Yeah?"

"I want what's right for you."

Manzie acknowledged that with an "OK," but im-mediately afterward his attitude changed toward Simmons in the conversation and he began to warm up to his old friend and lover. Simmons began once again to compliment Manzie and feed the boy's need for positive recognition. "You're smart," Simmons said. "You have a brilliant head. . . . Let us be hon-est, do you think I loved you because you were cute, darling and adorable?" he asked.

"Umm, yeah," replied Manzie.

"Naw, wrong," Simmons replied. "I liked you because it was fun to be with you because I can carry on a conversation with you because you had a brain."

He encouraged Manzie to stay with his psychiatric help and apply himself in school, saying he had potential to be in the top of his class. "Start getting your life back together," Simmons admonished, telling him he was a good young man, "basically a nice guy" and "good people," who, Simmons said, he hoped would have a professional future. "You have all the tools," Simmons said of Manzie, "but you just, like, leave them in the shed and you let them rust." Later in the conversation, Simmons said, "You think a little bit warped, but so do most people. . . . You've got to find a direction."

Manzie was still unconvinced but feeling increasingly guilty as he made another halfhearted attempt to get Simmons to say something inculpatory on tape. Simmons responded by saying he prefers somebody who has a brain rather than someone who has "a cute butt."

"I mean, you know, it's like a cute butt is good to fuck, but a brain at least you can make friends with and be with for a long time. It means a lot more. A cute butt will go in time, a pretty face will die in time, but a brain works."

Then Manzie said something that he had said dozens if not hundreds of times while on-line. "So you're saying you still like me?"

It was, in Manzie's mind, a legitimate question. He had said nasty things about Simmons, had written him a letter with the help of his girlfriend to tell Simmons to stay out of his life. But no matter how hard Manzie pushed and prodded, Simmons said he was still in Manzie's court.

"Of course I like you," Simmons said.

"You know why I called?" Manzie asked.

"What?"

"You know why I called, 'cause I miss ya," Manzie said earnestly.

The importance of that statement is hard to overstate. In a room full of cops, parents and recording equipment, Manzie had just told Simmons how much he cared for him. He had also called to set Simmons up and had thought all along with everything that had gone on in the chat room and the nasty letters that Simmons no longer cared for him. But here was a guy willing to stand by him, and unlike Manzie's parents, Simmons knew exactly what their son was all about. Simmons accepted Sam Manzie, warts and all—that's how Manzie saw it and he had never had the courage to be that open with his parents.

The tragedy was if Sam Manzie had only done so he may never have needed the emotional crutch that Simmons provided. Here was a human being, a pedophile, willing to still like Manzie despite all the violence, childishness and all the pranks he had pulled on him. "I never bought his line," Simmons later said. "He always tried to push those he loved away from him and I just said, 'Sammy, there's no way you can do that. I still care for you.'"

As the conversation continued, it became obvious, in retrospect, that the police investigation would go nowhere. Manzie apologized for sending a nasty letter to Simmons and then said he would never let his parents harass Simmons. He expressed concern for getting Simmons into trouble at work by sending the photograph to him at the T-shirt shop. Then the duo made plans to speak on-line again, with Manzie saying that he still loved Simmons and Simmons admitting there was still a "spark there" because Sam was special.

It was the perfect opportunity for Manzie. He knew the conversation was being taped and overheard by police and he could legitimately claim he was baiting Simmons. But in listening to the tapes, there is no mistaking the sentiment in Sam Manzie's voice; he still had powerful feelings for Simmons and the pedophile still had powerful feelings for Manzie.

This led to them talking about Manzie's parents, especially his mother, Dolores, and how much she may or may not have known about his and Simmons's relationship. Manzie lied and told Simmons his mother knew nothing and Simmons said he'd like to tell them but would wait until Sam was eighteen. "She blamed me for all your problems," Simmons said. "You didn't go to school because of me; you were depressed because of me; you turned gay because of me. You know we all know it's bullshit, but, of course, parents are parents and no parent likes to admit the fact that it could be their fault, or that it's nobody's fault."

But Simmons said he wasn't upset with Manzie's parents and told Sam that maybe by the time he was a legal adult, "They'll understand that they haven't done a bad job as parents, but they can't blame everyone else for your problems. You know a lot of your problems are because of you." As it turns out, that last statement by Simmons was as accurate as any made by any mental-health-care provider in Manzie's life. Indeed, most of his problems were ultimately of his own making.

They hung up after nearly a half hour of conversation, pledging to stay close. The police were more than happy with the results. According to Noble's subsequent report, Simmons made numerous statements referring to his sexual relationship with Sam Manzie, his knowledge that Manzie was under age and that he had destroyed pornographic pictures of the teenage boy. The clincher for the cops was when Simmons expressed a renewed desire to meet with Manzie again face to face.

The police completely missed the subtext of the conversation. "After the conversation was terminated," Noble wrote, "both Dolores and Nicholas Manzie, in their son's presence, were advised that the conversation was extremely productive and that evidence had been obtained. Samuel Manzie as well as his mother and father, Dolores and Nicholas Manzie, were quite pleased with the manner in which Sam had handled himself."

Hearing that he had successfully put the noose around the neck of the man he loved was not exactly what Sam Manzie wanted to hear. Simmons had been supportive and friendly during the conversation, and Manzie saw himself, in Catholic terms, as a Judas. It was the beginning of the end of the co-operation Manzie would give the police. He was feeling worse about himself than ever, not better. Everything he ever did seemed to go wrong. Simmons still liked Manzie—he'd said so during their conversation on the phone. It was there on tape for everyone to hear. Manzie could not rationalize hurting someone who apparently cared for him so much. It was a dilemma Sam Manzie couldn't face. He was, after all, still just a child; although bright, he was extremely vulnerable. He'd been manipulated by Simmons and now felt he was being manipulated even worse by the police. The cops may have been jubilant on September 17, 1997, but there is little doubt that Sam Manzie did not share the feelings of euphoria. He was, instead, beginning to feel suicidal once again. As was usual, he shared little of his true feelings with his parents.

He began his final, fatal spiral.

If he needed any further push, he got it the next day. Sam's parents agreed to let him travel to Suffolk County in New York to speak with detectives there—but only on the condition that the local New Jersey police allowed Sam to finish his counseling session scheduled that day. The police demurred and Sam Manzie found himself, after a lengthy counseling session, taking an even lengthier drive to New York and having to suffer through an equally lengthy interrogation by Detective Nicholas Severino. The New Jersey police escort was ever present. Arancio, Noble and Temple had Manzie in their custody for ten hours that day. Arancio noted that Sam was "calm, pleasant and cooperative throughout" the process.

Noble noted that Sam Manzie even joked with the detectives on occasion and seemed happy enough when they took him out to eat at an Olive Garden restaurant in Suffolk County. Perhaps the bright, moody and mentally disturbed Manzie was playing the detectives for fools. He certainly had other plans on his mind on September 18 and those plans had absolutely nothing to do with cooperating with the police any further.

Still, all was smiles and roses on Friday, September 19, when Arancio, Padula and Temple arrived at the Manzies' home for another attempt to contact Steve Simmons. The plan was to record yet another conversation between Manzie and Simmons and get Simmons to set up a firm date for the two to meet. The detectives would then show up at the meeting and arrest Simmons. Sam Manzie would never be anywhere in sight. It seemed like a fine plan on paper since Simmons had already indicated that he wanted to see the teen again, but plans aren't executed on paper and Sam Manzie was ready to put his own plans into action without the police knowing it.

It began shortly after the telephone call was placed. Manzie feigned indifference and Simmons noted that Sam sounded "somewhat tired" and was "just making small talk." He was. In fact, Manzie was trying his hardest *not* to talk about anything important. He felt he'd betrayed Simmons once. He wasn't going to do it again. So after a few minutes, Manzie cut the conversation short; then he told the detectives he was tired and had been up all night listening to music and hadn't slept well. All he wanted was a "couple of good nights' " worth of sleep, Noble noted, and Manzie swore he'd be ready to try again on Monday, September 22.

It sounded like a game plan to the police, who had no reason to suspect otherwise—after all, Manzie had been entirely cooperative up to that point and, according to the police, even pleasant. Manzie later disputed that, saying that he told the police he was not happy, but there is no indication or evidence to back that up. There is, however, ample evidence that Sam Manzie was again being duplicitous.

The next day, according to Manzie, he destroyed the recording equipment the police had left attached to his phone. When the second conversation had ended, Detective Padula had retrieved the tape. The police figured if Simmons decided to call back when they were not present, the best thing to do was to leave the recording equipment in place with a fresh tape so Manzie could use it. They apparently believed in Manzie enough, and trusted him enough, to do so.

Sam Manzie took advantage of that trust quite effectively. According to what he later told Simmons, his parents and his sister all left the house on September 20. Manzie told Simmons he took a hand ax to the front cover of the locked recording device in his room. Then he took the individual components out and took an ax to those. Next he poured cleaning fluid over the entire setup and planned to set the thing on fire. He was denied that final act of vengeance on the audio recorder only because his parents came home earlier than expected. Manzie retrieved the smashed equipment and put it upstairs in his room along with this note: "Sometimes in life we are faced with an important decision. We must go the way that we know deep down in our heart is right—even if you can get in trouble for that decision or even if everyone else says it is wrong."

No one found out what he had done until Monday, September 22.

On Sunday, September 21, 1997, Sam Manzie spoke on the telephone to Steve Simmons for the last time. It wasn't to trap him. It wasn't to help investigators and it wasn't to set up a time for the two to meet. Manzie decided he could only redeem himself if he helped out Simmons. He'd already left the note detailing how he had to do what was right. All that was left was to tip off Simmons to the investigation.

When he found time alone, that's exactly what Sam Manzie did. He encouraged Simmons to run for it and told him he was terrified of the police. "They told him if he didn't cooperate, they were going to arrest him as an accessory to my crimes," Simmons recalled. Manzie was nearly in tears. He couldn't run anymore from who he was, and it seemed he couldn't help out those he loved. He hadn't done right by his parents, hadn't done right by the police and certainly hadn't done right by Simmons. To top it all off, Sam Manzie was convinced the cops were going to bust him, too. Perhaps somewhere in the recesses of his mind he even felt he deserved to be arrested, though he feared it.

That Monday, September 22, on his regularly scheduled visit, Sam Manzie told his therapist everything that had happened that weekend. The therapist called in Sam's parents. Dolores and Nick were shocked and stupefied. They thought everything was under control. Sam hadn't let them know he wasn't cooperating with the police or didn't want to help them. He had never verbalized anything other than cooperation. It was typical behavior for Sam. His parents hadn't a clue what was going on in his head or in his life.

Sam Manzie's desire to help out the pedophile angered and pushed them over the edge. It did nothing for the police, either. During the last three weeks, Arancio and Noble had repeatedly commented that Manzie had cooperated thoroughly, honestly and gladly. He had shown no signs of instability or of ambivalence. "If he had done anything that led investigators to believe he couldn't help us, it would not have been done," Robert Honecker, the second assistant prosecutor, told reporters.

It was yet another example of Sam Manzie's perfected, duplicitous nature. At all times, he was at odds with everyone, including himself, and he could fool everyone in his life, including himself. He had fooled himself for three weeks by thinking he wanted to help catch Simmons. He'd certainly entertained the thought much longer than that as he'd reached out to Debby Mahoney and the Cyber Angels as much as six months before he went to the police.

He was constantly hiding things in his life from
his parents, the police and ultimately himself. He
had found an outlet in his therapists, but it only
served to exacerbate the problems in his life. When
he let out any dark secrets during therapy, he apparently hadn't gotten any help, only more pain. He'd
told about Simmons and suddenly the cops were investigating him. He talked about destroying the recording equipment and suddenly both the police
and his parents were on his back. He told his therapist he wanted to hurt someone and he felt as if he'd
been ignored. If Sam Manzie learned anything from
therapy at Shoreline, it was that he couldn't trust
anyone with his secrets. The next time he had a secret, he knew he'd have to be far more guarded
about telling anyone.

The fallout from Sam Manzie destroying the recording equipment was immediate, swift and crushing. The police began, in Dolores Manzie's words,
to "hound" them to help out in the investigation.
"It was as if they were threatening us with prosecution," Dolores later said. "The prosecutor from Suffolk County was calling, like, three or four times a
day." Dolores wasn't in the best state of mind at the
time, either, saying she was upset with herself, mad
at her son and feeling guilty for being mad and upset.

Sam Manzie felt this in a most direct manner. His
mother, later pointed out as the disciplinarian in the
family by police, got very upset with Sam. The two
got into a massive emotional argument as Dolores
Manzie saw the end of all hope in Sam's destruction
of the recorder. She was beyond reasoning with, beyond hope herself. She was emotionally spent and
her son felt her fury. But Sam gave as good as he

got and the whole mess ended up landing the
Manzies back at another hospital.

If that wasn't bad enough, the bad feelings continued and grew worse as the police became increasingly desperate to get Sam Manzie's attention and
renew his cooperation. Dolores Manzie said she
didn't handle the situation well, either. When Sam
busted up the recording equipment, Dolores realized that all the calm behavior had been a ruse and
had gotten them nowhere. "This was my breaking
point," Dolores Manzie explained. "I told Sam I was
sick with what he'd done." Sam's response was to
get up and walk out of the room.

Dolores Manzie was now close to suicidal herself.
She couldn't do any more and she couldn't endure
any more. She thought her son would eventually do
something horrible to her and nothing she had tried
to do to help him or stop the violence had worked.
The utter futility flooded over her like a cold bath.
It was something from which she felt she could never
rid herself. It was just going to be ongoing, numbing
and horrible forever. Despair mounted as did the
fear. She was deathly afraid of her own son.

Nick Manzie, who was out of town on business
again, was disappointed and disgusted with the turn
of events. When he got home, he saw a family beyond
help, it seemed. Dolores's nerves were shot, Sam
seemed to be in his own world and the police were
like the barbarians at the gate. The cops were angry
and threatening, and Dolores said one of the officers, either Noble or Arancio, called her up and told
her she'd better get her son to help them out . . .
or else. "I think they used a derogatory term for
Sam, but I can't remember it. I just know I told them
I didn't want them badgering us anymore. I told

them I couldn't get Sam to cooperate with them anymore. If the doctor could, then fine, but I couldn't."

Dolores and Nick Manzie couldn't offer the police any more than that. They weren't even sure Sam would testify to everything they'd uncovered in the investigation thus far, and that prospect turned the police, more than anything else, into a hostile force. Arancio and Noble had put in their time on the case and knew they were close to popping Simmons. But it wouldn't happen if Sam Manzie didn't testify. The case, at that time, amounted to little more than a handful of useless Polaroid snapshots of innocuous scenery, a few receipts that meant nothing without Sam Manzie and some suggestive photographs of the victim that couldn't be tied to Simmons without Sam's help.

It was a helpless, hopeless quagmire, an untenable case, and the more the police pushed for Sam Manzie to testify, the more furious he became and the more stubborn he got. Manzie was a human bomb waiting to explode. Steve Simmons was the fuse and the bungled police investigation was the match. All that remained was for someone to strike the match and light the fuse. A probation officer who worked for family court judge James Citta, as it turned out, was perfectly suited for the task.

Eight

Striking the Match

Sam Manzie's initial anger with the police began with the telephone call the investigators urged him to make on September 17, 1997. By then, the upset teen was beyond help, and after he'd destroyed the police recording equipment, the investigation into Steve Simmons effectively came to a standstill. But the police knew they still had a pedophile working the Internet and they did not want to let Simmons go. "Our feeling was that we had to take a chance and arrest Mr. Simmons before other children were harmed," said a member of the Monmouth County Prosecutor's Office, who requested to remain anonymous. "We knew it was a gamble because it was obvious that Samuel Manzie was probably not going to testify against him. But we figured it was better to get Simmons off the street."

While there was much wailing, pulling of hair and gnashing of teeth behind the scenes in the police department and at the Monmouth County Prosecutor's Office, there was a larger frenzy going on in the Manzie household. George Noble got a ringside seat to the main event. He found out about the smashed recording equipment after Guy Arancio called and told him he'd received a call from crisis workers at Paul Kimball Medical Center in Lakewood, New Jersey. That's where Sam Manzie and his mother were at the time. Noble wasn't sure what was going on, but all he knew was that Dolores Manzie was requesting the detectives get to the hospital "as soon as possible."

P. J. Wengen, the detectives later reported, met them when they arrived. According to her, Sam Manzie had a "violent outbreak" at home during the weekend. Making matters worse was Dolores Manzie, who was strung out, crying and screaming, too.

"OK, we'll take care of it," Noble told the social worker. "Can we speak to Mrs. Manzie?"

They found her in tears and pushed to the edge. She'd had it. The whole story of the smashed recording equipment came out in the open and Dolores Manzie felt comfortable enough to unload her fears on the detectives about the ramifications of her son's latest violent episode. She had pinned her hopes on catching Simmons and now it looked like that was a false hope, too, as much as everything else had been in the last year since Sam started his spiral into violence. She told the detectives she was not only feeling despair but fear "for her safety as well as the safety of her family," Noble said.

To the care providers at Kimball, it was Dolores Manzie, not Sam, who seemed the most stressed and out of control; Sam appeared calm. There was later speculation that it was an act of subterfuge by Sam. He did, in fact, lie to police that day when telling them he wasn't sure why he destroyed the recording equipment and called to tip off Simmons. Of course he knew. He was desperately in love with Simmons and didn't want anything to happen to his lover. Arancio later said he understood Sam Manzie's apparent contradictions; at one point, he was calling for help and at other points refusing the help and, in fact, standing by the man who molested him. At fourteen, the age Manzie was when he first made contact with Simmons, "we're about as vulnerable as any other time in our life."

Dolores Manzie understood that as well. She'd started out the day by taking her son to Monsignor Donovan High School for an interview, hoping to place him in school and in as normal a situation for a teenager as possible. School, therapy, the police and understanding parents, she surmised, would help put Sam back firmly on the road to recovery. Her hopes were shattered with the revelation of the busted recording equipment. She had maintained a fragile state of calm brought on by her sense of hope at finding Sam help. When she realized that hope was false, it destroyed whatever calm facade she was able to muster. By the time she got to Kimball (after a brief visit to Shoreline, where doctors agreed to transfer Sam to a residential program), Dolores Manzie was out of control.

"I just lost it in the office. I was crying. I knew I was mad and I was afraid we would have a fight at home," she told reporters. "I felt there was nothing we could do for Sam and I didn't want him around until he got help."

Sam Manzie, who had already vented his rage, was able to play it cooler than his mother and thus deflect some of the concern about his violent behavior.

During the meeting at Kimball, Dolores Manzie told police and social workers, "We have to put him away now." Kimball's emergency psychiatric unit serves as the emergency screening service for Ocean County's family court, so workers there try to observe everyone involved in a case. When Dolores Manzie began saying that she would "slit my wrists if you make me take him home," some of them were more concerned for Sam's safety should he return home than for Dolores's.

Appearance is not always reality and the intake workers there had no way of knowing, when the Manzies first entered the hospital, of the strife Sam had put his family through in the last year, ever since the ugly incident on August 10, 1996. They had no idea that Sam started fires, tortured pets and routinely punched holes in the walls of the family home. They did not know of his penchant for violence, or his dark fantasies of raping little boys, nor at first did they know about his molestation at the hands of a pedophile.

They only saw Dolores Manzie getting upset. She pleaded with hospital personnel to keep Sam for evaluation, but told Noble that the request was falling on deaf ears. "I'm not taking him home," Dolores told Noble. "Nobody will listen to me."

This was true enough. Wengen told Noble that "Sam Manzie is not suicidal nor homicidal," but in her opinion, Dolores was *more* of a threat than Sam because of how *she* had acted up when she arrived. Wengen's analysis, it was later revealed through the murder investigation, was based on only a 15-minute interview with Sam Manzie.

"The problem with what happened that night is so obvious," Dr. Pallone later said. "If the personnel at Kimball thought the parent was ineffective and irrational, that's even *more* of a reason to keep the child and not let that child return home."

Regardless, the Kimball assessment was obviously way off the mark, for Sam Manzie murdered Eddie Werner just a few days later and Dolores Manzie has maintained her sanity through three horrifying years of pain and suffering brought on by her mentally disturbed son. Perhaps the doctors at Kimball might have had a better glimpse into Sam's wounded mental state had anyone there ever bothered to take a look at his files from Shoreline. At Sam Manzie's sentencing, Mike Critchley, his attorney, said that "no one at that Kimball Mental Health Center ever took the time to adequately review the records and speak to the psychiatrist at Shoreline Medical Center."

Howard Golden, Steve Simmons's attorney, also blamed Noble and Arancio. "Why they didn't demand that the kid [Sam Manzie] be put away that night is beyond me," he said. "They had close contact with the child and should have known who the problem was in the family."

St. Barnabas Health System, the parent company of both Kimball and Shoreline, has never issued a public statement about what went on that night. But Noble had plenty to say in his report. He was allowed to take Sam Manzie aside and began talking to the troubled teen. Manzie told Noble he had an argument with his mother, but "could not account for exactly why he did what he did." He apologized and seemed calm and rational at the time. "I busted it up," Manzie told Noble, referring to the audio recorder in his room. "You might as well know I called Stephen and told him what we were doing," he added. Sam Manzie also told Noble that he "absolutely did not want to stay" at Kimball that night.

Noble shook his head and walked back over to the hospital personnel, hoping to get "both Dolores and Samuel Manzie some form of help," Noble later reported.

The case that Noble and Arancio had hoped would be so straightforward was by September 22, 1997, horribly twisted. The cops, instead of looking at a straight-up case of child abuse, were now looking at a horrible quagmire of emotions that they may or may not have had the training to handle. The fight that led Sam Manzie and his mother to Kimball had to be reported to the police department as a domestic violence incident. Sam Manzie had tipped off Simmons; Dolores Manzie was frantic; the case was in shards. Noble was getting frustrated as was Arancio. Nothing in this case seemed to go easily and nothing seemed to go as it was planned.

In retrospect, it is easy to see that the turning point for the cops came when Sam Manzie talked to Steve Simmons on the telephone for the police. Simmons still controlled Manzie. Manzie, in turn, was capable of enough duplicitous behavior to be able to play the cops and social workers in a limited fashion to suit his ends. Dolores Manzie, though, was through. She knew what her son had become and what he was doing and she could no longer cope with it. That she blew up in the way she did may have been as easy for Sam to calculate as a simple math problem. Certainly, her tirade was used by him to the best of his ability. She was upset; he played calm. She demanded something be done because of his violent and duplicitous behavior; he feigned ignorance.

Noble, it seems, was between a rock and a hard place, so he tried to strike a middle-ground position and finally got a staff doctor at Kimball to agree to hold Sam Manzie for at least twenty-four hours "for evaluation and screening." A day or two of cooling off between Sam and his mother, it was decided, would be best for all parties concerned.

"I was out of my mind," Dolores Manzie later said. "I was afraid they were going to let the pedophile go and I thought here was a man who abused my son and he's going to be free. They didn't have a case, you know, without the tapes. I didn't know. And I knew Sam was at the end of his rope and I was definitely at the end of mine. I just wanted some help and it seemed like no one could help."

Noble and Arancio certainly wanted to help. But they were also becoming distressed by Dolores Manzie's emotional reaction and the pressure on them to get an arrest. They also had acute feelings of discomfort about Simmons, and were beginning to understand the power Simmons had over Sam Manzie. "This man [Simmons] portrayed himself as a savior to this kid," Arancio later said in court. "Simmons could understand him in ways his parents could not." With the understanding came the power to manipulate and control.

"People like Steve Simmons are very good at coercion and manipulation," Debby Mahoney told reporters. She had originally worked Sam's case when he cried out for help to the Cyber Angels. "You take away the sex and these people wouldn't be anywhere near the kids. These guys manufacture more pedophiles. It's an imbalance of power and these adults use these children."

It was a power Simmons never gave up and Sam Manzie apparently couldn't or didn't fully understand. More than two years after Eddie Werner's murder, Sam Manzie offered to send Simmons money to help him out—even though Manzie was in prison at the time serving seventy years for murder and was dependant on his parents to supply him with money. It meant Manzie would once again have to deceive his parents in order to help out Simmons.

Simmons took offense to any characterization that he manipulated Sam Manzie. "I'm an evil predator that went out of his way to screw up Sammy's life? That's what really hurts," Simmons said. Those who knew Simmons best from his time in the internet chat rooms said at best Simmons lost his head for a young boy and at worst he was the "manipulative sleazeball many of us thought he was."

"That's not fair," countered Simmons, who said everyone should have left him and Sam alone in their relationship. "Sammy didn't mind it, and I didn't mind it; why should anyone else mind it?"

Since Sam Manzie had confessed that he'd tipped off the pedophile, Noble decided he'd have to move fast if he wanted to catch Simmons—after all, Manzie had urged him to flee. On September 23, 1997, Noble prepared the warrants charging Simmons with the sexual assault of Sam Manzie, as well as warrants for sexual contact and endangering the welfare of a child.

Meanwhile, Sam Manzie and his family continued dwelling in the hell created by Sam's deteriorated mental condition and his love for Simmons. His sister, a promising high school student, tried to spend as much time away from the home as possible. His father, who was still on the road quite a bit for work, tried to referee as best he could while also helping his daughter scout out potential colleges for an anticipated fall admission. It was Dolores who was having to take the brunt of Sam's violent outbursts and she wasn't handling it well at all.

On Tuesday, September 23, Sam Manzie was ready to be discharged, but Dolores Manzie wasn't ready for him to come home. "We wanted what was best for Sam, but what was best for him wasn't for him to come home to the same environment. I don't think I'll ever be nominated for parent of the year, but I knew my son needed help and no one was listening to me," Dolores said. "It was crazy. I was upset because of how bad Sam had become and it seemed like the people at Kimball were more upset that I was upset." When Sam was lucid, Dolores Manzie said he was the same sweet kid she remembered as a small child, but increasingly his lucid moments were fewer and far between, while the violent and duplicitous son was nearly omnipresent. Nick Manzie had noticed his wife's suffering and had tried to do something about the matter. That Tuesday he took time off from work and tried to find a more permanent solution to the family's problem: Sam.

Nick Manzie investigated a place called Kidspeace, an intensive residential program for children with emotional crises. Located in Allentown, Pennsylvania, it is a haven for the disturbed child, according to its brochure and the recommendations of social workers and doctors. It seemed like a perfect solution to the Manzies' problems.

Nick Manzie just didn't have the money. It cost nearly $350 a day, a far cry from the $90 a day he was paying for Shoreline. His insurance wouldn't cover the hefty sum, either, and so Nick Manzie was searching for alternative ways to fund a stay for his son. "It was a typical case of a family being let down by insurance red tape. It should've been covered," said a close friend of the Manzie family. "God knows they tried everything to get that boy help." When he was lucid, Sam knew that, too. "Can I take my CDs if I go?" Sam asked his mother when he discovered that he might go to Kidspeace. Dolores nearly cried. "He knew he needed help."

On September 23, Nick Manzie arrived home from a day trip out of town to a hornet's nest of strife and activity. Dolores was beside herself; Sam was about to be released, their daughter was upset; the police were trying to get the Manzies back on track to get an arrest of Simmons. To top it all off, no one wanted Sam to come home.

"It was the hardest thing I ever had to do as a parent," Nick Manzie recalled. "There was no way I could take him home the way we all were then. We needed some time and space." Nick told his son, regrettably, that he was going to try and find a place to put him. With the help of the police, the family secured an emergency bed at Harbor House, a county shelter for runaways. Since Sam Manzie wasn't a runaway, he could only stay one night. Nick hoped that would be enough for him to pull off some kind of miracle and get some additional help for his son. The folks at Kimball had referred the case to the family court system as a "juvenile-family crisis." On September 24, Nick Manzie was under the impression the court might help the family find a more suitable place for their son to receive therapy.

On Wednesday, September 24, 1997, the Manzies found themselves bounced to another person in the family court's family intervention unit. Sam Manzie was interviewed there by a probation officer, and Dolores Manzie said that particular interview lasted "all of about six minutes." The probation officer no longer works in that court system, but according to Nick and Dolores the sum total of the interview was the officer asking Sam if he wanted to go home. Sam nodded calmly and said yes, of course he wanted to be at home. Of course, Sam said, he loved his mother and father.

With that, Nick and Dolores Manzie were ushered

into family court, where they stood before Judge James Citta. It was an imposing, official-looking courtroom and commanding the attention of everyone was the man sitting on the bench. A round, balding man with a fleshy nose, Citta was well known in the community and well thought of in most judicial circles. It was a most intimidating way to spend the day for the Manzies.

Nick Manzie said he had no idea when he got up that morning that he was going to see a judge. *We haven't done a good job as parents or we wouldn't be here,* is what he thought as he stood in the courtroom, resigned to having his dirty linen aired in public. It was tough for him. A proud Italian-Catholic heritage was based on self-reliance and the ability to handle one's own problems. Here the Manzies were in front of a court telling a judge they couldn't handle their teenage son. "It was the first time in my life I was ever in a courtroom for anything," the soft-spoken Nick said. "Do you know what it took for us to get there?"

Apparently, Judge Citta wasn't quite sure why they were there, for he was told by the probation officer who also served as an intake officer for the family court system that she was made aware of the situation when Sam's parents refused to take him from Kimball. "So I didn't really have time to get into all the details," she told the judge. "In talking to Mom, it seems more like they're [Dolores and Nick] afraid of him than he's in any danger at the house. In talking to Sam, he says that he's not been violent and the two incidents that they [Sam's parents] talked about with throwing a remote, he didn't throw it at them, he just threw it and that was the only incident."

Again it seemed that Dolores Manzie had become

the focus of attention, rather than Sam. Her emotions were transparent, and as they were worn on her sleeve, the court worker had apparently painted her as fearful for no rational reason. Today it's easy to see how off the mark the assessment was. Particularly telling was the comment that Sam Manzie was apparently not dangerous around the house.

The officer also noted Sam Manzie had a good home to go to and was enrolled in Shoreline and "he has services already set up beyond what Family Crisis can offer to him. So my suggestion is that Sam go home today and the parents, you know, get involved in therapy to deal with this. It is a horrible problem and I can understand their concerns, but he is their child and he is their responsibility and he's going to get better faster if they help than they avoid it."

Nick and Dolores Manzie found themselves somewhat intimidated. They didn't expect to be in court in the first place and then they felt like they were scolded for not living up to their responsibility as parents. The intake officer made it clear that the parents should shoulder the blame and take a more active role in Sam's life. That didn't sit well with the Manzies. Nick had tried, he thought. When Sam had become addicted to the Internet, Nick had hidden the computer keyboard from Sam. Nick had cut off Sam's long-distance service. He and Dolores had done everything the experts had asked and had taken the parental initiative to try and find a solution. To say that the Manzies needed to take a more active role in their son's life seemed to be ignorant folly spoken by someone who really had no idea what was going on in the Manzie household.

Nick Manzie got over his intimidation of the court setting and the potential insult from the intake officer enough to tell Judge Citta exactly where he was coming from. He outlined Sam's abuse and told the judge he and his wife had only recently found out what actually occurred more than a year earlier when Sam had disappeared from the Freehold Raceway Mall.

"And the relationship in the house between my son and the rest of the family has quickly deteriorated and we are afraid of Sam," Nick told the judge, who sat on the bench nodding and listening. "Sam has violent moods. There is absolutely no parenting that Sam will allow us to do. He does not let me in his life at all, does not let me in his head, will not accept any, any counseling from me at all or anything. And he actually says that he's—well, he calls me names with F words in it just like, you know, total disrespect."

The doctors at Shoreline had told Nick Manzie that they thought Sam should be involved in a twenty-four-hour program. "It would be better for him and for the family," Nick told the judge, and offered to bring notarized statements to that effect into court. After all, he again said he did not know he was going to be in court that morning and felt the judge needed every bit of salient information upon which to make an informed decision regarding Sam's well-being. But the judge shook his head in the negative; he didn't think that was necessary as the hearing was, in the judge's own words, "not a formal hearing." The judge just wanted to figure out what was going on and figure out an amicable way to help everyone involved.

But Citta also said that the system had no way to "accommodate an inpatient," and the family would have to find alternatives to having Sam committed somewhere. Nick Manzie outlined his problem with insurance and told the judge he was trying to find a way to get Sam the help his therapists at Shoreline said the boy needed. Nick also told the judge not to get the wrong idea. "I want Sam back. I want him back as my son. I don't care where he's at with his sexuality or whatever it may be. He's my son and I love him. He just doesn't get that."

Nick looked at his son. As any caring father would in that situation, he felt carried away with emotions that only parents can understand. He knew Sam was sick and he knew Sam didn't accept him, but Nick Manzie wasn't ready to give up on his son. Far from it. Nick Manzie wanted Sam well, but he also had to think about his wife and daughter. The family, Nick feared, wouldn't survive if Sam didn't get some help. That's all he wanted was just a little bit of help. Some space.

"And he still has these fits of rage at home," Nick Manzie continued before the judge. "And I think he needs to be in a structured environment, which, obviously, we haven't been able to provide all these years or otherwise it would be different now," he added.

It was hard for Nick Manzie to get to that point in court, and harder, he remembered to swallow his pride and say what came next: "And we need to go to counseling also at the same time. And I don't know, maybe in three months, six months, this program out in Allentown [Kidspeace] is three to six months or six to twelve months . . . I would hope and pray that we can be a family again." No father could have done more or wished for anything better. Nick quite literally begged the court for help.

Dolores Manzie stood quietly with Nick as he poured out his problems and possible solutions, and then she told Judge Citta she thought Sam was making progress at Shoreline, but since it was only a five-and-a-half-hour program (in essence replacing school), when Sam came home, he had absolutely nothing in his life. The police had taken his computer, and Nick and Dolores had turned off his telephone service out of fear that he would continue contacting Simmons. "He has no one that he associates with in the neighborhood like other kids or anything," she said.

The judge seemed confused. Why wasn't Sam in school? Shoreline was the answer. Sam couldn't go to both places. Sam said he received some high school credit by attending Shoreline. Dolores said she'd taken her son for interviews at Monsignor Donovan High School, but that three weeks into the school year Sam was still not in school. Judge Citta wanted to know why private school was so important. What was wrong with public school?

"That was the only place I thought the judge acted a little weirdly," Nick Manzie later said. "He seemed obsessed with getting Sam into public school."

"Well, I wanted to go to Princeton, but I couldn't get in there," the judge said. "You know, I—what's wrong with public school?"

The bottom line as Dolores Manzie explained the situation had nothing to do with the ongoing debate about the quality of public versus private schools. Dolores and Nick weren't listening to G. Gordon Liddy on the radio and bobbing their heads in unison as Liddy attacked the nation's public school system. No, there was a bigger issue at hand; the caregivers at Shoreline had told the Manzies their son was not yet ready to return to school.

A short time later, the judge decided he'd heard enough. "Nobody here is going to like what I'm going to do," he warned the Manzies. Nick and Dolores wondered just exactly what the judge had in mind. "I want everybody to understand that, all right? And the reason that you're not going to like it, because it's not what I want and it's not what you want. But what I'm going to do is, I'm going to send Sam home with you, and I'm going to give him some very close instructions. How old are you now?" the judge asked.

"Fifteen," answered Sam dutifully. That took the judge back for a second; he commented on how tall Sam was for his age. "I don't know whether you're a violent guy or you're not a violent guy, I don't know whether you lose your temper and have trouble controlling your temper, and I don't know what you've been counseled for, and I assume that your counseling is helping you, all right, and I assume if you have a temper problem that they're getting it under control," the judge said. The judge also assumed Sam was still a "kid" and that he enjoyed doing things like going to school, having friends, hanging out, "doing whatever."

Out of all the assumptions the judge made that day, it was later pointed out that the only thing the judge got right was "doing whatever," which certainly was broad enough to cover everything Sam Manzie liked to do. But the judge wasn't done with his assumptions. "I also assume that you love your parents, and it's obvious to me that they care for you, but they're afraid. They're afraid for several reasons because they learned some things in the last couple of days that probably they didn't want to face, and you've learned some things in the last few days, or come to realize some things in the last few days, that you didn't want to deal with, and I can only assume, and I'm making an assumption that the destruction of that equipment that would have aided law enforcement to apprehend this gentleman because you didn't want to deal with it, and you, from your perspective, there was no harm, no foul. And I'm not getting into your personal life or your personal preferences or any of those kind of things because I'm not going to sit in judgment of that. Those issues are not before me, but I'm going to give you some ground rules and I want you to pay careful attention to what I'm going to say," Judge Citta said. He told Nick and Dolores to take Sam home, put him in school and advised counseling. He told Sam to "follow their [Nick and Dolores Manzie's] rules."

"But the bottom line is you know the difference between what's right and wrong, don't you? You're not retarded, are you?" the judge asked Sam.

"No," Sam said earnestly.

"No," the judge repeated. "And you're not mentally disabled in any way? You're not a psychopath? No? So you have some adjustment problems," the judge said, adding that Sam knew the difference between what was right and what was wrong and perhaps the family just needed counseling.

Making a nod to the Manzies' economic situation, the judge said there could be all kinds of talk about Shoreline and doctors, but maybe they could get through the situation without having to spend $350 a day on therapy. The judge also said he would not handle any insubordination from Sam. "I have little tolerance for young people who don't do the right thing," he warned Sam. He urged a "positive approach" to solving the family's problems and cautioned that "no man is an island" before wondering out loud who originally uttered that famous line.

Then he looked at Sam Manzie and again cautioned that he needed "the assistance and guidance of people who care for you and love you, and that's those two people right here." The judge pointed to Sam's parents. "You know how I know that, Samuel?"

"No," Sam said cautiously.

What Judge Citta said next was the only solace Sam Manzie's parents ever got from the legal system.

"Because I deal with people and problems from Family Crisis all the time, and it's very, very infrequently that when I look out in my courtroom from up here and these Family Crisis people are here and there's a young person or a young adult in front of me that I get to see one parent standing up and saying help, let alone two parents standing up and saying let's get some help. That's how I know," Judge Citta said. Sure, he said, Sam's parents may not always make the right decision, but what parents always do? The judge then said he had earned and spent more money than most people will make "in their entire lifetime" and cautioned the Manzies against throwing money at Sam's problems to solve them. But, he said frankly, that he didn't know what the solution to the problem was, he could only tell Sam "that you've got to do the right thing," and that if Sam didn't, "I don't have any tolerance for wise guys."

The judge said there was a real simple solution for Sam. All he had to remember to do was in the words of Spike Lee: "Do the right thing." If Sam Manzie remembered the difference between right and wrong, then everything would be fine. He just didn't want Manzie's parents to avoid their son's problems. That stunned both parents. To Nick and Dolores, it seemed like they were the only people willing to confront it. The therapists had passed the buck, they thought, the people at Kimball had passed the buck, the cops were pressuring them to assist in the investigation and Simmons was dramatically telling anyone who would listen how he was the only one who really cared for Sam, leaving Nick and Dolores stuck with a violent, mentally unstable teenager.

"I thought to myself, what the hell do we do now?" Nick Manzie said.

Nick just had to shake his head. No one understood. They didn't see how distraught Dolores was. They didn't see what the family had gone through. Nick wasn't sure what the judge saw, nor did he think the judge had a good handle on the situation. The judge had said that Sam Manzie appeared to be a "fine young man," and that the *family's* problems could be overcome if everyone in the family kept a cool head on their shoulders and a "positive approach, a positive attitude and understand that everybody's motivation is the same." Obviously, everyone's motivation was not the same and the judge prepared Sam for that, too, telling him he had no tolerance for "wise guys" and that if he continued to curse and fight with his parents or did anything "shocking and appalling" Sam would find himself right back in family court. It didn't seem like much of a threat to Sam Manzie, and Nick and Dolores seemed totally nonplussed. Finally Judge Citta said, "Trust me when I tell you, young man, that will not be a pleasant experience [coming back to family court] because I am a tough guy." With those prophetic remarks, the Spike Lee admonition and a few other choice invectives, the judge wished the family good luck and the hearing came to a quick close.

Nick Manzie shook his head in confusion and disgust. It was not the solution to the problem he had hoped for. He looked over at his wife, who was equally stunned and too numb to react after the outpouring of emotion during the last few days. To her, every day had been a horrible nightmare since she found Sam had destroyed the police equipment. There had been arguments, rage, uncaring and unmovable doctors. She was resigned to a state of perpetual hopelessness.

Sam was coming home.

"I began to think I'd overreacted," Nick Manzie said. "I mean, Dolores and I thought Sam was violent and a danger to himself and to others, but we couldn't get anyone else to believe us, so we began doubting it ourselves." So the first thing Nick did was reach over and hug his son. Maybe things would be all right. Instead, he was greeted with the same cold stare Sam Manzie had given him for the last year. Nothing had changed.

Nick Manzie knew then that the best thing, still, was to get his son into the Kidspeace program. The people he contacted at Kidspeace had told him there was a good possibility that either Sam's school district or the Department of Youth and Family Services might be able to pay for some of the cost of the Kidspeace program. That encouraged Nick, but the more he delved into that possibility, the more he became convinced that Judge Citta had let his son down.

The question raised in the newspapers after Eddie Werner's death was "Could Citta have done more?" The judge couldn't commit Sam Manzie to a psychiatric institution unless he was a danger by "reason of mental illness," according to New Jersey law. The judge had to rely heavily on the probation officer who interviewed Manzie just prior to court and she pooh-poohed the notion that the teenager was a threat. But the judge, according to the *New York Times*, could have transferred Sam Manzie into the care of a relative or friend, giving them temporary custody of the mentally disturbed teen. That seemed like a long shot, but he could have brought in the Department of Youth and Family Services and someone there could have either found extended foster-care options or perhaps a group home or shelter for a short time while Nick Manzie arranged for Sam to go into Kidspeace.

Kidspeace—it was like heaven to Nick. It was where he thought his son could heal and get better. It was the last chance the kid would have and it seemed like no one wanted to give it to him. All Nick was hoping for was a couple of days of reprieve while he figured out some way to get the financing lined up. Instead, the Manzies were told: "Take him home." The judge had asked Sam: "You're not retarded, are you?" It played like a Kafka novel in Nick's head as he ran through all the people who had denied him help in dealing with his son. He was at wits' end and no one, absolutely no one, helped out.

Meanwhile, the hammer was getting ready to fall on Steve Simmons. Nicholas Severino, the detective from Suffolk County, New York, had gotten the OK around 10:30 P.M. on September 23 to arrest Simmons, but as of noon on September 24, he still hadn't found Simmons. He'd also had a small bit of bad luck when he had prepared a search warrant for Simmons's home, only to have a judge refuse to sign it.

Severino, who bears a close resemblance to actor Harold Gould, is a well-dressed, well-mannered detective from the old school. Close to retirement when he took the Simmons case, he left the force long before the case ever made it to trial and came out of retirement to try and help hammer a few nails in Simmons's coffin, but instead nailed a few in his own.

On September 24, all he really wanted to do was arrest the pedophile. He got lucky and found Simmons at work at the T-shirt shop run by Joe Ferraro. Severino and his partner walked in and found Simmons calmly standing in the shop. "We identified ourselves and told him that we were conducting an investigation involving him," Severino said in his arrest report. "We asked him to accompany us to the fifth squad where we could discuss the allegations."

Simmons, previously tipped off by Sam Manzie, knew the cops were coming and said as much. If the cops were hoping to surprise him or in any way get a rise out of him, they didn't. Simmons went very peacefully from his work. He was cuffed and led unceremoniously and calmly out of the shop to the waiting police car. A very short time later, police said, Simmons confessed. Since it didn't take long to wheedle a confession from him and since he came so peacefully, it began to look to the police in New York and New Jersey that at least one part of the ugly tale was coming to a happy conclusion.

All still wasn't well at the Manzie home, though. On September 25, Sam Manzie returned to Shoreline and was reportedly calm. One worker who saw him there that day said he was even "lethargic." It was a deceptive calm, but Manzie was good at deceptions. He'd fooled social workers, judges, probation officers and his parents for a very long time. Simmons later said he thought Sam Manzie was going to commit suicide that weekend and there was some indication that Sam was contemplating it. He had thought about ending his life before and was certainly despondent enough to try it. He had visited violence on his family so often that it was becoming old hat. It was a well-traveled road that went nowhere. Simmons said he was worried at the time that Sam could turn inward and take his own life. Simmons's arrest would cause Manzie additional despair. Manzie had failed Simmons. He had failed his family and himself. Outwardly he was in good spirits on September 25 and 26, Dolores Manzie said.

Inwardly there's no question that Sam Manzie had reached critical mass. He was going to either implode or explode, and in all likelihood it was going to occur on the one day he knew he had a reasonable chance of being alone: Saturday, September 27, 1997—the one day a month his parents would work for a bus tour group going to the casinos. Nick Manzie said he had mixed feelings about going, as did Dolores, but Sam had been calm for two days following the court appearance and maybe, just maybe, they could hold out hope that they could get their son into Kidspeace. Maybe the weekend jobs would help. Maybe he would calm down. Maybe they could get some semblance of a normal life back.

"They told me he was no danger and finally I decided maybe they were right," Nick Manzie later said. "I wanted my son to be all right." The strict Catholic had prayed for it numerous times, but it wasn't a prayer that would be answered—at least not in the way Nick hoped.

On Saturday, September 27, just three days after Judge Citta and a probation worker who'd seen Sam Manzie for all of six minutes had declared him no threat to others, Manzie was ready to explode "in a paroxysm of violence," as he himself had described in one of his essays. Judge Citta, the probation worker and the police who arrested Simmons on September 24 had struck the match. It would have been a tragedy if Sam Manzie had imploded on himself. The Manzies would have been guaranteed a huge amount of guilt and pain had they come home from working that weekend and found their son dead by his own hand in their home.

But Sam Manzie didn't implode. He exploded and the only human being within range of the blast was an innocent child trying to sell enough candy to win a prize at school. Eddie Werner was just a normal eleven-year-old boy, unknown to his killer. That is the largest and hardest tragedy to face about the entire case. Simmons met Manzie in person on August 10, 1996. A little more than a year later, Eddie Werner was dead. There were signs and cries for help from everyone who ever knew Sam Manzie, who ever dealt with him or who ever loved him. Manzie had asked a teacher if he could perform fellatio on the teacher. He'd told about his affair with Simmons, cooperated with police, cried out for help on the Internet and saw numerous doctors, therapists and social workers. His parents literally begged anyone and everyone in the system for help. They didn't know how to get it for their son, but thought they were asking the right questions of the right people—and still Eddie Werner died.

Debby Mahoney remembered the first time when she put two and two together and read about Sam Manzie in the newspaper. She saw how Manzie had been molested by Simmons and read that they'd met on-line. A little bell went off in her head. Then she read that one of Sam's on-line screen names was "Sam82." She wanted to cry. "There it was. That was him. He was the boy who asked for help. I couldn't believe it," she said. "It was such a senseless, needless tragedy and we knew about it months before it happened."

As it turns out, the FBI never did anything with

Mahoney's call. The federal government was just the latest addition to the large list of agencies, doctors and officials who could've helped Sam Manzie and didn't.

Nine

A Mother's Intuition

Fall is a beautiful time in the woods of central New Jersey. The fall rains come and the weather cools, bringing with it occasional smells of the Atlantic Ocean, if you're fortunate enough to be close to the shore, and the sweet smells of falling leaves. It's a peaceful, passive time and you can almost feel the earth sigh as it gets ready for the coming holiday season. At least, that's how Ed Werner used to think of fall. Now he only thinks of his dead son.

The search for Eddie began at 11:00 P.M. on Saturday, September 27, 1997. By the following morning, there were people actively combing the neighborhood, knocking on doors, looking in the woods and walking the streets. It gave Dolores Manzie a scare; a shiver went up and down her back. She was afraid of and angry with her son, Sam, but she never thought his anger would lash out at someone outside of the family. As she watched people searching for Eddie Werner, she wasn't so sure anymore.

When the police showed up the first time to question Sam Manzie late at night the day after Eddie's disappearance, Nick Manzie wasn't so sure anymore, either. He was eager to help out the police in their search for Eddie—after all, he remembered well his own fears after Sam had turned up missing nearly a year before. He shuddered to think that other parents were going through what he and Dolores had to endure. He was more than eager to volunteer that Sam could help the police.

"I don't wanna talk to any cops," Sam told his father when Nick went back to the bedroom to ask him.

"What could I do?" Nick Manzie said in hindsight. "I didn't feel like it was the time nor the place to go into the entire history of Sam's emotional problems for the last year." So Nick Manzie told the cops that Sam was a little ornery and asked them to come back later.

The next day, Sam Manzie went to his therapists at Shoreline. When asked how his weekend had been, Sam said it had merely been "interesting." Dolores, though, was convinced it had been horrifying. However, when she spoke with the caregivers at Shoreline, they told her she was probably overreacting. Sam Manzie didn't have anything to do with Eddie Werner's disappearance, she was told. A few days later, when Dolores Manzie returned home from an excursion, she saw her son sitting on the porch smoking a cigarette. "They arrested somebody on that missing boy," he told her. Dolores breathed a sigh of relief, but it didn't last. "Everything that shocked me in my life occurred that night. I thought I'd been through a lot in that previous week, but it was nothing compared to what I had to go through after Eddie Werner was killed."

It was hell for anyone related to or who knew anything about Sam Manzie or Eddie Werner. The jarring, earthquakelike effect began when Eddie turned up missing during the weekend. By Tuesday everyone knew Eddie was dead, and police told the Werners they had a "very good suspect." On Wednesday Sam Manzie was arrested. That Thursday someone from the prosecutor's office stopped by to tell the Werners that Eddie had been sexually molested and Valerie went hysterical again. On Friday the Werners and the rest of the world found out about Sam Manzie's past and Steve Simmons's involvement. "The pain of losing my son was so intense and I was so numb," Ed Werner said, "but then every day we were hit with something else. I just couldn't believe it. Every day was a torture."

The worry the Werners felt when Eddie turned up missing became the universal nightmare every man or woman fears who has ever had a child; their son was never coming home. His toys would never be played with again, his bed never slept in, and his clothes would never be worn. Forever he would be frozen in his parents' memories as an eleven-year-old boy. He would not know the joy of growing up, dating, going to college, starting his own family. Nor would he ever know the joy of hugging his parents again. Sam Manzie had taken that all away from the Werners in one dark fit of rage spawned from the recesses of an extremely twisted and disturbed mind. In killing Eddie Werner, Sam Manzie had also killed the hopes and dreams of an entire family and propelled the Werners into a small but growing club of parents. It is a club, as John Walsh, the host of television's *America's Most Wanted*, often says, no one wants to join and once there no one wants to see any new members. Sam Manzie had caused the

Werners to join the club of parents whose children had been murdered.

Parents who suffer through such trauma are a scarred bunch. Marriages often shatter after the death of a child and the healing is rarely complete. The parents often torture themselves, struggling to find reason in the madness or constantly asking the question, "What if . . . ?" They blame themselves, they live in denial and there are tears and empty feelings that go on many times for the remainder of the parents' lives. Two years after a woman lost her only two daughters to a murderous rampage in an Austin, Texas, yogurt shop, the mother had life-size posters of her two daughters in their individual rooms. The rooms were made up as shrines; nothing had been changed or touched since the day her daughters died. "They say after your child dies you have to move on. No, you don't. My girls are still right here with me," the mother told an *America's Most Wanted* producer two years after the fact.

This was the reward Sam Manzie gave to the Werners for trying to raise Eddie, a vulnerable, typical preteen. This, too, was the gift that Sam gave his own parents, the guilt of raising a killer and the horrible pain of trying to understand what had happened and why. Nick and Dolores Manzie had struggled hard to find help for Sam before something drastic had happened. They did not feel the guilt of standing passively on the sidelines while their child, a boy who once picked the name "Job" for his confirmation, mutated into a psychopathic killer. They *knew* something was wrong. So apparently did detectives Arancio and Noble. According to Noble, after having the weekend off, he returned to work on September 29 to "assist an ongoing investigation that occurred during my absence over the weekend wherein information pertinent to this case may assist another agency in an ongoing criminal investigation."

Sam Manzie, never let on that he'd killed Eddie in his own home. Nor did he let his parents know about the suitcase with the boy's remains or the photograph and money in the dresser drawer. He went to Shoreline on Monday, dumping some of Eddie's clothes nearby.

After Sam Manzie became the focus of the criminal investigation, and his mother got him to confess to the crime, Dolores then had to take Sam in to make a statement to police. But first she had to tell the police what her son had told her. Not wanting to get anything wrong, and in an effort to protect themselves from future litigation, the police taped Dolores Manzie's interview that night. "It is a compelling statement," Mike Critchley, Sam's attorney, said. "It is full of emotion and full of pain. I planned on using it in Sam's defense in court."

Looking at just the facts of the case, Critchley said, reads like a tragedy.

Six weeks out of grammar school, Sam Manzie met and was molested by Steve Simmons. "At adolescence you are very vulnerable and at that point in time a forty-three-year-old man stuck his penis in Sam's anus. Imagine what that does to an already troubled teen. Every psychiatrist who ever examined Sam said he was suffering from a mental disability and I told him bottom line, 'Sam, you're sick.' He needed help." The normal route from child to teen is troubled enough, Critchley added, saying that Sam's involvement with Simmons was a "recipe for psychological disaster."

Certainly, the beginnings of Sam Manzie's mental demise and Eddie Werner's gruesome death began in August 1996. Critchley maintains that anyone, without even interviewing Sam, can see the deterioration that began once Simmons actively began exerting his influence on Sam. The boy apparently knew he needed help and reached out several times to get it, but was ambivalent when he got it. He remained torn until the very end, unable even to testify against the man who'd helped precipitate his violent spiral into murder.

When police, the press, lawyers, social workers and others began searching for answers to why Sam Manzie had protected the pedophile that had molested him, few if anyone found cogent answers. There was only speculation as to the hold Simmons had over Sam. But, perhaps, they overlooked the answer that Sam Manzie gave to that puzzle. In the end, it turned out to be said best by Manzie himself: "True Friendships Are Forever," Sam declared on his Web page. It was his award-winning essay that he wrote in eighth grade. It meant enough to him to publish it on the Internet. It meant enough to him that he proudly told the world he'd won an essay contest. The naive teen had mistaken Simmons's attraction to him as a "true friendship" and perhaps in Simmons's mind he believed that, too. Simmons turned out to be little more than a child in a man's body, while Sam was a boy trying to be a man. He couldn't or wouldn't see his own family as "true friends," but he would protect the one person he did see that way, much to the chagrin of his parents and to the delight of Steve Simmons.

Simmons has a far different take on why Sam Manzie murdered Eddie Werner. "I have no doubt in my mind that Sam was going to kill himself that day," Simmons later said. "Remember when the police made him make the telephone call to me. The first one. Sam had twenty-two minutes of me being on his side while he was stabbing me in the back. His guilt was immense because he loved me and trusted me and yet he was working with people he hated and didn't trust."

Newspapers, other police, doctors and therapists in the area, loath to agree with Simmons, reluctantly said that police pressure on Sam Manzie did indeed contribute to the stress in his life that may or may not have caused him to lash out at Eddie Werner.

"The prosecutor was nothing but blind to a boy's pain," said Dr. Pallone.

Simmons said the police should've just left everyone alone. "I knew Sammy better than anyone and if people could have gotten past the sexual thing, I think I could've helped Sammy out before someone got killed."

Simmons said he and Sam had talked about the two moving in together, and Simmons, indeed, saw some of the things in Sam his own parents had seen. "Sammy was a contradiction. Most gay kids are pacifists. Sam was aggressive and obviously violent. I made him feel comfortable and loved. He had no friends. He hated what he was. He was insecure with little self-respect. As such he couldn't give or share. He was like an unwatered houseplant. I can assure you that if Sam lived with me at fifteen he would never have been violent."

Meanwhile, Nick and Dolores Manzie had tried time and time again to reach out and help their son. They knew they had little control over him and even a smaller amount of influence on him. They hoped the professionals, whether it be professional lawyers, police officers, health-care providers, judges or any of a dozen of others they consulted, could help them in their desperate attempt to save their son. Time and time again, they were met with indifference and even hostility from those who were supposed to help. Judge Citta refused to commit Sam Manzie based on a systemic approach to the problem that worked efficiently and effectively "99.9 percent of the time," Critchley said. The law in New Jersey said at the time that individuals over fourteen cannot be committed to a psychiatric institution without their consent.

Sam Manzie, despite whatever attempts he'd made to reach out for help, wasn't about to consent to being committed. While Manzie may have told his parents he wanted help, the day he showed up in Citta's court he told the judge his desire was to return home. If he wanted help, really wanted help, he could've reached out then before the judge, but chose not to. Few, if any, fifteen-year-olds would want to voluntarily commit themselves and be put into a mental hospital. Ludicrous on the face of it, certainly in Manzie's case he didn't want to leave an environment in which he was not only familiar but also one in which he could exercise some control.

He could have been committed involuntarily under a temporary court order if two doctors, one a psychiatrist, certified the need for treatment. The people at Shoreline, according to Nick Manzie in Citta's court, had said Sam needed twenty-four-hour care, but the intake and probation officer at family court did not, and no other doctors were consulted. The recommendation was for Sam Manzie to return home and he had, to disastrous results.

The health-care workers told Nick and Dolores Manzie they were overreacting. Sam wasn't suicidal or homicidal, they told the parents. Some even mistakenly believed the parents were at fault and too emotional. The FBI never adequately checked out the leads. The problem of insurance coverage and its relationship to the health-care industry raised its ugly, greedy head as Nick Manzie was forced to shop around for health care he could afford for his son. That, too, was a tragedy many court observers in Ocean County, New Jersey, said was all too common. No one wanted to help, it seemed, and no one would unless the Manzies coughed up their life savings.

Sam Manzie had become frustrated, resentful and irrational. His parents were bullied and brow-beaten—by the system and most definitely by their son. On a number of occasions, Dolores Manzie told reporters, all it took to set Sam off was for her to "cook something he didn't want for dinner." The inside of the Manzie home looked like a war zone and while Sam had been sent to Shoreline, he obviously hadn't done well there. Manzie told his mother he killed Eddie to strike back at the people at Shoreline. They may have recommended twenty-four-hour care, but Manzie told his mother, "I told him [his psychiatrist] I was going to hurt somebody and he didn't do nothing about it."

Dolores and Nick grew to think it wasn't just Shoreline that had let them down. Arancio and Noble had known that Simmons gave Sam drugs, had more than one sexual liaison with Sam and at one point had tried to introduce another man into their tryst. Dolores and Nick were convinced if that information, which they were not aware of at the time Sam went to Kimball, had been known to them then or during the meeting with Judge Citta, then they could have gotten their son committed.

"Think about it," Nick Manzie said. "The cops knew much more than we did and they didn't come forward with it until after Eddie's death and then it was only to hurt Sam, not help him."

Had anyone told Citta, it's possible that things

might have been different. But there were many things that could've happened differently and didn't. Dolores Manzie remembered the day Citta returned Sam to her: "I saw him that day standing in court, and I just looked at him, and here everybody was saying, you know, 'There's nothing wrong with this boy,' and I'm thinking, 'God, what kind of mother am I to think I have a kid that needs to be put away?' "

"The Manzies had been crying out for a week before Eddie died and much longer," Critchley, their attorney, later said. "Everybody should step back and pause a moment before they put this kid on a pyre and burn him." According to Critchley, many people who could have helped failed to even lift a finger.

On October 3, 1997, as the news of the gruesome murder spread, Monmouth County prosecutor John Kaye began to feel heat from the local media for the way detectives Noble and Arancio handled the case. Kaye told newspaper reporters there was never any sign of trouble from Sam Manzie and if there had been he wouldn't have been used as a tool to go after Steve Simmons. "Eight days ago, he changed abruptly," Kaye told the *New Jersey Star-Ledger.* "We needed more information to corroborate allegations, and we were seeking the information when the machinery was destroyed and the boy stopped cooperating."

"The teen subsequently refused all psychological counseling," the paper also noted.

The Manzie family tried to stay away from all the furor during the first few days after Eddie Werner's death. They stayed in Northern New Jersey while they were vilified in their local community. "To tell you the truth, we didn't see a whole lot of the local papers then," Nick Manzie later said. "We knew they got a lot of things wrong, but it was too painful to read." Still, they wanted to set the record straight, so they agreed to talk to a national audience at the end of October. "I was nervous, but felt like I had to do it," Nick Manzie said. The Manzies chose as their forum ABC's weekly news magazine, *20/20*.

The appearance served to drive a wedge between the Manzies and the Werners. It wasn't so much what was said, although the Werners had trouble with that as well. It was the simple fact that the Manzies were invited and partook of the national media attention. The segment title "Sam's Story" didn't help the Werners much, either. After all, it was Eddie who was dead and not Sam Manzie. It was Eddie who would never play with his brother and sisters again. It was Eddie whose voice had been silenced forever. Valerie Werner "expressed disgust" at an ABC news release promoting the segment with the Manzies. The appeal for compassion for Sam Manzie and his family fell on deaf ears in the Werner household. A walk through their home where Eddie's clothes, toys and memories were still so painfully close was the reason why.

The appearance on *20/20* outlined some of the dilemma Nick and Dolores Manzie faced with Sam. They told how their son "knew he needed help" in the days before Eddie's death. Dolores talked about how lonely Sam was and how he had nothing in his life. She was happy when Sam began using the computer and communicating with people on-line. At least, she thought, her son was reaching out to *someone*. "He wasn't out playing like other kids. And it would break my heart to see them out there, and he [Sam] had nothing. So when the computer came into the house, it was like he had some kind of communication with somebody," Dolores said.

But then Sam turned violent, and for the first time, people got to hear from Dolores about the "living nightmare in our house." Nick told how he was in fear of his own son the day Sam threw a television remote at him. "The look in his eyes when he was looking at me was one of—I was terrified. Just his look, looking at me, as if he wanted to really hurt me bad."

In a world where teenagers had been known to kill their own parents, it wasn't an idle threat from Sam Manzie. It was a horrifying position for a father to be in: raise a hand to the child and the father might face charges of child abuse. Do nothing and the father could be a victim himself of far worse. Nick Manzie wasn't sure of the source of hatred he saw in his son's eyes, but thought that Sam's own "tortured" guilt over his sexual identity and Nick's own devotion to Catholicism may have had something to do with it.

It wasn't easy on Sam's end, either, as he struggled to relate to his devout Catholic father. After all, Catholics believe that homosexuality is a mortal sin. It couldn't have been easy for Sam, and that came across in the 20/20 interview, as did Sam's duplicity. Dolores Manzie told the national audience that Sam begged to get help. "He said, 'I'll go in a minute,'" Dolores said of Sam's desire to be committed. "He wanted help. He just didn't know how to do it. He didn't know how to ask for it." Unstated, of course, was that Sam Manzie had the perfect opportunity in front of Judge Citta to ask for help. Rather than do so, he balked and requested to go back home. Manzie was bright, no doubt about it. Perhaps he was afraid of being committed and sought the comfort of home as a solace to his problems. No matter how flawed his home life was—much of it because of his own actions—it was an arena where he felt safe. Perhaps it was an arena where he knew he also had some control. If committed, Sam Manzie would lose all control over his life. That couldn't sit well with him, so perhaps there were other reasons why he couldn't or didn't know how to ask for help.

Manzie's duplicity also showed itself in his actions before his parents in the days prior to the murder. "Sam was very docile those two days," Nick Manzie told the national television audience. He thought there would be no problems. The two days before the killing were "the best two days we had in one-and-a-half years with him," Dolores Manzie said.

The Manzies told the news audience that trouble began in August 1996 when Sam met Steve Simmons on-line and began a sexual relationship with him. Pressure grew in the household when Sam's therapist informed the authorities in Monmouth County of Sam's tryst with Simmons. When the detectives began using Sam, Dolores said, the trouble in their home became unbearable.

"They were giving us dates to come in for statements; they were coming to the house," she said. "Everything got so crazy that we forgot about Sam, his feelings."

That was a difficult admission to make on television as Dolores Manzie shouldered a heavy amount of blame. She and Nick had done everything the therapists and the police had told them to do. They had trusted those in authority who were supposed to be the experts. Looking back, she found herself lacking by trusting those experts too much. She thought she had neglected Sam.

Then came the destruction of the equipment and the visit to Kimball. Dolores said she begged the counselor there to keep her son for around-the-clock treatment. "I told her, 'Don't make me take him home 'cause something's going to happen.' And I thought it was going to be within the family 'cause he was so hard to control and his violence was getting worse and worse. And they said, 'You have to; you're the mother.' That if I didn't, I could be prosecuted or I could be arrested for abandonment.'"

Then the Manzies detailed their appearance in court and the judge's decision that rebuked everything the Manzies thought about their son. Dolores felt guilty about thinking her son needed to be committed. Nick stared at his son, thinking he was somehow wrong about the gangly teen standing before him. At that point, he told the national audience, he thought he was wrong about his son and *he* as a father had overreacted.

After Eddie Werner was murdered and Sam Manzie was arrested, the Manzies visited their son frequently, and Dolores told the television camera that "the very first time I saw him, he walked through the door and I was wanting to hug him, and just be with him. And he just looked at me right in the face and said, 'I need help.' " But Dolores said she wasn't sure Sam felt any remorse for killing Eddie. "I'm not even sure of that," she said. "I mean, I'm not sure of anything because he just stares blankly ahead. Like we're not even in the room with him."

If the appearance on national television was supposed to generate some sympathy for Sam, it certainly fell on deaf ears in the place sympathy was needed the most. Ocean County prosecutor E. David Millard didn't find any compassion for the Manzies. By the end of October, Sam Manzie found himself facing additional charges of first-degree robbery because of the candy money he had taken from Eddie. By then, Millard was also asking that Manzie be tried as an adult. The Werners were most decidedly for that action and the Manzies were against it. By December the Werners were publicly calling for a life sentence, the harshest that could be imposed on Manzie. Dolores and Nick, meanwhile, were still fighting to get their son psychiatric help.

The stage was then set for a legal showdown, which would take nearly a year and a half to play out. During this entire time, the Werners and the Manzies were distanced from each other, despite many similarities in their lives. Sam Manzie had destroyed both families, who were both devout Catholics. Eddie had minor problems with disabilities and sometimes had a hard time fitting in, as did Sam. Both families had been on a roller-coaster ride through the media, experiencing highs and lows as the story's ebb and flow swept them up and then left them alone in their grief. It was a mutual grief as the Manzies felt horrible for the Werners and experienced pangs of guilt as they realized what their son had done. The Werners could understand what the Manzies were going through, but the painful loss of their son was too much for them to empathize with the Manzies. They were two families separated by their mutual grief and the pain brought about by Sam's actions.

The only place they could find common ground was in their disdain for the way the system had treated Sam and their disgust with Steve Simmons.

Ten

"Do Something!"

His favorite color was green and in his death Eddie Werner was remembered by hundreds, perhaps even thousands, of green ribbons tied around trees, mailboxes, fences and posts all around the mid-New Jersey area. The Manzies posted one on the front of their house in the first few days after Eddie died, only to have it anonymously removed twice. It seemed no one, in the beginning, wanted to go out of their way to give the Manzies a break. After the newspapers began printing Sam's name as Eddie's accused killer, the Manzie family was on the receiving end of violent threats, some vague and some specific, which further drove them into isolation and alienation.

It was not the way Nick Manzie had been raised. It sure wasn't Christian, but there wasn't much he could do about it. He wanted to scream out that his family wasn't as monstrous as it was portrayed. He and his wife had raised two children in their household and their daughter was an honor student. She hadn't done anything wrong. Nick also wanted to let everyone know how sorry he was, but felt it would sound hollow, and besides he had no way of doing it. He and Dolores were getting no slack from the neighborhood, and police had to be posted in front of their home on a few occasions to make sure no one harmed the family.

Neighbors routinely described Sam Manzie as a "monster child" to whom no one would give the time of day. "He wasn't well liked," an older woman who lived on the same street as the Manzies said. "He was just mean."

Each day Nick Manzie had to shake his head as he came home to the circus engineered by his only son. On the day of Sam's arrest, Nick noted that the headlines on the front page screamed of his son's incarceration, while on the back page of the newspaper, almost in fine print, was a list of honor students at the local high school. His daughter was among them. On the day of Sam's arrest, the Manzies owned both sides of the local paper, but few were paying attention to the efforts of Nick and Dolores Manzie's daughter.

The world wanted to know about Sam Manzie and many, in the first few days of the case, were repulsed and fascinated as to why a fifteen-year-old child would attempt to sexually assault and then strangle another child who was only eleven.

It was a shot to the solar plexus for parents across the country and fodder for many a local and national talk show. "Are our children safe anywhere anymore?" was a theme that played itself out almost nightly on television news shows as Eddie Werner's last day on earth was recounted time and again. Jim Werner, Eddie's uncle, told a local reporter, "It was

five o'clock [the day Eddie disappeared]. It wasn't
even dark yet. You can't take an eleven-year-old boy
by the hand through life. You have to let him live."

The realization of the horror of Sam Manzie's
crime against Eddie brought other ramifications
from all over the country as people asked: what kind
of parents would raise a child as vicious as Sam Manzie? What was wrong? Who could we blame?

On October 2, word reached the media that Sam
Manzie had been the victim of sexual molestation
and that Steve Simmons had been charged on September 24 with the crime. While Sam Manzie was
still a juvenile, and even though he was the victim
of a crime himself, the newspapers continued to publish his name. It gave his parents no rest and no
comfort, but the new revelations enabled a scared
and vengeful public to vent its collective wrath on
someone other than the Manzies. It effectively
served to shift a lot of the blame onto a pedophile,
someone much easier to vilify than a fifteen-year-old
boy. It also made some sense to people who didn't
know the case. Many distant spectators across the
country could not fathom why one child could kill
another. The introduction of a pedophile into the
equation allowed many of those on the periphery of
the case to sleep easier.

"Can you see why I'm fighting so hard?" Simmons
responded to the attacks on him. "It's not for me.
It's for Sam; it is for the Werners; it is for the three
million gay teens. It's for the countless Eddie
Werners in the future. It would seem that the
Manzies and the Werners should be on my side. But
maybe the truth is only important to me. I'm an
idealist."

He was not seen as an ideal member of his community. While Sam Manzie owed his allegiance to

Simmons, few others did. Many saw him as a card-carrying member of NAMBLA, the North American Man/Boy Love Association. It is a group of pedophiles that publishes a monthly newsletter, lobbies to lower the age of consent laws and celebrates with joy all types of activities, most especially sex, between grown men and young boys. NAMBLA members have justified having sex with children as young as six or seven years of age and say that theoretically it is OK with children even younger. When police found out Simmons was a pedophile, they actively looked for NAMBLA literature among his belongings, but never found any.

"NAMBLA is full of sick perverts," Simmons said. "No way should children be having sex that young. I don't consider myself a typical pedophile. All I ever wanted was what was right for Sammy. I told him to get psychological help. He didn't get it before I suggested it to him."

Simmons said the community in New Jersey simply vilified him and hung him out to dry because they needed a "scapegoat."

"If the police had been where they were supposed to be and done their job right, things would have turned out a lot differently and that's what they conveniently want you to forget. After a while I got so disgusted, it was hard to follow my own case," Simmons said.

This could not be said of the Werners or the Manzies. After the initial shock of their loss, Ed Werner became determined to see the case through to the end, no matter how painful and no matter what the consequences. His boy was dead for no reason at the hands of another child. He did not want his son to die in vain, and both he and his wife struggled to make sure that would not be the case. Depression was a daily visitor for the Werners, as was the reminders that their son wasn't coming home. Sometimes all Ed or Valerie had to do was to look at one of Eddie's possessions and it could bring out a stream of tears.

Meanwhile, the Manzies' ongoing nightmare continued as well. Depression was an everyday houseguest for Nick and Dolores, too. Ostracized by some in the community, vilified and misunderstood by others, and helped by those who knew and loved them, the Manzies were under a great deal of pressure at the beginning of October. The Manzies had grief, the Werners had longing, loss and horror. It was no competition between the families. The despair visited both of them, plus the Manzies had the added horror of having lived through it for at least a year already and the desperation of trying to do something for their son and having nothing work out. Couple that with the realization that the problems were likely to continue for their family for the foreseeable future, and little wonder, then, that the Manzies seriously considered suicide. They planned it; they thought about how to execute it. However, they could not go through with it. Looking into the eyes of their beautiful daughter, and knowing that she would be devastated, kept them grounded. She became the biggest reason for staying sane and from delving too deep into the black hole of self-pity.

It wasn't easy. Public sentiment wasn't riding high for the Manzies, and the Werners weren't fans of the Manzie family, either. Even as the facts became public about Sam's molestation by Simmons, Valerie Werner, Eddie's mother, urged the public not to consider Sam Manzie a victim. She wanted him tried as an adult and punished to the fullest extent of the law. She did not feel predisposed to showing more

Victim Eddie Werner, 11. *(Photo courtesy the Werner family)*

Valerie Werner with Eddie in 1986. (*Photo courtesy the Werner family*)

Werner was a center forward on his soccer team. (*Photo courtesy the Werner family*)

Rescue dogs found Werner's body in local wooded
area two days after he disappeared.

Samuel Manzie, 15. *(Photo courtesy AP/Wide World Photo)*

Manzie's dark memories of his childhood do not show in these photos from the early 1980s. (*Photo courtesy Nicholas and Dolores Manzie*)

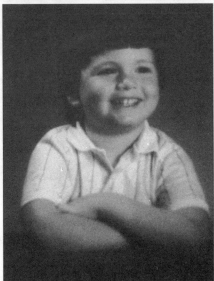

Manzie was confirmed in the seventh grade.
(*Photo courtesy Nicholas and Dolores Manzie*)

In 1996, Manzie designed his own Web site,
where he posted his essays about life.

Open window (*top left*) is Manzie's bedroom, where he strangled Werner.

Police believe Manzie hid Werner in suitcase behind fenced area near his back door.

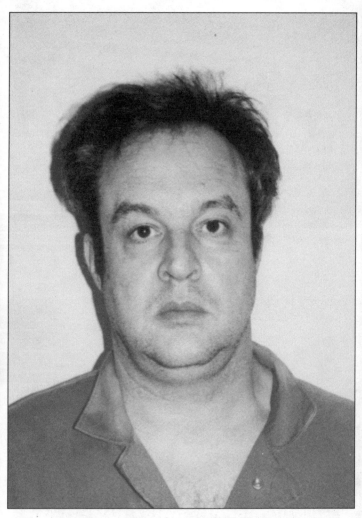

Convicted child molester, Stephen P. Simmons, 43, met Sam Manzie through an Internet chatroom.
(*Photo courtesy Monmouth County Prosecutor*)

Dolores Manzie.

Nicholas Manzie.

Dolores Manzie was thrown out of court on the
day her son Sam was sentenced.

Valerie and Ed Werner.

Ocean County, New Jersey, prosecutor E. David Millard.

Some of the protestors outside the courthouse felt Manzie's parents were to blame.

The controversial trial drew wide media coverage.

Press conference after Manzie was sentenced to 70 years.

Ed Werner and Pastor Tom Geoffrey on November 12, 1999, after Werner appeared with the Manzies to denounce Simmons at his sentencing.

Simmons received the maximum five-year sentence for
criminal sexual contact and child endangerment.

than the minimum compassion to Sam Manzie or to his parents.

Through this, Stephen Simmons sat in a jail cell reading about the latest news in the case with a deep interest and with good cause. He felt all eyes on him in jail. His fellow prisoners, the jailers, everyone, he said, looked at him with a blood lust in their eyes. There were plenty of inmates and jailers who were angry with him and hated him for who he was. As Simmons sat in his isolated cell, he began to believe the only way to stay alive was to talk, and he began doing that to anyone and everyone he could. Most especially he began talking to reporters.

The stain of Eddie's death continued to spread. Newspapers, radio programs and television talk shows all discussed whether or not it was OK to allow children to sell candy door to door. The Girl Scouts weighed in on the subject; a spokesman there said it is the policy of the Girl Scouts that adults must always accompany children. The National Parent Teacher Association said it was a bad thing for kids to sell goods door to door, and Maryann Kolbeck, president of the New Jersey PTA, said, "No child should ever sell, ever."

The furor over Eddie Werner's death was growing and far reaching. Then, as it seemed to hit a fevered pitch, everything came to a grinding halt for a collective sigh and community tear.

On October 4, hundreds showed up to pay their respects to Eddie's family at the George S. Hassler Funeral Home in Jackson Township. Mourners waiting to view the closed casket stood in a line that stretched outside along the side of the building.

Inside the somber chambers, there were hundreds of flowers. In the middle sat the casket and on top of it a small teddy bear. On an easel near the casket rested a poster with scribbled messages of love from classmates and friends. Another held a large picture frame containing snapshots of Eddie and his family. There was one of Eddie smiling while wearing a powder-blue baseball uniform with the name "Astros" scrawled across his chest. Another photo showed Eddie wearing a tuxedo and dancing at a family function. Still another showed him with his family while he was wearing a Tasmanian Devil costume.

The smiles on the faces of Eddie and his family members in those photographs stood in direct contrast to the somber events of his funeral. It was as if the pictures served as a reminder that all happiness is fleeting when one so young and vital is taken away so dramatically and senselessly. An Associated Press (AP) reporter said he stopped and openly wept.

The funeral service was held at St. Aloysius Church in Jackson Township, New Jersey, where more than six hundred people made the trek to hear the Werners bid Eddie farewell. Many of the mourners wore the green ribbons that had become indicative of Eddie's search and later his death. The burial service was marked by the emotions of many people who had only come to know Eddie in death. Distraught children cried and wiped at their faces, trying to tug away the tears. Adults joined them. "You don't have children to have them die like this. It's horrible," moaned one woman to an AP reporter.

All was quiet as the closed casket draped in a white linen cloth and embroidered with crosses was rolled up the aisle. When a fifteen-member choir and organist rendered the hymn "Be Not Afraid," the congregation collapsed in tears. It was as if, according to one reporter present, "grief hung over the congregation like a dark cloud." Governor Christie Todd Whitman and her husband, John, sat in the first pew opposite the Werners, as did several township officials and the Ocean County prosecutor, E. David Millard.

The forty-five-minute service had no eulogies. The only speaker was Monsignor Casimir Ladzinski. He told the congregation that Eddie loved to go to mass, and recalling the boy's baptism, he said, "God made a promise that Eddie would live forever. We say God, be God. And take care of Eddie forever. Forever. Forever."

At one point, Valerie Werner, who swooned throughout the service, apparently collapsed. Ed Werner caught her before she hit the pew. The monsignor went on. "The last few days, people have been asking, 'Why? Why?' and I don't have all the answers."

The service ended with the choir singing "On Eagles' Wings" as Eddie's parents and his younger sister walked arm in arm down the aisle behind his casket. Valerie stared blankly ahead, one arm around her husband and one arm around her daughter. They were dissolved in tears. When they got outside, they were ushered into waiting limousines as a dozen television cameras recorded the grim scene.

"Why? Why?" the monsignor had said, echoing the thoughts of everyone in Jackson Township that day. "I don't have all the answers," he had said. No one did. Many of those so close to the gruesome murder were numb and raw. On Wood Lane, just a few hundred feet from where Eddie had been found, there was a growing shrine for the slain boy. Mounds of green ribbons, bows, gifts of fresh flowers, candles and dozens of heartbreaking letters from area children were placed at the informal shrine. They were written on construction paper, napkins, single sheets of loose-leaf paper and cardboard. Sentiments profound and banal made their way to the shrine. It seemed hard for anyone to understand Eddie Werner's death. The shrine became a cathartic means of release for many. One sign read EDDIE'S PLAYING WITH THE ANGELS. A necklace, which hung on a tree, stated EDDIE, WE LOVE U AND MISS U.

It was a meaningful gesture to the Werners, who appreciated that Eddie had touched so many people, many of whom he'd never met. But it was a bitter gesture, too, for it brought home the very real fact that Eddie would never be coming home. It was a surreal scene to them, that shrine, and it only served to make the Werners understand how very hard and painful reality was.

There was a political spin to the events, too. As it became increasingly obvious the Monmouth County Prosecutor's Office was going to take some heat for using Sam Manzie to get at Simmons, there was a fear that things would be "misinterpreted" and that the office would catch some heat John Kaye felt his office didn't deserve. The *Asbury Park Press* reported on October 5, 1997, in the story about Eddie Werner's funeral that Kaye had said that "five days before Manzie allegedly killed Werner, detectives who were worried about the teen's mental state tried unsuccessfully to get him to see a counselor." Kaye did not identify Manzie by name, but Sam's name was out in the public eye nonetheless.

The statement in the paper was a real slap in the face to the Manzie family. Besides being a shadow of the truth, the Manzies also saw it as the prosecutor's office trying to say, "See, it wasn't our fault" when all along the Manzies had felt pushed and prodded by the investigators. Besides, if Arancio or Noble had felt the need to get counseling for Sam, there was more than ample opportunity, as had been previously mentioned, to assist the Manzies at Kimball the night Sam and his mother ended up there. There had also been a chance to turn over information to Judge Citta when the Manzies landed in his courtroom. "There are so many layers of hypocrisy in all this," Mike Critchley, the Manzies' attorney, said later. "We're very good in this country at blame and punishing, but not very good at assisting and helping."

Critchley, with an authoritative countenance and a slight New Jersey accent, didn't at first think he would get involved in the Manzie case. He'd read the newspapers and watched the beginning of it from the sidelines. "It didn't seem like there would be much lawyering going on. It looked to be very simple." He had been notified by a friend that the Manzies were interested in talking to him, but Critchley wasn't all that interested. He did, however, decide to meet with the Manzies—more out of courtesy, he added, than anything else. It was a meeting he wouldn't soon forget.

"If anything, they downplayed and understated everything they'd gone through for the last year," Critchley said. "I felt they were either exaggerating or they had gone through a tragedy." The Manzies recounted to Critchley everything they'd undergone and they kept basically to the facts. The more Critchley heard, the more he became interested in the case. At the end of the first meeting, though, he wanted to remain cautious. He had to check out much of what the Manzies had told him. He explained that to Nick and Dolores and then told them he would contact them once he'd done so. It wasn't long before Critchley decided he wanted in on the case. "They [the Manzies] had just undertaken this absolute effort to take care of their son. Everyone who was someone told them what to do and they had followed it without question. When the school said Sam had a problem, the Manzies didn't say 'Not our son.' They never balked. They did what we all say good parents are supposed to do."

Critchley was not only interested in what had transpired in the Manzies' lives during the year before Eddie Werner's murder, he began to see it as a cautionary tale of hypocrisy and systemic neglect. "The more I got into it, the more troubling it became."

In the early part of October 1997, Critchley did not yet know how troubling it would become, but he had an idea and it all boiled down to a prosecutor who wanted to try Sam Manzie as an adult. That plan would bring yet untold additional grief upon the Manzies, who had struggled to find help for their son.

It certainly kept Sam's name in the spotlight and in that way also took a toll on the Werners, who were still having trouble with their own grief. Besides Valerie Werner's open emotions at her son's funeral, the Werner family continued to go through a living hell. Guilt plagued them unnecessarily as Ed and Valerie went over and over in their minds what they could have done differently. The rising national debate over allowing children to sell candy door to door only exacerbated the problem. If only Eddie had been with someone else; if only Ed had gone; if only Eddie hadn't gone at all. If only. It was torture. Adding to the torture were the questions from Eddie's siblings. There were still three other children in the Werner family, an eight-year-old girl, who remembered her oldest brother better than her siblings and was present during the funeral, a six-year-old boy, who was developmentally disabled, and a three-year-old girl. The Werners weren't sure how they would get through the funeral service, let alone get back to any normal kind of life with their remaining children.

Sam Manzie's arrest only hurt the tenuous hold the Werners had on a "normal life." Ed Werner said when he first heard the news of Manzie's arrest, it just didn't compute. "How could a child kill another child?" Ed asked. Manzie wasn't known to Eddie. Eddie had never done anything to Sam Manzie. There was no cause for it. There seemed to be no rhyme or reason for it. It was as if Eddie had been struck down instantly by demons sent to torture the family for sins they couldn't comprehend.

The Werners' mourning was eased by the hundreds and thousands of green ribbons and an outpouring of emotion from people throughout the state, including Governor Christie Todd Whitman. The governor also publicly thanked the FBI, state and local law enforcement and the hundreds of volunteers who searched and helped in the investigation into Eddie's death. There had been thousands who pitched in. They were friends, family members and acquaintances; people who visited the Werners and those who stirred soup on top of propane grills; those who handed out soda, water and food; those who searched. It had been a community effort and the community grieved with the Werners. Richard Kanka, the father of Megan Kanka, for whom "Megan's Law" was named, showed up and helped.

In the first part of October 1997, there didn't seem to be anyone that little Eddie in his death hadn't touched. "No one can explain why something like this happens," said Jackson Township mayor Vicki Rickabaugh shortly after Eddie's funeral. "In our shock and disbelief, it is easy to cast blame, but it is our responsibility to endure the pain, begin the rebuilding process and to always remember Eddie by ensuring that something positive rises from the tragedy that befell him. We must all work to bring our town together as it has never been together before."

No public words of encouragement were offered the Manzies. While the mayor had said it was easy to cast blame and the community should try to rebuild, there was precious little of that going on. The Werners were grief stricken, but they had an entire community, even a state and nation, on their side. They would have preferred to have their son instead of the empathy, but they could find some solace in the goodwill of strangers. That could not be said of the Manzies, who remained numb, raw and isolated from the community because of the actions of their mentally disturbed teenage son.

On October 7, Ocean County prosecutor E. David Millard said he wanted the case against Sam Manzie transferred from juvenile court to New Jersey superior court because of the violent nature of the crime and to prevent similar crimes by others.

Millard wanted to make an example out of Sam Manzie. At a news conference that day at his office, Millard told the media, "There is a need for deterrence both as to this defendant individually and general deterrence to dissuade others in society, including juveniles, from committing such horrible acts of violence."

An investigator involved in the case said that Sam Manzie was an unbearable child. If one ticked off the traits for potential serial killers, Sam, like the villain in the cult film *Headless Body in Topless Bar*, absolutely "had them all," the investigator said. "The boy was a disaster just waiting to happen."

The scene was now set. If Millard had anything to do with it, Manzie was going to become demonized and prosecuted to the fullest extent of the law in order to "dissuade others" who might decide to follow him down the road of sin and perdition. The fact that Manzie was emotionally troubled, a victim of a horrendous and offensive crime himself, did not come into play. Sam Manzie was a criminal. Sam Manzie was going to pay, and through paying he was going to scare the hell out of any other bad boys out there who wanted to kill little kids. It may have made for excellent newspaper fodder, but did it make sense? Mike Critchley, for one, was critical. He noted that Millard had thirty days to make such a request. The insinuation was that Millard had been more interested in grabbing headlines and revenge rather than seeking justice. "This is a case that cries out for more time and consideration," Critchley told the *New York Times.* "It's a constantly evolving case."

Part of the learning curve for Critchley and why he wanted more time to consider the case was, of course, the Stephen Simmons factor. But it wasn't limited to that, either. Sam Manzie's treatment by health-care workers and the system was also a large part of what Critchley considered to be meaningful circumstances that had an impact on the case.

Under the motion filed by Millard, the presiding judge of the family court would have to conduct a hearing to determine if Sam Manzie could be prosecuted as an adult. To prevent the transfer, the defense lawyers had to convince the judge that Sam Manzie, at the time just fifteen years old, could be rehabilitated in the juvenile justice system before he reached the age of nineteen. That seemed like a long shot, and it appeared that Sam Manzie was headed for superior court and trial as an adult.

Meanwhile, the Jackson PTA came under fire for Eddie Werner's solo sojourn to sell candy. School fund-raisers were halted just two days after the murder, and the local newspaper published an article touting "safe selling tips" for children.

The Association of Fund Raisers and Direct Sellers, a trade group representing about half of the more than 1,500 companies that work with school and youth groups, had already adopted, prior to Eddie Werner's death, a policy against door-to-door sales, and a spokeswoman for the National Association of Elementary School Principals told the *New York Times* her organization was "totally against" door-to-door sales. Jackson Township school district spokeswoman Stephanie Yusko jumped into the fray as well and told the press that sales kits issued to Eddie and other children participating in the PTA sale included warnings to sell only to "family, friends and neighbors with whom you are familiar."

The spreading trauma caused by Eddie Werner's death looked to be even larger as counselors were brought into Eddie's school to help his classmates cope with the loss. Many of those children also visited the impromptu shrine erected near the site where the body had been found and discovered some solace in the gesture. But solace was something the Werners themselves were not yet feeling.

Everyone involved in the Eddie Werner/Sam Manzie/Steve Simmons case at one point or another found themselves yelling to themselves and to anyone who would listen, "Do something!"

For the Manzies, it had all been about doing something for Sam before he went off the deep end, and doing something about getting Simmons out of their life. After the murder, the Werners wanted the prosecution to do something about Manzie; the Manzies still wanted something done about the pedophile and at the same time urged the system to do something about their son. In November 1997, a psychologist told a judge of Sam Manzie's suicide tries. "Do something about that," the Manzies cried, as did the Werners.

For many involved in the case, it became a large paper bag that no one could find the right way to split open. Despair and heartache cloaked everyone. The Werners could take it no more and in December they put the Monmouth County prosecutor on notice, along with many of the caregivers and police who were involved in the Simmons case. If no one else wanted to do anything, Ed Werner was determined that he would. He told all of them they may be sued for the action they took in regard to Sam Manzie, action, he believed, that led to the death of his son Eddie.

Editorials in the local newspaper only seemed to back up the call of "Do something." Critical of Judge Citta, a perspective piece written by Gil Spencer in the *Star-Ledger* pointed out that Sam's "terrified parents alleged violence, cybersex. If you can think of better reasons to have had Sam Manzie committed, send the judge a list."

The tension in the air was palpable and under such strife bad things often happen. That's exactly what the Manzies believed occurred next, for the one person left at that time who could do something was the prosecutor Millard. He was ready, willing and able to do something and was about to do it with elan. But it wasn't going to be anything to bring joy to either the Manzies or the Werners. More pain and suffering were in store and it was about to get nasty, personal and vindictive.

Eleven

The "Trophy Photo"

If Nick and Dolores Manzie or Ed and Valerie Werner thought their suffering would ease any during the early days of October 1997, they were sorely mistaken. The case was scaling the heights of media frenzy as all the sordid details came out into the light. In the middle of October, the *Asbury Park Press* ran a story with the headline JACKSON BOY'S SLAYING REPORTEDLY DRAWS HOLLYWOOD INTEREST. Executive Assistant Prosecutor Gregory J. Sakowicz said he hadn't received any calls, but the paper reported that producers had contacted the Werner family.

The same article took notice of the fact that William P. Cunningham and Ronald L. DeLigny had been assigned as prosecutors in the case. Cunningham's zealous behavior would insure the case stayed before the public for the next several months. He, in particular, became seemingly obsessed with making sure Sam Manzie was tried as an adult, to the delight of the Werners and to the horror of the

Manzies. The fact of the matter was that Cunning-ham had a high-profile case that screamed for justice dropped in his lap, and some who were not directly involved in the case shouted for vengeance. That cry never came from the Werners. Still, plenty of people not associated with the case donned hand-painted placards and marched in front of the courthouse, making it a point to use the death of Eddie Werner as a rallying cry to get tough on criminals. If you can't be safe in your own neighborhood in broad daylight, these people reasoned, then the person responsible for such a heinous crime should suffer the direst of circumstances. The prosecutor seemed to play into the hands of the most vengeful of those on the sidelines.

Thus, the Manzies were sullen about their chances of keeping the case in juvenile court. It had already received far too much media attention and was far too gruesome a crime, it seemed, for the judge to keep it a juvenile matter. The growing public sentiments against the Manzies certainly didn't help, either.

Meanwhile, another judge was feeling the heat of the Manzie case. Judge James Citta, the fifty-year-old former municipal prosecutor, assistant county prosecutor and criminal judge, was getting it good from an editorial in the *Star-Ledger*, as did many others involved in the Manzie/Simmons case. The thrust was that the family court in New Jersey had to be changed. It was a seed planted that would grow wildly after Eddie Werner's death. Manzie and his parents, the editorial stated, ". . . were entitled to a few basic things. They were entitled to a crisis worker who had time to learn the basics of the case before making stern and firm recommendations. They were entitled to have those who treated him present, or at least have the full benefit of what they had learned about the young man. They were entitled to a judge who paid more attention to what was going on and insisted on knowing the facts. They got none of it."

The alternative press and gay and lesbian publications also weighed in heavily on the case, sometimes to the horror and chagrin of Manzie's parents. A Web site designed to support Manzie was denounced by Nick and Dolores after they came to find that questionable people were behind the Internet address. NAMBLA publications addressed the Simmons/Manzie case as well as others. Many of these publications were openly bitter and critical with the police for going after Simmons. "The police in their own earnest stupidity wanted to believe if they sank their heads deep enough into the sand (quicksand?) surrounding the Manzies, questioning a very disturbed, frightened boy about things that they themselves found disgusting, then they, in effect, would not have to deal with any of the lives they had destroyed," one such publication offered.

Some of these publications defended Simmons as coming from "a gay perspective" and others denounced him for taking advantage of Sam Manzie and causing the death of Eddie Werner. Many of these publications were also very vitriolic in their criticism of the Manzies—sometimes referring to them as "soft" and calling their lifestyle a "vapid, strangling suburban setting." The Manzies were accused of not setting enough limits for their son by giving him his own telephone line and allowing him to have time by himself. They were accused of homophobia and because of their Catholic upbringing, seeing Sam's sexuality as just a "phase" he was going through. Some of these publications gave the Manzies credit for raising Sam in an environment and giving him a lifestyle "that most kids would love to have," but they also said the Manzies displayed a "sense of benign detachment," with little touching or even closeness with Sam. In one article, the Manzies were even compared to the inquisitors during the Inquisition. "Heretics would be talked to sweetly, offered the use of a priest, last rites, moments of prayer. All of this would make the proceedings much nicer for the assembled believers and the scene at the stake a little easier to watch."

Meanwhile, the lawyers were jockeying for position in an upcoming rehabilitation hearing. During that hearing, the attorneys on both sides of the Manzie case would argue whether or not Sam could be rehabilitated by the time he was nineteen years old. Psychiatric testimony would be offered and Sam could testify without worry of it being used against him during a criminal trial. The hearing would decide whether or not Manzie would be tried as an adult. In November Sam Manzie was reported to be severely depressed, suicidal and had tried to harm himself. In a ruling, superior court judge Robert A. Fall said that press coverage of a rehabilitation hearing might push Sam Manzie over the edge.

In a ten-page opinion, Fall cited a psychiatrist who said Manzie had cut himself with an aluminum-foil dessert dish, punched the walls of his cell and hid a shoelace from one of his sneakers in an apparent futile attempt to commit suicide. Manzie was up to his old tricks again, but this time his parents were out of the loop. They could only sit and watch on the sidelines as their son displayed the same behavior for the court system as he'd displayed at home for the last year and a half. "It was exactly as they [the Manzies] warned them it would be," a friend of the Manzie family said. "Finally someone else saw what they saw, but it was too late from them and too late for the Werners."

Fall also said that one of the reasons he wanted the rehabilitation hearing closed to the public was because some new and sensitive testimony might be heard about Sam's possible abuse as a small child; Sam's early childhood incident in the day-care center might come up and the judge felt the press didn't need to know about that.

As the year drew to a close, the Werners and the Manzies also found themselves swimming through the miasma of pop culture. Touted as the heroes or the goats of the moment, they found themselves and their sons used as either icons of virtue, evil or victims of the moment and thus used by legislators across the country to validate new laws governing the Internet.

Representative Robert D. Franks, R-New Providence, New Jersey, said the Manzie case "is just the latest instance where the Internet was one tool used to stalk someone." Franks advocated federal legislation requiring Internet service providers to notify law enforcement authorities when they suspect child sexual abuse, such as the transmission of child pornography or solicitation of minors. The issue, Franks said, was of vital importance to parents and would be better addressed by the federal government than by individual states. He cautioned against the "dark and seedy side to the Internet."

It was the campaign tool of the moment, ready made to exact sympathy for those proposing the law and perhaps generate some needed votes come re-election time. It was also incredibly naive to think that most Internet providers could do as the bill asked. There simply was no effective way to capture, store and disseminate all the information the bill

asked for. Nonetheless, the Manzie case was getting
to be a rallying cry for concerned parents, misguided
politicians and paranoid people across the country.

None of it brought back Eddie Werner and none
of it helped either the Werners or the Manzies sleep
better at night. In fact, by December the Werners
had decided to take to the airwaves themselves,
partly in response to the Manzies' appearance on
national television, partly to sway the judge into ruling Sam Manzie should stand trial as an adult and
partly because of the continuing lunacy of the daily
media pressure.

Their venue was *Dateline NBC* and on that show
the Werners said they had a message for anyone who
believed Sam Manzie deserved a break: "Let him live
next door to you." They were upset and disappointed by those who were making excuses for people like Sam Manzie. "Society's got to stop doing
that, making excuses for these things because that's
never going to stop. Nobody will ever be safe,"
Valerie Werner said. It became another wedge between the Manzies and the Werners. Catholic ideol-
ogy, the teachings of Jesus and the idea of turning
the other cheek all seemed to be exercises in rheto-
ric and of little real consequence as both devoutly
Catholic families descended into and struck out
from the safety of their pain.

The Manzies seemed confused and upset that they
had been singled out for the Werners' wrath. They
even began to believe the Werners were exacting
small slices of revenge against them. The Werners,
hurt and miserable because of their son's death,
could think nothing but the worst about the
Manzies. "Why had they allowed Sam to be alone
that day if they thought he was so dangerous? Why
hadn't they done more?" Valerie Werner asked on

more than one occasion. The Werners didn't know everything that the Manzies had gone through and really only knew what was being published in the media. But it seemed to be enough to them. They were convinced early on that the Manzies were somehow at fault for Sam's horrifying actions.

Simmons, too, seemed to be weighing in on the side of the Werners, a move that angered the Manzies and riled the Werners. After all, as Ed Werner and Nick Manzie both reflected, "Who wants a pedophile on your side?" But Simmons said the Manzies must've done something wrong. Perhaps they didn't listen to Sam enough. Perhaps they didn't care. Who knew?

On December 19, 1997, Simmons reentered the limelight when he was indicted. Since the end of September, he'd been sitting in a cell and had awaited the inevitable. It came less than a week before Christmas, less than a week before Eddie Werner's birthday. Upon reviewing all of the evidence—most of which was supplied by Sam Manzie, a grand jury indicted Simmons on nine different counts. The first charge was for criminal sexual conduct and had to do with the clandestine rendezvous between Manzie and Simmons at the Freehold Raceway Mall on August 10, 1996. The second charge was for endangering the welfare of a child and accused Simmons of "sexual conduct which would impair or debauch the morals of a child," and that, too, had to do with the August rendezvous. The third, fourth, fifth and sixth charges against Simmons were alleged to have occurred on September 29, 1996, and included sexual assault, illegal sexual contact and two charges of endangering the welfare of a child—one of which had to do with the lewd photos taken of Sam Manzie at a local hotel. The final three charges against Simmons included sexual assault, sexual contact and endangering the welfare of a child "on or about and between October 1, 1996, and November 30, 1996."

As Simmons had already been sitting in jail under a $225,000 bond, which he readily admitted he couldn't afford to make, John Kaye, the Monmouth County prosecutor, said there had been "no critical need for speed in this case." At least that's what Kaye said when reporters asked him about the gap in time between Simmons's arrest in September and the indictment in December. Kaye also said he had reached an agreement with the Ocean County prosecutor and would wait to take Simmons to trial after Sam Manzie's murder trial. "We don't need the victim Manzie to prove our case," Kaye said ominously. Sam was no longer "Sam" to the prosecutor. He was a cold-blooded killer and the Monmouth County prosecutor strove to distance himself in every way from Sam Manzie. Kaye may have wanted the headlines for prosecuting Simmons, but not for the price he had to pay. The Manzie case had tainted the prosecution and would continue to do so for at least two more years.

Meanwhile, Kaye wasn't especially interested in dealing with Simmons, either, while Simmons actually seemed to enjoy the spotlight surrounding him by his arrest, no matter how bad it got. When Pulitzer Prize–winning cartoonist Steve Breen, at the *Asbury Park Press,* lampooned Steve Simmons on the editorial page, Simmons was ecstatic. Though the cartoon was less than complimentary, Simmons didn't complain. He just wanted an autographed copy. As he sat in jail, Simmons didn't hesitate to contact the local press, talking with anyone in any newsroom who would accept his collect phone calls. Local reporters were stunned at the easy access to an accused pedophile. When they pointed out in print that Simmons had two previous convictions for sexually abusing minors, in Brooklyn in 1984 and in Florida in 1986, Simmons didn't hesitate to explain himself.

When they wanted to talk about the current case, much to the dismay of his attorneys, Simmons eagerly discussed those charges as well—telling most reporters the charges would never stick and the prosecutor was out to get him. Simmons seemed upbeat and certain of his vindication at a time when no one else would've given a nickel for his chances and at a time when life in jail wasn't easy for him. The accusations against Simmons, his history and his notoriety made his stay in jail uncomfortable at the very least. With his penchant for drama, he outlined to anyone who would listen how dangerous he thought it was. He was stuck in a small cell and surrounded by those who thought of him as a sick pervert. Even the guards, he said, wanted to get him. But Simmons remained defiant, challenging the guards, writing letters to his attorneys and to the press. If he felt threatened, as he most assuredly did on several occasions, he quickly fired off letters to the press. "I wasn't about to let them do something to me," Simmons later said. "And I knew even if the press didn't like me, they would print the truth."

Simmons also defiantly remained on Sam Manzie's side. "We all live with our guilt. I will always be looked at as part of a troika with Eddie and Sam," he later wrote. "Some will blame me and some won't. It matters not. I tried. God knows I tried as I'm still trying to prevent Sam's death and that the truth should come out. My part in it and my relationship with Sam and me being gay is between me, my conscience and my God. Nobody, absolutely nobody involved, ever thought anything like this could happen. It we did, we all would have done different things."

Perhaps, Simmons mused, if Hitler had invaded England in 1940 "as he should have," then Eddie wouldn't have died because Simmons would have been killed or never been born.

It seemed like a stretch to blame Adolf Hitler for Eddie Werner's death, but Simmons thought he had a point. "The facts are Eddie is dead, Sam killed him. We all contributed to some degree. We can never let it happen again." Simmons even talked about writing a book while in prison, a handbook for parents to recognize and keep their children away from pedophiles—written by someone with a knowledge of the subject: a pedophile.

Simmons still denied ever having sexual contact with Sam Manzie in October or November—the basis for the bulk of the most serious charges against him. He claimed he and Manzie ate pizza and cuddled that day—nothing else. He said he committed no crime. Afterward, Simmons said, when the two stopped meeting and the parents and police got involved, only then did Manzie turn to violent fantasies. "It was then I began pushing him to get help," Simmons said. "I failed. That's my real crime. I failed to get him help." Simmons's proclamations to the contrary, he failed to mention that he was aware of Sam Manzie's violent fantasies prior to the police involvement in Sam's life. Simmons only said he wanted nothing more than to help Sam.

But once Simmons went to jail, he had little chance of helping Sam Manzie and instead struggled to help himself. He said it wasn't easy. On his second day in jail, he said, "the inmates wanted my hide." He said his jail guards told other inmates that if "I was to have an 'accident,' they would never see it."

Simmons claimed his mail was read and intercepted, religious material was thrown out and he had his belongings and his body searched repeatedly. He claimed he reported his guards' recalcitrant behavior and was ignored. When he called his attorney to complain, he claimed the jailers wrote him up for "loud and belligerent behavior. I never had a hearing and I demanded one but was ignored."

He said he actually pressed charges against a jailer for terroristic threats, but the complaint was dismissed. Time and again, Simmons claimed, his civil rights were violated. His response, he said, would be to sue just about everyone involved in the case, including, but not limited to, Oprah Winfrey, Prosecutor John Kaye, the *New York Post,* the *Asbury Park Press,* Nick Manzie, the jail and various parts of the prison medical establishment. At the time, few took Simmons's complaints, let alone his threats of legal action, seriously. It was all sound and fury, the rantings of a pedophile riddled with guilt, many thought.

It is an understatement to say that Simmons felt he was unfairly portrayed in the media as a predator and molester. His response to this portrayal vacillated from the sublime to the ridiculous, and his vociferous denunciations of his portrayal only served to alienate him even more from the community as time wore on. No one involved in his case wanted to be associated with it or Steve Simmons, and that ultimately included his own attorney, Howard Golden.

As the year ended, Simmons was swept back under the rug while the Sam Manzie problem took center stage. It was a difficult Christmas in the Werner household as Valerie and Ed struggled to make it a special, happy holiday for their remaining children.

They desperately wanted it and needed it themselves, but no amount of toys, love or Christmas cheer could erase what had happened to them in the last three months. Melancholy memories of Eddie hung like a sullen ghost over the entire Christmas season. Just a few blocks away, the Manzies were dealing with similar pain while they struggled to get their son more help.

Dolores and Nick Manzie, while never shying away from the awful crime their son had committed, were convinced that Sam was insane. The picture of Eddie that he kept in his drawer was enough to convince Dolores of that. Nick cited holes in walls, fires started in Sam's room and the memory of a television remote sailing past his head to convince him of Sam's need for mental help. Eddie's death only sadly reminded them that they had been right about their troubled son all along, but it was a revelation that brought them little solace. They did not want an innocent child to have to die just so they could be proved right. They had wanted help for Sam. They had wanted help *before* Sam killed Eddie, and with Sam in prison and charged with the crime, they wanted the help even more. They desperately fought off the prosecution's attempt to have their son classified as an adult.

That high drama came to a head in mid-February 1998. Senior Assistant Prosecutor William P. Cunningham wielded the sword, which turned out to be the photograph of Eddie Werner that Dolores gave to the authorities.

Superior court judge Robert A. Fall listened as Cunningham made the case for having Sam Manzie stand trial as an adult. Wielding the Polaroid photo, Cunningham marched through court as he retold the sordid and sad story of how Eddie spent his last day trying to sell candy and gift wrap in a door-to-door effort to get a set of walkie-talkies. Then he met the demon Manzie, a fiend who sexually assaulted the boy and then took his life, in Manzie's own words, in "a paroxysm of violence."

During the forty-five-minute hearing, Cunningham also produced a psychological report and a fifteen-page statement from Dolores Manzie, who had told police her son had confessed to killing Eddie. Judge Fall listened intently to the prosecutor and looked at the photograph. "The photograph depicts Edward P. Werner laying facedown, unconscious or dead, on a brightly colored carpet with a man's necktie around his neck, as well as an electrical cord around his neck and attached to a clock radio, with plain underwear or shorts on," the judge wrote in his subsequent ruling.

Ed and Valerie Werner sat in court that day listening to the evidence. More than ever, they wanted Sam Manzie tried as an adult. The photograph, which they'd seen "well in advance" of the hearing, only cemented their feelings that Sam Manzie needed to spend the rest of his life in jail.

It was a surreal and sickening moment for the Werners to face, to actually gaze upon a photograph of their dead son, to have to look at that photograph and realize that it was the last image they'd have of their son and to know that dozens of other people would see it, too. The Werners wanted to reach out and change history by simply touching that photograph, hoping it was all just a bad dream they'd wake up from. Those thoughts fueled the Werners' desire to see Sam Manzie tried as an adult.

Sam Manzie sat in court that day, shackled and dressed in a navy-colored jail uniform. Most of the time he had his head down, as if ashamed to face the facts in court that day. He knew what he did and his Catholic guilt was eating away at him. Already suicidal and in protective custody, Manzie looked as pale as the living dead as he sat in court and listened to a recitation of the monstrous events he had unleashed the previous September.

Cunningham outlined how Manzie had disposed of Eddie's clothes at Shoreline and how he'd picked the area to dump Eddie's body because he had walked his dog in that woods. As Cunningham waved the photograph around the courtroom, Manzie heard it referred to as a "trophy" photo of the young victim, Eddie Werner.

The photo, as it turned out, was all the prosecution needed to get Manzie to stand trial as an adult.

A short time later, Mike Critchley, Sam's defense attorney, and Judge Fall asked Manzie if he understood what had happened in family court that day; the case was going to be transferred to criminal court. Manzie bowed and barely said, "Yeah." There was no emotion in the response.

Outside of court, the Werners were happy with the outcome of the hearing. Finally they thought the hearing was putting things back into perspective. The Manzies had gotten extremely favorable media play with their appearance on *20/20*, a segment that particularly incensed the Werners. With the ruling against Sam Manzie that took the murder case into adult criminal court, the Werners said they were awaiting more spin control from the Manzies.

"I can only brace myself for the performance that we now can expect until the trial," Valerie Werner told a reporter. There were no immediate statements from the Manzies. Nick and Dolores had sat quietly in the courtroom during the hearing, on the opposite side of the Werners. They left through the judge's chambers immediately afterward. Dolores was simply too pained to face reporters that day; she felt betrayed.

She'd gotten the confession from Sam. She retrieved the photograph, told the prosecutors where the clothes were, related to them how the body had been disposed of and had given a fifteen-page statement to the police. There wasn't any investigating left to do. Dolores Manzie had provided the prosecutors with everything they needed to secure a conviction against her own son. She'd done it out of a sense of justice and hoped that by providing the information Sam would finally get the psychiatric help she knew he needed. She was the first person, other than her son, to look at that horrible picture of little Eddie. But she didn't see a "trophy" photo; she saw the product of insanity and thought it was obvious to anyone who cared to look at it with compassion.

Dolores Manzie felt she'd been betrayed yet again. The prosecutor was looking for headlines and promotions, she felt, not justice. "Maybe my son needs to go away for the rest of his life," Dolores said to reporters. "But doesn't he deserve the chance to heal?" Dolores thought so. She didn't shirk away from the demonic acts her son had engaged in; she still just wanted to get Sam some help.

The next day, Nick and Dolores Manzie felt composed enough to speak to a local newspaper reporter and dutifully told the *Star-Ledger* exactly how they felt. "When I heard them say that it was a trophy picture, it hurt," Dolores said in a mixture of anger and tears. "I gave it to them. A trophy picture? I don't think so."

Nick and Dolores spent many more days in tears. "We had so many questions," Dolores said. "Had we done wrong by Sam? Should we have refused to cooperate with authorities? Where was it getting us? Everywhere we turned we felt cornered and stymied. Would it ever get any better? The system failed us. When we were in crisis, they turned their backs on us."

In a house a few streets away, the Werners, seeing only the newspapers and fed information from the prosecution, were unsympathetic to the Manzies. "They say they wanted their son in a supervised setting; then they deliberately left him unsupervised," Ed Werner told a reporter. "The best thing that can happen to Sam Manzie is to be incarcerated for life. That's the only way we're going to make sure he never rapes anybody again."

The Manzies and the Werners were now set on a painful course of action. Neither had approached the other about the events that were sweeping both families away. Instead, both families had vented their rage and pain to local reporters all too eager to include the quotes in their stories. The more the case progressed, the farther apart the two families appeared to be.

It was still going to be a long, agonizing wait for both the Manzies and the Werners. The trial would be several months off as Sam Manzie would be transferred to an adult jail and the case would be transferred to criminal court.

Twelve

Fresh Wounds

The long wait for Sam Manzie to go to trial was, for the Manzies and Werners, like being in a slowly tightening vise grip. The pressure was turned up a notch each day and the hope for any semblance of a normal life seemed to seep slowly away. If there wasn't something new to report on psychiatrists, therapy or some gory detail of the crime, both families got to read or hear about Steve Simmons. If that weren't enough, the nation's parents, teachers and youth organizers continued having their own apoplectic fits over fund-raising.

There was also just the horrible daily grind of it all. The Manzies were having to spend day after day looking into health care for Sam, consulting with attorneys, trying to cope with the recriminations and struggling to make life normal for their daughter.

The Werners were still struggling with the loss of their oldest child while raising three other children, who didn't quite understand what the family was going through. It was a pressure cooker and Ed Werner sighed, thinking about it. Everyone wanted a piece of him for something. He desperately wanted to "get engaged" and help out, valiantly trying to make sure his son's life and death would "mean something." But he was torn apart by requests. After the community and the country began to learn the true nature of the crimes that occurred in Jackson Township, Nick Manzie, too, began getting requests. The Cyber Angels and others saw Nick and Dolores as effective tools to be used in the hunt for chicken hawks and other predators on the Internet.

It was exceedingly tough on both families to watch their lives broadcast over the airwaves each day. "I'd just sit there," Dolores Manzie said. "I'd watch the television and my whole life was out there. Just my whole life."

Sam Manzie's group of attorneys, which grew to include Critchley, John Vazquez, and death penalty expert David Ruhnke, decided the best thing they could do for their client was to have Manzie claim he was legally insane at the time of the killing. Critchley, who had spent an increasing amount of time with the Manzies, had come to the same conclusion Dolores had; Sam Manzie wasn't right in the head. Being held at the Ocean County Jail in lieu of a $500,000 bond, Manzie was a child in an adult nightmare of his own making. He was segregated because he was a juvenile, but he was constantly the target for jeers, death threats and physical abuse.

Nick and Dolores Manzie were visiting Sam three days a week; the visits were torturous. "For the fifteen minutes we see him, he can be pretty calm, unless other inmates or guards jeer him," Nick told a local reporter at the time. "Then he goes into a protective shell and doesn't talk. They jeer him about his sexuality and what he's done. Threats."

The Manzie routine was one of visiting their son, trying to work, taking care of their daughter, trying to talk to lawyers and eventually trying to find the right therapists for Sam. Eddie's death was never far away from the Manzies as they tried to put their life together.

It was a horrendously fiendish nightmare for the Werners as well. Eddie was the oldest—bright, outgoing and a loving brother. To say he was sorely missed around the Werner household was a cruel understatement. Ed and Valerie were having a hard time explaining to their smaller children why Eddie wasn't around anymore. The children and to a lesser extent the parents couldn't really comprehend it. The children only knew their big brother was gone. Why wasn't he coming back? Why couldn't they be together again? Each day brought the inevitable questions, the odd moments when Eddie seemed to be around and wasn't, the almost dreamlike moments when they wanted to call out for Eddie and half-expected him to be there.

Finally Valerie repainted Eddie's room and took down his bunk bed. Ed couldn't do it, couldn't bring himself to that final good-bye. Valerie had to. She moved her girls into the room Eddie had shared with his brother, took down the bunk bed and gave her only remaining son, a developmentally disabled child, his own room.

There is an extremely strong bond between a father and his firstborn son. It is something most men dream of from the time they are small boys and playing ball with their own fathers—having a first son to carry on one's name and to teach how to play ball. There are so many "firsts" a father dreams of: the first time a son picks up a baseball glove, the first time he shaves, the first time he kisses a girl, his first date, the first time he drives a car and the first time he takes his dad into his confidence to ask for advice "man to man." Ed Werner was denied almost all of those experiences. He could never sit across from his son and be proud of the man Eddie had become. All Ed had were memories, and the only thing he had left to connect him to Eddie was Sam Manzie's trial. Ed vowed to go through all of it. It was a weak substitute for having Eddie to hold and to talk to, and it seemed like the trial would be delayed forever. "It's very difficult, but I want to be here for every second of it, to see it through," Ed told reporters as the trial wound its way slowly through the court system.

In February 1998, after Sam Manzie was told he would stand trial as an adult, Critchley brought forward to the press his assertion that Sam was insane at the time of the killing. Critchley mentioned Sam's long-standing psychiatric problems and the fact that Sam had been medicated and had been an outpatient at Shoreline.

The day before Critchley pleaded for leniency in Manzie's case, the hearing had taken place; in hindsight, it's easy to see why Critchley went to the press. Things didn't go so well for him and his client at the hearing. Manzie had showed up in a prison uniform, shackled and handcuffed, and had met the proceedings woodenly. He had been scolded by the judge for refusing to come out of his cell for food and medication. He met that scolding as woodenly as he had everything else. Meanwhile, the prosecution had produced the "trophy" photo. It didn't do anything for Manzie, and his reaction at its presentation was just as wooden as any other reaction or emotion he displayed that day. "He's a nut job," some of the spectators said as they watched the proceedings unfold. That was exactly the point Critchley made the day after to the press, and since Sam Manzie was to be tried as an adult, the assertion that Manzie was insane was the best defense Critchley could put together. But that assertion went nowhere with the public, some of whom still clamored for Sam's head.

Meanwhile, in his effort to give meaning to his son's death, Ed Werner teamed up with Maureen Kanka, the mother of Megan Kanka—the seven-year-old girl who had been raped and killed by a neighbor in Hamilton Township in 1994 and the namesake for "Megan's Law." Megan's father had been involved in the search for Eddie and the bond continued. Ed and Maureen appeared together at the statehouse in Trenton to make a strong pitch for legislation that would ban door-to-door fund-raising sales by public school students. They appeared together the same day Critchley announced Sam Manzie would plead not guilty and that he was insane the day he killed Eddie Werner.

Ed Werner was torn. He went to Trenton to try and help other children. "We have to make sure people like Sam Manzie never get out of jail," Werner said as he spoke out for the bill that Hudson Democrat Joseph Doria introduced. But Werner wanted to be home with his wife and children, just wanted to hug them and hold them. A reporter asked, Had Ed Werner talked to the Manzies? Ed replied, "They haven't reached out to us yet, maybe they will have the decency to try." Ed Werner was still among the walking wounded.

That same day, Manzie defense attorney Michael Critchley said, "We are a collection of our life experiences, and his [Sam Manzie's] life experience at the time of the incident was a nightmare." Critchley could've been talking about Ed Werner, Valerie Werner, both Nick and Dolores Manzie and all their children that late winter day of 1998.

It looked as if nothing would happen at all on the case for several months. Judge Peter J. Giovine, who would hear the case, set a date in August for motions to be heard. That was a long time from February, and both the Werners and Manzies didn't know what those months would bring.

At about the same time all of this was going on, Steve Simmons decided to plead not guilty to sexually assaulting Sam Manzie. Simmons said nothing as his lawyer, Anderson Harkov, soon to leave Simmons and be replaced by Howard Golden, entered the plea during a hearing before superior court judge Michael D. Farren in Freehold. Nick and Dolores Manzie attended the hearing, but quickly left— avoiding the reporters gathered to watch the sideshow that the Simmons case had become. Simmons himself did not talk to the press at the hearing, but with his usual aplomb, he did make quite an impression as his face registered a number of reactions during the course of the proceedings.

Harkov, however, did appear before the media. "Mr. Simmons is concerned about Sam Manzie and his treatment by the justice system," he told the assemblage of reporters. To which Michael Critchley, Manzie's attorney, had a ready-made answer: "It's ironic that Mr. Simmons would feel sorry for Sam's treatment in the system when it is he who caused Sam's greatest harm."

In April 1998, yet another shoe dropped. The media found out that Sam Manzie had reached out to the Cyber Angels and to Debby Mahoney, the founder of Safeguarding Our Children, an Internet child-protection service.

Again Sam Manzie and Eddie Werner were tied together in a mountainous media onslaught. Debby Mahoney, in hearing about the Sam Manzie case, had cruised the Internet and found Sam's Web site and came to find out that he was the same "Sam82" who had contacted her. "I started shaking," she said. The FBI admitted it had received information in its Maryland office, but a "spokesman declined to say what action the bureau took or didn't take," it was widely reported. "We are prohibited by the Justice Department from discussing our techniques," Special Agent Larry K. Foust of the Baltimore FBI office told the AP. "But I assure you we will take the appropriate steps to address criminality if we find it."

Mahoney expressed her disappointment that the FBI hadn't done much in helping Sam Manzie. Didn't it mean anything to Bureau agents that a teenage boy was confessing to an affair with a forty-three-year-old man? "I wish I could say more," Foust told a reporter. "But if we tell everybody the progress of the case, even the people who give us information, it won't be long before the wrong people know what we are doing."

By now, Nick and Dolores Manzie were too numb to be surprised. The FBI spokesman sounded like every other well-meaning cop, lawyer and doctor they'd dealt with in the last two years. There was a lot of talk about wanting to help, but curiously nothing was done. How hard, Nick Manzie wanted to know, would it have been for an FBI agent to contact America OnLine and request the owner of the "Sam82" account? Could the whole ugly debacle have been averted with one phone call? When he read the paper, Nick Manzie was disgusted. To him, it was just another example of someone in a position to make a difference doing absolutely nothing.

Sam Manzie was moved from the juvenile detention facility in April to the county jail, and another battle began. From the first day that Manzie had been housed in a juvenile facility, the Manzies had continued their struggle to get him psychiatric treatment. Nick and Dolores had asked the county to provide emotional and psychological treatment for their son, but the officials at the detention center refused the request. In New Jersey, officials noted, there is no mandate for an institution to provide mental treatment.

It had been another slap in the face, and one that Nick sighed over and accepted. Then he and his wife went out and found their own therapists for their son. It wasn't an easy search. Many of the professionals in the area wanted to have nothing to do with Sam Manzie or the media juggernaut the case had become. "They gave varying reasons for why they could not treat Sam," family attorney Critchley said in papers filed before criminal court. "Some were simply too busy. Others would not travel to the detention center, and some said that Sam's case was outside their area of expertise. Others simply stated that they did not want to get involved due to the media attention given to the case."

By December 1997, the Manzies were still searching for a psychiatrist for Sam. Initially Shoreline Behavior Center was supposed to assign someone to help, but the center backed out after it was made public that Sam said he was really strangling his counselor at Shoreline when he killed Eddie because the counselor didn't take Sam's threats to commit violence seriously. The obvious insinuation from that revelation was that the Shoreline people could later

end up at the wrong end of a lawsuit brought by the
Manzies. Maybe on another level, they didn't feel
like exposing themselves to Sam Manzie anymore; if
he already wanted to strangle his caregivers from
Shoreline, he probably wouldn't be too receptive to
their help anymore—or maybe he might just try to
strangle someone.

Finally the Manzies had managed to find two doctors to come and treat Sam. Dr. Ellen Zupkus was
his psychologist, and Dr. Donald Oh became his psychiatrist. They treated Sam—Zupkus once a week
and Oh once a month beginning in January. But in
April, after Sam's transfer to an adult jail, the warden
there, Theodore J. Hutler Jr., refused to have either
doctor visit Sam Manzie. It was a liability issue, said
Hutler. Neither of Manzie's doctors had visiting
privileges at the jail, and Hutler wanted Manzie to
use someone who did. According to papers filed in
court, Hutler said the jail could be held liable if Sam
Manzie were inadequately treated.

Jail officials wanted Critchley to turn over all of
the medical and psychological records on Manzie so
jail physicians could begin treating him. Critchley
was vehemently opposed to that scenario. He
planned to use Manzie's diminished mental capacity
as part of his defense and he said that the two doctors Sam had treating him were essential to that plan.
Besides, how constructive would it be to take away
two doctors whom Sam had just become comfortable
with and replace them with two strangers on the pay-
roll of the state? Sam Manzie's reaction to that could
be frightening.

Critchley filed papers in May with the court to
overturn that decision. During this time, Sam Manzie was still not receiving the treatment his parents
wanted him to have. Dolores said Sam wasn't even

being provided schooling, "which by law he's entitled to," she claimed. The jail did provide him with
schoolbooks, "but for a sixteen-year-old to be expected to teach himself is ridiculous," Dolores said.

On Friday, May 29, 1998, Judge Giovine, who
would hear the criminal case against Sam, set aside
time to hear Manzie's attorney argue to keep his physicians while awaiting trial in jail. Michael Critchley
handled the arguments for Manzie while Ocean
County counsel Steve Nemeth handled the chores
for the county. Nemeth's argument against Sam
Manzie keeping his doctors boiled down to emergency contingencies. In other words, if Manzie had
some kind of a "breakthrough" while in the care of
his own therapists, the jail staff wouldn't know how
to handle Manzie because they'd been kept in the
dark. It was an emergency situation the county just
couldn't be prepared for—as if Manzie would suddenly have a screaming moment of clarity and the
jail would be unprepared for whatever action the boy
would take. Meanwhile, Critchley argued that Manzie had just begun to trust his new therapists and
that forcing him to change doctors would have a
"devastating" impact on his mental condition. In the
end, the judge ruled that Manzie could keep his own
doctors, a move that brought a small measure of relief to his parents and his attorneys.

But the case was getting more drawn out as each
day passed and it began to look like it would never
get to trial in 1998. The delays were caused by a busy
court calendar, the pretrial motions, Sam Manzie's
need for continuity in his doctors, coordination with
the Simmons case and numerous other reasons. But
the bottom line was that the longer it took to get to
trial, the worse things became for the Werners and
the Manzies.

In September the attorneys on both sides of the
Manzie case met in the judge's chambers. Sitting in
the courtroom were Ed Werner and Nick Manzie.
They didn't speak to each other, but sat staring and
watching the morning activities in court with rapt
interest. Sam Manzie never showed up and the case
was continued again.

"It's very difficult, but I want to be here for every
second of it, to see it through," Ed Werner told the
reporters assembled outside the courtroom. He
dropped his head and left the court when it became
clear nothing was going to happen that day. It
seemed like a never-ending nightmare to him and
one from which he couldn't wake up. It had been
nearly a year since his son had died and it didn't
seem like anything had changed since the day Eddie
had been found slumped over in a muddy stream
with Sam Manzie's footprint on his back. Ed just
wanted it to be over. So did Nick Manzie, who left
the courtroom after Ed. He was corralled by an AP
reporter and told him the same thing Ed had been
thinking. "I'm still waiting to wake up from this
nightmare," he said sadly. He walked away from the
proceedings quietly.

At their respective homes, Dolores Manzie and
Valerie Werner took the latest delays stoically, but
not indifferently. Dolores was angry and bitter with
the way she'd been treated and often thought back
on the visit she made with Nick and Sam to family
court. "Maybe if I sat in front of the courtroom and
put a gun to my head, maybe they would have treated
me a little bit more seriously," she said. Meanwhile,
her daughter was going to college. Her husband continued to work. Life went on, but so did the agony
and pain.

Valerie Werner was dealing with similar pain and

agony in her household, just blocks away from the Manzies. "Going to court and seeing the Manzies, a lot of the horrible feelings get dredged up in that setting," Ed had said. But Valerie hadn't gone. She was dealing with the pain of trying to keep three other children in line, get them to school, feed them, clothe them and care for them. Life went on for her, too, but the pain and agony were always in sharp focus when her children would inevitably talk about Eddie, or when she saw something that reminded her of him. Eddie had been a center forward on a youth soccer team and it had been one of the joys of his young life. Nearly a year after her son's death, Valerie Werner couldn't face looking at other youth soccer players in her neighborhood. A mere glance at a child in a soccer uniform brought back a flood of memories about her son Eddie.

Just as the Manzies and the Werners got used to the daily pain of waiting for the murder case to come to trial, the Simmons case came again to the forefront.

Howard Golden, Simmons's attorney, disclosed that the second telephone conversation recorded between Sam Manzie and Simmons had been erased by the prosecutors. It was the second telephone call Manzie had made that had been an abortive attempt to get Simmons to say something inculpatory. It was also the telephone call in which Manzie had tried his level best to avoid getting Simmons to say anything inculpatory. The police said erasing that telephone call had been a simple error and it didn't mean anything anyway because nothing of substance had been said during the conversation.

But Simmons had his own interpretation of events. It was evidence of how bungling the prosecution was and indicative of how unprofessional the police were—at least according to Simmons. Steve Simmons also said it was no surprise that the tape had been erased since it had recorded a conversation that showed Simmons was more caring for Sam than intent on having sex with the boy.

Golden was stuck between a rock and a hard place. He didn't like it when his client spoke to the media— it only brought more attention to the case. Since Golden thought, as did many others at that point, that Sam Manzie would not testify against Simmons, Golden was looking at the possibility of a plea bargain. However, since the case was so high profile, and since his own client was making it even more so, Golden had little hopes of getting an acceptable plea deal. The prosecution and police don't like pedophiles to begin with, and they really don't like unrepentant pedophiles who run their mouths in the press. Simmons was hurting his chances at a plea deal by refusing to shut up.

In a closed hearing before Judge Michael D. Farren in Monmouth County, Golden moved to have some of the evidence against Simmons suppressed. The machinations of the Simmons trial all but guaranteed that Simmons would keep his name in the media and closely associated with Sam Manzie for many months to come. That made Golden's job problematic at best and next to impossible at worst. For Golden, a family man and former prosecutor, it was a nightmare.

"It's not just our case alone; it's that it's tied into the Manzie case," Golden said. "It's become impossible to separate the two."

The Manzies and the Werners found that to be a true statement, but it certainly didn't help them out of the box of pain in which they'd been dwelling.

A year had passed since Eddie had died; an entire

year without their son had come and gone and Ed and Valerie Werner couldn't believe it. "I remember his smile," his father said. "And it doesn't feel anywhere near a year ago that I saw him smile, saw his whole face light up. He had a really infectious smile. It could light up a room."

Valerie Werner was beyond numb as she recalled the year that had just passed. "Sometimes it seems surreal, like it never happened. It definitely doesn't seem like a year ago. When I think that a whole year has gone by without Eddie, it's too much. It's too overwhelming."

The Werners spent the anniversary of Eddie's death visiting the cemetery where Eddie was buried.

As the year drew to a close, neither family was looking forward to the long, drawn-out trial that was sure to come in 1999. Neither, as it turned out, was Sam Manzie and he was about to make a decision that would drastically change the life of everyone involved in the case, yet again.

Thirteen

The Defense Wants Out

As 1998 came to an end, so apparently did any influence Michael Critchley and David Ruhnke had on Sam Manzie. Nick and Dolores had long ago given up any hope of influencing their son, but they had hoped the professional attorneys could deal with Sam, at least on a legal level.

Shortly before the anniversary of Eddie's death, however, Nick and Dolores heard from Sam that he wasn't planning on following his attorneys' advice. Sam wanted to change his plea to guilty. "It was a shock, to say the least," Nick said when he heard his son wanted to change his plea. It may have been a surprise, but something Dolores and Nick both came to see as consistent with Sam's character. They kept it quiet for weeks from Sam's attorneys as they tried to talk their son out of his determined course of action.

It was to be to no avail. Sam Manzie, who was considered an adult in Ocean County where he was to stand trial for murder, was considered a juvenile in neighboring Monmouth County where he was the victim of sexual abuse at the hands of Steve Simmons. He was betwixt and between and didn't feel comfortable in either position. Since he'd been seeing his own therapists, Manzie had been put on a new mixture of psychotropic drugs. He was taking Paxil, an antidepressant, Tegetrol to treat bipolar disorder (manic depression) and BuSpar, a tranquilizer used to ward off anxiety. The result of the medication was a calmer, more lucid Sam Manzie, at least according to his mother and father. "Finally I have a son I can relate to and he is behind bars," Nick Manzie said. "Eddie Werner would be alive today if only Sam had that medication in September [of 1997]." Dolores Manzie said her son was a completely different person once he was properly medicated and she bemoaned the fact that Eddie had to die for her son to get the care he needed.

But with Manzie being more lucid, it evidently also brought with it massive feelings of guilt. The child who'd written about true friendship could not escape what he'd done to Eddie Werner. Nor could he escape, in his mind, the feeling that he'd treated his *only* true friend in the world, Steve Simmons, in less than a friendly manner. Sam had time to think, had time to digest what had happened to him and had time to realize that he wanted to be punished. More importantly ultimately for Steve Simmons, Sam Manzie wanted to help the pedophile avoid punishment.

What happened to Eddie Werner was also never far from Sam's mind, nor was it far from the thoughts of Sam's parents. "Not a day goes by that I don't think about it," Nick said. "What my son did is always in my head and I don't know how I would be acting now if I were Eddie's parents."

Nick reserved his anger for the court system, which he believed let down both children. Dolores saved her anger for the same target, and became an extremely vocal critic of the system—which would later cause both of the Manzies emotional trauma in an open courtroom, but at the end of 1998, they both tried to keep in mind what was best for Sam. Dolores had seen some improvement in him during her many visits to jail and on the odd occasion when Sam called home. She desperately wanted him to get help and perhaps be able to get out of jail while he still had some time left in his life to lead a life. "I don't know if he would be all right in ten or fifteen years. I just don't like the thought of him coming out an old man and not having anyone left. We could all be gone, and what kind of life would that be for him?"

Nick Manzie was upset as the prospect of his son changing his plea came closer to becoming a reality. He'd broken up his retirement annuity to pay for expert testimony to benefit Sam and he'd poured a lot more money into the defense fund. Nick and Dolores were slowly going broke and it seemed like it didn't matter at all to Sam. The boy was going to do what he wanted to do.

The last chance to change his mind came when Nick and Dolores told Michael Critchley, the defense attorney, in November 1998 about Sam's intentions to change his plea. Perhaps, his parents thought, the attorney could talk some sense to him.

"I told him, 'Sam, we don't let seventeen-year-olds vote, drink or smoke cigarettes,' " Critchley said. "A jury should weigh this case. You shouldn't do this."

Critchley tried to reason with Sam Manzie, tried

to cajole him and tried to show him why it was important for a jury to consider the case. In sealed court documents, Critchley got to the heart of the matter. "We are confronted here with whether a juvenile who is suffering from a mental disability, under the care of a psychiatrist . . . , should be allowed to enter a plea of guilty which results in a custodial sentence as great as if he went to trial and was found guilty on all the charges. If an adult not suffering from a mental disorder desired to take such action, it would be cause for hesitation, or for pause. The same pause and hesitation is heightened when a juvenile, under medication and suffering from a mental disorder, requests to proceed in such a bizarre manner," Critchley wrote.

There were other ancillary issues in the case that also compelled it to be heard before a jury. There had been several systemic problems that had been stripped naked for the world to see, if the case went before a jury. No one was saying Sam Manzie didn't kill Eddie Werner, but Critchley reasoned that the case was far more important than that. Sam should pay for what he did to Eddie, but the system's weaknesses should also be exposed in a trial setting and before the full glare of the media and a jury.

In a world where horrendous problems with children were on the rise, Critchley hoped something valuable could come of a jury trial; he wanted to make sure other children didn't get caught in the same trap that had snared Sam Manzie and ultimately an innocent bystander by the name of Eddie Werner. In his own way, Critchley was struggling to put meaning into the death of Eddie Werner. If the system's weaknesses could be exposed, then perhaps change could occur and that change could insure that in the future children like Sam Manzie would be taken care of before they turned on a murderous rage.

As Critchley reasoned, the doctors should've seen the problem with Sam Manzie. The police should've been more careful with Sam. The family court should've listened more to Sam's parents. The insurance companies should've helped the Manzies with extended care for Sam. The FBI should've done more to help. The list went on and on. Almost everyone who could've done something didn't. Critchley became determined to see that all of those issues and more were brought up in the appropriate venue.

But Sam said, "No."

By February 11, just one year and nine days after Judge Robert A. Fall ruled that Sam Manzie would stand trial as an adult, it was apparent that Critchley and his partners were not going to be able to convince Manzie to continue to plead not guilty as they planned. Manzie then told Critchley that he was angry because Critchley wouldn't let him plead guilty.

"I got upset with that contention," Critchley said. "We sat down and talked, and I said, 'Sam, I don't care what you think. Take it from me, you're suffering from a mental disorder.'"

"No, I'm not. I know what I'm doing," Manzie replied. He further threatened to fire Critchley and his partner if the attorneys didn't carry out his wishes promptly. Then Manzie planned to contact the judge or the prosecutor directly.

Critchley was unconvinced. "Look at it at face value. We have a kid who wants to plead guilty with no benefit to himself. It's a plea bargain, but there's no bargain involved. He was sixteen at the time. He wasn't old enough to vote. He can't drink. That's because in our society we recognize that normal children can't make those decisions, so how could we allow a child who has obvious mental problems to make a decision like this, which will affect the rest of his life?"

To prepare for the trial, which ultimately never came, Critchley had bought $1,400 to $1,500 worth of psychiatric books and read them all. "I knew that the case would be won or lost on my cross-examination of the state's psychiatrist and I didn't want that to descend into psychobabble."

What Critchley wanted to do, and what he ultimately only did to Sam, was to hold up a mirror to Sam and ask the jury to "use some common sense. You may not know *what* is wrong with Sam, but you know *something* is wrong with him." Two different state's doctors had examined Manzie and each one of them came up with a distinctly different diagnosis. One even said Manzie had a "gender identity" problem, said Critchley. But the bottom line, as Critchley pointed out, was that all the professionals said that "there was something mentally wrong with Sam."

"The science of psychiatry is silly. It is based on a subjective viewpoint and on bias," Critchley said, "but we all know when something isn't right with a person."

Critchley tried to point this all out to Sam, who stubbornly refused to yield. To make matters worse, Sam wanted to be able to talk to Simmons and lobbied, again, to testify on *behalf* of Simmons during the pedophile's trial. Critchley roundly rejected that. He, in fact, had planned on calling Simmons into court and asking the pedophile, point-blank, if he'd stuck his penis in Manzie's anus. Manzie was aghast at that possibility. It would hurt his beloved friend, Steve Simmons, more than he cared to think.

In disgust, Critchley went into a closed-door hearing where he and Ruhnke asked the judge to excuse them from the case. A guilty plea, they were convinced, was not in the best interest of Sam Manzie. Judge Giovine's response was to impose a gag order on all the attorneys in the Manzie case, so no one in the media knew for sure why the defense attorneys were asking to leave. Speculation ran wild.

David Ruhnke would not discuss anything to reporters standing outside, waiting to find out what was going on. "We're not at liberty to discuss the contents of the motion as they are placed under seal by the trial court judge," he told inquisitive reporters. It was a roundabout way of telling them it was none of their business, but it made a more official-sounding quote in the newspapers.

The ramifications of a guilty plea were far more disastrous to the Manzies than they wanted to think about. Sam could effectively spend the rest of his life in jail, being ineligible for the death penalty since he'd committed the murder when he was a juvenile.

Sam Manzie certainly knew what the ramifications were; his attorneys had told him often enough. Still, he didn't budge. He wanted to plead guilty and was determined to do it. But Critchley was adamant. "In essence, he has nothing to lose by going to trial," Critchley wrote to the judge. In a status conference in Judge Giovine's chambers on January 19, 1999, and in a letter dated February 4, 1999, from Judge Giovine, Critchley was directed to obtain a defense psychiatrist to examine Sam Manzie to see if he was competent to "plead guilty and waive his mental-health defenses."

Critchley did so, but requested the judge reconsider his decision. "It is my understanding of the relevant law that when there are issues concerning a defendant's competency to stand trial or to enter a plea of guilty . . . it is generally within the province of the court to order an independent examination of the defendant. . . ."

Critchley also filed a complaint against the prosecutor William Cunningham who was being widely portrayed as a loose cannon on the deck in the way he was handling Sam Manzie's prosecution. According to his motion, Critchley said Cunningham had indicated to the court that even Critchley thought Manzie was competent to enter a plea of guilty, hinting, of course, that perhaps Manzie's mental-health issues were all a ruse.

"Mr. Cunningham in his memorandum of February 4, 1999, attributes to me," Critchley wrote, "an opinion regarding Mr. Manzie's competence by stating 'It is clearly implicit that Mr. Critchley knows the defendant is competent under law.' In addition to being bold and reckless, such an opinion is wrong. Lest there be any doubt as to what my opinion is, let me state it rather than Mr. Cunningham. I am of the unequivocal and unambiguous opinion that Mr. Manzie, for the reasons previously stated, is incompetent to enter a plea of guilty in this matter."

Further, Critchley wrote, "I am of the opinion that Sam Manzie is a very sick boy. I believe that he has suffered for a greater part of his life, and continues to suffer, serious mental illness."

Finally Critchley vented his rage on the actions of the state's prosecutor. "I did not invite the prosecutor to express such an opinion or characterization and considering the sensitive nature of the issues involved it was reckless for him to have done so and I request he refrain from any such future action."

All of the motions, which included very sensitive information about Manzie's condition, were sealed until well after the trial. Then it was Critchley himself who asked they be unsealed so he could proceed to use the information in preparing an appeal on Manzie's behalf.

All of the legal maneuvering meant little or nothing to Sam Manzie, of course. His mind was set on his course of action. He was simply following his conscience; in his mind, he was doing what was right to protect those he loved most.

At about the same time Manzie was going through his crisis of conscience, Ed Werner was going through some crises of his own. He'd wanted to do something to make sure his voice and the voice of other crime victims could be heard. He'd appeared in public to speak out for legislation to do so on one occasion and liked the response. It seemed only natural to him to take the next step.

A registered Democrat, Ed Werner had always enjoyed politics. Now, it seemed, was the time to do something with it. At the beginning of 1999, Ed Werner announced he would run for the state legislature on a platform of victims' rights. He didn't fool himself. He knew he was a long shot. He was a political unknown campaigning against a very conservative tide, but he had hopes of winning due to his own celebrity and through a cause he thought was just. He couldn't bring back his son, but in every way he could, Ed Werner tried to make his son's life and death mean something.

He looked askance at the permutations of the Manzie case. In many ways, it continued to be a surreal circus to which he was only a sideshow. He had vowed to get on with his life and being immersed in the Manzie trial didn't seem to be a proactive way of doing that. Sometimes he said he almost wished it would go away.

Of course it did not. On February 17, superior court judge Giovine denied Critchley's and Ruhnke's requests to be removed from the case. He sealed all requests related to the lawyers and ruled that another upcoming pretrial hearing for Sam Manzie would be closed to the public. That hearing had to do with Manzie's mental state.

The die was now cast. The next time Sam Manzie would be seen in public was scheduled for mid-March of 1999.

It wasn't entirely clear at the time what the result of the closed hearing was, nor what the issues were. But it became increasingly clear who'd won: Steve Simmons. If Sam Manzie would plead guilty, Simmons would never have to testify in open court in Ocean County as to the extent of his sexual relationship with Manzie. If Manzie pleaded guilty, then it was a reasonable conclusion that he would never testify against Simmons. If Manzie pleaded guilty, Simmons would be protected from most of the harsh consequences of his sexual activity with Manzie.

For Steve Simmons it was a win-win scenario. It was Sam Manzie who was going to pay, and Sam Manzie alone. He was willing and able to stand up in a court of law and tell the world he'd killed Eddie Werner and he was willing to tell all about the gory details.

It was a hell he was willing to go through, but to Sam Manzie it made sense. Aren't you supposed to sacrifice for those that you love? Aren't you supposed to have a conscience? If by pleading guilty Sam Manzie was able to protect Simmons, then maybe, just maybe, Sam could obtain some absolution for his own wicked acts.

It was a twisted logic, but as Critchley had said, Sam Manzie wasn't in his right mind and hadn't been for most of his life.

Fourteen

"Remove Her from the Court."

Friday, March 19, 1999

It was cold in Ocean County, New Jersey, and the aging courtroom looked like it was sagging beneath the weight of the spectators who came to see Sam Manzie stand trail as an adult for murdering Eddie Werner. There had been rumors and speculation as to what Manzie would do when he got into court, and the latest rumor would turn out to be the truth; Manzie was indeed going to plead guilty and avoid a lengthy and painful trial.

If Manzie had continued his not-guilty plea based on some diminished capacity, the trial could've dragged on for weeks. The prosecution's side would actually be limited and probably quite short. There was the confession by Manzie, the statement by his mother, the photograph and much of the circumstantial evidence. It was a pretty tight case against him, thanks to the excellent detective work done by his mother and her willingness to trust in the judicial system. But the defense had much more to explore, and it would be during the defense phase of the trial that Critchley and Ruhnke would bring up all the mitigating circumstances, the pain in the family, the therapy, the pedophile and the family court problems. Critchley said he wanted to put the system on trial and he had planned a beautiful case to do so. But it just wasn't going to happen.

In the end, Sam Manzie had his way again.

The proceedings got under way then with that speculation rife in the air. A half a dozen or more still and video cameras were allowed inside and the dimly lit, pale courtroom filled almost immediately. On one side of the aisle sat the Werners and on the other side sat the Manzies.

Puffy-eyed and tearful, Valerie Werner looked increasingly pale as the court proceedings got under way. She nervously jiggled her leg and watched the judge, the attorneys and especially Sam Manzie. He looked like a devil to her. Black-haired, tall, gangly and with a deep voice and deep-set eyes, he seemed so calm, and Valerie Werner seemed so distressed. Her eyes could not mask the pain she felt. The day before the hearing, she told reporters she was happy Manzie would plead guilty so that a trial would not be necessary. "Obviously, sitting in court and dredging up everything would be very difficult, hard for the kids, the family and his friends. I'm just glad we won't have to go through that," she said. But as she sat in the courtroom that day it was obvious even without the trial she was reliving all of her pain in its entirety as the abbreviated proceedings commenced.

Just twenty feet away sat Dolores and Nick Manzie. Dolores sat still with her red-rimmed eyes, looking, as one reporter described it, as "the eyes of an old-world statue of a crying saint—rimmed with tears in perpetuity." Both Dolores and Valerie would have greater reason to cry before the plea was done. Dolores had prayed for a trial to at least show the world that her son desperately needed help. In some way, perhaps she also wanted to be exonerated by those who'd said such foul things about her family during the last year and a half. She'd raised two children under the same roof and one of them had turned out OK. One of them was an honor student and in college and well adjusted—with the exception of the pain she'd dealt with via her brother. Dolores Manzie also wanted everyone to know that there was nothing the Manzies wanted to hide. It was Dolores who turned in her son, it was Dolores who'd done most of the work for the prosecution and she'd done everything with a strong sense of justice to guide her. She wanted to see it through.

Judge Giovine began the proceedings with little fanfare as it was obvious he wasn't surprised that Sam Manzie was going to change his testimony. He'd been conducting closed hearings with the attorneys on both sides for months. Manzie's intentions were well known and the judge was prepared for what was to follow. It was a plea bargain that would keep Sam Manzie in prison for at least thirty years, but in return Ocean County prosecutors agreed to dismiss nine charges, including rape, kidnapping and robbery. In return, the prosecution wanted to hear in open court Manzie's confession, sans the attempted sexual molestation.

"I took him [Eddie] into the upstairs bedroom," Manzie said as he glanced around at his mother, father and other spectators. The Werners caught his eye briefly and then he looked down at his nails before looking back to the judge. "I proceeded to strangle him with an electrical cord from an alarm clock . . . for approximately forty minutes. I put the body inside a suitcase. I took his body inside the suitcase across the street . . . behind my neighbor's house."

As Sam Manzie spoke, Valerie Werner began to rock back and forth, grabbing her husband's hand and clasping it tightly. It was as if each word Sam spoke brought her physical pain. She grimaced and quietly sobbed.

Then Nick Manzie stood up and shouted in the courtroom. "Ask him those questions when he's off the medication," he said in an uncharacteristic booming voice. He waved his finger at Judge Peter J. Giovine and then finished his interruption. "He's a different person when he's off the medication."

Dolores, dissolved in tears, seated next to her husband, looked to be a mirror image of Valerie Werner, sitting so short a distance away. "You know he's right," she yelled in defense of her husband. The implication was, of course, that Sam Manzie may have indeed known that he did wrong now, but did he know the ramifications of his actions when unmedicated? It was unlikely that without the medication Sam would have a foot in the real universe, and Nick was upset that no one seemed to care about that.

Nick and Dolores shattered the calm demeanor of the courtroom and Sam looked on quietly. His parents were sure their son did not know the ramifications of changing his plea and felt he had been railroaded yet again. Dolores carried the additional

guilt of knowing she'd helped the prosecution prepare such an airtight case against her son.

But the Werners weren't sympathetic. The outburst sent Valerie running from the courtroom in
tears. The assembled crowd gasped and then stood
mutely by as Ed Werner chased after his wife, effectively putting an end to the court proceedings. The
judge had lost control of his courtroom while Sam
Manzie stood by, watching all the drama unfold with
a placid look of acceptance on his face. His parents
hurriedly tried to compose themselves.

Outside of the courtroom was a different story.
Moving through a gauntlet of reporters and photographers, Ed Werner chased Valerie down a secluded
hallway, sealed by armed court officers, to try and
calm down. Valerie and Ed Werner, adorned in
green ribbons in memory of their dead son, took
several minutes to get themselves under control.

When they reemerged and walked into the courtroom, the Manzies apologized for their outburst.
They had been thinking of Sam and clearly had forgotten, for the moment, the pain Sam had visited
upon the Werners as well as themselves. With the
tension so palpable the air felt thick and sticky, Judge
Giovine then resumed the plea hearing. The judge
addressed Nick's concerns but said he was satisfied
Sam knew the consequences of his actions by refusing to go to trial. Critchley just bowed his head. He
had a very strong and viable psychiatric defense
planned and it was going absolutely nowhere.

Meanwhile, Judge Giovine pointed out that Sam's
medication didn't interfere with the boy's "above
average" intelligence and he could accept the guilty
plea.

Again, Sam Manzie stood passively next to his attorney, listening to it all. He kept most of his answers

short and to the point, answering "yes" or "no" to most everything the judge and his own attorney asked him.

"We've advised you not to plead guilty," Critchley said.

"You have," Manzie said as a reply.

"Despite our advice, you chose not to go to trial," Critchley added.

"I did," Manzie said.

Then Manzie bowed his head. "I know it was a violation of the law," he said, regarding the murder.

Outside the courtroom, the Werners were not jubilant, but at least they had cause to smile. "This is the only way within the law to make sure that Sam Manzie never murders or rapes again," Ed Werner told the throng of reporters. "There's no visible sign of remorse. I see no sign he can turn it around."

Indeed, because of the medication, the Sam Manzie the world saw that day was a calm, composed young man. It was nearly impossible to see a killer lurking inside. But E. David Millard, the Ocean County prosecutor, said Sam Manzie was a vicious, evil killer, nonetheless. "It's certainly no day of celebration," he said in an afternoon news conference. "It's a tragic occurrence. There was no viable defense. From the beginning, this office would not accept any plea to anything besides open-ended murder."

The arrogance of that statement is overwhelming to Critchley, who noted that it was Dolores Manzie who made the prosecution's case for them. It was the Manzies who cooperated the entire time and it was the Manzies who agreed their son needed to be put away. The only difference was they wanted their son to get much needed psychiatric help so if he ever were able to turn his life around he might have a chance of getting out of jail and leading a semi-normal life.

Dolores was incredibly angry after the plea. "This isn't a plea bargain. Where's the bargain?" she asked. "The prosecutors talked about a 'trophy' photo. Do you know what that really was? My son told me that he did not know whether what he was doing was a dream or real, and so he took a photograph so that when he woke up, if the photograph was there, he would know. He's sick. But, you tell me, is my son the monster, or are these people who have the degrees who don't know what they're doing?" The remarks stunned, stung and angered the prosecution. Cunningham would have time during the sentencing, and later took it, to respond to Dolores Manzie.

Critchley agreed with Dolores, but said so in a less emotional way. He said he could prove that Sam Manzie lacked the ability to comprehend the ramifications of pleading guilty and of his actions when he killed Eddie. He had submitted evidence that Sam Manzie had extensive psychological troubles dating back to the sixth grade. Critchley also remembered what had been said about Sam when he was so young and a teacher described him as a "sad little boy" who liked to fight a lot.

"I thought it was so telling and so sad. It was very touching," Critchley said. But what was angering to Critchley was the way the police in Monmouth County had used Sam Manzie to try and get to Steve Simmons. It was that action, Critchley contended, that ultimately put Manzie over the edge.

The plea was puzzling to Sam's parents. Their son had never listened to reason and they told local reporters that Sam apparently had been overcome with guilt and grief. They lived with the speculation and the pain for another month before Sam's sentencing. During that time, the drama continued and would culminate at the sentencing hearing with a low view of the prosecution that startled and angered many New Jersey residents.

Meanwhile, the community had to get past the sentencing. It wasn't easy for anyone living in the Jackson, New Jersey, area. Some eighteen months had come and gone since the murder, but the area still felt the pain visibly. It could be seen in the torn and frayed green ribbons that still hung all over town on mailboxes and lampposts. It could be seen in the fresh ribbons that were still worn on lapels of adults and children all over the county. Take a trip to the neighborhood bar or stop for a quick jug of milk at the nearby market and likely as not you'd find someone wearing a green ribbon and talking about Eddie Werner or Sam Manzie. Jackson mayor William Allmann said, "People don't take anything for granted anymore. It's taken precaution to another level."

Terrence R. Kenney, the principal of Christa McAuliffe Middle School, where Eddie Werner once was once a student, said, "People are still very cautious. I don't think you can go through something like this and not be. I know I'll never be the same again. You can't be this close to losing someone and expect things to be the same. I was always a stickler for safety for the school. I'm almost paranoid now."

The fear and scarring were greatest because Eddie Werner had not been killed by an outsider but by a neighbor. To those of devout faith, it seemed almost like a biblical parable. Who could look at their neighbor now and not be fearful or mistrusting? Eddie's death, Manzie's life and the pedophile Simmons played into everyone's worst fears.

* * *

Wednesday, April 14, 1999

Nick Manzie walked into the courtroom of Judge Peter J. Giovine not really knowing what to expect. He knew his son would face at least thirty years in prison and he hoped the judge would be merciful. He also knew the media would be in attendance; after all the story of how Sam had killed Eddie had taken on a life of its own. In some ways, it had been overshadowed by the Steve Simmons case, but the two cases combined were fodder for a greedy public as well as those who saw the two cases as the living embodiment of a parent's worst fears.

But Nick Manzie was still surprised. "What the hell is this?" he remembered thinking as he walked into the Ocean County Courthouse. Someone came up to him and asked whether he wanted to be placed on "the victim's or the defendant's side." It was as if the bailiffs were ushers in some bizarre wedding fete. "And then I thought to myself that after a year and a half, didn't they [the bailiffs] recognize that I was Sam's father?" Nick said.

He sat down in the front row with his wife. Dolores was already close to tears as she walked into the courtroom that day. All eyes, she felt, were on her and she later said she felt that among the dozens gathered in court that day, some couldn't help but look at her and cast at least some blame her way. She felt guilty, tired and scared. More than that, she was consumed with the thought of what was going to happen to her son.

The Werners made a late appearance in court, being ushered quietly down the center aisle to take a position on the left front row, just a dozen or so feet away from the Manzies. Neither family spoke to each other or acknowledged the other's existence. Yet, they mirrored each other almost exactly. Nick, in a gray suit, slightly balding and quiet, had his right arm around his wife, who appeared in a very fragile state. Across the aisle sat Ed Werner, in a dark suit, slightly balding and with a calm demeanor. He had his left hand around his wife, who appeared to be in a very fragile state.

The predominant sound in the courtroom as the families entered was the ubiquitous sound of shutters releasing on the silver and black cameras being handled by the photographers from the various daily newspapers and magazines sent to cover the sentencing. Someone coughed, but few said anything as the spectators watched the Manzies and the Werners file into the room. Somehow, as the families sat down, the air became thicker, more oppressive.

Then the judge entered and the tumultuous proceeding began. Using Sam Manzie's own words, William Cunningham and Judge Giovine gave a blow-by-blow description of Eddie Werner's murder based on Sam Manzie's interviews with psychiatrists. Nick Manzie sat there, shaking his head, "Why drag the Werners through all of that?" he asked himself. The pain it caused them had to be great. He looked over to his left and saw Valerie Werner in tears, clutching a bouquet of dyed-green roses wrapped in a green ribbon. Ed Werner was desperately trying to help her keep her composure.

Critchley countered by recounting all of Sam Manzie's psychological troubles and told the judge that "one after another these events took their toll." Finally, according to Critchley, "because of his load he snapped and because he snapped we're here today. I ask this court to sentence appropriately and ignore the call for revenge."

Manzie's mother, Dolores, also pleaded for leniency. "I don't know what's going to happen, but I'm asking you today to have some mercy on my son. He is my only son, and I am dying here today knowing that he may go to prison for the rest of his life." Unspoken but not unfelt was the fact that Dolores had provided all of the ammunition the prosecution would use against her son. She only hoped to be treated fairly because of her and Sam's cooperation.

But there was blood in the air and Cunningham was particularly vengeful. He practically sneered as Sam Manzie rose shortly after 2:30 P.M. to give his statement. Manzie approached his sentencing as he had everything during the trial—passively, calmly and detached. Somber and with his head hanging down, Manzie said he was "sorry for all the suffering I put people through," and that "I need to take responsibility for what I did. I still can't figure out why I did what I did. I still think about it every day." He apologized, looked briefly back at his parents, then toward the prosecution and then he was silent. The courtroom was as well.

"You have spoken well on your own behalf," the judge said, breaking the silence, but it didn't seem to affect the judge much, nor the prosecutor at all. Cunningham had already said that Sam Manzie was a "pedophile and a predator. He feels he is programmed to have sex, rape and kill."

But Cunningham wasn't done and what he said next put the court in a state of pandemonium and chaos. Cunningham blamed Dolores Manzie for everything. He accused Dolores of trying to dump her son on health-care professionals and he accused the Manzies of neglecting their duties as parents.

"A lot of institutions have been put under indictment," Cunningham said. "I want to clear the air. He wasn't seeking help. His mother wanted to get rid of him, and I am quoting, and these are quotes from the report from Mrs. Manzie."

Cunningham paused briefly for maximum dramatic effect. "Quote: 'He's here because I don't want to take him home.' Quote: 'I don't want the kid anymore.' Quote: 'Basically, I can't be around him.' Quote: 'I'm past the point of being mad.' Quote: 'Whenever he decides how he feels about anything, that's the way it's got to be.' Quote: 'I get the crap all the time; I'm not going to do it anymore.' Quote: 'I'm going to have a nervous breakdown.'"

Each statement was a pungent slap in the face. Dolores Manzie blinked and seemed to visibly recoil as Cunningham spat out each word. "The notes go on to read, the mom threatened suicide three times while she was there [at Kimball Medical Center in Lakewood the night Dolores found Sam had destroyed the police equipment] if they didn't take him—and they thought she was the one that needed the referral, not him. Let's make no mistake about it as to who wanted to get rid of who." Cunningham said this loud enough to be heard all across the courtroom.

"Excuse me, who the fuck is on trial?" Nick Manzie said loudly as he vaulted into an upright, standing position and tried to defend his wife. The courtroom fell into a shocked silence. Even the judge was nonplussed.

"You take him home for a week," Dolores Manzie challenged Cunningham as she, in turn, stood up and pointed her finger at the prosecution and began to yell. "Take him off the medication. Tell me you would be able to handle it."

Cunningham looked on quietly, with only a hint of a smirk on his face. Sam Manzie remained as placid as he had during the entire proceeding. Nothing, it seemed, would bother the calm induced by his psychotropic medication, even the sight of his mother being verbally assaulted by the prosecution.

The judge cleared his throat and spoke up. "Mr. And Mrs. Manzie, madam. Madam. Take your seat," he said. Then louder, "Take your seat. I'm telling you now, madam, I'm telling you now."

But Dolores Manzie wasn't done. She'd *handed* the case to the prosecution. Sam *handed* the plea to the prosecution. They, in turn, were thanking her for her cooperation in a most Machiavellian manner. "Your Honor, I didn't, I couldn't handle my child anymore. At least I admitted it." She was tired, scared and in tears, not to mention close to being hysterical. Dolores Manzie had not expected nor could she handle such vitriol from the prosecutor. She was already riddled with enough self-doubts about her ability as a parent. She didn't need the prosecutor to dump any more on her. She began to cry profusely.

"Remove her from the court," the judge said. "Remove her from the courtroom. Remove her from the courtroom."

But Dolores Manzie was stubborn. "I'm going nowhere. I am staying here. I'm not going. I am not going."

The judge looked out at Dolores, crying and yet standing like a statue. The bailiffs had surrounded her, but no one actually wanted to physically grab her. If she'd been a three-hundred-pound man armed to the teeth and ready to pounce, that would have been one thing. The bailiffs would have quickly acted. Instead, she was a thin, tired, scared woman, with hair suddenly awry, who couldn't physically have fought off her teenage son if he'd attacked her.

She stood naked in her weakness and emotional trauma, and no bailiff had the temerity to touch her.

Sam Manzie just looked on passively while the Werners looked at the scene through their own set of tears.

"Mr. Manzie, would you help us here?" the judge said pleadingly to Nick. Clearly, the judge had lost control of his courtroom.

But Dolores Manzie continued to say she wasn't going to go anywhere, and Nick didn't look like he wanted to cross his wife, either. "I won't say any more," Dolores finally said in a futile struggle to remain in the courtroom. "He was a lot of . . ." she said, and then pointed to her son. "He can judge me. I was at the end of my rope. No one was helping us. I'm not going to take it because, I'm telling you, I went there, I told them that night. . . ." She seemed to dissolve into tears as she refused to leave yet again. "Why don't you just try and destroy the family a little more?" she asked in anguish at Cunningham, who seemed to derive pleasure from the outburst.

She was done. She couldn't find any more words for her pain. If the prosecutor was right, it was all her fault. She visibly slumped, and with that gesture all of her rage was spent, which allowed a group of ten beefy bailiffs to assist her from the courtroom. It was a ludicrous sight. The bailiffs still looked like they were ready for and perhaps even preferred physical confrontation—with anyone but Mrs. Manzie. Despite her proud countenance, she looked spent and emaciated. Nick followed behind and stayed with her in the hall of the courthouse for a time before returning.

"I could not believe he did that," Critchley said afterward of Cunningham's attack on Dolores Manzie. "I couldn't believe what I was hearing. I tried never to press those emotional buttons and believe me I could have. I always tried to play it as professionally as I could."

Apparently, Cunningham thought it was important to vilify Dolores Manzie. He certainly never apologized for it, and while James A. Churchill, the executive assistant to prosecutor E. David Millard, later said that Cunningham may have overstepped his boundaries, Cunningham was never sanctioned or punished in any way. "Did he go too far? Maybe he did" was the extent of Churchill's remarks.

The sad effect of Cunningham's comments, according to many close to the case, was that they did nothing to help bring the Werners and Manzies together. The comments only seemed to drive them more and more apart. Whatever Cunningham's intentions in castigating Dolores Manzie, healing definitely wasn't a part of it, and hurting the Manzies was.

It was important, the judge said, that the proceedings take place with the "utmost dignity." He was not happy, and said, "This woman disrupted these proceedings and knew what she was doing."

Nick Manzie returned alone to the courtroom after settling his wife down, who waited outside and chatted with reporters. "I'm sorry that happened," he told the court. He got back in time to hear that not only was he a bad parent, his wife a bad parent, but his son was evil incarnate. While Critchley had used the information from psychiatrists who interviewed Sam Manzie to conclude that he was mentally ill, the prosecution saw it otherwise and so did the judge.

Recounting the horror Eddie Werner must've felt when Sam Manzie turned and locked the door on the little boy, prompting a cascade of tears, Cunningham said, "That makes you scream until your skin crawls." Utilizing the doctors' reports, Giovine concluded that the reports "support the fact that he [Sam] knew exactly what he was doing."

As for Steve Simmons, the prosecution said he didn't matter. The case of Eddie Werner was not about Steve Simmons. There was a revelation in the courtroom that Sam Manzie was initially attracted to Eddie Werner because the little boy wore all black, and both Sam and Steve Simmons had worn all black on the day they first met face to face. But Simmons had nothing to do with Eddie Werner and Sam Manzie, the prosecution claimed. "I am not here to serve as an apologist for what did or did not happen. We could talk about what-ifs—those are not appropriate to this case. I'm here to judge this young man," the judge said.

Cunningham noted that from an early age Sam Manzie liked to set fires, tried to hurt kittens in the home by stuffing them under cushions and at the tender age of eleven confessed he wanted to have sex with an eight-year-old boy at summer camp. Cunningham said Sam Manzie made the boy touch his penis and Manzie touched the boy's penis and anus. All of this occurred, Cunningham stressed, before Manzie ever met Steve Simmons; ergo, Simmons had nothing to do with Manzie killing Eddie Werner.

The parents of both boys sat and watched in the courtroom with haggard looks of revulsion, disgust and resignation on their faces. Dolores Manzie may not have been in the courtroom, but her presence was certainly felt by everyone there.

Before Judge Giovine proceeded to pronounce the sentence against Sam Manzie, both of the Werners finally got their opportunity to speak.

Valerie, fragile yet determined, dressed in a cream-colored knee-high dress, got up and said, "Nobody should have to go through this pain." She dabbed at her eyes, sniffed occasionally and sat back down. Many of the parents in the courtroom audience were close to tears.

Ed Werner got up, tugged at his dark suit, cleared his throat and spoke up. "Sam Manzie doesn't seem to understand the pain he caused," he said, looking directly at Sam, who remained quiet yet attentive.

"I can only wonder about the pain my son felt," he said, recounting the agonizing moments after Manzie closed the door and locked it on Eddie. Ed Werner said he constantly thought about the moment Manzie stretched the alarm clock cord taut against his son's neck. "When the cord was wrapped around his neck, did he wonder, 'Is this the last thing I'll ever see?'"

Ed Werner was now close to tears, but his voice did not betray him as he struggled to finish. "You feel pain in ways you don't think you can," he said, noting that at the "brief time between wake and sleep, I have a recurring dream. The bedroom door opens and Eddie walks in and I hug him and tell him my horrible dreams, and my son says it's OK and gives me a hug. Then I fully wake up and the nightmare becomes reality."

The entire courtroom, including Nick Manzie, was in tears. The judge waited for a few moments while Ed Werner, his wife and the rest of the audience were able to compose themselves before he went on. Perhaps he needed a moment for himself as well.

Judge Giovine looked up and acknowledged the many letters that he'd received in support of Eddie Werner and Sam Manzie, and then he complimented the Werners on their behavior. Finally he proceeded to go over the mitigating and aggravating factors of the case. Noting that Sam Manzie appeared to have "little or no concern for others" and recounting all of the heinous things Manzie had done in his life, the judge sentenced Sam Manzie to seventy years in prison. It would be fifty-nine years and six months before Sam Manzie would be eligible for parole. He would be an old man, a very old man, if he lived to be released.

"I am trying as hard as I can to keep my faith," Edward Werner had told the judge. "When I ask, Judge, to give a life sentence, it is not revenge, not to do evil. It is the only way, Judge, to make sure that Manzie never kills any more dreams or makes any more nightmares come true, that he never brings this kind of pain again."

Werner had, in effect, got what he requested from the judge. He took little comfort from it. After all, his son was still gone. But at the very least he was convinced Sam Manzie could harm no one else anymore. He and his wife walked slowly from the courtroom and addressed the throng of reporters and cameras gathered outside of the courthouse. The Werners stood defiantly and proudly as they addressed the reporters.

That was in direct contrast to Nick and Dolores Manzie. Dolores, still beside herself with grief, shunned the reporters and cameras and fled to their nearby car with cameras in tow, clicking away as their grief was starkly visible on both of their faces. The prosecutors and other court watchers had sneered at the Manzies again, saying that Dolores's outburst had been staged for the cameras. In front of the cameras, Cunningham was particularly disdainful to the Manzies' pain. It didn't mean much to him.

But the Manzies' pain was about to increase, be-

cause one of the ramifications of Sam's sentencing
was that the focus would now shift back to Monmouth County where Steve Simmons sat in court,
waiting for his turn and relishing the opportunity to
get more attention. "I only want what is right for
Sammy," Simmons had said on numerous occasions.
That statement was about to be tested in ways even
Simmons couldn't anticipate.

Fifteen

"I Do Not."

There was unending speculation throughout Freehold, Ocean and Monmouth counties as to why Sam Manzie changed his plea, opening himself up to the harsh sentence he received. Ultimately, though, the motivation may not have been that difficult to understand.

"Sometimes in life we are faced with an important decision. We must go the way that we know deep down in our heart is right—even if you can get in trouble for that decision or even if everyone else says it is wrong," Sam Manzie had written in his note left with the destroyed police recording equipment.

His plea and his placid acceptance of his sentence was nothing more than the living embodiment of what he felt he had to do—what he knew was right and everyone else knew to be wrong. Again he protected his friend and lover, Steve Simmons.

The day after the sentence, the Freehold area was in upheaval. "What if the information presented to the judge who gave Sam Manzie seventy years—such as a doctor's report that Manzie wanted to kill a child—had been offered to the judge who decided it was safe to send Manzie home three days before the fifteen-year-old did kill?" That was the lead sentence in a *New Jersey Star-Ledger* editorial after Manzie's sentencing. Another editorial in the same paper castigated Cunningham's vitriol against Dolores Manzie as the prosecution's "coup de disgrace."

The judicial system was under heavy attack, as it was pointed out in the newspaper, further driving the horrendous crime against Eddie Werner into the background. The Manzies had sought out help. They had struggled to put an end to Sam's reign of terror and had been unable to do so. Cunningham's vilification of Sam's parents was seen as an "unjustified and inexcusable effort to defend the failure" of the institutions that had let down the Manzies and ultimately the Werners.

The town was split. Protestors had shown up during Manzie's sentencing eager to have his neck at the end of the rope. There were those who thought the Manzies were as horrible a pair of parents as any who'd ever lived, as well as those who thought they were horribly abused by the system.

The tension was still thick in the area the day after the sentencing and in the middle of the assessment of guilt and casting of blame across the board, there was increasing speculation that Steve Simmons would admit to molesting Sam Manzie and avoid an embarrassing trial. It was only assumed that it would be embarrassing for Simmons. "I don't think that there will be a trial," Prosecutor John Kaye had told the press at the end of March 1999. For months Simmons had wanted to plea-bargain with the prosecution, and for some reason, Kaye seemed to think he had greater bargaining power once Sam Manzie had been sentenced.

There was also a renewed attack against the Monmouth County Prosecutor's Office for the way they handled the Simmons case by using Sam Manzie, a troubled teen, in their investigation. "I just don't think it's ethical at all," Janice Levins, executive director of the Safer Society Foundation, told the local media. "This young man is already under tremendous strain because he is in this relationship. And on top of that he is asked to sabotage the relationship."

The prosecutor's office in Ocean County was being hammered for what was said about Dolores Manzie—who'd been openly critical of the prosecutors in both Ocean and Monmouth counties—and now it was time for the Monmouth County Prosecutor's Office to be hammered. The monstrosity of the Werner/Manzie/Simmons case was devouring reputations right and left. No one in the judicial system seemed safe and no one in any of the three families was safe, either.

During the height of this tumult, Sam Manzie was quietly and quickly whisked away to Trenton State Prison. According to Jack Terhune, the state commissioner of corrections, Manzie was received at the facility at 6:20 P.M. the day he was sentenced to seventy years. It effectively meant that he went straight from the courthouse to the state facility with only minimal time at the county jail to collect his things and get processed. It wasn't unusual in high-profile cases, Terhune said, for the state to take such measures.

But it didn't seem that way to Nick and Dolores Manzie. They were told late Wednesday night that their son was still at the Ocean County Jail. They had planned to visit him the day following his sentencing. That night when he failed to call, Nick and Dolores feared the worst. There had been continuing threats against the boy; now with the sentence complete, Nick and Dolores feared inmates had exacted their own justice on Sam. It would not have been unheard of and it was a fear Nick and Dolores had been dealing with since Sam's arrest.

Nick Manzie picked up the phone and called the county jail. "We called him and were told by people at the jail that he was sleeping," Nick said. He didn't know until the following day his son wasn't even *at* the jail that night. When they found out what really had happened, the Manzies were unsettled to say the least. Meanwhile, Judge Giovine had similar concerns about Sam Manzie's health. He ordered sheriff's officers to stay with the teen wherever he went. In a psychiatric report given to the judge by Michael Critchley, the contention was that Sam Manzie would pose a danger to himself and others. There was talk of a suicide watch. "I hope they do that," said Dolores, who feared Sam would take his own life.

Once Sam Manzie got into the state system, however, the sheriff's deputies would not tag along. Manzie had to go through the classification process. Once brought into the massive state penal system, Manzie would be staying at Central Reception, an area of the prison that can house as many as seven hundred prisoners. It is there that most prisoners stay for a brief period of time while they are accessed and assigned more permanent lodgings. Any medical reports accompanying the prisoner are evaluated, and as Terhune later said, it is during that classification process that an inmate will be assigned to protective custody if needed.

The needs of all the prisoners were evaluated in

exactly the same manner. Sam Manzie ceased to be Sam Manzie when he got into the state system. He was a prisoner with a number and would be treated as everyone else in the system was treated. In an odd sense, it was as democratic as possible and the fairest treatment Manzie would encounter since his arrest.

In a few weeks, he was settled in, and his parents said he actually seemed to be calmer, more attentive and gradually became the son they wish they always had. It broke their hearts that it only came after he had killed another child.

The Werners tried to get on with their life at the same time, confused and angry that Sam, his parents and most especially Steve Simmons had become the focus of the attention in the media. It wasn't for selfish reasons, but they wanted people to remember that the real tragedy had been the loss of an innocent life. Simmons had steered the press away from that. His cause was that of the gay teen and how he had struggled to assist the troubled Sam Manzie in getting in touch with who he really was. His argument was that society wasn't accepting of gay teens and the tragedy was that Sam had to kill someone before anyone ever noticed there was trouble with the boy.

But Simmons's arguments seemed to fall on deaf ears and he said he became despondent. In May 1999, in what some later said was a desperate bid for attention, Simmons tried to take his own life. At least that's what the headlines intimated. Simmons had hidden and hoarded in his jail cell ten antidepressant pills he had been prescribed. On Saturday, May 1, while revelers celebrated the "Running of the Roses" at Churchill Downs in Louisville, Kentucky, Simmons had his own little race going on in his prison cell.

The race was between the medication Simmons had swallowed and whether or not it would incapacitate or kill him before doctors pumped his stomach or gave him medication to counteract the pills.

Simmons had handicapped this race considerably. Shortly after noon, mere minutes after he chugged his pills, he told jail guards he'd taken them. At first surprised, the guards reacted quickly, taking Simmons to Central State Medical Center, where he stayed briefly until his medical condition stabilized and then he was whisked back to his cell in Monmouth County.

A local reporter covering the story had to make an unfortunate trip to see Simmons after the overdose. Apparently, one of the side effects of the overdose was akin to a massive dose of Viagra, and Simmons noted with pride as the reporter showed up to interview the prisoner that this side effect had taken place. "I'm surprised you didn't notice," Simmons said, and then went on to tell the reporter how he'd also become infected.

Whatever the reason, whatever the cause, no matter how puerile, no matter how embarrassing, Simmons couldn't help but talk to and tell all to the press. He reveled in the attention. After his attempted suicide, he was going to get a lot more.

Ever since Sam Manzie's sentencing, the speculation had been growing as to whether or not he would testify against Steve Simmons. Now that Manzie's case was over and the drama shifted from Ocean County to Monmouth County, that speculation also took center stage in the seemingly never-ending sad saga of events that led to Eddie Werner's death.

It was an expected turn of events. Simmons was seen as the demon who destroyed Eddie's life through Sam Manzie. It was Simmons who was still, apparently, manipulating Manzie. The speculation and tension were palpable as the summer months dragged on. Most casual observers knew that Manzie had participated with and supplied the bulk of information to Arancio and Noble to help make the case against Steve Simmons. It was going to boil down to Manzie's word against Simmons's. In that kind of confrontation to a jury of adults—many of whom would probably be parents—there was little doubt in anyone's mind what the outcome would be.

The spit was ready and Simmons would be the barbecued pig.

Sam Manzie knew what the prosecution had in mind and didn't seem to be interested in helping John Kaye or Marc Fliedner roast Steve Simmons, but outwardly the prosecutors continued to hope that he would help out their case.

Another player in the unfolding drama of the Werner/Manzie/Simmons case had his turn to be barbecued. Judge Citta, who'd been the butt of many jokes and the target of many letters to the editor, was up for judicial review. The judge had to be seen before a State Senate Judiciary Committee so it could be decided whether Citta could continue to work at his current job.

The hearing was part of the regular review of judges, and while it coincided with the upheaval of the Manzie case, it wasn't directly related to it. However, the Manzie case would dominate Citta's bid for tenure. On Thursday, June 17, 1999, in his only public comment on the Manzie case, Citta told the senators: "That one particular case is a terrible tragedy. We're all aware of that. I would suggest respectfully to each of you that you cannot imagine the number of times I've reviewed the evidence that I had before me that fateful day in 1997. Every day, a family court judge is required to make difficult decisions . . . based on the evidence before them. I have made every effort to assess thoroughly all of that evidence. That's what I did then and that is what I do in every case."

Three people, however, showed up to speak against Citta, including the executive director of the League of American Families, who suggested that Citta had information before him that indicated Sam Manzie had sexually molested another boy, that he had abused a young child by forcing him to drink cleaning fluid and that he had tortured animals.

The judge found himself at the center of the controversy surrounding the Manzie case. His critics were vocal and blunt. In letters to the editor at the *Asbury Park Press* and the *Star-Ledger,* Citta was described as both negligent and inept. Bernard Laufgas, a Barnegat, New Jersey, resident who is a frequent critic of jurists in New Jersey, was quoted in the *Asbury Park Press,* saying even stronger things about Citta. "The most frightening judge is Judge Citta. He's cold-blooded. He has no respect for the law." Laufgas said Citta should've listened to the Manzies' plea to have their son hospitalized.

Other critics said the judge was indifferent at best and ineffective at worst. "The governor's renomination of Judge Citta is grotesque. To approve this nomination would be nothing short of an obscenity," said one citizen who came to testify before the senate committee.

All of that flew in the face of the judge's past record. "He doesn't take any shit in his courtroom," most of his backers said. Indeed, his record had shown that Citta was a most capable jurist. Being nominated to a lifetime appointment was an investment for the state, not a cost to the state, they argued.

All three Ocean County senators supported Citta's renomination. Those who supported Citta said he ruled the only way he could on September 24, 1997. They urged that the laws be changed and that a good judge be protected. The Ocean County Bar Association backed Citta as well—a valuable endorsement to any jurist. "We believe Judge Citta is an exemplary judge, in all areas of the law," Patricia B. Roe, who headed the county bar's family law committee, said. "He is a fair, no-nonsense judge."

The State Senate Judiciary Committee put off until the following Monday a decision about whether or not Citta deserved tenure.

Valerie Werner, when questioned, tried to stay out of the thick of the latest controversy. "I don't believe that anything Judge Citta did caused the death of my son. I believe that he sent Sam Manzie home with his parents so they could be parents to him and help him. But he could have taken a little more time in looking at the whole picture. He could have been a little bit more thorough."

The Manzies, on the other hand, particularly Dolores, were delighted to see that someone was finally listening to the criticisms they'd had all along about the family court system. When Dolores read in the newspaper about the continued hearing, she decided to attend the following Monday. She and Nick had taken an initial pass at participating in the hearing because they said they had been "beaten down" whenever they tried to get anyone to listen to their complaints about the system. That they were not and would not be the only voices of dissent was encouraging to them.

It was discouraging, to some extent, for the

Manzies to read about the support Citta had and how many of those supporters, upon reviewing the transcript of the Manzies' visit to family court, had concluded Citta had "done the right thing."

"No one knew Sam the way we did," Dolores said. "No one watched the violence the way we did. No one saw how it got worse and worse and no one ever got it. Nobody ever listened."

But, as it turned out, Citta couldn't have listened to the problems of cleaning fluid ingestion, sexual molestation and tortured animals because he'd never *seen* that information. While it had come out in the criminal case against Sam Manzie, the judge had not been given the information when he ruled that Sam should go home with his parents three days before Eddie Werner's death. He couldn't have asked for it, either. He simply couldn't act on information he didn't know existed.

The problem was far deeper in the family court system than most realized. Ten years prior to the judge's renomination, a panel of family court judges had examined the system and found that New Jersey's family court needed more judges, staff and mandatory training for all in the social sciences related to their responsibility. The New Jersey legislature had never acted on the suggestions and the chickens had finally come home to roost in the Sam Manzie debacle.

The state had known for at least ten years that there were major problems in the family court system. "Ten years that our family courts, the ones that deal with the most important issues in the world for most people, are understaffed, undertrained and less than competent," a *Star-Ledger* editorial noted. "We know it and we let it continue."

The Manzies, meanwhile, continued to take heat

from the judicial system. That angered Sister Laura Long, principal of the Holy Family School in Lakewood. She had first met Sam Manzie when he was a kindergartner at her school and she had visited him and written to him regularly since he had been arrested. "He has his parents who are absolutely devoted to him," she remarked.

The furor over Citta and the accusations against the Manzies began to die toward the end of June 1999. Citta was given his tenure and the Manzies were happy to retreat from the limelight while they wrestled with their son over his intention to testify for Steve Simmons in his upcoming trial. Ed Werner, on the other hand, was gearing up for his state legislature race.

Life lurched forward in fits and starts for the Werners and the Manzies. Their next big obstacle would come in July. On July 8, 1999, the die was cast. Simmons was set to go to trial the following week, despite all of his overtures about a plea bargain. Apparently, the prosecution hadn't offered anything Simmons would accept and Simmons's counteroffer to drop everything but the first two charges (the ones that carried the least amount of punishment) was not acceptable to Kaye, either. But no one, not the prosecutors, not Simmons's lawyer, not even Sam's parents, knew then whether Sam would testify at the trial. It was a big gamble for the prosecution.

"He's so back and forth on this," Dolores Manzie told reporters. "You're probably going to know the day they bring him into court." She wasn't sure, she said, because she and Nick didn't discuss Simmons much with Sam. "I don't like that man [Simmons]," she said. "He could be the greatest man in the world, but he's still a child molester."

Monmouth County prosecutor John Kaye outlined for the public what to expect. He said before the trial would start Manzie would be put on the witness stand and quizzed about his intentions. The defense would try everything they could to keep Sam Manzie from testifying while the prosecution would do everything in its power to make sure Manzie testified. Manzie was once again going to be pulled in different directions. So were his parents. In Ocean County, Manzie had been certified as an adult and was sentenced as an adult for killing Eddie Werner. In Monmouth County, Manzie was still regarded as a juvenile and a victim. "All this makes me want to throw up," Dolores said of the irony. Time and again, she said, she was confronted with examples that Sam remained a juvenile under law, but had still managed to be sentenced as an adult.

It seemed like a nice Orwellian concept—the ability to hold two completely contradictory thoughts in one's head at the same time and believe both of them. John Kaye told a local reporter that "I feel sympathy for her [Dolores Manzie]." It didn't change anything, however.

Meanwhile, the discussion revolved around what would happen if Sam Manzie didn't testify. Defense attorney Howard Golden said he would probably ask for a plea deal if Manzie didn't testify, but Kaye said there would be no deals made. After months of speculating about a deal, Kaye was apparently convinced he had a great case without Manzie, which included pictures, witnesses and even some hearsay testimony, which Kaye said he might try to get admitted.

The time to find out if Kaye was bluffing was on July 14, 1999.

On that sunny morning, Sam Manzie, serving seventy years in prison for murdering Eddie Werner, walked into Judge Michael D. Farren's courtroom in shackles and handcuffs. Sporting a pallor indicative of too much time under the inadequate lights of a dank prison, Manzie appeared calm and relaxed. He strode with a resigned look into Farren's courtroom.

Even his own parents didn't know what to expect next. They had, of course, spoken about that moment when Sam got up to testify, but always the issue was unresolved. "He wavered on what he was going to do," Nick Manzie told reporters. "We talked to him about ten minutes beforehand and he told us what he planned to do, but we weren't sure until we got into the courtroom and heard what he had to say."

The court room was silent as Sam Manzie was brought in. The tension was thick and resonant in the small, stuffy courtroom. Windows lined the right side of the room, allowing sunlight in, but they were closed and the air-conditioning didn't seem to work right. If it came on at all, it seemed to drown out the voices at the bench, so consequently the air-conditioning wasn't used at all.

Stuffiness seemed appropriate, however, for what would ensue. Sam Manzie, a convicted murderer, was being put on the stand to be asked if he would testify against the one man many believed helped to put him behind bars, a pedophile. Steve Simmons sat in the courtroom, quietly watching Sam, with a small smile on his face. He either knew something most of the spectators did not, or was perhaps wistfully thinking of better times with Manzie.

Both had come a long way since their first meeting in August 1996. Sitting in a courtroom, both were in shackles and handcuffs, while their whole lives were played out for the press and public. It was not necessarily where Manzie wanted to be, but Simmons had seemed to thrive on the attention. It was becoming apparent that without the benefit of a trial for Sam Manzie, the emotional catharsis of the denizens of New Jersey would only be served by the trial of Steve Simmons. After the April 1999 sentencing, it became increasingly clear that Simmons was going to reemerge on center stage for an encore.

He played it as best he could, calling every local reporter who'd listen to him, much to the chagrin of his beleaguered lawyer and, some said, to the detriment of his own defense. This didn't stop him of course. "He thinks he's the smartest guy in the room," Howard Golden said on numerous occasions. "He's smarter than all of us," he added with a sideways grin to let you know he wasn't serious.

But Simmons was serious. Like every actor who's ever played summer stock or had aspirations of picking up an Oscar, Simmons played his time in the limelight with poise and hamminess. As he sat, waiting for the curtain to go up on the latest demonic act in the tortured play, he wore a smile, perhaps one of pure enjoyment. His life was in the balance, and that moment when Sam Manzie got up to testify was the test. If he had any sway over Sam at all, Simmons was confident the boy wouldn't testify against him. It was a moment of drama an actor could not help but notice and even enjoy.

Manzie looked at Simmons and then nodded to his mother and father. In his khaki prison garb, he looked vulnerable but defiant. He was not intimidated by the court proceedings; he was far beyond the ability to be swayed by officialdom or any threats, real or imagined, they could bring down on him.

"Do you intend to testify in this case as to what allegedly occurred between you and Mr. Simmons?" the judge asked bluntly.

"I do not," Sam Manzie replied defiantly. Simmons smiled.

"Do you understand that you have no privilege that would permit you not to testify? Do you understand that?" the judge asked.

"I will dispute that" came the clipped answer.

"What is the reason you refuse to testify?"

"I'm asserting my Fifth Amendment privileges," Manzie said. The boy was convinced he had the constitutional right to protect himself from self-incrimination, but the judge just shook his head as Sam's parents watched openmouthed and numb.

"Do you understand that you have no Fifth Amendment privileges in this case?" the judge asked.

"I intend to dispute that," Manzie said curtly.

Reporters were now shaking their heads. A quick glance at Simmons showed his small smile had begun spreading across his face. Meanwhile, Sam's parents exchanged glances with each other and then looked back at their son.

"I'm going to order that you testify in this case as to what allegedly occurred between you and Mr. Simmons," Judge Farren said sadly in response to Manzie's defiance. Farren looked like he already knew that wouldn't work. "Do you still refuse to testify?"

"I do" came the short and swift reply.

Farren then did what he thought he had to do; he found Sam Manzie in contempt of court and sentenced him to serve an additional six months in jail that he would have to serve if he was ever paroled. "Big deal" seemed to be Sam's response as he shrugged his shoulders and was quietly led out of the courtroom. What's six months compared to seventy years? Why should he testify against Simmons? In Manzie's mind, Simmons had remained true to him, and Manzie saw the courtroom setting as a way to remain true to Simmons.

Outside of the court, in the horribly lighted, tiny hallways of the courthouse, Nick and Dolores Manzie greeted reporters once again. Through her tear-stained eyes, Dolores expressed her greatest fears about Simmons. "He's going to get out of jail and have sex with another fourteen-year-old boy." She knew Sam could've helped put Simmons away and she shook her head as she confronted that issue. "I wanted him to testify," she said. "But Sam's a victim. Why was he sentenced for not testifying? He's been traumatized. Doesn't that mean anything to anybody?"

Nick said he was disappointed Sam hadn't testified, but said he wanted to support his son. "I love him. But it hurts to know that all this work that's been done, [it] is for nothing. Who knows where it's going to go now?"

Dolores shrugged as she listened to her husband, and noted that "cooperating with authorities gave my son seventy years. This is the first time I've seen a victim held in contempt for not testifying against their molester. That tells me they don't care what happens to Sam. It tells me they don't consider him a victim." Dolores was back to doing what she did best—pointing out how the system had failed.

Legal authorities across the state of New Jersey weighed in on the side of the Manzies in that regard. The former president of the state's Association of Criminal Defense Attorneys told a local reporter he'd never heard of a case in which a victim who refused to testify against an alleged molester was held in contempt.

"I have a live son with a dead life," Dolores said through tears. She'd shed so many during the last

two years. It was inconceivable to many of the reporters who'd come to know her how she was capable
of shedding any more. Yet, she did.

Simmons was appropriately giddy about the pros-
pects of Sam not testifying. As he saw it, that left the
bulk of the charges against him not provable.
Howard Golden, Simmons's attorney, shrugged during the break and over his shoulder told reporters
that, of course, he was relieved that Sam Manzie
wouldn't testify. The question then facing Golden
was whether to pursue a jury trial, or simply have
Simmons tried in front of the judge. His gut feeling
was to go for a jury, because as he said, he would
get "two bites of the apple." He could plead questions of the law before a judge and play the jury's
sentiments for everything else. But even Golden admitted he thought he had little chance against a jury.
"Who was going to be supportive of a pedophile?"
a reporter asked. Not many people would, Golden
admitted.

After Manzie was sentenced and court broke,
Marc Fliedner, the prosecutor assigned the case, still
tried to be upbeat about the prosecution's chances.
They appeared very slim, though. Without Manzie's
testimony, there were only a handful of pictures, a
few peripheral witnesses—the most powerful of
whom were Sam's own parents—and, of course, Simmons's confession. If that's all the prosecution had,
reporters speculated, Fliedner didn't have much. It
was surmised that he must have some ace up his
sleeve. But no one knew. Fliedner was all smiles as
he walked out of court and predicted that all would
be well and he had an ironclad case. Everyone
wanted to believe him, but few did.

"Any evidence I can keep out that prosecutors
want to use helps the case," Golden told reporters.

"I think Sam Manzie is the only source of evidence for a number of the charges in this case."

Any casual eye could see that the prosecution was damaged beyond repair, but for some reason, John Kaye's office wouldn't give up. Nick and Dolores Manzie were still hoping for a miracle, and since Kaye didn't drop the case, they continued to hold out hope that something good would come of all the hell they'd been put through during the last two years. The whole Simmons case was what many saw as the catalyst that led to Eddie Werner's death. For it to end with no conviction was almost unthinkable.

"First Sam warned Simmons, then smashed the machine," Nick Manzie said of the recording equipment and the past actions his son had taken. "Today was his way of again saying 'I'm sorry' to Simmons. It's obvious Sam didn't testify because he still has feelings for him."

That night Simmons sat in his cell ecstatic. He knew what Sam's refusal to testify meant for him; he was going to get out of jail a lot sooner than most people thought he would. He called a local reporter, cheering Sam's actions. "What does that say to all of these people who have been giving him advice for two years? After all this, I'm still the one he trusts. He did what he felt was right."

The statement served only to inflame the public and the Manzies. It seemed defiant, ugly and boasting. Golden wasn't too happy about it, either, when he read it in the next morning's paper. "I wish he would just keep his mouth shut," Golden said. It wasn't the type of case Golden, a former prosecutor and father, wanted to take on anyway. But he was bound ethically to give Simmons his best defense and Simmons wasn't doing anything to help out. The judge, the prosecutor and anyone else who happened to read Simmons's statements in the media would be angered by the comments. Dealing with angry and petulant judges and prosecutors is not what any competent defense attorney wants to do.

The proceedings were bound to just get uglier.

Sixteen

Who's Miranda?

The sight of a pale, composed and defiant Sam Manzie in the courtroom wasn't the only surprise to be thrown at the public during the course of the Steve Simmons trial, but it was an accurate prediction of things to come. It was as if once the prosecution, defense and judge reached that ugly precipice of sentencing Sam Manzie to additional time in jail for not cooperating with them, there was no place to go but down. Down it went—sordidly, callously and very loudly.

Jury selection was a speed race through ninety potential jurors during two days with only a brief questioning of each of them about the case. Many of the jurors who were excused were sick or had scheduling conflicts. One was excused after being asked about whether or not the testimony about a gay sexual encounter would upset him. "I'm not too happy about it," he said candidly, and he was gone.

Another young man, an electrician who was good-looking enough to be a male model, was excused by Golden, not because of anything the prospective juror said, but because Golden was upset with his client. "Knock it off," Golden told Simmons as Simmons made comments about the electrician. Simmons was interested in the electrician, but not necessarily to serve on his jury.

Otherwise, the selection moved rather quickly and Howard Golden and Steve Simmons didn't seem to mind. Everyone wanted to get the trial over. Marc Fliedner, the prosecutor, was stuck with a difficult case without Manzie and knew it. His best hope was to find a jury who just wouldn't like Simmons and would be willing to convict him even without adequate evidence. Golden had no stomach for his client's sexual tastes and didn't want to be around Simmons for any great length of time, yet he wanted to do the best job he could. The judge, Michael Farren, wasn't exactly enthusiastic about having to preside over the case, either. With Manzie already sentenced for killing Eddie Werner, the Simmons trial would take center ring in the three-ring media circus the Werner/Manzie/Simmons case had become. Judge Citta had already been raked over the coals because of his participation. Judge Farren had no desire to join Citta on the fiery spit.

The only one who seemed to enjoy the proceedings was the accused. Simmons waved to reporters, enthusiastically continued communicating with them and enjoying his moment in the spotlight. One reporter, cracking wise, said he wouldn't be surprised if Simmons walked into court and took a bow.

By 2:15 P.M. on July 14, Fliedner and Golden had agreed upon a jury of ten women and four men, two of whom would be the alternates, and Fliedner began with his opening statement. It was rancidly hot inside the courtroom and dry and hot outside. New Jersey was in the middle of a drought, and there would be as much of a drought of information in Simmons's case as there had been in Manzie's. Fliedner outlined in great detail all the lurid aspects of Simmons's accused criminal behavior as he told the jury how Simmons and Manzie had met on the Internet and how the two had consummated their affair.

"He was fourteen years old. . . . I think it's important to keep this in mind in this investigation," Fliedner said of Sam Manzie. "We're about as vulnerable as any other time in our life." Fliedner echoed Mike Critchley and Nick and Dolores Manzie when for the first time since the August 10, 1996, incident, which led to Sam Manzie's downfall, someone finally appeared to be taking Sam's side.

Fliedner said Simmons portrayed himself as a "savior to this kid. . . . He could understand him in ways his parents could not." Fliedner said Simmons was nothing but a crass manipulator and that he used Sam Manzie and then urged him to cover up their sexual activities because Simmons "knew he was wrong."

"There is a darkness around this case," Fliedner said, then told the jury how Sam Manzie sent Polaroid photos of himself to Simmons at Simmons's place of employment, and how Simmons, in turn, took photographs of Manzie—some of which showed Manzie posing naked. "You're going to listen to definitions of penetration as it relates to anal and oral sex," Fliedner warned the jury. He also told them how much Steve Simmons liked to talk and that Simmons talked for hours on end in an attempt to manipulate Sam Manzie.

His opening statement was neither lengthy nor

was it dull. In approximately fifteen minutes, he suc-
cinctly outlined his case and succeeded in shocking
the jury with the prurient facts. Fliedner had an exceptionally easy time doing this. Being young, with
an all-American look—complete with sandy-red
hair—Fliedner had many in the jury convinced Simmons was a total degenerate before he ever presented a shred of evidence.

Golden had a more difficult opening statement
to make. To his credit, he didn't try to con the jury
at all. He didn't try to convince them of Simmons's
innocence nor did he try to tell the jury what a great
person his client was. In a short and sweet introduc-
tory statement, he merely said, "I submit the state
will not be able to prove these charges." He urged
the jury to watch the evidence carefully and not be
convinced by emotional arguments. He asked them
to consider the facts.

With that, he sat down and all the cards were on
the table. Sam Manzie would not testify. According
to Fliedner, that meant that Simmons's own confession made to police in Long Island after his arrest
would be "the centerpiece of the case." According
to Fliedner, it was all anyone would need to convict
Simmons of nine different crimes. Simmons didn't
see it that way.

"How many times have I said it? I met Sam Manzie
and, yes, I inappropriately touched him," Simmons
said in a jailhouse interview to reporters following
his first day in court. "I'm not lily-clean. We've never
argued that fact. We know that I'm not going to walk
away scot-free. I'm willing to do five years. We've
never said that I'm a sweet, innocent victim here. I
should never have met Sam. I never should have laid
my hands on him. But convict me for a crime I did."

The first witnesses in the case were Detectives Ar-

ancio and Noble, who talked about how cooperative
Sam Manzie was in the beginning of the case and
how much he wanted to testify. A couple of hearty
objections from Golden kept them in line, and when
they tried to get the naked pictures of Sam Manzie
entered in as evidence, Golden successfully objected
to it because without Manzie's testimony there was
no way to know who took the photos. The instant
messages sent via AOL were read into the record
and entered as evidence and the entire car trip
around Monmouth County was discussed. Without
Manzie's testimony as to the importance of the car
trip, the detectives' testimony about where they went
and why was vague. Their testimony sounded like a
travelogue. They visited the amusement park and
they visited a hotel. They stopped at a deli and they
took pictures. There was no testimony concerning
sex or pedophiles—that would've been hearsay since
Sam Manzie wasn't going to testify. Arancio and Noble sounded more like disgruntled tourists than cops
as they talked about all the places they went trying
to retrieve records, for what purpose the jury did
not hear.

This was more than Golden could bear. He asked
for a mistrial and a dismissal of all but the first two
charges against Simmons. The judge just shook his
head. "I let the attorneys try their case," Judge Farren said as he turned down Golden's request.

From the beginning, there was a very tense and
adversarial relationship between Golden and the
judge. Part of it was brought about by Golden's client. Simmons antagonized and angered the prosecutor and the judge by simply sitting in the
courtroom with a smile and a defiant air about him.
Simmons also continued to engage in his discom-
fortable habit of trying to talk to everyone—the

judge, the bailiffs, the prosecutor and the assembled reporters—while in the tiny courtroom. It was a universal sign of disrespect for the process, which angered all the officers of the court, but something that Golden could not control. "Will you please inform your client I do not wish to have a conversation with him?" Fliedner admonished Golden on one occasion. "I will talk to him up there," Fliedner said, pointing to the witness stand, "but not down here." The thought that people didn't like him or didn't want to talk to him seemed either an alien concept to Simmons or something he thought he could charm his way past. Either way, he was not popular in the courtroom, and as the specifics of the case began to unravel and the jury, press, spectators and judge got to see the nature of the crimes Simmons was accused of, the harder it was for the officers of the court to be civil to him.

It was also impossible to divorce the case from the Eddie Werner case. Everything that was said and was done in the courtroom only seemed to further drive home the point that Steve Simmons had become sexually active with a boy who ended up killing another child. While Eddie Werner was seldom mentioned, there was no mistaking the fact that his presence was keenly felt in the courtroom every day of the trial.

Consequently, almost every time Golden stood up to object to something, he was overturned. Early on, there was a question about Simmons being given his Miranda warning properly. The judge dismissed Golden's concern. "Having an attorney doesn't necessarily preclude that individual from being questioned," Judge Farren told Golden as he overruled his objection.

It was all an innocent misunderstanding, apparently. Andrew Quinn, who was a Monmouth County corrections officer, had questioned Simmons for classification purposes shortly after Simmons was brought down from New York. In trying to determine if there were any prisoners Simmons needed to be kept separate from, Quinn said he asked Simmons if he had any codefendants. After all, it would not do to have two quarreling codefendants trying to knife each other with a homemade shiv in the joint. Simmons had said no, he was the sole defendant. Quinn didn't buy it. He'd read in the newspaper how more than one person had been involved with Manzie. Quinn may have, mistakenly, thought that Simmons's fifty-nine-year-old live-in lover had also been involved with Manzie.

But Simmons was adamant. "He stated to me that he had sex with a fifteen-year-old boy all by himself," Quinn said. That was what got Golden upset and he objected to having the testimony entered as evidence since Simmons had not been read his Miranda rights prior to making that inculpatory statement. But the judge didn't care and allowed the testimony to stand. The upshot was each individual juror had to decide whether Simmons was merely naive when he said what he said to Quinn or had been defiantly proud. The look on each juror's face gave the obvious impression they weren't about to give Simmons the benefit of the doubt.

Golden managed to score some points on cross-examination with other witnesses. With Noble, Golden got the policeman to admit that the lewd photographs of Sam Manzie had nothing in them that would indicate who took them or when they were taken. In addition, although the prosecution had tried to intimate that the photos were taken by Simmons for his sexual gratification at the Days Inn

Motel in Freehold, the room as depicted in the photos did not match the decor at the Days Inn.

Later, as Noble recounted a tale of receiving the photographs of Sam Manzie in various states of undress, he told the court there was a pack of Marlboro cigarettes in one picture and he knew that Simmons smoked Marlboro cigarettes because he had done so during a ride from a jail in New York to the jail in Monmouth County. No one paid much attention, but Simmons seemed to hop up and down in his seat at the defense table as if he were a first grader anxious to answer a tough question from his teacher. Simmons wanted to point out that there were no cigarettes in the car that day because he'd been shipped from a nonsmoking facility and didn't have any cigarettes on him when he rode with the officers. To Simmons, it was a beautiful indication of how the police would tell any lie to convict him. Golden finally had to get him to calm down and sit down before Simmons again angered the judge.

On July 15, 1999, Nick and Dolores Manzie finally got their chance to confront Steve Simmons. They were the strongest witnesses the prosecution could call to the stand and they told a very heartbreaking story, leaving one jury member teary. Both parents recounted the agonizing descent into madness by their son, Sam, that had begun on August 10, 1996.

". . . And he looked at me with such a look of hate on his face that I'd see for a whole year after," Nick Manzie said of finally finding Sam after a fruitless search in Freehold.

Outside of the courtroom during a break, Nick Manzie took a couple of local reporters to the side and asked them not to say that his son Sam "raped" Eddie Werner. He had tried to fondle the boy, but didn't rape him, Nick said. "It could be a matter of survival in jail for Sam," Nick explained.

Inside the courtroom, Nick Manzie walked a jury, who looked more than sympathetic, through the hell he and his family had gone through during the last three years. He talked about the phone calls and the calls he made to Simmons. He outlined the violence in the home and the duplicitous nature of his son. All of it, Nick said, could be traced back to August 10, 1996, and Steve Simmons.

On cross-examination Simmons pulled and prodded at his attorney's arm until finally Golden asked Nick if he smoked. The intimation from Simmons was that somehow if Nick smoked Marlboros that perhaps it was Nick who had taken naked photos of his son. Sadly, Golden asked the question, although he and everyone else in the courtroom firmly believed, even without proof to the contrary, that Simmons took the photographs of Sam.

"I stopped smoking for thirteen years until August the tenth. . . ."

"I object," Golden said as he walked away from Nick Manzie, and shook his head.

"Sustained," said the judge, giving Golden one of his rare victories.

"But it's true!" Nick said as he looked over his shoulder at the judge.

The most emotional testimony of the day came from Dolores Manzie as she methodically retold her story of family violence, the horrible confrontation at Kimball and every other horrible act that had occurred to her during the last three years. "If you let him come home, I'm going to slit my wrists," she admitted saying to health-care workers that night at Kimball just days before Sam killed Eddie. Dolores explained that she was simply and undoubtedly at the end of her rope. Sam had been troubled from early in life, but since the incident in August 1996, he'd been so troubling that Dolores felt like she was in a living hell.

As she recounted her bouts with her son—the lying, the manipulation, the threats, the violence, the fires and $3,000 worth of drywall repair work that had to take place because of holes he had put in the walls of the family home—many of the parents sitting on the jury looked at her with empathy. If the case went to the jury, it was increasingly apparent that Steve Simmons didn't have a prayer of getting off. Fliedner saw that, too. His case was marginal, but it was hitting all the right buttons.

The story about the holes in the wall and the fires really touched some of the jurors, and at the end of the day, the Manzies looked better than they had in months. For once, they got to tell their side of the horrible story in a court of law, and people actually listened to them without getting angry and tossing them out. It was a milestone of sorts and Nick said he felt satisfied that he could finally tell someone what had happened to his family.

Steve Simmons, as usual, also talked to anyone and everyone after the end of court that day. When asked to explain the statement Quinn had taken from him, Simmons pooh-poohed it. "You have to understand the condition I was in that day," Simmons said. "I think it was taken out of context. You can't take things out of context and make them work."

That rationale didn't fly for most court observers. "How can you take that out of context? Simmons said he had sex with the boy all by himself. It's pretty self-explanatory," a bailiff offered in the courtroom after she read the article in the local newspaper that had printed Simmons's interview.

The weekend, therefore, rolled around with few—if any—court observers, spectators or local citizens rallying behind Steve Simmons. The jury watched the first few days of the trial with mounting disgust evident on their faces. The judge had consistently ruled against Simmons's attorney on almost every objection Howard Golden had made. The prosecution, while sparse, had managed to score points with Simmons's confession and the testimony of a prison guard who said Simmons confessed to him in person as well.

Nick and Dolores Manzie had sat for most of the trial in the small courtroom's front row, intently watching the trial unfold. Sometimes holding hands, sometimes simply staring agape at Simmons as the tawdry details were aired in public, they went into that weekend with the most hope they'd had in many months. But it had been a difficult two days, especially for Nick, who became agitated as the physical aspects of Simmons's relationship with his son were heard. Several of the men and women on the jury had turned to look at Nick during these crucial moments in the trial. Nick Manzie stared straight ahead, sometimes grinding his teeth. A seething look overcame him as he watched Simmons, but Nick did not show any other emotion in the courtroom, and unlike the spectacle in Ocean County with their son, neither Manzie got up and said anything out of turn in Freehold during the Simmons trial.

Outside the courtroom was a different matter. Nick had to leave during one particularly disgusting and vile juncture as a sex act between Simmons and Manzie's then fourteen-year-old son was described in detail. Going out into the hall of the courthouse, Nick paced back and forth for a few seconds before he found a suitable wall and punched it. Heavy brick, concrete and mortar being what it is and human flesh being what it is, Nick Manzie only took that avenue once and deeply regretted it. He didn't break his hand, but he was quite sore for days on end.

As court reconvened on Tuesday, there were plenty of things to talk about in the courthouse hallway. It was the thirtieth anniversary of mankind's first walk on the Moon. John F. Kennedy Jr. had disappeared in a plane with his wife and her sister. All across New Jersey a parched brown landscape was a constant reminder of the area's worst drought in years. "It's not just the heat, it's the humidity" was such a universal call that it ceased being a joke and instead became a cry of anguish.

None of it mattered in the Monmouth County Courthouse, sitting on a small rise above the tiny town of Freehold, back among some trees and in a residential area. Those who gathered around that courthouse in July had nothing on their minds but the trial of Steve Simmons. The pressure had been building for months and the newspaper and television coverage of the trial only helped to build the expectations that Simmons would be put away for a long time.

There was just one problem: Simmons had other ideas. He would not go gentle into that good night, and he had an attorney who knew what he was doing. Early in the proceedings, Howard Golden had raised the issue of Simmons's Miranda rights. The prosecution had answered that adequately, or so Marc Fliedner thought. But as court reconvened on Tuesday, July 20, 1999, that issue was about to blow up on the prosecution.

Simmons later gloated that he knew it all along. His rights had been violated and he had been the victim of an attempt to railroad him into jail. He never claimed to be innocent, but instead said what the police had done to him was far worse than what he had done to Sam. At first few were willing to give a pedophile a break, but as the facts came out in the courtroom, one reporter remarked that the police had managed to do the impossible by generating sympathy for a pedophile.

It all began because the police acted like they had no idea what the Miranda rights were, and although they had close to two years to get their story straight, no witness called on the stand that Tuesday would tell the same story.

The bottom dropped out of the hope that the Manzies had taken with them into the weekend.

Seventeen

A Time to Hurt

From the beginning Marc Fliedner told the jury that the most important piece of evidence in the case against Steve Simmons had been his confession given to police in New York. Of course, Fliedner had to say that. Since Sam Manzie had refused to testify, it was not only the most important piece of evidence, but the *only* piece of evidence to substantiate many of the charges against Simmons.

On Tuesday, July 20, 1999, Fliedner lost most of his critical evidence against Simmons. For starters, Howard Golden got the judge to strike some of the confession from the record, particularly lurid testimony of sex acts that apparently occurred between Manzie and Simmons in New York State. Golden argued successfully that those acts had nothing to do with the charges in New Jersey. Judge Farren, who had excused the jury to consider the proposition, read the details out loud in the courtroom before the press and the spectators, including Nick and Dolores Manzie. The statement included many of the details of the sexual events that occurred when Simmons took Manzie to Long Island on their first encounter. For the first time in his life, Nick Manzie got to hear the complete details of what had occurred to his son while he and his wife had searched for him the night he was missing. This was the statement that the detectives had told Nick would be interesting for him to read. It was at that point in time when Nick got up, excused himself from court and, walking out into the hallway, decided to relieve his frustrations on a very thick wall.

The day's witnesses included a morning visit with Joe Ferraro, the T-shirt entrepreneur who ran his silk-screen empire from his home in Long Island. He had been Simmons's boss and it was in Ferraro's basement office where Simmons had been arrested. Ferraro told the court that Simmons was a Marlboro cigarette chain-smoker, a question Fliedner apparently felt compelled to ask since Simmons had raised so much fuss about the placement of Marlboros in at least one of the lewd photographs taken of Manzie. Ferraro also said Simmons admitted to having oral sex with Sam Manzie, and later when recalled as a witness told the prosecutor that Steve Simmons had been read his rights at the T-shirt shop while he had stood by and watched.

Ferraro, an amiable-looking man in his late thirties, seemed very friendly with the Manzies and very displeased with his former employee. He outlined how he had received a letter at his company address from Sam Manzie and became curious because it looked like it was written by a child. Ferraro knew of Simmons's penchant for young boys and Simmons's homosexuality and since his company name was on the envelope, Ferraro decided to open it up.

Inside he found an innocuous photograph of Sam and immediately called the Manzies and expressed his concern.

After that, the prosecution didn't have much luck. First they called Steve Padula on the stand, the technician who had helped record a conversation between Manzie and Simmons. Padula had to admit that the second conversation between the pair had been accidentally erased. Simmons told everyone who would listen that it had been no accident. "The second conversation showed how much I cared for Sam and they probably erased it on purpose," he later said.

That aside, the remaining recorded conversation didn't paint Simmons in an unfavorable light, either. While he did call Sam "my love" and talked about cute butts, Simmons's tone was one filled with concern for Sam, a fact even Dolores and Nick Manzie noted when they spoke with the press outside of the courtroom that day. Stone-faced and sallow-looking, they sat through the playing of the tapes, but as it progressed and Simmons talked about getting Sam help, it did touch the parents. It was sad, some later noted, that a pedophile was the only other person on earth besides Sam's parents who showed any interest in helping him.

It was a fact the parents did not overlook. "You have all the tools, but you leave them in the shed to rust," Simmons admonished Manzie during their phone conversation. Nick Manzie had his eyes closed and rubbed his temples as he listened to it. Sam's problems had been obvious to his parents, and apparently obvious to the pedophile Simmons. Nick Manzie later said it was horrifying for a parent to see that a man exploiting their son at least cared enough about him to advise him to stay in therapy.

"What if Simmons hadn't been a pedophile, but just someone who cared?" Nick speculated in front of the press. The thoughts, the fears, the frustration, were all intolerable as the parents saw Simmons in a slightly different light. "It's hard to do, but if you take away the sex, it's obvious to see that he cared for my son in some regard. I have to give him that," Nick said.

But Simmons still had the ability to annoy everyone and did it quite often. Following a lunch break, he tried to get himself a cup of water and did so in such a melodramatic manner, complete with gesticulations, smiles and assorted sounds, that the judge felt compelled to say, "Mr. Simmons, that's very distracting. . . .." Simmons smiled, apologized and still got his water.

There were many distractions for Judge Farren, who presided over the case with a firmness that had been sorely lacking in Judge Giovine's court. Farren was also exceedingly fair to all sides, although it was clear he was going to give the prosecution as much leeway as possible to prove their case. On Tuesday, though, the prosecution had been fed enough rope that it hanged itself and there wasn't anything the judge could do to prevent it.

The trouble began when Nicholas Severino, the retired detective from Suffolk County, New York, got on the witness stand and testified about the day he arrested Steve Simmons. According to Severino, he arrived at Ferraro's place of business and found a "very calm and laid-back" Steve Simmons; the suspected pedophile told Severino that he was expecting a visit from the police. This was natural since Simmons had been tipped by Sam Manzie that the cops would be coming.

At first, Severino testified, Simmons denied having

a sexual relationship with Manzie. But just a few minutes later, the retired cop said Simmons said, "OK, I'll tell you what happened." After Simmons confessed, Severino arrested him and then took him to the police station.

Golden watched Severino testify with rapt attention. According to Severino's report, Simmons had been given his Miranda warnings at Ferraro's T-shirt shop *prior* to a confession. But according to Severino's testimony, the confession came *first* and then the Miranda warning.

Severino then said that he began interviewing Simmons at the police department and advised him of the allegations and read him a statement by Sam Manzie. Then Simmons said he would again talk about the allegations and again confessed. "I then advised Simmons of his rights," Severino said.

Golden jumped up quickly, as it seemed he finally had the cops. The judge just shook his head and cleared the jury from the courtroom. Marc Fliedner was at an uncharacteristic loss for words. Arancio and Noble had to be brought back in and put on the stand, and the entire Miranda issue had to be revisited. Noble and Arancio, who'd sat quietly listening to Severino destroy their case, were not very happy. "I can't stand working with New York cops," Arancio said from the back row of the courtroom. "Yeah, you guys had two years, you think you could get your story straight," a reporter offered.

But the cops couldn't. According to Arancio and Noble, who testified with Severino out of sight and probably secured away in a soundproof booth, Severino had Mirandized Simmons prior to the confession. That coincided with Severino's official report, which said Simmons had been Mirandized prior to the confession. But on the stand, Severino stubborn-

ly stuck to the story that he had given Simmons the
warning after the confession, but before a formal
confession had been written down.

Now the judge had two conflicting stories to con-
tend with, but the conundrum was far from over.
Fliedner, seeing his case was on the ropes, brought
in another detective, Richard McKillop, who was
with Severino at the time of the arrest. He told a
completely different story from the other detectives,
giving the judge three different versions of what had
occurred to mull over. Golden looked upon the
muddled mess with grim determination. Simmons
had a look of glee on his face as the prosecution
dissolved into anarchy.

According to McKillop, Severino read Simmons
his Miranda rights at Simmons's workplace and
again read Simmons his rights immediately before
the pedophile gave a formal, written statement. At
first, McKillop said, Simmons had denied his involvement with Sam Manzie. "After he denied involvement, he was read his rights at the precinct." Golden
cocked his head, trying to make sure he heard
McKillop correctly. Was this now a fourth story? It
was apparent the cops couldn't decide when, if ever,
Simmons had been read his Miranda rights. McKillop's testimony, far from straightening the problem
out, only exacerbated it. He testified at various times
that Simmons was read his rights at the T-shirt shop
and at the precinct prior to a confession; still other
times he contradicted himself and said the second
warning did not take place.

As a backup, Ferraro was brought back to the
stand and said Severino read Simmons his rights as
he stood by, but by then all was hopelessly lost. From
where the spectators sat, it looked like a command
performance of the Keystone Cops. "The horrible

thing was, these are professional police officers who issue Miranda warnings almost daily. There should never have been a mix-up like this. It made us all look bad," said a member of the Monmouth County Prosecutor's Office, who declined to give his name.

An erased tape, a bungled investigation and suddenly Simmons's claim of a lynch-mob mentality on the part of the cops didn't look so unbelievable. That was the most frustrating thing for Fliedner. He was trying a guy who had admitted his guilt repeatedly in the press and suddenly it looked like Fliedner wouldn't and couldn't get a conviction.

That development frustrated the Manzies and outside of the courtroom a reporter told Dolores, "Well, now I can see why Sam didn't want to cooperate with them. My God, how could you all have gone through all of that?" Dolores Manzie smiled, but it was not enough to ease the renewed pain.

Dolores and Nick Manzie were angry with the cops and angry with Simmons. Simmons's recorded conversation included Simmons advising Sam, "I mean you weren't gay, you didn't turn gay because of me, and you didn't turn gay because of them [his parents]. You were gay because you're gay." That passage alone brought out the fight in Nick. As Simmons was being led out of court, Nick shouted in the hallway after him, "This isn't about gay. This is about pedophilia," and then turning back to the assembled reporters, Nick Manzie said, "He is a disgrace to the gay community."

Nevertheless, the prosecution was looking mighty rocky and the next day, July 21, Fliedner got to find out just how bad it was. The day began as Judge Farren, in a sour mood because of the lack of professionalism on the part of law enforcement, walked into court to find no clerk and no defendant present. "We have a real first-class operation here," he said sarcastically. He was in no mood to put up with anything from anybody and was extremely uncomfortable with being placed in the middle by the prosecution. If the prosecution wanted to railroad Simmons, Judge Farren had no intention of being the engineer who'd ditch the Constitution to do so.

Severino was brought back on the stand and almost immediately recanted everything he'd said the day before. He also mistakenly referred to Steve Simmons as "Richard Simmons," which brought a belly laugh from even the judge, but serious heads were to prevail and there were no more belly laughs offered as Severino said that since he'd slept on it he'd had a chance to rethink his previous day's testimony and decided that yes, indeed, he had given Simmons his Miranda warning at the T-shirt shop prior to the confession. He even managed to say it with a straight face and Fliedner managed to get the question out without looking too sheepish, but it didn't wash with Golden. After all, as Golden noted, Severino had spent a night in a hotel with his partner McKillop and had ample opportunity to be coached by all the other cops in the case.

"What is this, like, the third or fourth or fifth different story now?" Golden asked as he heard Severino change his tune.

Noble sat in the back of the courtroom extremely upset. "New York cops are sloppy" was all he could say as he watched Severino try to dig himself out of a hole by going deeper with a shovel. Severino then said Simmons waived his rights at the T-shirt shop. He told the court he couldn't quite remember everything he had testified to the previous day, but with sudden clarity he remembered Mirandizing Simmons nearly two years ago at the T-shirt shop.

Severino tried to use his notes in answering questions, and Golden didn't want him to, as a way of testing Severino's sudden clarity. As Golden approached the witness without permission, Farren let him have it. "Don't turn this into a circus," the judge said. "You stay ten feet away from the witness. Don't grab anything from the witness."

Golden apologized and continued questioning Severino, who then said he didn't recall saying the day before that he had failed to give Simmons his Miranda warnings until Simmons had confessed. As Golden pointed out, Severino couldn't remember what he said *the day before*, but suddenly with great clarity could remember what he told Simmons many months ago. "That really stinks," Golden said.

Golden felt like throwing his hands up in disgust, but thought better of it considering the judge's demeanor. Then Fliedner wanted to recall another witness. "Judge, I don't understand this whole process," Golden said by way of reply. "The whole rules of court don't seem to apply." Golden said it was obvious the prosecution was just recalling witnesses in a naked and poorly conceived attempt to fix the problems it had caused itself the previous day. The judge characteristically overruled Golden and Fliedner argued that Severino's failure to initially recall giving Simmons his Miranda rights at the T-shirt shop was all Fliedner's fault. The prosecutor said it was because of the manner in which he'd asked the question and because Severino, a police veteran, was "nervous."

There were other discrepancies that Fliedner addressed. Severino said Simmons left without being cuffed; another cop and Ferraro said he had been cuffed. Someone said Severino had a card with the Miranda warning printed on it that he read to Simmons; another cop said he didn't remember a card. Finally the court had enough and Judge Farren took a break. Shortly after noon, Farren came back and said that it first came to light that Steve Simmons wasn't read his rights the day before and that "this was a surprise to the defense and quite frankly to the court," giving a good indication as to where the judge was headed.

Then he lowered the boom. Ferraro's testimony wasn't credible, the new testimony from Severino wasn't credible and the judge believed beyond a reasonable doubt that Simmons hadn't been properly Mirandized—until Simmons was faced with signing his confession.

A short time later, Golden asked the judge to throw out the case. Saying that "the court does not find the state has met its burden of proof," Judge Farren threw out seven of the nine charges against Simmons, including all of the charges that would have cost the pedophile serious jail time. What was left were the first two charges against him, which Simmons had long claimed he would plead guilty to, but to which the prosecution never considered accepting a plea.

Now Fliedner had to accept in disgrace what he could have claimed in victory months earlier and could've saved the taxpayers thousands of dollars in the process had he done so. It was without a doubt the single largest victory for anyone involved in the Werner/Manzie/Simmons affair and it was won by the pedophile. Dolores and Nick Manzie, sitting in court, watched Judge Farren lower the boom and again they were numb. "Have you seen anything in this case go right yet?" Dolores asked of the reporters in her characteristically cavalier manner. "I'm totally numb. I can't believe it. What were the cops thinking?"

Nick Manzie wondered the same thing and noted that "Simmons is going to be out on the street in less than five years because of this mistake. He's going to be doing it to kids again. You watch."

Gone from the case was all circumstantial evidence, including a hotel receipt that showed that Simmons stayed in Freehold Township at the Days Inn on September 29, 1996. Farren said, "There is insufficient proof the defendant had any contact with the victim on September 29, 1996." That concurred with Golden, who said, "There is nothing proving that Sam Manzie was in the motel or anywhere near Freehold Township that day." Gone were the photographs because there was no way—without Manzie testifying—to prove who took them. The judge also said there was even less evidence to support three other charges of unspecified sexual encounters in October or November 1996 in other motels. All that was left for Simmons's jury to consider were the charges of sexual contact and child endangerment that were based on Simmons's confession that he fondled Manzie in a movie theater and parking lot before he took him to his home on August 10, 1996.

The judge let the confession stand, despite the obvious problem of when Simmons was Mirandized. The judge reasoned that it was OK to keep the confession because Simmons was eventually advised of his rights prior to signing the confession—one of the few facts about the confession that wasn't in dispute. The other facts not in dispute had to do with the first two counts against Simmons concerning the fondling of Sam Manzie. Since the beginning of the case, Simmons had agreed to cop a plea to those charges. The rest of the charges, the judge reasoned, had no evidence to support them, even if the confession stood. There simply was no evidence to corroborate many of the charges without Sam Manzie's testimony. So the confession stayed, and the charges went. The judge had remained true to his word and allowed the prosecution to present its case. In the end, Marc Fliedner just didn't have much of a case to present.

Outside the courtroom, the Manzies again found themselves angry. This time Nick vented his frustration on Golden as the two men and several court spectators gathered in the hall. "All you care about is getting your client off," he yelled at Golden.

"My interest is seeing that the Constitution of the United States is upheld," Golden shot back with equal vitriol.

Golden had been in an unenviable position. "I'm not happy. I'm a human being. I've got kids and grandkids. But all of that is gone when I enter the courtroom. It's like a doctor who has to treat somebody he hates. I have to do it." He had done his job well, a fact noted by both the prosecution and the judge. He could hold his head high, but he was one of the few who could make that claim.

The prosecution looked pathetic and the police even worse. In their zeal to go after Simmons, they had done everything as badly as Simmons claimed. Suddenly the Manzies' claims of coercion, pressure and a lack of sympathy gained much more credence. The police and prosecutors had sullied the Constitution, run roughshod over procedures and changed their story so many times on the stand that no one watching the trial could say who had lied or when, but everyone knew something hadn't been done right. "This only proves how screwed up it's been all along," Nick Manzie said as he left the courtroom, feeling disgusted and depressed.

On Thursday, July 22, 1999, Steve Simmons pleaded guilty to the two remaining charges against him. The plea meant Simmons could be freed in as little as eight months, although he faced up to five years in prison. The sentencing was scheduled for October 15, but it was ultimately delayed another month. A dejected Fliedner left the courtroom that day. "It was a very frustrating case" was all he would say.

Nick and Dolores Manzie, though, had plenty to say. Dolores was upset that her son had been sentenced an additional six months in prison and wondered why it hadn't been overturned. Nick said his life had a new goal: to keep Simmons off the street. He said he was sickened that Simmons had also requested the six-month sentence based on the boy's unwillingness to testify be dropped: "Molest your child and then ask the court to take away six months. Anybody who molests a child, they take their soul away from them."

Ed Werner, who never attended the trial but watched from afar, was also questioned about the Simmons case. He said the outcome was tragic. "Simmons has a history of pedophilia. From the quotes I've read of his, he apparently doesn't see anything wrong with it. It's just a horrible result that he's going to be allowed to be free again. It's very predictable that he'll continue to prey on minors. It's tragic that the prosecution ended that way."

It was the first kind word Ed Werner had sent to the Manzies since the murder of his son Eddie.

Meanwhile, Simmons remained unrepentant and vowed to continue to fight for the rights of gay teens. "I take my responsibility as a pedophile seriously," he said after the verdict. "I feel some guilt for what Sam did. What he did was illegal, but what the police did was horrible." Simmons was standing on his soapbox, tall and bright now, and telling everyone that he came out the big winner in the Werner/Manzie/Simmons case. He predicted he would be out "very soon" and within weeks of pleading guilty was seeking ways to abandon that verdict and ask for a quick release.

Every time Simmons opened his mouth, he brought with him a mountain of pain for the Manzies, and as he became bolder and began talking about Eddie Werner, he brought a mountain of pain to the Werners as well. He said he meant well, but never seemed to get the point. After the verdict against him, the Manzies seriously began to wonder if their pain would ever end.

Then they received the news: the Werners had filed suit against the health-care establishments that had cared for Sam prior to Eddie's murder. The Manzies were being sued, too.

Eighteen

And a Time to Heal

Ed Werner is not a man given to maudlin displays of anguish, nor did anyone who ever knew him in conjunction with the case that centered around the death of his son ever believe him to be a fool Yet, Ed himself said he felt foolishly maudlin during the fall of 1999.

It had been two years. When Ed Werner looked at his home, or backed his car out of the driveway, or when he looked in his backyard, he could still see Eddie. Eddie was always there in his thoughts and hopes. "He would've been a teenager by now. I wonder what kind of teen he'd have been?" Werner asked himself.

Werner found himself often thinking about his son and missing him more as time went on. Valerie, too, seemed caught up in her emotions, her yearnings, her desires to see her son again. No mother wants to bury her own child. Few mothers can face that fact when the child is taken so young, so tragically and horrifyingly as Eddie had been taken.

The pain never ceased.

Sam Manzie, the boy convicted of killing Eddie, had been sentenced to seventy years in prison. Steve Simmons, the pedophile who molested Manzie and, police argued, started him down the slippery slope that led to murder, had been found guilty of two minor charges and was awaiting sentencing. Nick and Dolores Manzie had been sued by the Werner family along with most of the health-care institutions that had failed the Manzies. Ed Werner was running for the state legislature and each day memories of Eddie were fading from his younger brother's and sisters' minds. In the hot and dry late summer of 1999, Eddie's memory seemed to evaporate and float away from his siblings like so many wisps of water vapor.

But not for Ed and Valerie Werner. Their pain remained all too fresh and the tears still came too quickly. They'd worn the pain for two years, cloaked in it like an old overcoat. But it had never become comfortable. Something, Ed Werner said, had to change.

Nick and Dolores Manzie, during their many conversations with their son and in their visits to him, had felt the same thing. For the last two years, the Manzies and the Werners had been at each other's throats in the press, the bitterest of enemies. It isn't hard to understand why. The Werners were victimized in the truest sense of the word. They were completely innocent. They had known nothing of Sam Manzie. They had done nothing to Sam Manzie and their world was so far removed from the hell Sam had created for his own family that it seemed unlikely the two would ever cross paths. But they had and it's easy to see why the Werners thought the Manzies should have done more to get help for Sam.

For two years, Pastor Tom Geoffroy of the Christian Life Fellowship Church, near Jackson, had been talking to the Werners about their grief and their enmity toward the Manzies. Several times they had expressed a desire to put it all behind them. But apparently by the late summer of 1999, they still hadn't got to a place where they could reconcile with the Manzies. The Werners had filed suit against everyone and every institution that had been involved in Sam Manzie's life. The only group kept out of the suit was the government entities involved. There was widespread speculation that was done because Ed Werner was running for state office, but the Manzies never agreed with those assessments.

What they did react to was the constant mention in the media that the Werners were suing the Manzies. Nick and Dolores couldn't understand it. "We don't have anything. If they want our mortgage, they can have it," Nick said often. Not that he was surprised that the Werners had sued him. "They put us on notice at the very beginning through their lawyers," Nick said. "We kind of expected it. We were always waiting for that shoe to drop." When it did, it didn't make the Manzies any less upset. They may have known the blow was coming, but at the time they were faced with more arduous torture in the courts brought about by their son. Only after the blow came did it sink in: the Manzies were being sued by the Werners. Hurt, but wanting to talk, Nick had made overtures, suggesting that he and Dolores meet with Ed and Valerie.

A few blocks away, the Werners weren't feeling any better about suing the Manzies, either. So the weekend of the second anniversary of Eddie's death, Ed

Werner picked up the telephone and called his friend, Pastor Tom Geoffroy. Maybe, Ed reasoned, Nick had the right idea.

Ed Werner was near tears. "This has got to stop," he told Pastor Geoffroy, who listened with hope.

"He's a very sincere, honorable man," Geoffroy said of Ed Werner. "His pain was too great and he asked me how we could go about getting in touch with the Manzies and coming to some kind of reconciliation." Geoffroy wasn't surprised that Ed Werner had called, but he was surprised at the timing of the call. The pastor figured out why Werner called when he picked up his newspapers that had remained untouched for the previous two days. It was then that he saw the headlines regarding the lawsuit and figured out why Werner wanted to meet with the Manzies.

Geoffroy happily made the telephone call to Nick Manzie. He'd seen Nick, of course, several times during court appearances, but had not talked to him. He didn't know how Nick would take the call, but wanted to assure him that things were going to be OK. "He was very cautious," Geoffroy said of the telephone call to Nick Manzie. "He'd been named in the suit and was afraid he might say something that could cause him problems in court. He was really quite shocked, but I assured him that only good was going to come out of the telephone call."

"We had been hoping for something like this for a long time," Nick later said. "We had no grudges against the Werners, but we thought they would never want to speak to us. I was floored when I got the telephone call." Through the media, Nick Manzie had often said he wanted to meet with the Werners. Until that day, the Werners had always declined. Ed Werner himself had mentioned meeting the Manzies to the press on several occasions, but had thought the Manzies had declined to reach out to him.

A day before the second anniversary of Eddie's death, Geoffroy arranged for the two to meet on church property, a wooded area in New Jersey that is the site for a future church. It was a bright, sunny day. The weather was almost the same as the day Eddie had died and Ed Werner had told the pastor there was a strong sense of déjà vu in that day. The colors of the trees were the same; the smells in the air were the same.

Nick Manzie remembered driving down a tree-lined lane, almost a "tunnel of trees" into a small clearing. He got out of his car and saw the pastor there. Ed Werner drove up behind Nick, parked and got out of his car. It was one o'clock on a Sunday afternoon and things were about to change. Nick Manzie and Ed Werner had worn their pain so plainly on their faces for the last two years that both men could immediately recognize how they felt by looking at each other's face. When they got out of their cars, the pastor said, the two men immediately recognized their mutual pain. The men simply walked up to one another, saying nothing, but immediately they embraced.

Nick Manzie said he was sorry for what Sam had done and Ed Werner eagerly and easily accepted it. They cried and held each other even harder. The pastor let them have their moment together. "God was present," Nick Manzie later said. "I felt God there in that moment. There is no doubt."

When the two were done, they prayed with the pastor, and Nick and Ed both wondered what the next step should be. They decided on a mutual press conference. "The media were so anxious to talk about bad news," both Nick and Ed said, "let's see how they react to this."

It was a remarkable about-face, which touched many who saw it on television or read about it in the newspapers. The bitterest of enemies had made peace with each other and saw in each other a reflection of themselves. "There've been too many hard feelings," Ed Werner said. "It was time for healing."

Geoffroy was happy with the outcome and hoped it would spark forgiveness among other parishioners. "Most people would say Christians should not be angry. But the Bible says we can be angry; that's an emotion God has given us. But once people have vented, they can get to a place where they understand they need to release the persons they hold the bitterness toward," the pastor said. Geoffroy said usually when he preaches about forgiveness, people's eyes "glaze over," but after the Werners and Manzies reconciled, he made a point of mentioning to his congregation that he was inviting "anyone who had bitterness or unforgiveness in their hearts" to come forward in his church. To his delight and surprise, nearly three-quarters of the congregation did so. He said at least once a week he will get a message from someone at his church who tells him, "If the Werners can forgive the Manzies, then I have to let go, too."

Geoffroy describes the meeting of the Werners and Manzies as something "ordained by God." He, too, believed, as did Nick, in the presence of God at the moment the two men met. The next day when the two couples got together, and Dolores Manzie met Valerie Werner, Geoffroy again felt the hand of God. "There was a moment of deafening silence as the two mothers met," Geoffroy said. "And afterward their demeanor changed completely. Ed said a tremendous weight had been lifted, as did the Manzies, and I think afterward came a time of peace and resting. God made that all possible."

Dolores Manzie had been openly critical of the Werners just a week prior to meeting Valerie, and so their husbands questioned what kind of demeanor both women would bring to such a get-together. "Our family was wrapped up in our own pain about knowing what our son had done," Dolores later said. "We were never able to put our pain aside and fully realize what they [the Werners] had gone through and are going through with their family. We talked about that today. I wanted her [Valerie Werner] to know that if I never expressed it, it's because I wasn't able to or never had the right words. I don't know if I have them yet."

Valerie Werner, the most publicly soft-spoken of the four parents, was characteristically succinct. "I felt like a weight was lifted off me," she said at the news conference that followed.

Almost immediately the press asked about the lawsuit. Dolores had angrily questioned how the Werners could insist all along that Sam alone was responsible for the murder, then file a wrongful death suit that attempted to spread the responsibility. It had been that anger that, in part, had prompted Ed to seek peace. Suing the Manzies "had never been in their heart," Geoffroy told the assemblage, so the Werners dropped the Manzies from the lawsuit.

For the first time in two years, both the Manzies and the Werners were able to take a breath without the numbing pain they'd felt every moment since Sam killed Eddie. The press, which had covered so much of the Manzie/Werner case, had covered the reconciliation with equal aplomb. WERNERS AND MANZIES TEACH US ALL A LESSON was the headline in a perspective piece in the *Star-Ledger*.

For the entire community, it was a breath of fresh air. The tension had been palpable in court hearings and everywhere in the community since Eddie Werner's death. Certainly, everyone close enough to venture a learned opinion on the case had noted how the two families had much more in common than they realized. It just remained unthinkable to most people that the Manzies and the Werners would ever reconcile.

After they did, the level of tension dropped dramatically in the community and in the courtroom. Of course, as with everything in the case, their new friendship would be quickly tested. Steve Simmons, for one, wasn't buying it and told reporters that it was only done on Ed Werner's behalf because Ed Werner was running for political office.

"He's taking advantage of his dead son to run for office," Simmons said from jail. That statement did not gain Simmons any new friends, but it was a portent of things to come.

A few weeks after the guilty plea, Howard Golden, beholden to no one, including his client, filed a motion to vacate the plea Simmons had entered.

Golden had become increasingly upset with the prosecution and the cops in the case. The obvious lies, the changing of stories, the misplaced evidence, were proof to him of malfeasance or at the very least misfeasance. Golden, of course, had experience to say that. He was a former prosecutor from Elizabeth, New Jersey, and knew intimately what prosecutors and policemen had to do and what they did do.

"I was told when I came down here that the prosecutor runs this county [Monmouth]," Golden said one afternoon. "If so, he's doing a horrible job of it. The cops in this case cared nothing for the law, the Constitution nor anyone's rights or the rules of procedure. Steve Simmons shouldn't get off because he's innocent, but because the prosecution abused his Constitutional rights in going after him."

The Manzies were back and forth on that issue. "You take away the sex from the relationship, the homosexuality aspect of it, and you can see that Simmons cared for Sam," Nick said on more than one occasion. "But he groomed Sam. He took Sam away from us and it was for his own purposes. I can't forget that."

Dolores was equally ambivalent. "He [Simmons] seemed to care more for Sam than the cops," she said. But she, too, was upset with Simmons because Sam never seemed to grasp what Simmons's true nature was. Simmons also continued to vilify the Manzies, saying that Nick had verbally abused his son and perhaps physically admonished his son in too strong a manner.

As for the Werners, Ed and Valerie luckily didn't have too much to do with the nuts and bolts of the Simmons case. Ed couldn't grasp what Simmons was all about; he had not attended any of the court functions in the Simmons case and his knowledge was limited to what he'd read in the newspapers or seen on television. But he offered this cursory view of Simmons: "He's scum. He was a major factor in my son dying."

Meanwhile, Ed Werner continued his uphill struggle as a candidate for the state legislature. The local newspapers, noting that he was a political neophyte, didn't count him out of the race because of his locally high profile. The Democratic Party, too, liked Werner's chances. Party leaders contributed heavily to Werner in an effort to oust the GOP incumbent in a heavily Republican district.

"He has name recognition and a powerful message," said Julie Roginsky, the director of the Assembly Democratic campaign, about Ed Werner. "When he talks about issues like community safety, he knows what he is talking about." In a state race, the stakes were quite high. Ed was running a campaign with a budget exceeding $200,000.

Werner used part of the money to put together campaign literature and television commercials, some of which mentioned Eddie's tragic death. He declared he wanted to make sure a similar tragedy didn't strike another New Jersey family. Werner had also jumped on the bandwagon very early when the National PTA and other organizations discussed banning door-to-door selling by schoolchildren. He criticized his Republican opponent, saying the incumbent never did anything about that. But Joseph Malone, the Republican incumbent, said, "He can criticize me, but he never talked to me about it."

Otherwise, very little negative campaigning was done against Ed Werner. There was a contention that the thirty-eight-year-old lawyer, who did securities work as well as personal injury and real-estate work, didn't pay certain annual dues to the Lawyers Fund for Client Protection in a timely fashion, but the GOP readily admitted they had to tread on eggshells when it came to criticizing Ed Werner.

"There are campaign strategies we may have used with other candidates we may not use against Ed," said George Gilmore, the Ocean County GOP chairman. "Ed comes into the equation with higher name recognition than most previous candidates in the area. What happened to him was very unfortunate and tragic."

Ed and Valerie had talked about the campaign, saying they realized it would take time away from the family to run, but Ed said it was something he needed to do. He needed to be connected and wanted desperately to be involved. Ultimately, it did not work. Werner lost the election, but remained hopeful of keeping his son's name alive.

In mid-October, Superior Court Judge Peter J. Giovine unsealed the documents that showed how angrily Sam Manzie had argued with his attorneys about changing his plea to guilty. Manzie had appealed his sentence as being excessive, so needed the supporting documentation and the appellate court materials that were also sealed to make his case. Giovine had said the records did not have to be unsealed for the appellate panel to consider them, but John Vazquez, appearing for Sam, pushed for them to be opened.

"The court was somewhat taken aback" by the motion to unseal the documents, Giovine told Vazquez, but agreed to unseal them because senior assistant Ocean County prosecutor William P. Cunningham had no position on the motion. In fact, Cunningham had strongly opposed sealing the records to begin with, saying the public had a right to know what was in them.

Giovine had said the public had no right to know the status of plea negotiations prior to the plea. He said they were "dramatic" and potentially "explosive" and could have prejudiced a jury and deprived Sam Manzie of his right to a fair trial, if the trial was later held.

Back in February, over the objections of the media, Giovine had closed the hearing in which

Critchley and Ruhnke had asked to be removed from the case. But now, late in October, it was all coming out.

Meanwhile, Vazquez and Critchley filed a suit on behalf of the Manzies against the same health-care workers the Werners had sued. Absent from their suit was a mention of Judge Citta. Nick Manzie said he just couldn't blame the judge.

"The main reason we didn't sue the judge is I really feel if the hospital provided the proper documents as they were supposed to do, Judge Citta might have acted differently," he said.

"The court did not have the proper information before it concerning the severity of Sam's mental and emotional condition," the lawsuit maintained. "Accordingly, the court erroneously ordered the Manzies to take Sam home, over their objections, as opposed to placing him in full-time inpatient treatment."

The Manzie suit also laid out Sam's troubled history, which began in nursery school and worsened in the seventh and eighth grades. By then, Sam was suffering from erratic sleep cycles, decreased concentration, tremors, vivid nightmares, racing thoughts, suicidal and homicidal feelings as well as depression. Toss in the Steve Simmons sexuality issue, the lawsuit maintained, and there was a nice recipe for disaster.

According to the lawsuit, some forty different people had an opportunity to observe or help Sam Manzie, and the defendants "carelessly, recklessly and/or negligently examined, diagnosed and treated Sam," the lawsuit claimed. Nick Manzie said the experts all failed to accurately diagnose Sam's illness and should have recommended Sam be placed in residential treatment, especially the night Sam and Dolores ended up at Kimball.

All of these revelations, machinations and ruminations occurred after the Manzie and Werner reconciliation. When it was learned that Golden was claiming prosecutorial misconduct, asking for Steve Simmons's plea to be reversed and further asking for the charges to be dropped against Simmons, the community held its collective breath. In the past, all of it would have caused the Manzies and Werners a tremendous amount of grief and stress.

But as the late fall of 1999 rolled around, both families felt better. They could handle whatever came along. They had weathered the worst part of the storm and somehow they both had survived. Things had to get better.

Nineteen

"I Am Not an Evil Person."

November 12, 1999

Ed Werner got a good glimpse of hell by watching Steve Simmons in court. "Is he always like that?" he asked a reporter, who nodded in the affirmative. It was the first time Werner got to see exactly what his new friends Nick and Dolores Manzie had put up with for more than three years.

With the Manzies and the Werners allied, they decided to show their newfound friendship at the sentencing of Steve Simmons. Ed Werner wanted to show up to get a glimpse of the man many were convinced put into motion the fatal wheels that led to his son's death. His wife, Valerie, couldn't bring herself to go. But Dolores and Nick were there with Ed Werner and approached the sentencing in lockstep. Nick was more than ready and eager to see Simmons punished to the fullest extent of the law. "Simmons interjected himself into my family, tore out its soul and stole my son from me," Nick Manzie said. As he walked into court that day, he was hoping Judge Michael Farren would recognize that fact.

Judge Farren was also eager to get the case over. He had expressed his anger with the prosecution for putting him in the middle so many times during the course of the trial. He wasn't happy with the job the police had done and he wasn't happy to have to side with Simmons in dismissing the worst of the charges against him. But he never had any other choice. Howard Golden had maneuvered with the skill of a veteran and Marc Fliedner, an excellent trial attorney, had been left with very little room to maneuver—the lack of Sam Manzie's testimony and the actions of the police had effectively destroyed the case against Simmons.

It all boiled down to a maximum of five years. With time already served, it meant that Simmons would be eligible for parole in March 2000. It was a bitter pill to swallow for those who'd suffered because of the pedophile. Even more bitter would be the speech Sam Manzie would be allowed to make as a victim. Victim impact statements are rarely used to ask for leniency for the accused, but Sam Manzie had it in his mind to do so.

The sentencing was scheduled to begin at 9:00 A.M. The secretary of state of New Jersey and Curtis Sliwa, radio personality and head of the Guardian Angels, joined the Manzies, the Werners and Pastor Geoffroy, who had brought the two families together, in court that day. It was a media circus waiting to happen. ABC News Magazine *20/20* provided the one pool camera for all the television stations in the world who wanted to broadcast or tape the event. Two photographers with zoom lenses the size of which are often seen at NFL games sat in the front row ready to take still shots to feed to any newspaper who cared enough to want a photograph. The small courtroom was packed and the air rife with tension. The tension usually came because when the Werners and the Manzies were in a packed courtroom the enmity between the two was palpable. On the day Simmons was sentenced, the tension was there as everyone waited for the circus to begin. Everyone knew Sam Manzie was going to speak and everyone had a pretty good idea as to what he was going to say. The tension also existed because Howard Golden had put a motion before the court to withdraw Simmons's guilty plea. If the judge ruled in his favor, that meant Simmons could literally walk out of the courtroom a free man.

It was a horrible prospect for the Manzies and the Werners; both families had come to see Simmons as the trigger behind Eddie's death. Considering how the judge had already dismissed seven charges against Simmons because of huge prosecutorial blunders, it was well within the realm of possibilities that Simmons would walk out of court that day free to live his life unfettered by law enforcement. Simmons himself thought he had an excellent chance of doing so. The Manzies and the Werners prayed it wouldn't happen.

Twice delayed because the state prison system couldn't get Sam Manzie to court on time, the proceedings finally began a little before the noon hour in a cramped, hot courtroom filled with people praying for the best and expecting the worst.

Steve Simmons arrived first in the courtroom and was placed in the jury box as close to the witness chair as possible. Adorned in shackles and handcuffs, dressed in khaki prison garb and wearing black tennis shoes, Simmons ignored most of the crowd assembled before him. He concentrated on eating a muffin in a flamboyant manner, which provided the still photographers ample opportunity to take abundant pictures of Simmons in very undignified poses. Several, with his tongue sticking out, were used by the local papers the next day.

Sam Manzie made his appearance after Simmons was settled. He, too, was wearing shackles, handcuffs and a khaki prison uniform. Unlike Simmons, though, Manzie also wore a matching set of khaki-colored laced-up boots. The beefy bailiffs attending to Manzie put him at the opposite end of the jury box from Simmons and closer to the crowd. Sam Manzie acknowledged that crowd and even smiled and waved to his parents as the court session began. Meanwhile, Simmons, who had been told not to look at Manzie, continued to eat.

When the judge entered, the crowd rose. Finally the proceedings began. Howard Golden was the first to speak. He brought before Judge Farren a thirty-page motion accusing the prosecution of "prosecutorial misconduct" and asked for the judge to allow Simmons to vacate his guilty plea so the judge could dismiss all charges against Simmons.

It was a mouthful to say for Golden, and the courtroom remained still as he did so. Manzie was rapt with attention at the proposal, while Simmons sat quietly chewing his food. Golden, a kind, gentle man, didn't want the judge or the media to misinterpret his motion. He wasn't a Steve Simmons fan. Quite the contrary. He said Simmons's acts had sickened him as they would any normal person. But Golden was convinced the prosecution's acts were potentially more dangerous to society. In a recent newspaper article, Second Assistant Prosecutor Honecker had stated that Mr Simmons's act was

". . . also an assault on our society." Golden noted that he thought the prosecution's acts were a "far greater assault on our society."

Golden went on to say that the prosecution fabricated much of what they said about Simmons. They didn't take pictures in the one hotel room where they had a receipt from Simmons. They knew that the photographs Simmons allegedly took of Sam Manzie did not take place in the hotel room as they claimed. Golden also accused them of making up stories about Simmons smoking cigarettes in the car ride after his transfer from a nonsmoking jail facility.

"We are a nation of laws, not individuals," Golden told the judge. "We cannot abide by illegal acts from the prosecution." According to Golden, Detective Noble "knowingly made up testimony," an act Golden said was "egregious behavior." Golden further accused Noble and Arancio and the rest of the prosecution of being a "vigilante group or lynch mob out of control."

Sam Manzie sat still and listened, slightly nodding his head. Simmons didn't move. For many in the courtroom, the accusations had an air of truth to them; certainly, the Manzies felt the prosecution had put them through the wringer in trying to go after Simmons. But the problem was no one wanted the prosecution's lack of professional demeanor to be a basis for dismissing the charges against Simmons. If it was a choice between the lesser of two evils, the Manzies and every other spectator gathered in the courtroom, with the possible exception of Sam Manzie, wanted to err on the side of the prosecution. Mind you, many of those who said that publicly also said privately they were appalled with the demeanor of the detectives and the prosecution in the Manzie case. It just all boiled down to the fact that no one

wanted Steve Simmons to walk out of the courtroom
a free man. While Golden could empathize with that
feeling, his thought was that jailing Simmons with
the amount of misconduct that he alleged occurred
by the prosecution was tantamount to turning one's
back on the Constitution. Most of the assemblage
didn't agree and viewed Golden's motion with a mixture of fear and revulsion.

They didn't have to worry. Judge Farren dismissed
the accusations against the prosecution from Golden
as "nothing more than a last ditch effort to embar-
rass the prosecutor's office." The assembled crowd
in the courtroom nodded silently. "Funny," one reporter said to another during the stillness, "I
thought the prosecution did a fine job of embarrassing themselves." A small smattering of quiet laughs
ensued.

With the worst-case scenario for the Manzies then
dismissed, the judge got down to brass tacks—the
sentencing of Steve Simmons. Marc Fliedner, the
prosecutor who had been saddled with the unenviable task of prosecuting Simmons, tried to deflect
the statement he knew Sam Manzie was going to
make prior to the sentencing. "Sam Manzie is still a
teenager and doesn't have the perspective," Fliedner, who looked little older than a teen himself, told
the judge. Sam Manzie, he warned, was coming from
a "very dark place" to speak to the judge, and Fliedner asked the judge to take into consideration the
fact that Sam Manzie had refused to testify against
Steve Simmons during the trial, which directly led
to the reduction of charges against Simmons.

As for Simmons, Fliedner barely acknowledged
the pedophile's existence in the courtroom with little more than a nod, but said, "His unique perspective will show he is still a danger to the community."

Fliedner characterized the relationship Simmons had with Sam Manzie as "the relationship from hell," and pointed out that Simmons went on-line to have sex with young children and to "participate in predatory conduct."

Fliedner went on to outline all the damage he said Simmons did to Sam Manzie, characterizing the relationship with the boy as manipulative and diseased. Sam Manzie began to believe that Simmons "was the only one on earth who understood him," Fliedner said as he gesticulated toward Simmons. This relationship was forged by Simmons, Fliedner continued, then added that Simmons had done a great job on Sam, "effectively cutting him off from those who cared. He sealed Sam Manzie into a dark world," where Fliedner noted Sam still dwelled. "Steve Simmons still doesn't get it, and when he gets out, he'll do it again."

Fliedner went over Simmons's previous convictions and told the judge that "everything about his history is a chronicle of predatory behavior."

It was unusual for a prosecutor to argue that a judge ignore a victim impact statement, but Fliedner was backed up against the wall. If Sam Manzie were to come out, as Fliedner and everyone else thought he would, and speak in favor of Simmons, the prosecutor had to deflect all of the support Simmons would get from Sam Manzie.

Fliedner's arguments before the judge were the most concise and cogent he made during the course of the Simmons trial and far more effective than any of his witnesses. But it still remained to be seen what, if any, effect they would have following Sam Manzie's statement.

As Fliedner sat down and the judge motioned for Manzie to get up and make his own statement, the courtroom crowd again fell silent as they stared at the now seventeen-year-old Sam Manzie. He was pale but well groomed and in apparently good health. He sported a few pimples on his otherwise clean-shaven face and looked as innocent and as docile as any teen who aspired to be the captain of the high school chess team. If he had a pocket protector and was dressed as any other child with his interests, it would be hard to see the quiet boy as a killer. He had no mark of Cain on him to tell the world he was a murderer, and his soft-spoken behavior, perhaps induced by his psychotropic diet, did not allow anyone to see the beast that lurked beneath the surface.

Nick and Dolores Manzie knew the dark side of their son, though, and watched anxiously as Sam stood up to make his statement. He slowly and methodically opened a manila envelope as best he could under the constraint of the handcuffs and then pulled out several yellow sheets of legal-pad paper. He then thanked the judge and with grace and a sort of quiet dignity tried to explain to the court his relationship with Steve Simmons.

According to Manzie, his relationship with Simmons was not only a good one, but one in which Simmons had become a "role model" for him. He denied that Simmons ever manipulated him and said the police had aggravated the situation by demonizing Simmons, someone Sam Manzie said is "a person I love." Racked with guilt, Manzie said he regretted ever turning on Simmons to save himself.

"I begged him to leave town," Manzie said as he talked about telling Simmons to leave town during the investigation. "I don't know why he didn't."

He was upset, Manzie said, with investigators who characterized the relationship as manipulative.

"How can you assume it was manipulative if you weren't there?" By the time the investigators came onto the scene, Manzie said, he had put the relationship with Simmons behind him. "It was just a fond memory," he said of the sexual abuse and the never-ending fights in the gay chat room.

Ed Werner and Nick Manzie sat side by side in the front row of the court, silent and aghast as Sam continued. Dolores, a small frown betraying her calm demeanor, sat with her eyes glued on her son. Sam Manzie was far from done. He said the abuse he received at the hands of the police department was far worse than anything they claimed Simmons had done to him. "They reprimanded me harshly for getting nothing on the second telephone call," Manzie said, which was contrary to what the investigators claimed they said to Manzie. " 'You're a screwed-up kid,' " he said they told him. This angered Manzie, who termed the relationship with investigators as "frustrating and stressful." He claimed he "never did more than I wanted" with Simmons. "I never regretted the relationship."

The police activity led him to alcoholic drinking, Manzie said, and smoking too many cigarettes. After the night at Kimball, Manzie claimed Noble came to him and said, " 'You've really fucked up this investigation.' " It was the first public claim Manzie made against the prosecution in that regard.

As Manzie fumbled through the pages of his impact statement, it was clear he was still enamored of Simmons. He still considered Steve Simmons the one true friend in his life and understanding why Manzie defended him was readily apparent to anyone who had read his award-winning essay posted on his Web site. "A true friend is hard to find, but once you have found one, the friendship can last forever," he wrote. "A true friend will stick by you, even when the popular crowd doesn't." Sam Manzie, in his own naive way, had recognized Simmons as a true friend and was struggling hard to make sure he remained true to that friend. There seemed to be little doubt that Sam had not progressed beyond needing, wanting and loving Steve Simmons.

Manzie again thanked the judge at the conclusion of his statement and reinserted the papers, from which he'd read, back into the manila envelope and sat down. Across the audience there was a quiet gasp and a smattering of heads shaking back and forth. It was a stunning moment. The confessed murderer was absolving everyone but himself. He had accepted his own guilt for killing Eddie Werner, and he didn't want anyone else to feel that guilt. Most assuredly, he wanted Steve Simmons to feel guiltless and he had struggled to maintain some kind of dignity as he spoke on Simmons's behalf—hoping to impress the judge enough to show some leniency.

After Sam Manzie sat down, the judge cautiously nodded and thanked him for his statement. Showing no emotion, he then urged Steve Simmons to come forward with his own statement. It was time for Simmons to take center stage and he did so with the panache for which he had become well known to most reporters and court watchers.

Simmons began by saying he hadn't spoken publicly for the last two years, by which he meant he hadn't said anything on the record in a court of law. He most definitely had spoken to reporters time and again. But because he hadn't yet spoken in court, he begged the court's indulgence as he had a lot to get off his chest. Marc Fliedner remembered wincing as he heard Simmons speak. "When he begged for the court's indulgence, I thought, 'Oh, boy, here it comes.' I thought it was going to be a long show."

Fliedner braced himself for the worst as did the rest of the audience, some who visibly grasped at the benches on which they were sitting as if to keep themselves steady in a strong wind.

"I wish we were here to sentence me," Simmons began, saying he was convinced that Sam's crime "overshadowed" everything that had happened, so his response was to dive right in and give his considered and learned opinion on the entire fiasco. "I don't think it is possible to separate the two crimes, so I'm going to address it [the Eddie Werner/Sam Manzie case]," Simmons said dutifully.

"We can blame the parents for not being there," Simmons said with a gesture of his expressive hands. "We can blame everybody, but the fact is a crime was committed. I committed a crime." With that move, Simmons placed his hand near his heart for dramatic effect. Simmons said how he was going through life with his crime on his conscience and the fear that he could've stopped Sam Manzie's horrible crime but did not. "Nobody did what they did to hurt anybody," he said by way of explaining his relationship with Sam. "My intention wasn't to hurt Sam Manzie," he added with outstretched hands.

Simmons was rolling as he said that he encouraged Sam always to be as open as possible. "Tell them everything," he said when he heard Sam was going to the cops and to therapists. "I could have said, 'Hey, don't mention me,' but I didn't," Simmons claimed. It was, of course, a lie. There was a matter of a written on-line conversation with Manzie that had been entered as evidence during which Manzie and Simmons had both conspired to hide their physical relationship. But Simmons either conveniently forgot that as he spoke before the judge that day, or he deemed it irrelevant because he claimed before the court he was always for full disclosure of everything to try and help Sam Manzie. "If I could give up my life to bring back Eddie Werner today, I would," he said defiantly. He spread his arms wide again and looked directly at the judge. "I am not an evil person," he implored, adding that the prosecutor wasn't evil, either, nor were Detectives Noble, Arancio or anyone else involved in the case. "Deep down we're all at fault," he said.

Then again he said that nothing was done by anyone involved "to hurt anybody." On that point, Simmons flailed away desperately. "Is it so hard to believe that I care about him?" Simmons asked as he gestured toward Manzie without looking at him. Manzie looked back at Simmons with little emotion while his parents and Ed Werner sat in the front row of the courtroom, grimacing at Simmons's speech.

"I will not step on your parents' feet," Simmons said to Manzie, after having already done so. "This child is not evil," Simmons went on to say about Sam. "He's basically a good boy." Despite getting in trouble in the past by calling Sam Manzie, Simmons said he would indeed do it again in the future, saying he was going to stay in touch with Sam and that he cared for him deeply.

Simmons said he'd also "learned my lesson" through Sam. No more getting involved with young boys sexually, he said. After all, a child had died and Simmons had that on his conscience for the rest of his life. That, of course, did not mean that Simmons was repentant. "I will not stop fighting for gay kid's rights," he said defiantly. "I know if I can change things, I will."

Then silence. As Simmons sat down, the courtroom crowd seemed numb. The gathered crowd had just heard from a victim who professed to love his abuser, and a convicted pedophile who claimed to still love his victim and had also vowed to continue to fight for "gay teens," whatever that declaration meant.

The judge seemed to take it right between the eyes without flinching. He calmly thanked Simmons as he had thanked Manzie and then proceeded to sentence Simmons to the maximum amount of time he could give him. It added up to five years, but also meant that in a little more than four months from the date of sentencing Simmons would be eligible for parole. The judge quickly added that Simmons probably wouldn't make parole on that date because of his defiant and unrepentant nature, but noted that Simmons probably would make parole before he maxed out his time in prison.

There was just an afterthought to handle following the sentencing. John Vazquez, representing Sam Manzie, asked the judge to reverse himself on the contempt-of-court charge that Judge Farren had imposed on Manzie for his unwillingness to testify against Simmons. Vazquez noted that it was rare for a victim to be held in contempt and suggested that Sam Manzie was still in a "dark place" regarding Steve Simmons. "Hopefully, down the road, with experience, he's going to look back and understand that he was manipulated," Vazquez told the judge. Judge Farren nodded and, noting that Sam's statement seemed to come from the heart, decided to dismiss the contempt charges against him.

The nightmare that began on August 10, 1996, was finally over. Simmons had finally been sentenced. It wasn't as much as the Manzies had wanted; it wasn't anywhere near adequate, according to their desires. But as they gathered for the cameras outside of court that day, they had smiles on their faces. It was quite a far cry from the way they looked as they bolted from court the day their son had been sentenced. That had been quite a scene, but the sight of Ed Werner standing with the Manzies as they denounced Simmons was as close to a Hollywood happy ending as anyone had hoped to come in the case of Sam Manzie/Steve Simmons/Eddie Werner.

"Simmons is a truly disgusting person," Ed Werner told the assemblage of more than thirty television cameramen, still photographs, print and radio reporters. "There's got to be a way to keep people like that in jail," he said as he shook his head. "It makes me physically ill to hear that piece of filth utter my son's name."

Pastor Thomas P. Geoffroy was even blunter, if that was possible. Geoffroy said that Simmons was an evil man, contrary to Simmons's claims. He said that Simmons had been touched by Satan, was demonized and needed to repent before God. Nick and Dolores Manzie, angered for years with Simmons, took a more Christian approach. Nick said that he was going to be committed to seeing that Simmons serve every day of his sentence and said that he and Ed Werner were "locked arm and arm" in doing so. Dolores said Simmons was "beyond madness," but added that she saw him as "a very sad, lonely man. His life has led him down a lonely street."

That lonely street included the possibility of additional charges in Suffolk County, New York. Authorities there said they planned to prosecute Simmons for molesting Manzie in Simmons's Long Island home. Simmons still faced charges of third-degree sodomy, which carries a maximum of four years in prison, according to a spokesman there. But Suffolk

County faced the same problem that authorities
faced in New Jersey. Without Sam Manzie as a witness, it would be problematic at best in obtaining a
conviction against Simmons. Still, it was obvious on
the day Simmons was sentenced that the system was
not ready to let him go. The public had been denied
much in the prosecution of Eddie Werner's murder.
The Simmons trial had been the only catharsis available and there was still much bad blood in the water.
Simmons wasn't likely to make parole on his first
chance, and it looked increasingly like he was going
to be made to pay again, not only for his role in
Eddie's death but for his seemingly defiant attitude
toward authorities.

Some of those authorities were facing the music
as well. A hastily called news conference in the prosecutor's office followed just a few short hours after
Simmons's sentencing. First assistant Monmouth
County prosecutor Alton D. Kenney, a man with
more than a quarter of a century of experience in
prosecuting cases, was tapped to stand in for John
Kaye, who always seemed to be curiously absent
when questions were asked about the Simmons case.

Kenney defended the actions of the investigators
and prosecutors in his office during the course of
the Simmons trial, saying they were all highly trained
and sensitive people who were not the "vigilante
mob" Golden had described. "Their first rule is to
do no further harm to children who are victims,"
he said. That, of course, did not explain the pressure
the cops put on Manzie, or their attitude toward
him, or their accusing Manzie of "fucking up" their
case. For that, Kenney simply denied that it happened and accused Manzie of fabricating that encounter. Outside of the news conference, however,
in front of prosecutor Marc Fliedner and a reporter,

another prosecutor—upon hearing what Noble and Arancio reportedly said to Manzie that night at Kimball—added, "Sounds like something they'd say."

Kenney, a tall man of stout frame and distinguished-looking appearance, was solid on his defense of the county's actions in regard to Sam Manzie. Although Manzie had taken sole responsibility for *everything* that had occurred, Kenney said that Manzie was "looking for someone else to blame for what he did" by accusing the detectives of cursing at him. The only mistake that Kenney admitted the county may have made, and he flinched at even calling that a mistake, was that he said the county was "not clear" on the emotional commitment Sam Manzie had to Steve Simmons.

"We did everything we could to get the child help," Fliedner said to the reporters. As for the assertion from Dr. Nathaniel Pallone from Rutgers, a man quoted heavily, and vocally critical of the Monmouth County Prosecutors Office, in the *New York Times* and various other publications, Kenney decided to shoot the messenger. He dismissed Pallone's criticism of the department as coming from a man he'd never heard of. Never mind the criticism, Kenney seemed to say, for it came from someone he'd never worked with. "I'm not being critical of his credentials," Kenney said. "He may be a brilliant man," it's just that he had never heard of Pallone.

Kenney did point out that he thought Manzie had been deceptive with the prosecution, but never adequately explained how a teenager managed to dupe the seasoned and caring investigators sent to help him. The bottom line simply seemed to be, as far as the prosecutor was concerned: "It wasn't our fault."

Oddly enough, the prosecutor found himself the mostly unlikely of allies, Steve Simmons. While Simmons didn't come out and praise the Monmouth County Prosecutor's Office, he did say that Fliedner and Kenney were right about one thing. "In conclusion, Fliedner put it best," Simmons later said, explaining that the prosecution was right in that it misjudged the emotional commitment Manzie had to Simmons. "That's my point exactly," Simmons said. "If the boy doesn't complain, don't make it a crime. It's that simple. If the boy goes to the police, then arrest. The man deserves it. Is it that hard to understand that we all have different tastes? I am twenty-eight years older than Sam. We met. We had a fling. We separated and stayed friends—which is more than many men who go through a midlife crisis do with women twenty to thirty years younger."

Simmons was as unrepentant weeks after the sentencing as he was the day he was sentenced. "Please understand that I will do whatever is needed to keep this story alive and to get justice for Sam. It is still my main objective," he wrote. He accused the judge and the prosecutor of being corrupt and crooked. He vowed to appeal his sentence, writing that "I don't appeal for lost time, but for truth." Simmons accused Ed Werner of being duplicitous because Werner had called him "filth."

"If I'm such filth and the cause of Eddie's death, then publicly ask for Sam's sentence to be reduced. We both can't be responsible," he claimed. Simmons also accused Sam Manzie's soft-spoken father, Nick, of being a tyrant, and said he, Simmons, was the only one "doing positive things."

Simmons couldn't resist a little gloating, either. "Believe it or not, I'm the winner (I wish Sammy was, but in time he will be). They have used everything they can [sic] now I'm walking in 400 or less days. They still have to answer questions and defend themselves," he wrote.

Although Simmons was unclear as to who "they" are, he clearly had no sympathy for either the Werners or the Manzies since they both showed up in court to show their solidarity against him. Simmons also renewed his vow to write a book that will outsell any other because "people are morbid and Sam's description of Eddie's death will sell like Jerry Springer. It should not be, but it will be. My conscious [*sic*] is clear because I'm giving away two thirds of my share to Sam's defense fund and children's charity in Eddie's name (I would have given it to the Werners to pass out but not now). Who knows? I may even get to play myself in the movie. But I'll never stop trying to get Sam free, to get the laws changed, and to help gay teens in this country."

Lost in Simmons's zeal for gay pride and justice was the one thing that brought such notoriety to the case in the first place—Eddie Werner had been brutally murdered by a troubled teen who'd been sexually involved with a pedophile. In the ultimate question of "Who is to blame?" there seemed to be plenty of accusations to toss around everywhere. But ultimately Sam Manzie had absolved everyone else of guilt but himself.

Sam Manzie thought he was standing by his only friend in the world when he refused to testify against Steve Simmons. It was a sad and poignant moment in court when Sam Manzie, then seventeen, stood up to defend Simmons. Many people in the courtroom couldn't understand why he would do it. Why would Sam Manzie stand by a man with whom he'd fought so bitterly, a man with whom he'd tried at different junctures to have imprisoned? It was Manzie who contacted the on-line help group; it was

Manzie who told his psychiatrist about Simmons; it was Manzie who began to cooperate with authorities. While Manzie's parents had come to suspect he'd been involved with Simmons, it was only Sam Manzie's confession that the affair had occurred that spurred law enforcement into action.

Sam Manzie himself had reached out for help and retreated from that help when he saw it as an uglier, ultimately more terrifying prospect than a pedophile who'd befriended him and sexually molested him. That Manzie saw the system that was there to protect him as ultimately more evil than the man whom the system was there to protect him from speaks volumes about our society.

In the end, it caused the death of Eddie Werner. That should give us all reason to pause and reflect.

Epilogue

Since Steve Simmons was sentenced, effectively bringing to an end the dark human drama that culminated in Eddie Werner's death, there has been no end to the gnashing of teeth and knee-jerk reaction on the part of parents, lawmakers and school officials.

It was, indeed, a horrible revelation that Sam Manzie brutally murdered Eddie Werner. It was also brutal to learn that Manzie had been molested, manipulated, befriended and loved by a pedophile.

There had been talk of reforming school fundraising, talk of new laws and endless talk about the ramifications of the case. If Eddie Werner is remembered and all the proposed judicial reforms take place, there will be some meaning attached to his death.

That, of course, can never be solace to a parent who has lost a young child. It can be of little comfort. However, there were so many uncomfortable things about the case and so many cultural taboos questioned that the case promises to be discomforting and discussed for many years to come.

Central to all of it is the relationship between Steve Simmons and Sam Manzie. What role did it play in Eddie's death? If the two men (Sam became a legal adult as of January 2000) still claim to love each other, what do we as a society do about that? Was it wrong? Did getting law enforcement entangled in the event cause more stress? Should the cops have seen the warning signs? Why didn't the cops share their information with the judge and the hospital? Why, in the ensuing months after the trial, had precious little been done to reform a system everyone knows is broken? Also, how are prosecutors, police and other investigators able to look at themselves in the mirror each night and not feel some amount of guilt at what happened to both Sam Manzie and Eddie Werner? Never mind the systemic problems that the case raised. How, as parents and adults, do those in law enforcement justify their actions in this case? The facts show that those who were supposed to help did little to.

Simmons continues to look forward to leaving jail sooner rather than later and he continues to question all of those who demonized him during the last few years. He maintains his love for Sam Manzie and his dedication to finding justice for him.

The Manzies have become more politically active. Nick has begun training to be a "cyber angel" so that he may patrol the Internet, looking for pedophiles and assisting those manipulated by pedophiles.

The Werners' tragedy continues. As in many cases where a child has died, the Werners' marriage also died—though both Valerie and Ed remain in an amicable relationship. Ed Werner, although losing his race for the statehouse, gained recognition and a name independent of his dead son. With his voting base, he may be a power in New Jersey politics in the future if he chooses to be. Valerie continues working and trying to raise her remaining children, holding them close to her and showing them love and affection. She still mourns the loss of her oldest son, and still continues to struggle with the attention Simmons and Manzie got because of her son's death. To her, the only true victim was her son. Eddie certainly got lost in the shuffle as the perverse revelations concerning Manzie and Simmons came into the public light, but the fact does remain that the person who paid the highest price was an innocent child whose only crime was trying to sell enough candy and wrapping paper for a school project so that he could get a walkie-talkie set. Eddie Werner is lost to all of us forever.

There are many disturbing questions left unanswered by Eddie Werner's death. Unfortunately, both the Werners and the Manzies have to live with these.

At least, at the very least, they have made peace with each other and themselves and it is both heartwarming and uplifting to see that it occurred. It gives all of us a cause to hope.

The case of Eddie Werner, Sam Manzie and Steve Simmons may never really be finished. The ripple effects alone were enough to cause the New Jersey legislature, the governor's office and the judiciary system to take a long hard look at the way the state conducts business on several different fronts. It is hoped they will actually do something about those problems.

There was the problem with Sam Manzie being

released into his parents' custody despite their protest. There was the problem of the police not adequately telling the courts what they knew. There was the problem with the prosecution underestimating the emotional commitment Sam Manzie had to Steve Simmons. There was the problem of children being unsafe selling candy door to door. There was the problem of pedophiles trolling for kids on the Internet. There was the problem of parents being afraid of their own children.

But in the end it really all boiled down to the death of one little boy. Eddie Werner never knew what his death would mean to his friends, family and people he never met.

His laughter and his smiling face will long be missed by his family. Hopefully, the hard lessons learned by the horrible circumstances that brought about his death won't long be forgotten by the rest of us, either.

Just after Thanksgiving, on November 30, 2000, Sam Manzie got the best news he'd received since the entire nightmare had begun. A three-judge panel in the state of New Jersey tossed out the requirement that Manzie, then eighteen, serve eighty-five percent of his sentence before becoming eligible for parole. In what amounted to a very controversial decision, which was later appealed by the prosecutor, Manzie was determined by the judges to be eligible to leave prison after serving thirty years of his sentence. That meant that Sam Manzie might still be able to lead some sort of life, and that he would be free to walk the streets before he was fifty, perhaps as young as forty-seven.

The Manzie case was back in the headlines and

again making history. The impetus for jailing Manzie for at least eighty-five percent of his sentence was a New Jersey law called the "No Early Release Act," or NERA. It was adopted in 1997 and was imposed by the sentencing judge when Manzie was sentenced on April 14, 1999. However, the three-judge panel that reviewed the case determined that murder cases were exempt from the new law. So not only was the Manzie case thrown into doubt, but so was every murder conviction and sentence since 1997 in which the sentencing judge had used the NERA standards to determine a sentence.

Not only did Ocean County, New Jersey, prosecutor E. David Millard appeal the decision, but those in his office said they were flabbergasted that Manzie could possibly be freed. "He deserves to rot in a cell for what he did to Eddie Werner," one prosecutor said, demanding anonymity. "To think that he did such a horrible thing and could be out walking the streets and still have the capacity to hurt others is a terrifying thing." But Manzie's attorneys praised the court, and Dolores Manzie managed a slight smile and sigh of relief. She had long contended that had the court system functioned the way it should have, a mental-health intervention would've kept her son off the streets and out of harm's way. She had struggled so hard to get her son help, and she never felt vindicated for all her travails until the three-judge panel ruled to help out her son. "None of that was considered by the judge, and Sam got seventy years," Dolores told a local reporter at the time. "He did a horrible thing, but it never would have happened had everyone done their job. He was a fifteen-year-old kid at the time."

* * *

On July 18, 2001, the State Supreme Court of New Jersey denied Attorney General John J. Farmer's request for a rehearing on the ruling that overturned Sam Manzie's seventy-year jail sentence. Manzie will be eligible for parole after serving thirty years.

AUTHOR'S NOTE

In order for me to write this book, an eleven-year-old boy had to die and that's not a fact that sits well with me—the parent of an eleven-year-old boy.

Within this book are described some of the more despicable acts that human beings can perpetrate upon each other. The language is as graphic as the testimony in court, which was extremely blunt and coarse. This book is not for the faint of heart and deals with issues many parents would never wish to confront. Yet, it covers issues that many of us need to grasp and deal with if we are to do our children justice.

This was without a doubt the most difficult thing to write I've ever attempted. It is because of the nature of the crime, the people involved and the issues discussed. No one was more victimized by the series of events that ended in Eddie Werner's death than Eddie Werner himself. Some people, most especially *not* the Manzies, have tried to say otherwise or have intimated otherwise. That isn't the case. Eddie Werner was killed before his time and probably never understood why Sam Manzie, another child only four years older, would want him dead.

Sam Manzie was a ticking time bomb and his parents knew it and desperately tried to defuse him. They got little if any help. The courts didn't help them, the hospitals didn't help them and ultimately the police didn't help them, even though they tried.

Sam had fallen prey to a pedophile and had done so under the collective eyes of his parents. Steve Simmons never understood what it was all about. His homosexuality and pedophilia are not what the case was about, nor what was most angering about Simmons.

The bottom line with Steve Simmons is that for a year he claimed to know Sam Manzie better than anyone. He can be heard in an audiotape recording, which was entered as evidence in his subsequent trial, encouraging Sam Manzie to seek psychiatric help. On that recording, he admitted that he knew Sam at the very least was suffering from "depression." If Simmons knew Manzie as well as he claimed, then Simmons's greatest sin was in becoming sexually involved with a person with a mental disability and then manipulating that person to lighten his own load in prison.

I don't care who Simmons is attracted to, and while I personally find the idea of being attracted to young boys a repugnant fact, I am far more concerned with the fact that Simmons cared for himself far too much and for Sam far too little. I believe he did care for Sam, but believe the facts show that he was always more concerned about his own hide a little more than Sam. Simmons preached he was an idealist and a martyr for the cause of gay rights. Nothing could be further from the truth. He was a naive man who took advantage of an emotionally disturbed person and conspired to hide that fact. When he could have stepped forward and sacrificed himself for Sam—if indeed he really did care for him—he chose to hide.

That is not to say that Simmons, in his own mind, did not have the best intentions at heart. I believe he did. It is this contradictory nature of almost everything that took place in Sam Manzie's life that makes this case so fascinating to me.

It also makes it hard to categorize. In a world where we increasingly enjoy pigeonholing things, categorizing them because we like things neat and tidy, this case is very disturbing because nothing in it was neat and tidy.

It is haunting, tragic, sad and in so many ways the ultimate parental nightmare that engulfed and threatened to destroy not one but two different families.

I grieve for the Werners, though I never knew Eddie. I grieve for the Manzies, though I never knew the hell they went through. But as the father of three children I do know one thing unconditionally:

There but for the grace of God, go I.

Brian J. Karem

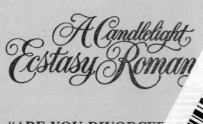

A Candlelight Ecstasy Roman

"ARE YOU DIVORCED

"No, I've never been marri   ured,
bemused by the way Thad ling   e—as if
he were savoring the sound o

"Never came close." Thad opened his m   as if he were
going to make some additional comment. Then, reconsidering, he shook his head and took a sip of wine. After a
few moments of silence he said, "I'm surprised you were
never married. Any special reason why?"

Laura smiled wryly. "Didn't your mother ever tell you it's
impolite to ask a question like that?"

"Sure she did. But you know how it is," Thad drawled.
"I've done lots of things Mother told me not to."

"Well, then, did anyone ever tell you that even if a woman
feels inclined to get married, she might decide not to when
she finds out how many frogs she has to kiss to find a
prince?"

A CANDLELIGHT ECSTASY ROMANCE ®

BRISTOL'S LAW

Rose Marie Ferris

A CANDLELIGHT ECSTASY ROMANCE ®

Published by
Dell Publishing Co., Inc.
1 Dag Hammarskjold Plaza
New York, New York 10017

Dell ® TM 681510, Dell Publishing Co., Inc.

Candlelight Ecstasy Romance®, 1,203,540, is a registered
trademark of Dell Publishing Co., Inc.,
New York, New York.

ISBN: 0–440–10803–9

Printed in the United States of America
First printing—January 1984

To Our Readers:

We have been delighted with your enthusiastic response to Candlelight Ecstasy Romances®, and we thank you for the interest you have shown in this exciting series.

In the upcoming months we will continue to present the distinctive sensuous love stories you have come to expect only from Ecstasy. We look forward to bringing you many more books from your favorite authors and also the very finest work from new authors of contemporary romantic fiction.

As always, we are striving to present the unique, absorbing love stories that you enjoy most—books that are more than ordinary romance.

Your suggestions and comments are always welcome. Please write to us at the address below.

Sincerely,

The Editors
Candlelight Romances
1 Dag Hammarskjold Plaza
New York, New York 10017

CHAPTER ONE

The Minnesota north woods were full of big bearded men, especially during the tourist season. What was so special about this man that Laura Powell should want to look and look at him?

Of course, it went without saying that he was wickedly attractive. Although he hadn't glanced her way, and Laura had seen him only in profile, she knew that he would rate a second glance—even a third—from any woman.

But if he looked as if he knew all the answers, Laura had long since stopped asking the relevant questions. And besides, she had known other men who were just as attractive, just as big and bearded and commanding as this man, and she'd never felt compelled to stare at any of them. So why did she feel that way now?

It's useless to wonder about it, Laura told herself. Nevertheless, she continued puzzling over the matter as she knotted a length of string around the last of the balloons Trina Gunderson had asked her to blow up.

When she'd let Laura into the house, Trina had been in such a rush, she'd hardly stopped to say hello. She'd simply waved Laura through to the patio, hastily explaining, "Phil's out there with Thad. You've heard me mention Thad Bristol, haven't you?"

Laura hadn't, but Trina went on without waiting for her answer.

"Thank God they volunteered to broil the hamburgers. I don't know what I'd have done if they hadn't offered to help. The kids are beginning to arrive, and I haven't even begun to decorate the cake. I couldn't drag myself out of bed till ten this morning."

"Was it morning sickness again?" Laura inquired sympathetically.

"Worse than ever. Be an angel, would you, Laura, and take care of the balloons while I finish making the frosting?" With a beleaguered smile at Laura, Trina had added, "Oh, and would you keep an eye on the children? Phil said he would, but you know how men are. If he and Thad get to talking—"

"Consider it done," Laura had agreed with alacrity. She marveled that petite, dark-haired Trina, though in the early stages of pregnancy, had enough energy and ambition to organize a birthday party for a dozen or more preschoolers—and on the hottest day of the summer to boot!

Just before she'd walked across the street to the Gundersons' house, Laura had showered and changed from her shorts and work smock to a backless halter dress. She might have presented the appearance of cool elegance, but with the hot August sun beating down and the temperature hovering in the nineties, even crossing the street had made her feel uncomfortably sticky. The dainty ice-blue challis of her dress had lost its crispness within five minutes.

The heat was a bit less oppressive on the Gundersons' patio, for the backyard was shaded by tall evergreens, and an occasional breeze rustled the leaves of the birch trees on the lakeshore, but the fact remained that the afternoon was sweltering.

Sighing, Laura impatiently pushed her fingers through her sun-streaked honey-blond hair, lifting it away from her flushed cheeks. Her hair was finespun and silky, but it was also very thick. Today she had left it loose, brushing it away from her face so that it fell to a point just below her shoulders. Though she had always prided herself on her long, shining tresses, today she'd wondered why she'd never had the good sense to cut them all off. At least she should have braided them or pinned them up as she usually did in hot weather.

A thoughtful expression ruffled the smoothness of her brow and turned her eyes more blue than gray as, despite her resolve not to, she stole another glance at Thad Bristol.

She envied his being able to wear nothing more than a pair of brief khaki shorts that rode low on his narrow hips, leaving his long legs and smooth, muscled chest bare. In fact, because the shorts were only a shade or two lighter than his skin, he might have been almost naked.

Arrested by the disturbing image this thought brought to mind, Laura continued watching Thad covertly.

He and Phil Gunderson were tending the barbecue at the far end of the patio, and she realized there was no need to worry that he would detect her watchful gaze. Both men were looking at the group of children who were playing in the sandbox some distance away. The two men appeared to be completely engrossed in their conversation, and when Thad threw his head back and laughed at something Phil had said, Laura studied him openly, brazenly.

For the space of a few pulsebeats she was startled by the keenness of her interest in this man. It seemed that no detail of his physical appearance must escape her attention.

She had already registered that he was tall and dark and clean-limbed. She had decided that he was probably twenty-three or twenty-four and that he wore a beard so that he would look a bit older. She had known the first instant she'd seen him that every angle, every line of his hard, rugged body conveyed a supreme self-confidence,

11

but now she realized that he also exuded sexuality. The aura of raw animal magnetism about him was so potent, not even she was immune to it.

Merely seeing Thad Bristol's coal-black hair and tawny eyes gave her an oddly intense, almost tactile pleasure. His skin was tanned to the rich ruddy bronze of the outdoorsman, and she knew that it would be wonderfully smooth and warm to touch. Her fingers itched to outline his full lower lip, to trace the bold slant of his eyebrows and the bridge of his nose.

Transfixed by the earthy rumble of his laughter, Laura stared at Thad, and she saw that he radiated good-humored warmth as well as uncompromising masculinity. She saw the way his eyes crinkled, the way his lean cheeks creased, the way the muscles in his throat worked as he laughed. She noticed how strong and even his teeth were, how dazzlingly white they appeared in contrast with his jet-black beard.

It was only when four-year-old Kit Gunderson abandoned his playmates and climbed out of the sandbox that Laura realized how intently she had been studying Thad.

Attracted by the sound of laughter, Kit came hurtling toward the patio, running as fast as his sturdy little legs could carry him. When he reached the men, Thad scooped Kit into his arms and cradled him against his chest, and the little boy squealed delightedly.

"Uncle Thad! Mommy said you wouldn't be home in time for my birthday."

Thad swung Kit up to perch on his shoulders. Laugh lines fanned out from the corners of his eyes as he grinned at the four-year-old.

"Well, tiger, that just goes to show you that Mommy doesn't know everything. Not quite anyway."

"For heaven's sake, Thad, don't tell him that," Trina pleaded with mock solemnity as she joined the three by the barbecue. "He'll find out his parents aren't all-knowing soon enough as it is. . . ."

"And when he does," said Phil, "there goes our last advantage over him!"

Tangling his small, chubby fingers in Thad's dark hair, Kit pulled at it to get Thad's attention.

"Uncle Thad, what's a 'vantage?"

"According to your mom and dad, it's something you have plenty of, youngster."

"Oh." Kit nodded sagely, as if he had anticipated Thad's answer and completely understood it. Then, speedily changing the subject to one of higher priority, he asked, "Did you bring me a present?"

Chuckling at Kit's childish candor, Thad shrugged off Trina's apology for her son's rudeness and replied, "You bet I did. It's over there with the others."

They turned toward the table where Laura stood near the stack of gaily wrapped packages, and for the first time Thad saw her. His smile faded, leaving his expression unexpectedly sober. His eyes narrowed speculatively, then widened with a shock of recognition that mirrored her own, and for long moments his tawny gaze held her smoky-blue one captive.

The very air between them seemed to be charged with mutual awareness. Futilely Laura tried to tear her eyes away from his, and when she discovered she couldn't look away from the excruciating intimacy of his gaze, she was shaken by a cold frisson of alarm.

Before she could stop herself, one hand had fluttered to the base of her throat to hide the wildly pounding pulses there, but she resisted the impulse to moisten her lips, to pat her hair into place, to smooth the full skirt of her sundress over the gentle swell of her hips.

Thad's knowing smile revealed that it was too late to prevent his seeing how deeply—how dangerously—she

13

was drawn to him, but she could at least make it plain that she was capable of resisting his appeal.

Stubbornly refusing to give in to the urge to avert her face, Laura lifted her chin and forced herself to smile faintly. Admittedly her smile was a bit tremulous at first, but she pressed her lips together and tried again, and this time she managed to project the hint of cool condescension she'd hoped for.

Now she lowered her eyes purposefully, allowing her gaze to trail downward over Thad's powerful shoulders and chest to his lean waist. When she arrived at his hips, she paused briefly, as if she were assessing his virility. At last, with a great show of reluctance, her eyes returned to his. She made no attempt to hide her appreciation of his body, and in response, he raised a cautioning eyebrow at her.

She had thought Thad would be put off by her frank appraisal of him, but she was disappointed. On the contrary he was annoyingly undaunted. His smile was actually approving, and his eyes shone with admiration for her performance. *Well done,* they seemed to say.

Aloud he said quietly, "Who's the pretty lady, Kit?"

"Oh, my God!" Trina cried, casting a stricken look at Laura. "You two haven't met, have you? What must you think of me—"

"That's just Laura, Uncle Thad," Kit remarked, interrupting his mother's self-reproachful wail matter-of-factly. "She's Groucho's mommy."

"Groucho?" Thad repeated. His eyebrows shot up. He looked so startled that Laura had to stifle a laugh as she disclosed, "Groucho is my *cat,* Mr. Bristol."

"I'm relieved to hear that," said Thad. "Groucho's an okay name for a pet, but it's a mighty strange handle to give a child."

"I agree," Laura returned gravely. "Although Groucho Marx did very well with it."

14

"So he did." Thad's tone of voice matched hers for gravity, but a smile played around the corners of his mouth. He seemed to be unaware that Kit was pulling at his hair again, trying to monopolize his attention. "With a name like that, though, it was probably a case of over-compensation. I mean, he'd have had to become a comedian, wouldn't he?"

"I must admit you have a valid point there."

"Would you also agree that Kit could use a lesson in elementary biology?"

"Yes, Mr. Bristol, I would."

Laura was surprised to find herself enjoying Thad's easy banter. Her blue-gray eyes sparkled with merriment until he lifted the wriggling Kit down from his shoulders. Setting the little boy on his feet, Thad gave him a light swat on the bottom to propel him toward the sandbox and came toward her, his stride long and supple.

"That's the second time you've called me Mr. Bristol," he remarked thoughtfully.

"Isn't that your name?" asked Laura.

"Yes, but please call me Thad." His eyes dared her not to comply with this request.

"Very well . . . Thad."

"And do you have a last name?"

Laura nodded. By now he was standing so close to her, she had to tip her head back to see his face, and she was mesmerized by the intimate message she saw in his eyes. It was as if his eyes were communicating on one level—an elemental, almost sexual level—while his voice communicated on another, purely social level.

It had seemed safe enough to flirt with Thad when they were separated by the length of the patio, and the Gundersons were present, but now that he had accepted the challenge she'd been foolish enough to give him, Laura decided that things were getting out of hand. She took a step away from him, but he immediately closed the gap.

15

"Would you tell it to me?" he inquired softly.

He smelled of fresh air and sunshine and of some tangy, woodsy men's cologne, and his breath stirred a tendril of hair at her temple when he spoke.

It was impossible to think coherently when he was so near, and she moved away from him again, but again he pursued her. Step-by-step she eased her way around the table and began backing away from him, but it was only when her cautious retreat was blocked by the wall of the house that Laura realized how dangerously out of her depth she was with Thad Bristol.

She darted a frantic glance over Thad's shoulder, hoping to find someone to rescue her, but Phil was busy arranging the hamburger patties on the grill, Kit had run back to his playmates, and Trina had returned to the kitchen.

She made a reflexive move, trying to step around Thad, but he forestalled this action by propping his hands on the wall at either side of her head and leaning toward her so that she was effectively trapped in this deserted corner of the patio, and when she tried to duck under his arm, he moved even nearer.

Now Laura could feel the hot imprint of Thad's thighs against her own and she experienced another twinge of alarm. She flattened herself against the wall, attempting to avoid touching him, but pride made her ignore the impulse to cross her arms in front of her breasts.

Schooling her expression to reveal nothing of her turbulent emotions, she looked directly into Thad's eyes. Her heart skipped a beat when she saw that the pupils were dilated so that his eyes were nearly as black as his hair.

"What is it?" he repeated.

"What?" she replied numbly. She was frighteningly aware of the hard strength of his body as he towered over her. "I'm afraid—"

Her breathless murmur faltered into silence when

Thad's eyes left hers to settle on her mouth, and her heartbeat accelerated when he gently ran his forefinger along the vulnerable curve of her mouth. His gaze wandered slowly over the graceful arch of her throat and the flawless slope of her shoulders, finally coming to rest on the rounded fullness of her breasts. She opened her mouth to protest, but the words lodged in her throat as Thad moved even closer and smiled lazily down at her.

"Your last name," he prompted. "I intend to call you, Laura, of course, but in case I have to look up your phone number or something—"

Finding her voice, Laura broke in coldly, "Don't bother. My last name is Powell, but if this is an example of your technique with women, Mr. Bristol, I'd advise you not to waste your time phoning me." She drew in a deep, calming breath before she went on. "And now, if you'll excuse me, I really must see if Trina needs my help."

Thad was not discouraged by the cool disdain in Laura's voice, but when he saw the panic in her eyes, he tensed with dismay. This time he made no effort to stop her when she ducked under his arm and walked away from him, leaving him to frown after her.

Initially she had seemed relaxed and interested. He could have sworn that she was as attracted to him as he was to her; she had parried his lighthearted teasing, and she'd seemed an informed and willing participant in the flirtatious game they were playing. Then, in the blink of an eye, she'd become reserved, remote, unattainable, and he was perplexed by her abrupt change of mood, and more intrigued by her than he cared to admit.

Several hours had passed, however, before he had an opportunity to solve the riddle Laura Powell presented. By one means or another she managed to avoid him all during Kit's birthday party, but when Laura said good night to the Gundersons and began the short walk to her own home, Thad fell into step beside her.

17

Without preamble he said, "I'm sorry I misread my cues and came on too strong for you earlier."

"Apologies accepted."

She had replied airily, as if she had already forgotten their encounter on the patio, but she didn't stop walking. And neither did Thad.

"I really would like to see you again," he persisted.

Laura's steps slowed, then stopped completely. She turned to look at Thad, confronting him stiffly. At some time during Kit's party, he had put on a shirt, but the image of his broad naked chest lingered. Her blue-gray eyes were clouded and her face was pale in the twilight.

"Why?" she asked tersely.

"Damned if I know," Thad answered truthfully. "Maybe it's because I don't believe in running away from a challenge." There was a long silence during which he studied the delicate modeling of her upturned face. "Then again," he added as if he were thinking out loud, "I've always enjoyed mysteries, so maybe it's just that you've aroused my curiosity."

"Is that all I've aroused?"

"No." Thad's appreciative chuckle told her he was amused by her directness. "At the risk of offending you again, I'll confess that you turn me on, Laura Powell. And why not? My male instincts are in excellent working order, and they tell me that you're a very desirable woman. You have the face of a Renaissance angel, a fantastic figure, and besides being lovely to look at, you're interesting to talk to. You're bright, witty—"

"I'm thirty-three," Laura said crisply. "And *you're* exaggerating."

"I'm twenty-five," Thad returned smoothly. "And if you refuse to believe all my compliments, feel free to accept whichever ones you prefer."

In spite of her resolve not to encourage him, Laura laughed. The tension drained from her, making her feel

18

slightly giddy with relaxation. She started walking again, strolling across the Gundersons' lawn toward the street, and Thad walked beside her, shortening his much longer stride to keep pace with her. When they stepped into the street, he took her elbow, but he was careful to keep his touch light and impersonal, and she did not pull away from him.

"At least your honesty is refreshing," she murmured, half to herself.

"It's nice to know there's something about me you approve of," Thad said dryly.

"Oh, there are quite a few things about you I approve of."

"Then why not go out with me? Have dinner with me tomorrow night."

Laura sighed. "Look, Thad, I hate to state the obvious, but I'm eight years older than you."

"So when you're one hundred, I'll only be ninety-two! Unless you happen to be discussing wine or cheese, what the hell does age have to do with anything?"

By now they were almost at Laura's front door, and with Thad grinning at her so engagingly, she was finding it increasingly difficult to decline his invitation.

If only he weren't so likable, she thought. But he was. He was too likable. And far too attractive.

It was time, she decided, to disillusion him—before the temptation to see him again became too great to withstand.

"All right," she said flippantly. "Since you insist, we'll talk about wine. We both know that wine improves with age—"

"*Some* do, and some turn to vinegar."

At this mocking qualification Laura's steps dragged to a stop. Her hands curled into fists. Inwardly she was seething because Thad had intuited her thoughts and deprived her of landing the first blow. His barbed comment stung. She wanted to scream at him, but more than that, she wanted to retain some dignity, so she gritted her teeth, counted to ten, and produced a semblance of a smile.

"If you were a wine, Thaddeus Bristol, I'd say that you were robust and that you would have a certain adolescent appeal."

"Gee, thanks!"

Laura held up one finger, signaling that she hadn't finished her comparison. "But," she continued evenly, "I'd also say that you're extraordinarily presumptuous and that you're memorable mainly for your impertinence."

"Ouch!" Thad yelped. His mouth turned down at the corners and for a few moments Laura thought she had succeeded in disconcerting him. Then his expression brightened, and he said hopefully, "If that means you won't go out with me tomorrow night, how about Thursday?"

His audacity left Laura gasping. "Good Lord!" she cried. "I don't believe this. You are the most . . . the most—"

"Insolent?" Thad suggested.

"Yes!"

"Annoying?" he provided.

"Exactly!"

"Impossible?"

Laura nodded her head so vigorously that her hair flew about her shoulders and a few wayward strands clung to her cheeks in enchanting disarray. Her confusion deepened when Thad chuckled.

"Poor baby," he crooned. "I shouldn't have baited you that way. My comment about vinegar really struck a nerve, didn't it?"

Laura wanted to reply, but before she could think of a suitably cutting response, Thad went on.

"Would it make you feel any better if I told you that

you're incredibly sexy when you're angry? Your cheeks are as pink as peonies, and those gorgeous eyes of yours are shooting off blue sparks—"

"My eyes are gray," Laura cut in heatedly, "and the thing that would make me feel better would be for you to leave me alone!"

"They're blue when you're angry," Thad said equably, "and all right, I'll leave."

Laura was openmouthed with astonishment that Thad should have given in to her demand that he leave with such unflattering haste, but her surprise was mingled with a certain healthy skepticism and some other emotion. Could it be disappointment?

In her bewilderment she hadn't the presence of mind to turn her face away when Thad leaned down and touched his lips to hers. His beard tickled, but pleasantly so, and the kiss he gave her was light and sweetly tentative—even shy—and far too brief to be threatening. When Thad raised his head and smiled at her, she stared up at him wordlessly.

"I'll leave, Laura Powell," he declared softly. "And I'll even promise not to bother you again—unless you want me to, that is—if you'll ask me in for a drink right now."

21

CHAPTER TWO

Somehow Thad talked his way into Laura's house. Laura was not sure precisely how he accomplished this, but she had a sneaking suspicion that his refusal to take no for an answer had simply worn down her resistance. In the short run it seemed easier to ask him to come in for a drink than to stand on the doorstep debating the subject. As for the long run, no doubt she'd have cause to worry about that later.

After having been closed all afternoon, the house was stifling. For the first few minutes both Laura and Thad were occupied with opening windows and doors to catch the evening breeze off the lake. Then Groucho appeared, meowing strident demands for his supper. Laura fed the cat while Thad found the bottle of Chablis in the refrigerator and poured a glass for each of them.

They carried their wine to the screened porch off the kitchen, where it was a bit cooler, and by the time they were settled, Thad lounging on the glider and she seated in the basket-weave chair across from him, Laura's feeling of strangeness at having succumbed to Thad's blandishments had passed.

The sweet-pungent smell of raw lumber drifted out to the porch, and Thad asked, "What's all the remodeling at the back of the house?"

"It's going to be my shop," Laura replied proudly. She was still rather tense, and to fill the silence she told Thad

22

about her plans for the gift shop, but she didn't tell him how long she had been planning it. Neither did she tell him how she'd scrimped so that she could bank every extra penny of the money she'd earned as a production potter, saving for the day when she'd have enough of a nest egg to open her own ceramics studio.

For more than ten years she had worked at her wheel, turning out scores of bud vases, hundreds of dinner plates, thousands of coffee mugs, and dreamed of having her own studio.

"Of course, production pieces are a potter's bread and butter," she told Thad. "I'll still have to do lots of vases and coffee mugs, but I'll be able to design them as I think they should be designed, and I'll have more time for creative things. Eventually I hope to sell a whole range of craft items on consignment. I've already been approached by a local woman who weaves absolutely beautiful wall hangings and place mats, but I'd like to stock candles and stained glass, paintings and sculpture, jewelry and wood-carvings. . . ."

The previous summer, Laura's savings had accumulated to the point that she'd decided she had enough for a down payment on her dream. For months she'd spent weekends scouring the countryside for the perfect locale, and the minute she'd seen this house near Ely, she'd known it was exactly what she'd been searching for.

The house was situated on the shore of Shagawa Lake, a few miles northeast of Ely, so there was quite a lot of traffic past the property. The lot had only modest frontage, but it was sufficient to make the kind of commercial development she was contemplating seem feasible. In fact, because of the way the road wound along the lakeshore, it was almost like a corner lot.

There were drawbacks, of course. She'd had to apply to have the property rezoned, and governmental red tape had prevented her being open for business earlier in the summer. Structurally the house was sound, but it was old, and it had taken extensive remodeling to make it usable as a combination residence and shop. And although she'd done as much of the work as she could, she had refused to cut corners. As a consequence, the remodeling had been even more expensive than she'd estimated it would be.

She'd tried to plan for every contingency, but just now her savings were sadly depleted. She would have to operate on a shoestring until the store began making a profit, but she was determined to hang on—even if she had to take a temporary job to see her through the winter.

Next Monday she would be celebrating the grand opening of Powell's Gallery of Gifts, and it would be worth every cent of her investment just to see her dream become a reality.

Since the middle of June, when she'd moved out of her cramped efficiency apartment in St. Paul, each day had seemed like a gift. She awakened every morning to the sound of birdsong—unless Groucho chose to wake her by jumping onto her pillow and howling a hungry complaint that he was ready for breakfast.

From the windows of her studio she had a breathtaking view of the birch trees and the lake, and the house itself was surrounded by green and growing things. The yard was full of stately old maples, and the maples were full of squirrels' nests and birds' nests. Rhubarb grew in the garden, and she had her very own blueberries and raspberries and an asparagus bed as well.

As for the shop, it was everything she'd dreamed it should be, right down to the bright red geraniums in the window boxes.

Because she had gone over budget on fixtures for the shop, most of her living quarters weren't furnished yet, but she had taken special pains decorating her bedroom. She had painted the walls a creamy ivory, renovated the handsomely detailed woodwork, hung frilly white curtains at the honest-to-God bay windows, and made a sunflower quilt for the brass bed she'd picked up for a fraction of its real value at a garage sale.

As a bonus, she'd discovered she had neighbors like Trina and Phil Gunderson, who were friendly and caring, expressing an interest in her, but minding their own business; and Emily Carruthers, a garrulous widow who exhibited all the symptoms of being a died-in-the-wool busybody, but who was too nearsighted and hard of hearing to be very good at it.

And with this discovery had come a feeling of having shed the past; of being free of old concerns, old constraints, old hurts. Despite its big-city anonymity Laura had never felt nearly as free in St. Paul, and after all was said and done, perhaps that was the real reason she'd invited Thad into her home tonight. Perhaps she had merely felt a need to test her newfound freedom.

They had been talking only desultorily, and now, while twilight gave way to darkness, as if by mutual consent, their conversation trailed into a companionable silence.

The ghostly white trunks of the birch trees along the lakeshore glimmered more and more feebly through the gathering dusk. Somewhere in the distance a loon cried. The moon rose, full and round and oddly fluorescent. Cicadas chirped. Fireflies appeared. The breeze grew stronger, veiling the moon with thin, gauzy clouds.

Thad got up to refill their wineglasses, but neither of them spoke until Groucho wandered out to the porch, jumped onto the glider next to Thad, and sat there, licking the last crumbs of his dinner off his whiskers.

"Careful. He's not very friendly with strangers."

Laura issued the warning automatically, for the cat could be painfully aloof. He had been known to scratch people who attempted to pet him without his approval, but tonight, as if to make a liar out of her, Groucho elected to curl up in Thad's lap.

25

"He seems friendly enough to me," Thad observed. "One might even accuse him of being mellow. Why do you call him Groucho?"

"Because of his mustache," Laura explained.

After two full glasses of wine she was beginning to feel rather mellow herself, but she held her breath when Thad scratched the cat under the chin. She was afraid that Groucho might change his mind about their guest after all, but instead of hissing and arching his back, the cat purred and obligingly stretched his head back to give Thad access to more of his chin. This also permitted Thad to see the oblong splotch of black on the white fur just below the cat's nose.

"I see what you mean." Thad laughed. "His mustache is like Groucho Marx's."

Laura managed some inanity in agreement. She watched Thad beneath her lashes as he continued petting the cat, fascinated by the rhythmic stroking movements of Thad's long, sunbrowned fingers. His hands were big-boned and capable-looking, Laura noticed. They were strong. His wrists were thick and powerful, yet he handled Groucho so gently.

Before she could stop herself, Laura had recalled how it felt to be touched by Thad, and the recollection brought her wool-gathering to a sudden halt.

Grow up! she scolded herself silently. Don't be an idiot. How can you possibly envy a cat?

But, improbable though it seemed, she did envy Thad's display of affection for Groucho, and this realization made her want to laugh at herself for being such a fool.

"Tell me," she said brightly, "do you happen to have a cat?"

That would account for Groucho's uncharacteristic behavior, even if it didn't explain her own.

"My kid sister does," Thad replied.

"Until today I didn't know Trina had any brothers or sisters."

"She doesn't," said Thad. "I think of Trina as a sister because we lived next door to each other when we were kids, and my folks practically raised her, but we're only cousins." At Laura's inquiring glance he added, "Trina's father was killed in a hunting accident when she was three, and her mother couldn't seem to get her act together after that."

"How very sad," Laura sympathized. "But at least Trina was fortunate to have your parents nearby."

"Yes, she was."

"Do you have other sisters?"

"I have three," Thad replied with a grin. "Two older and one younger."

"But no brothers."

"No. No brothers. Just my three sisters and Trina."

He lifted the bottle of Chablis, offering her more wine, but she quickly covered her glass with the palm of her hand, and while he refilled his own glass she set hers aside.

So Thad was the only son in a family of four, thought Laura. Five if you included Trina. No wonder he was so knowledgeable about women!

"I'll bet your sisters spoiled you outrageously," she conjectured.

"Sure they did—when they weren't ganging up on me." Thad's grin broadened. "My kid sister, Angela, was an afterthought. She's nine years younger than I am, but the rest of us were stair-stepped. When we were growing up, we went through stages when we had some royal battles, but for the most part we were fairly close."

"That sounds very . . . jolly." Laura's face was pensive as she inquired, "Are you still close to your sisters?"

"Not really. Oh, I suppose there'll always be a certain amount of closeness between us, but we're not as insepara-ble as we once were. Lila and Connie married men from

27

out of state, so they live on opposite sides of the country. Lila and her husband settled in Maine, and Connie's in Southern California, and none of the Bristols are terrific letter writers. We have a standing arrangement for a conference call every other month, and during the off-season I make the circuit of boat and recreation shows, which means I see them maybe once a year, tops, although this year is an exception. They're both going to be here next month for Mom and Dad's thirty-fifth anniversary. But how about you, Laura Powell?"

Unprepared for the abrupt change of subject, bemused by the way Thad lingered over her name, as if he savored the sound of it, Laura murmured, "Pardon me?"

Chuckling, Thad said, "What I want to know is, is it Miss or Mrs. Powell, or is it Ms.?"

"It's just Laura."

"From that reply I take it you don't have a husband who's likely to come barging in and misinterpret what's going on here."

"You take it correctly."

"Are you divorced?"

"No, I've never been married. Have you?"

"Never even came close." Thad opened his mouth as if he were going to make some additional comment. Then, reconsidering, he shook his head and took a sip of wine.

After a few moments of silence Laura's curiosity got the better of her. "What were you going to say?" she asked.

"Before I had second thoughts, I was going to say how surprised I am that you were never married. I also wanted to ask if there's any special reason why."

Laura smiled wryly. "Didn't your mother ever tell you it's impolite to ask a question like that?"

"Sure she did. But you know how it is. Over the years I've done lots of things Mother told me not to."

"Well, then, did anyone ever tell you that even if a woman feels inclined to get married, she might decide not

28

to when she finds out how many frogs she has to kiss to find a prince?"

"Okay, Princess," Thad drawled. "I get your drift." Trying unsuccessfully to look chastened, he inquired, "Would you consider it rude if I ask whether you have brothers or sisters?"

"I'm an only child," Laura answered shortly.

Thad's glance sharpened, making it obvious that he was baffled by her reticence, and she hastily expanded her reply.

"I was a change-of-life baby. Before I was born, my mother had had several miscarriages. She was well into her forties when I came along, and my father was three years older than her."

"Are your parents still living?"

In a carefully neutral tone Laura replied, "My father is, but I haven't seen him for quite some time. We aren't very close. He doesn't really approve of me."

And that, Laura thought ruefully, was a gross understatement. It might be accurate enough to say that she had been a disappointment to her mother, but her father's feelings toward her were not nearly as mild.

To Selby Powell, with his unbending pride and rigid moral code, she was an affront. From the time she was eighteen, he'd regarded Laura as if she were a blight on the Powell family tree. Through no fault of her own, she had become, quite simply, an embarrassment. And it hadn't helped that she had inherited more than a little of her father's pride. Now that she thought about it, if either of them had been a bit less proud, they might have reached a compromise. As it was, they'd arrived at an impasse, and she had become an outcast.

Laura's eyes were fixed on the wineglass Thad was turning absently between his palms, but she sensed his scrutiny of her.

"I didn't mean to pry," he said quietly.

29

"It's all right."

"No, really," he insisted. "If my mother were here, she'd read me the riot act for asking such personal questions, but she'd also tell you that I can be a damn good listener. If you ever decide you want to talk about whatever happened between you and your father, I'm available."

Laura looked up at Thad and smiled, shaking off the dark mood that seemed inevitably to accompany memories of her father.

"Yes," she said evenly. "I'll just bet you're available."

"Not to everyone," he qualified.

"Naturally not," she agreed.

Thad heard the skepticism in her voice and pulled himself erect. "You sound as if you have your doubts about that," he remarked.

"Well, Trina did mention that you're considered the most eligible bachelor in Ely. . . ."

"Ely's not that big a town," Thad cut in dismissively.

"Maybe not, but Trina led me to believe that you have quite a reputation with the ladies."

"And when people gossip in a small town, it's often a lot of—"

"Please, don't." Now it was Laura who broke in. "I don't know why I said that. Your love life is certainly none of my business."

"No, it isn't," Thad declared firmly. "But my reputation must bother you, otherwise you wouldn't have brought it up, and since you saw fit to raise the issue, I'm going to tell you about it, then we'll consider the subject closed."

The springs of the glider squealed a rusty protest as Thad shifted position again, leaning toward her with his elbows on his knees.

"I'd have to be pretty damn stupid if I didn't know I'm supposed to be quite a catch," he began. "I've been pursued by girls—by women—ever since I was in junior high.

30

Lord knows why hopeful mamas encourage their daughters to set their caps for me, but they do."

If Thad had given her a chance, Laura could have come up with a plausible explanation for this phenomenon, beginning with his dark good looks and finishing with the fact that, if Trina could be relied upon as an informant, Thad was an astute and prosperous businessman. He might be only twenty-five, but Trina had said he owned several sporting goods stores in the state and was one of the major canoe outfitters in the Boundary Waters area.

But Thad paused only long enough for Laura to wonder if he might be putting her on. She barely had time to marshal her thoughts before he frowned reflectively and went on. "Maybe it's because the Bristols are an old respected family in this community, but whatever the reason, quite a few opportunities come my way, and when I was younger, I took advantage of most of them. I fooled around as much as any of the other guys did—probably a little more—until experience taught me to be more selective. Nowadays . . . well, I might not live like a monk, but contrary to popular belief I'm not exactly a swinger either."

Thad had completely abandoned his indolent pose. He studied her intently as he asked, "Does all of this make any difference to you, Laura Powell? Would it make any difference if I told you I knew you were thirty-three before I asked you to see me again?"

"You knew?" she said incredulously. "But how?"

"I pumped Phil for information about you—just as you must have asked Trina about me."

A warm tide of color washed into Laura's face. She tried to turn away from Thad, but he stopped her, tilting her face toward his with one finger hooked beneath her chin.

She could very easily have avoided his touch, but she didn't. He held her immobile more by the force of his personality than by the light pressure of his hand against

31

her chin. What's more, she knew she should move away from him before it was too late, before she was so captivated by him that she would agree to anything he suggested. But for some inexplicable reason, she didn't move away.

"I'm right, aren't I?" Thad exclaimed softly. "You did ask Trina about me."

Laura wished she could lie. Failing that, she wished she could honestly say that she hadn't spoken to Trina about him, but with Thad grinning at her so disarmingly, with him looking at her so possessively, she could only answer "Yes. Yes, I did."

Thad's deceptively boyish grin faded, leaving him strangely solemn. His hazel eyes were deeply shadowed, smoldering with barely suppressed urgency as he said, "Go out with me, Laura. I've got a feeling we'll both be missing out on something terribly important if we don't get to know each other better."

"P-perhaps later." Good heavens! Now she was stammering, Laura thought.

Leaping to her feet, Laura made herself take several steps away from Thad. She stopped only a few yards away from him, but even that short distance allowed her to rally her defenses.

"I'm very busy just now," she offered coolly, and although she sounded rather prim, she thought that was an improvement over being breathless and indecisive. "Perhaps after the shop is open for business, when I have more free time . . ."

"What's keeping you so busy tomorrow?" Thad asked brusquely. He'd sounded angry, but she was afraid to look at him, afraid that if she saw him, her fragile composure would melt like snow beneath the warmth and intimacy in his eyes.

"Well," she said huskily, "tomorrow I'd planned to fire the kiln for the first time, and I'm also going to do a little painting and put the final coat of sealer on the pine paneling in the store."

"I'll help."

She realized that Thad had got to his feet, and when she spun around, she saw that he was striding toward the kitchen. He stopped by the sink to deposit the wine bottle and both of their glasses on the counter.

Over his shoulder he called, "I'll be here first thing in the morning. Is eight o'clock too early for you?"

"Eight o'clock is fine," she replied dazedly. "I mean, I'm usually up with the sun, but—"

"Good! I'll see you in the morning then."

"God, but you're pushy, and—"

"And you don't like it," Thad finished for her.

"No," she responded crossly. "No, I don't."

"Then you'll have to help me break that particular habit, won't you, Laura?"

Now Thad was heading for the door. Shaking herself out of her stupor, Laura hurried after him.

"Since you have so much to do tomorrow," said Thad, "I doubt that you'll feel like fixing dinner, so we'll go out somewhere. You can choose the place." Having made this announcement, he stopped walking so suddenly that she ran into him. Pivoting on his heel, he smiled down at her and prompted, "That's your cue to say 'All right, Thad.' "

Too stunned by his steamroller tactics to argue, Laura echoed faintly, "Uh—all right, Thad."

"Now, see how easy that was?"

Thad nodded approvingly, as if she were a child he'd coaxed out of a tantrum, but before she could reply, he had opened the door and stepped outside. He paused to say softly "Sweet dreams, Laura Powell, and may they all be of me." Then with one long bound he was down the stairs, jogging across the lawn toward the Gunderson house.

Laura watched after Thad until he had disappeared into

the darkness. She went through her nightly routine of closing and locking the doors and retraced her steps to the kitchen, automatically turning off lights as she went.

She was standing at the sink, rinsing the wineglasses, when Groucho rubbed against her ankles.

"Traitor," she muttered.

She glared at the cat accusingly, but he seemed to understand that her anger wasn't directed at him. He gave a consoling little chirp that was a cross between a meow and a purr, and when she knelt down and gathered him into her arms, his wide green eyes narrowed into slits, and he began purring in earnest.

"I'm in deep, deep trouble," she whispered brokenly.

Tears prickled at the backs of her eyelids, and when one tear spilled over and trickled down her cheek, she buried her face in the ruff of soft white fur at the cat's neck and cried, "Oh, Groucho, what in the world am I going to do?"

CHAPTER THREE

For all his look of worldly wisdom, Groucho was only a cat, so it was not at all surprising that he couldn't answer Laura's question.

That night, for the first time since she'd moved from St. Paul to northern Minnesota, she slept fitfully. When she'd been planning her studio, she had tried to foresee every possible problem that might arise, but never in her wildest dreams had she imagined that she would meet a man like Thad Bristol.

Over the last fifteen years her wariness of romantic entanglements had become a deeply ingrained habit. How could she have known that in Ely, of all places, she would meet a big, bearded man who would make her want to break the habit? Just the memory of the evening with Thad made her want to run away and hide—for the sake of her sanity if not for her life. When she'd been with him, however, another part of her had wanted to curl up in his lap and purr just as Groucho had.

Thad had implied that he was intrigued by the mystery she presented, but it was he who was the real enigma.

Why should he be so eager for her company?

Of course, she couldn't help being aware of the sexual tension between them. It was terribly potent. But if he was in the market for a new mistress, there'd be no shortage of applicants for the role. And Thad must know that. He must know perfectly well how attractive he was to women.

35

Trina had boasted that he'd had to get an unlisted number for his home telephone because he received so many unsolicited calls from women.

So why should he waste his time with Laura when she was uninterested and unwilling and—heaven help her!—more than anything else, she was uncertain.

Thad was the sort of man who was completely outside her experience. He came on as if there were no tomorrow. There were moments when his self-assurance bordered on being insufferable. He'd refused to recognize the brush-off that had proved so effective with other men, and he hadn't been intimidated when she'd pretended to be brazenly aggressive.

But if on the one hand he was brash and cocky and stubborn, on the other hand he could be so damnably, devastatingly appealing.

He was also, Laura reminded herself, eight years younger than she.

This thought restored a measure of her self-confidence, and she clung to it as if it were a lifeline. Surely the age gap should give her at least one advantage over Thad.

By the next morning when she was carefully stacking the final tray of pottery into the kiln, Laura was no closer to knowing what to do about Thad than she'd been the night before. Her eyes were shadowed with weariness, but she grinned when she noticed that this tray contained coffee mugs and bud vases.

There was a certain irony in that, Laura mused, even though these mugs were altogether different than the ones she had turned out in her job at St. Paul: the new mugs were gracefully proportioned and designed for serving Irish coffee, while the lines of the bud vases had a lovely fluency.

The lower trays held an assortment of beer steins and earthenware casseroles, larger vases, several cachepots, some candle holders, and wonder of wonders, an umbrella stand shaped like an elephant's foot.

Laura laughed out loud at this recollection. The umbrella stand contrasted with the rest of her pottery as surely as night contrasts with day. The evening she'd made it, she had been trying out her wheel. She'd had a glass of wine to celebrate the occasion and she'd been feeling whimsical, in the mood to experiment, and she had got carried away.

The piece was unremittingly ugly, but she had decided not to destroy it because it had a character all its own. She thought that after it had been bisque-fired and glazed it might be a good conversation piece for the shop.

Laura lowered the lid of the kiln, propping it ajar with the kiln post. As she adjusted the thermostat she saw a flash of movement out of the corner of her eye, and she looked out the studio window in time to catch a glimpse of Groucho as the cat streaked across the lawn in pursuit of a dragonfly.

Then she saw Thad. His hair shone blue-black in the sunlight as he walked toward the house with his loose-limbed athletic stride, and her pulses quickened at the sight of him. He was dressed for work in chinos and a faded red T-shirt that fitted him like a second skin, but in spite of his well-worn clothes, he managed to look dashing and even more attractive than she'd recalled.

He saw her watching him through the window, smiled, and waved. As Laura raised one hand to return the greeting, she realized she had regressed to a habit she'd broken years ago and bitten several of her fingernails.

When she saw how ragged and unkempt her nails looked, she expelled her breath in a sigh. Her hands were unsteady as she removed her denim apron and hung it on its hook near the potter's wheel, and it was only her long years of training that enabled her to remember to check her wristwatch before she went to let Thad in.

This was the first time she'd fired the kiln, and until she was thoroughly acquainted with its idiosyncracies, she intended to take it slow and easy. She was satisfied that the pieces in the kiln were fairly well dried, but increasing the heat too rapidly could cause greenware to explode, and that would be disastrous.

"Good morning," Thad called cheerfully when she opened the door.

"Good morning," she returned brightly. "You're very punctual."

"That's just one of my many fine qualities!" Laughing, Thad crossed the porch and entered the shop without slowing his pace, but once he was inside, he stopped and looked around, assessing the interior of the shop with an expert's eyes.

"This is nice," he said. He nodded appreciatively, noticing the arrangement of shelves and counters, the hand-hewn ceiling beams, the Franklin stove in one corner, and the herringbone pattern of the wide-planked pine paneling on the walls. "*Very* nice," he repeated.

"The shop is going to be carpeted," Laura explained enthusiastically. "I thought it would help keep the place warmer in the winter and cut down on breakage too. They're supposed to deliver the carpeting tomorrow, then I can install the gondola cases and run in my stock."

Thad nodded again, as if he were envisioning the way the shop would look when it was finished. "I'm glad to see your store is air-conditioned," he remarked. "Today's going to be another scorcher."

"Yes, it looks that way," Laura replied. "Have you had breakfast?"

Thad turned toward her, grinning and patting his flat belly. "Sure, but if you have any coffee, I wouldn't mind having a second cup while you tell me where you want me to begin."

The way he was looking at her, the open admiration she

38

saw in his tawny eyes as they lingered on her long, slender legs and bare midriff, made Laura acutely conscious of her own body. She could feel him watching her as she led the way toward the kitchen, and she walked rather stiffly, trying not to swing her hips.

She wished she were wearing something less revealing than shorts and a sleeveless cotton blouse with the shirt-tails knotted below her breasts for coolness, and she was promptly exasperated with herself for the thought.

She was a perfect idiot to attach so much importance to Thad's opinion of her, especially since she had resolved to call his bluff by asking him to help with all the grubby jobs she could think of. Jobs she'd been putting off doing because she dreaded them, such as—Such as organizing the storeroom!

The storeroom *wasn't* air-conditioned, and after spending a few hours moving hundred-pound sacks of dry clay around, Thad should be more than happy to see the last of her.

Instead of diminishing her irritation, this idea seemed to add to it. She poured coffee into Thad's cup angrily, so that it sloshed over the rim into the saucer. This meant that she had to get a clean saucer from the cupboard, and she had to fight against the impulse to slam the cupboard door shut, but she made herself smile at Thad as she handed him his coffee and placed the creamer and sugar bowl within easy reach on the table in front of him.

Thad smiled his thanks in return.

"I brought a paint sprayer along," he said. "It's in my pickup. If you'd like, I can put the sealer on the walls."

"That would be fine—for a start."

Thad stirred sugar into his coffee, tasted it, and put his cup down, all the while eyeing her suspiciously, as if he'd read her mind. Or perhaps it was only that her conscience was troubling her.

"What else is on your agenda for today?" he inquired blandly.

"Nothing much really." Feeling guilty, Laura busied herself at the counter. "Just a few—uh, odds and ends."

CHAPTER FOUR

Nearly twelve hours later Laura had cause to wonder who had called whose bluff. Not only had Thad applied the sealer to the pine paneling and cleaned up the storeroom, he'd also painted the shutters at the shop windows and trimmed some low-hanging branches off the locust tree nearest the street so that her sign would be more visible to passersby.

And he'd done all these chores well and cheerfully. She had made the mistake of looking in on him while he was at work in the storeroom, and he'd actually been whistling!

The storeroom had been like an oven today, so he'd stripped off his T-shirt and tied a blue and white bandanna around his forehead as a makeshift sweatband. He'd been perspiring freely; his hair and beard were liberally coated with clay dust; and his skin was dust-streaked too. Beneath a fine, even layer of clay, his face was ruddy from heat and exertion, yet to Laura he'd never looked more attractive.

She'd stood just inside the door watching him, fascinated by the ease with which he handled the dead weight of the heavy sacks. His body was lean and hard, without an ounce of superfluous flesh; the muscles of his back and shoulders and chest were well defined. He was, she thought, graceful and beautiful.

When Thad saw her watching him he paused to flex his shoulders and stretch some of the kinks out of his back.

"Just call me the gray ghost," he joked, referring to the color of the clay that disguised his golden-brown skin.

"Would you like a cold drink?" she inquired. "I made some lemonade."

"Sounds great," said Thad, mopping his face with the bandanna, "but I'll finish up in here first." Inclining his head toward the half-dozen sacks of clay he'd aligned against the far wall, he asked, "How'd you manage to get 'em in here?"

"The truck driver who made the delivery brought the sacks in with a dolly, but he said that his contract didn't call for anything beyond curbside delivery, so he'd only stack them by the door."

"It's a good thing I insisted on helping you, isn't it, Laura?" Thad said laconically. "It's also fortunate that I'm used to toting canoes and camping gear over long portages."

She'd been flustered by the knowing light in his eyes, but she had managed to murmur a feeble agreement. As she left the storeroom, she'd heard Thad chuckling, amused by her hasty retreat. She'd wanted to run, but she'd forced herself to walk sedately along the hall to her studio.

By the time she'd reached the studio, she'd been so frustrated that she hadn't been able to keep from slamming the door, but if closing the door to her studio had shut out the sound of Thad's mocking laughter, it hadn't silenced the inner voice that taunted her for her inability to send him away.

If she really didn't want Thad around, the surest way to get him to leave would be to tell him calmly to get lost. That was simple, direct, and to the point.

What's more, she was sure that, despite his obstinacy, Thad would not ignore such a demand.

If the demand were genuine. *If* she made it.

The problem was, Laura was not at all certain she wanted Thad to leave. But she was even less certain that she could cope with the consequences of his staying.

Her one excursion into romance had ended in disaster. Even when Brian had worked up the courage to break their engagement, he hadn't had enough courage to be honest with her. Perhaps by then he hadn't cared enough, but his defection hadn't been clean or swift. It hadn't been merciful in any respect.

In retrospect Laura attributed much of Brian's callousness to his youth. They'd both been so very young; so hopeful and innocent.

Of course, it had all happened years ago. She was no longer haunted by memories of Brian. In fact, except for such general details as coloring and body build, she couldn't remember what Brian looked like. But because he had deserted her at a time when she had desperately needed his love and support, she remembered vividly how wounded she'd been when they'd said good-bye; how defeated she'd felt afterward.

In the intervening years she had picked herself up by her bootstraps and risen above the defeat. She was proud of that. And the wounds had healed, but the scars remained.

Brian's betrayal had eroded her fragile self-confidence. She'd been left questioning her own judgment, doubting her worth, mistrusting men—and with a peculiar sense of her own vulnerability. But the experience had also taught her a valuable lesson.

If she couldn't depend on those closest to her, if she couldn't rely on her father or Brian, it seemed unlikely that she could rely on anyone else. Therefore she had done her utmost to develop a protective shell of self-reliance.

For the most part this seemed to work. Certainly being independent had helped restore her self-respect. It was only now and again that she felt lonely—an awful, aching loneliness that casual friendships could not assuage.

Recently, for instance, she'd wished she had someone to share her happiness about the shop. Her defenses were down, and this was why she couldn't bear to think about what might happen if she continued seeing Thad. Not just now at any rate.

Seeking distraction from her troublesome thoughts, Laura uncovered the ball of clay on her worktable and turned her attentions to it.

She slammed the clay down on the wooden tabletop as hard as she could to force out any air pockets. She worked it between her fingers, folding and kneading the ball of clay as if it were dough, enjoying its honest earthy odor; enjoying the cool, damp, spongy feel of it in her hands. Gradually her thoughts became less frenzied, and her hard-won tranquillity was reflected in the way she handled the clay.

Smiling ruefully, Laura told herself that one good thing about working with clay was that it was therapeutic. Her work provided a much needed outlet for her emotions.

When Thad knocked at the studio door an hour later, she was still working with the clay. Her rebellious fingers had begun modeling a man's head, and she flushed when she recognized the striking similarity to Thad's strong features.

Hurriedly, before she answered the knock, she rolled the clay into a ball again. Finally, satisfied that she had obliterated the evidence of the turn her wayward thoughts had taken, she called, "Come in."

Thad opened the door enough to look in at her. "Excuse the interruption," he said, "but it's getting kind of late."

Laura glanced at her wristwatch and was stunned to see that it was nearly seven o'clock. "I'm glad you interrupted!" she exclaimed. "I should have turned the thermostat up half an hour ago."

While she got to her feet and crossed to the kiln, Thad came into the room. With Groucho scampering close on his heels, Thad wandered about, pausing to admire the porcelain ginger jars on the drying rack. There were three of the jars in graduated sizes, and Thad bent closer so that he could examine them at eye level.

"I like these," he said softly. "You're very talented, Laura."

More pleased by his praise than she cared to admit, Laura limited her reply to a negligent "Thanks." As she adjusted the thermostat, she remarked, "I wondered where Groucho was. He usually pesters me for his supper long before now."

"He's been helping me in the storeroom," Thad said dryly.

"Oh? How so?"

"Well, for one thing, he curls up by the door while he's watching me work."

"So?"

"So he makes a good doorstop."

Laughing, Laura turned to face Thad. "Did you want something else?" she asked.

Thad nodded. "I just wanted to let you know I'll be gone for a while hauling those tree limbs to the dump. After that, I thought I'd stop by my place and grab a shower, which means I should be back here by eight thirty or so to take you to dinner."

"Oh, yes," Laura said, hoping she sounded nonchalant. "Actually I meant to talk to you about that earlier."

"Why? Is there some problem?"

"Well, no, there's no problem, but I really shouldn't leave the kiln until I've finished the bisque-firing."

"How long will that take?"

"Several hours at least. It might be as late as midnight before I'm done here."

"I see." Thad leaned one shoulder against the window

casement and folded his arms across his chest, but the steely glint in his eyes belied his casual stance. "In other words you're trying to welsh on the agreement we made."

"No, I'm not," Laura objected. "I'd never do a thing like that—not intentionally anyway. It's only that this is the first time I've fired the kiln, and I don't want to take any chances with my pottery."

"Very well," Thad returned smoothly. "Since you won't leave, I'll bring our dinner here. What would you like? Chinese food? Pizza? Chicken?"

Laura shook her head more adamantly with each suggestion he made. She wished she could stop staring at him. She wished he were wearing his T-shirt. She wished he were a few years older, a bit closer to her age.

"I—uh—I'm not at all sure that would be wise," she began hesitantly. Then she saw the stubborn set of Thad's mouth, and she went on more firmly. "That is, I appreciate all the work you've done today. You've been a tremendous help, and I can't begin to tell you how grateful I am—"

"I don't want your gratitude, Laura," Thad broke in harshly.

"What *do* you want then?"

"Damn, but you're suspicious!" Shifting impatiently, Thad straightened away from the window and demanded, "How many times do I have to tell you that I want to have dinner with you—get to know you better?"

"And that's all?"

Thad shrugged. "That's all for now, and since there's nothing even remotely sinister about my plans for this evening, what are you worried about?"

"I'm worried about what comes later," Laura replied heatedly. "Maybe you'd be less eager to get to know me better if I told you that I don't sleep around!"

"Who the hell asked you to sleep around?" Glancing at Groucho, who had curled up on the windowsill, Thad gestured wildly with one arm as if he were waving at an invisible crowd of onlookers, and inquired, "Hey, Groucho, old buddy, did you hear anyone ask Laura if she'd sleep with them?"

Her face rosy with embarrassment, Laura insisted, "You know very well what I mean."

"You bet I do," Thad agreed flatly. "Among other things you've just insinuated that I'm easy."

"Of all the—" At a loss for words Laura faltered into silence. Then she saw the smile lurking in Thad's eyes, and she realized that he was teasing.

"Of course," he allowed, grinning lazily, "it had occurred to me that eventually our relationship might progress to a more intimate one. At the risk of offending you, Laura, I have to admit that if I found you in my bed, I wouldn't kick you out."

By now Laura was blushing so violently that her face felt as if it were on fire. "For heaven's sake, Thad," she cried. "Will you please, *please* be serious!"

"Okay, Laura, if that's what you want, we'll play it straight for a while. Will you go first, or shall I?"

Laura frowned. She was perplexed by Thad's unexpected concession until it dawned on her that he might have maneuvered her into an exchange of confidences.

"Wait a minute, Thad Bristol," she said. "If this is another one of your 'can't lose' deals, you can deal me out!"

"Christ! What does it take to convince you that I'm not some sort of villain?" Thad muttered disgustedly. His expression dark as a thundercloud, he stalked angrily toward the door, and Laura was dismayed to realize that she didn't want him to leave.

"Please, Thad," she called, her tone conciliatory.

He stopped in the doorway, swiveled around, and looked at her expectantly, waiting for her to continue.

"It's only that I wondered—"

"Go on," he prompted when she lapsed into silence.

"Well," she went on weakly, torn by indecision, "I wondered how you could afford to take so much time away from your business."

"That's one of the perks of being the boss. Besides, I just got back from my annual tour of duty as a guide up North, in Quetico Provincial Park, so I'm entitled to take it easy for a few days."

Laura smiled. "Do you consider what you've been doing today taking it easy?"

"Believe me, Laura, compared to guiding a pack of greenhorns over the Poohbah portage, today was a breeze. But I think what you really want to know is why I'd go to so much trouble for you when we've only just met."

"Yes," Laura agreed. "Yes, that is what I'd like to know. I mean, it's very kind of you to help out, but I can't help wondering—"

"About my motives."

Laura nodded eagerly. She had purposely left her question unfinished, and she was relieved that Thad had supplied the ending. She hadn't wanted to hurt his feelings, but she had more than a few doubts about him. Not only were her misgivings ungracious, she'd have sounded downright paranoid if she'd had to state them in so many words.

"I'll confess I do have one ulterior motive," said Thad. "I had hoped to spirit you away from here tomorrow or Friday. I thought, if we got the shop ready for your opening, you might like to go canoeing with me, maybe do a little sight-seeing."

"But why me, Thad? Trina says you have your choice of the eligible young women in town, so why me?"

"I have this theory, Laura," Thad answered steadily. "I've thought about it for years, and I even have a name for it. I call it Bristol's Law, but I've never tried to tell

48

anyone about it before, so I'm not sure I can explain it. Not so you'll understand."

"You'll never know unless you try me."

"All right then. Here goes." Thad inhaled deeply. "Do you know how sometimes you read a poem or hear a song or see a sunset—or a stretch of white water or a piece of pottery—and something very rare and magical happens? You feel as if you're in perfect harmony with nature. You feel at peace with yourself. You feel spiritually refreshed, and so enriched by the experience, it's as if the whole were greater than the sum of its parts."

"I think I follow you, except for that last bit," Laura remarked tentatively. "I'm not sure I understand that."

Thad grinned sheepishly. "I'm not putting this at all well. I don't mean to sound pompous or preachy, but I guess what I want to say is, sometimes all you have to do is *see* someone and you get the same sort of feeling about them. You sense that, if you were with that person, one and one would add up to a lot more than two. It's as if, if you were together, you might transcend yourselves and create an infinity of ones. You might even become inviolable, like a number that's indivisible except by itself. A perfect entity—"

Thad stopped abruptly. For a few moments he was silent, then he shook his head and laughed self-consciously.

"God!" he exclaimed. "You must think I'm an idiot. I wanted to sound poetic, and I sounded like an accountant."

"Don't say that! I don't think you're an idiot at all, and you sounded very poetic . . . very idealistic."

The cynic in Laura cautioned that Bristol's Law was nothing more than an elaborate line, but everything feminine in her responded to Thad's explanation, and in this instance, the woman in her had won out.

"The truth is," she confided, "I can't remember *ever* being so idealistic."

"Will you answer a question for me then?"

Laura glanced at Thad inquiringly. They were separated by the width of the studio, but she felt as if he'd embraced her. His eyes were intent, yet they were warmly appealing.

"That depends on the question," she answered warily.

"Naturally," Thad countered smoothly.

"What is it you want to know?"

"I'd like to know what happened to make you so suspicious of men," Thad said gently. "Somewhere along the way, someone must have hurt you terribly—"

"Perhaps someday I'll tell you about it," Laura said coolly.

"But not just now?"

"No, not just now." She smiled at Thad, but her smile was overbright. "I will answer your first question though. If you still want to buy me dinner, I could go for some pizza."

"The dinner offer is still good." Thad smiled crookedly. "If you don't trust me enough to open up with me, I guess that answer will have to do. I can't pass up the chance to prove my theory, but I'll let you set the pace, Laura—for now."

His protectiveness made her feel secure, but his choice of words rankled.

"I've been on my own for nearly fifteen years," she retorted. "I'm quite used to making my own decisions and setting my own pace. I don't need your permission."

"Sure, Laura. I'll try to keep that in mind."

With his easy concession Thad let her know in no uncertain terms that he thought she had overreacted. Her spirits plummeting, Laura acknowledged that he had also snatched the wind from her sails and stolen the initiative.

CHAPTER FIVE

Thad was as good as his word. He hauled the tree limbs away, made a side trip to his own place to shower and change clothes, and by eight thirty he was back at Laura's house with pizza, a tray of antipasto, and a dusty bottle of Lambrusco.

As he uncorked the bottle Thad said, "A connoisseur would tell you Lambrusco is a pedestrian choice and that it's best drunk when it's young, but I never could resist buying a wine when there's dust on the bottle. That little hint of age adds to the wine's mystique."

Laura took a sip of the Lambrusco and immediately followed it with another. "Pedestrian or not, I like it," she announced.

"Good." Thad nodded approvingly. "So do I."

"But tell me," she said, "is there a moral to the story about your affinity for dusty wine bottles?"

Giving her a villainous ogle, Thad drawled, "I guess it's just my way of saying that I can't think of a more potent combination than young wine in a vintage bottle. Can you?"

"Not at the moment," she laughingly retorted. "But give me time and I'll come up with several."

The next afternoon, after the carpet had been delivered, Thad helped Laura move the display gondolas into the shop and install the stock.

Later he returned to the studio and went through the

pieces of pottery she had discarded, wondering why she'd thrown them away.

"What's wrong with this one?" he asked, holding up one of the vases.

"Turn it over and you'll see," Laura replied.

Thad upended the vase and studied it from various angles, but the irregularity in its foot was invisible to his untrained eye. Laura had to point out the flaw before Thad could see it.

"God," he marveled. "You're really a perfectionist."

When Thad saw the clay figure of Groucho she'd finished that morning on the drying rack, he grinned as if he knew that his chance comment about the cat's making a good doorstop had inspired her, and when he saw the elephant-foot umbrella stand, he laughed outright.

On Friday with everything in readiness for the opening of Powell's Gallery of Gifts the following Monday, Thad spirited Laura away from the shop as he'd promised he would.

She packed a picnic lunch, and they drove through the lush green countryside, aimlessly following winding back roads and finally stopping when they came to an idyllic grassy glade on the shore of Snowbank Lake.

Thunderstorms had put an end to the heat wave the night before, and although a few leaves on the maple trees bore traces of the russets and golds of fall, it was a glorious summer's day. The temperature had moderated, the sky was a crisp rainwashed blue, and the sun sparkled on the sapphire waters of the lake.

After they'd eaten, they walked along the edge of the lake until they came to a narrow white-sand beach. The water was enticingly clear, and when Laura kicked off her sandals and waded along the shore, she found that the water felt like warm silk against her skin. She would have enjoyed a swim, but when Thad offered her the choice of swimming or canoeing, she opted for canoeing.

Surprised by her choice, Thad asked, "Didn't you bring a bathing suit?"

"I'm wearing one under my clothes. It's just that I've never been canoeing, and I've always wanted to try it."

She'd answered with bogus enthusiasm, but the truth was that she was strangely reluctant to strip down to her bikini now that she was alone with Thad.

As they were returning to the pickup Laura chided herself for her foolishness. Her bikini was really quite modest as bikinis went, and she knew she had the sort of softly rounded figure that men found appealing. She'd thought she had overcome the last remnants of self-consciousness about her body ages ago, but Thad's admiring gaze made her intensely aware of the frankly feminine contours of her breasts and hips.

Vanity was not one of her failings, but when Thad looked at her, she was glad that her waist was trim, her derriere neatly rounded, and her thighs sleek and nicely tapered.

When they arrived at the pickup, Laura watched while Thad unloaded the canoe. He tilted the craft, keel up, on one end, and ducked under, centering himself beneath it. Within a matter of seconds he was balancing it effortlessly on his shoulders.

"Can I help?" Laura asked belatedly.

"You can bring the paddles and life vests if you'd like," Thad replied.

He carried the canoe to the water's edge and launched it as easily as if it were a toy, and she marveled at the graceful economy with which he handled it. It struck her that, with his dark hair and Gallic features, if Thad had lived a century or two before, he might have been one of the lusty band of French-Canadian fur traders who had plied the thousands of miles of wilderness canoe trails in the Great Lakes region. When she said as much to Thad,

53

he laughed and said dryly, "I take that as a compliment, Laura, but I'd never have made it as a voyageur."

"Why not?"

"For one thing, I'm too tall," Thad replied. "The average voyageur wasn't much taller than you. They were five feet six, maybe five-seven at most, and they were also very stocky. This canoe isn't that heavy. It weighs only about seventy-five or eighty pounds, but in a routine working day the voyageurs had to portage anywhere from a few hundred yards to nine miles while carrying a couple of ninety-pound bales of furs on their backs. Some of them were able to carry more than that, so they had to be as strong as bulls."

Thad steadied the canoe while she climbed in and moved cautiously to the bow. When she was seated, with one lithe movement he shoved the craft away from the beach and stepped into the stern.

As Thad paddled smoothly toward deeper water, he went on with the story. "Most of the voyageurs didn't survive very long on the job, but contrary to the Hollywood version of the story, the majority of them weren't killed by Indians or wild animals. Injuries caused the greatest number of fatalities and, tough as they were, such small things as insects were probably their biggest problem. At certain seasons of the year they had to coat themselves with goose grease to ward off the mosquitoes and no-see-ums."

"Ugh!" Laura wrinkled her nose with distaste. "I've been thinking of them wearing fringed buckskins and wide sashes and plumes in their caps—you know, like Pasquinel in Michener's *Centennial*—but that doesn't sound terribly romantic."

"No, it doesn't," Thad agreed. "They must have been fairly rank even before the grease turned rancid! But still, they did dress as colorfully as rock stars, and from what history tells us, they were even more famous for their singing and hell-raising abilities than they were for their strength and endurance, so it would have been interesting to have traveled with them

"Incidentally," Thad said, digressing, "you don't have to keep changing the side you're paddling on. I can set our course with my paddle."

Laura nodded, and after watching her for a few moments, Thad continued his narrative as if there had been no interruption.

"I remember reading a quote from one of the voyageurs when I was a boy," he said. "It went, 'No portage was ever too long for me. Fifty songs could I sing. I have saved the lives of ten voyageurs. Have had twelve wives and six running dogs. I spent all my money in pleasure. Were I young again, I should spend my life the same way over. There is no life so happy as a voyageur's life.'" Smiling, Thad added, "Even allowing for a certain amount of exaggeration, I have to admit that *does* sound romantic to me."

"No doubt," Laura remarked sourly. "Especially the part about the twelve wives."

Chuckling, Thad countered, "You'll notice, though, that he put his wives ahead of his running dogs and spending all his money in pleasure."

Laura laughed, but she chose not to reply. Instead, she trailed one hand in the water and watched the tree-studded shoreline drifting by.

After a while, Thad said softly, "This country must have been something to see in those days, before everybody and their brother discovered the wilderness."

Surprised by the proprietorial note in Thad's voice, Laura glanced at him over her shoulder. He, too, was watching the scenery gliding silently by, and his face was fiercely proud, as if he were personally responsible for the pristine beauty of the country that surrounded them.

Her own voice was subdued as she said, "You really love it here, don't you?"

"Yes, I do," Thad admitted quietly. "In my opinion anything north of the Laurentian Divide is about as close to paradise as a man can get on this earth."

"Is there some spot that's a special favorite of yours?"

"There is one place on the Cascade River," Thad replied. "My dad used to take me there when I was a boy, and you wouldn't believe how plentiful the wildlife was. Around here it's not uncommon to see beaver and moose and timber wolves, but up there we saw otter and mink and eagles."

For a few seconds Thad was silent. Then he sighed and exclaimed, "Those were the days, Laura! Instead of air mattresses we'd sleep on beds of reindeer moss or balsam boughs, and we had one campsite where the forest floor was literally paved with lady's slippers. In the spring the swampy areas would be covered with marsh marigolds, and there were spots in the woods where we'd come across whole acres of violets. Sometimes we'd go for a week or more without seeing anyone else. On clear nights we'd watch for the northern lights, and the skies were as thick with stars as the fields were with wildflowers, and on still days the silence seemed absolute."

Laura was astonished that one moment Thad could be factual, and the next so unabashedly sentimental. Taken aback by his lyrical description, she rested her paddle on her knees and gazed across the water at the trees on the shoreline.

Even before that Friday afternoon at Snowbank Lake, she had suspected that Thad could be full of surprises, and in the weeks that followed, this suspicion was confirmed.

She was surprised at how similar their tastes were and at how much they found to talk about. She was impressed by Thad's rare ability to laugh at himself, by his shrewdness, by the consideration he showed her.

They saw each other several times a week, and although

for the most part, they were remarkably compatible, they did have one argument over her refusal to have dinner with him at a restaurant in Ely.

"What's wrong, Laura?" Thad jeered. "Are you ashamed to be seen with me?"

"It's *me* I'm ashamed of," she answered tartly. "If we go someplace so public, I'm afraid I might be arrested for contributing to your delinquency."

"Fat chance!" Thad grimaced derisively. "Before you could be arrested, you'd have to do something illegal, and I can't even get you to be even slightly immoral."

Smiling blithely, Laura returned, "Well, sweetie, that's the price you pay for keeping company with an older woman. But if it's action you want, there doesn't seem to be a shortage of candidates who'd be more than happy to provide it. And you have my blessings!"

As soon as she'd made this rejoinder, they both broke out laughing because there was a sizable element of truth in it. Wherever they went, women of all ages swarmed around Thad like so many bees to a blossom.

"Okay," Thad said when their laughter had abated. "Now tell me the real reason you won't go to the Embers with me. It can't be that you don't like steak, because I know you do, and they have the best T-bones in Saint Louis County there."

"You're right," Laura conceded. "I do like steak, but I don't like gossip, and I like it even less when I'm the one who's being gossiped about. In a town this small if we're seen having dinner together, there's bound to be talk."

"But look at the bright side," Thad countered, smiling. "It might help your business if we gave the gossips something to talk about. Lots of people subscribe to the notion that any publicity is good publicity."

"I know," said Laura, "but I'm not one of them."

Her adamancy put an end to the argument, and afterward Thad appeared to respect her wishes. He didn't try to persuade her to attend events in Ely with him, and she was amazed at how agreeable he could be.

Thad behaved almost like a brother toward her, and she found this reassuring. She began to feel safe with him. She began to think she might have misinterpreted his interest in her. She began to trust him.

It was not until they had been seeing each other for several weeks that Thad's brotherly attitude began to pall.

He didn't make any passes. He didn't pressure her to allow him intimacies she was not prepared to grant. He hardly even kissed her. He treated her carefully, as if she were as fragile as blown glass, as if he were afraid she might shatter, and she began to wonder what it would be like if he were to kiss her—not the tantalizing, all too brief embraces with which he customarily said good night, but *really* kiss her.

Had Thad planned for that to happen? Laura wondered. Was that why he'd rationed his affections so strictly?

Laura had no way of knowing, but by the first week in September, after they'd shared more than half a dozen cozy suppers for two, after a month of Sundays spent picnicking and canoeing and hiking through the woods with Thad, his behavior was as infuriatingly restrained as ever.

Her decorum, on the other hand, was beginning to wear a bit thin. She badly needed someone to talk to about Thad, and it came as a relief when Trina Gunderson paid her a visit one morning and revealed that she had discovered that Laura and Thad were dating.

"How did you find out?" Laura demanded. "Did Thad tell you?"

"He never said a word," Trina replied staunchly. "In fact, Phil and I have hardly even seen Thad since Kit's birthday."

"Then how did you know?"

"Elementary, my dear Laura! Thad's pickup is parked on the street in front of our house several nights a week and most Sundays. It's not us he's coming to see, and I know he wouldn't be calling on Mrs. Carruthers that often. Since you're our only remaining neighbor, it had to be you."

Trina had been smiling, but now she frowned. "What puzzles me, Laura, is why you're so secretive about seeing him."

"In case it's escaped your attention, Trina, Thad is younger than I am."

"Oh, well, eight years." Trina shrugged dismissively. "That's nothing."

"I notice you have it all figured out though."

Trina colored. "I'll admit it took me awhile to get used to the idea of Thad going out with you—and vice versa. Then Phil pointed out that there's nothing unique about a woman seeing a younger man. If Thad were eight years older than you, I wouldn't have given it a second thought."

"But I'm the one who's older, Trina. You did give it a second thought, and so would most people. The truth is, they'd be less understanding than you and Phil."

"I don't see why!" Trina exclaimed indignantly. "I think you and Thad are wonderfully well suited to each other. Besides, Thad's always been wise beyond his years. Why, when he was only a junior in high school, one of the teachers made the mistake of betting Thad's science class fifty dollars that no one could hit a golf ball a mile. Thad asked if that included the distance the ball would roll after it had landed, and when Mr. Crosby said yes, Thad thought it over and decided to take him up on his wager, provided Thad could name the time and place.

"To make a long story short," Trina said with a laugh, "that fall when Shagawa Lake had frozen over, the class came down to the lake, and Thad won the bet. Since the ice created so little friction, the ball actually traveled more than two miles before it finally stopped rolling."

Smiling, Laura inquired, "Did Mr. Crosby pay Thad?"

"Sure he did! There was no way he could squirm out of the deal—not when the whole class had witnessed it. So, Laura, you can see for yourself that not only has Thad had a good deal of responsibility, he's also had a lot of experience. He's very mature for twenty-five."

Trina didn't actually say that Laura seemed younger than her age. She didn't tell Laura that her concern about public opinion was less adult than Trina would have expected, but that accusation was implicit in her comments.

"The only person who might give you a hard time about seeing Thad is his mother," Trina confided. "He's the apple of her eye, and while Aunt Dorothy claims she wants to see him settle down, if she had her druthers, he'd marry some sweet young thing she could lead around by the nose."

"If Thad's mother should find out about us," Laura said flatly, "I'd appreciate your telling her that she needn't worry on my account. The subject of marriage hasn't come up, nor is it likely to. Thad and I are good friends, nothing more."

"And the moon is made of green cheese, and in six months or so, I'm going to find a baby under a cabbage leaf!" Trina laughed gaily and patted her slightly rounded abdomen as she exclaimed, "For heaven's sake, Laura, you don't have to lie to me. If you weren't serious about Thad, you wouldn't fret about the age difference—you wouldn't care if he were twenty years younger. I've been in love myself. I still love Phil, so I recognize the symptoms, and lady, you've got it bad!"

"Stop it, Trina!" Laura clapped her hands over her ears, underscoring her refusal to listen to any more of Trina's nonsense. Her voice shook with the force of her denial as she cried, "Thad and I are friends, that's all. *Friends!* Period. End of report. Do I make myself clear?"

Still laughing, Trina agreed. "Sure, Laura. Whatever you say."

But her laughter told Laura that Trina was humoring her. Obviously, from Trina's point of view, the lady was protesting too much.

CHAPTER SIX

The opening of Laura's shop had gone well, and sales were brisk. If the afternoons continued to be so hectic, she would have to find part-time help soon. She had made arrangements with craftsmen who supplied the store with custom-made candles and leather goods, and she was negotiating with one artist who did beautifully authentic wildlife paintings and another who worked with stained glass.

She was busy planning improvements, finding new merchandise for the shop, and creating her own, so she should have had enough on her mind, but thoughts of Thad intruded at the most unlikely times.

In the midst of talking with a customer or writing up a sale, she would think of Thad's smile or of the devilry in his amber eyes. She would remember something he'd said; the rough timbre of his voice; the sound of his laughter. She might recall the way his hair grew at the back of his neck, or one of his mannerisms.

When they talked, for instance, he had an endearing way of cocking his head to one side. All the while he was listening to her, he looked at her in a way that made her feel very special, as if she were the only thing that mattered to him.

One evening when she was supposed to be entering a column of figures in the ledger, she found herself listing the pros and cons of seeing Thad. Below the PROS heading, the ledger page was blank, while that beneath the CONS was full, but some perverse part of her would not be swayed by her own logic.

On another evening she was working at her wheel when something jogged her memory, and she recalled the way Thad walked—silently and with a predatory grace. She thought of how he'd looked when he was paddling the canoe. She envisioned the fine coordination evident in the slightest gesture he made; the supple play of muscles in his shoulders; the crisp dark hair on his chest; the way the sunlight burnished his skin, shone on his hair, and seemed to gather in his eyes.

Try as she might to banish thoughts of Thad, she couldn't get him out of her mind. There were days when she could think of nothing else, and bad as the days were, the nights were worse. That was when images of Thad's kissing her, of his touching her, making love to her, were most disturbing.

She would lie in her darkened room and try to concentrate on other things, but the seductive images persisted. Sometimes they tormented her so, she abandoned her bed and prowled around the house until she could barely keep her eyes open. But when she managed to fall asleep, thoughts of Thad lingered like an erotic mantra that she couldn't elude even in dreams.

On nights like that she was grateful she had a single bed. A double bed would have seemed so empty.

All of her anticipation should have prepared Laura for the moment when Thad actually kissed her, but it didn't. And afterward she realized that nothing could have prepared her for it.

Thad's kisses were a drug to which she had no immunity; they were like a jolt of liquor for which she hadn't built up a tolerance. One kiss was all it took, and she was hooked. After one touch of his lips—one heady, intoxicating taste of his mouth—she was hopelessly, helplessly addicted to him.

She should have said good night to him at the front door that night as she usually did. If she had, he wouldn't have protested. It had been a long and trying day, and both of them were travel-weary.

They'd left for Grand Marais at the crack of dawn so that she would have time to set up her booth before the art fair opened. Thad had helped her with the display and waited patiently for her all day and, since she couldn't leave the booth unattended, he'd even brought her lunch and dinner.

By the time they arrived back in Ely, it was after midnight, and it had seemed that the least she could do was invite him in for a nightcap.

Having bent the rules to that extent, she shouldn't have sat beside him in the glider. She should have sat in the basket-weave chair across from him as she had the first time he'd been in the house.

Was that why he'd kissed her? Had he taken her departure from routine as a sign that she was ready to advance to the next step in their relationship?

She should have moved away from him when he'd put his arms around her.

Why hadn't she? Was she so hungry for affection? And if she was, was it Thad's affection she craved, or would any reasonably presentable man's have done just as well?

She should have moved away from him after his first kiss, but his arms were warm and strong, and his mouth was hot and exciting. She had been battling against the magnetic pull of Thad's appeal for so long that it seemed as if she had been battling it forever, and she was tired of denying her own instincts.

Somehow it seemed only natural to run her fingers through his hair, to cradle his head in her hands and invite him to kiss her again, and in the instant he did, she was utterly, irretrievably lost, for now it was Thad who set the pace. He pulled her even closer to him and assumed command of the kiss, and when her lips softened and opened beneath the tender persuasion of his, the sweet domination of his mouth seemed natural too.

He touched the tip of his tongue to hers, invading her mouth slowly, as if he savored the slightest nuance of her surrender, and even as he deepened his invasion of her mouth, he shifted his weight, pressing her downward and following after her so that they were half reclining in the glider. She felt the cushions at her back give beneath her as he moved over her, blanketing her with the weight of his body, and suddenly they were lying mouth to mouth, breast to breast, their hips and thighs touching, bound by a single desperate need, and mere compliance was not enough.

Thad's body was hard and delectably warm. Her body was languid, liquid with desire as she melted into his embrace. She held him tightly in her arms while her body conformed to the demanding thrust of his. She welcomed the blissful ravishment of his tongue, fanning the flames of his ardor with her own passionate response, and for Laura time seemed to telescope. The rest of the world spun away, leaving them tangled together, stranded in a molten sea of sensation.

Laura was not certain where Thad's second kiss ended and the next one began, nor did she know when her blouse parted company with the waistband of her skirt. She knew only that all at once Thad was caressing the bare skin of her back. His hands moved over her slowly, alternately molding her closer to him and learning the secrets of her body. His hands explored the satiny texture of her skin and traced the fine bones of her spine. Then they were trailing over her shoulder blades, wandering over her rib cage.

With the same deliberate slowness he eased one arm

from underneath her. He found the softness of her breasts and fondled them gently, teasing and coaxing the nipples to tautness with a knowing delicacy that left her trembling at his expertise.

But if his expertise was exciting, it was also alarming. She was, she recognized, way out of her depth. Her fascination with Thad might have caused her to dream about his lovemaking, but there was a vast difference between reality and fantasy.

In her fantasies she hadn't lost her composure, not for a moment. She had been cool and sophisticated. She had been in control.

In reality she was overwhelmed and more than a little frightened by her unbridled response to Thad.

Laura no longer clung to Thad. She tried to wedge her hands between them, attempting to push him away, and when that didn't work, she let her arms fall stiffly to her sides.

Twisting her mouth free of his, she gasped, "Please, Thad. No more."

Thad tensed with surprise. For a moment he remained immobile, wondering if he might have misunderstood her. Then he rolled away from her. Bracing himself on one elbow, he stared down at her face, searching for verification that her needs rivaled his own.

He had not withdrawn his other hand, and her heart was racing beneath his palm. He circled her nipple with his fingertips, rolling the sensitive bud with the ball of his thumb, and when he saw that the expression in her eyes was soft and unfocused, he smiled.

"Why not, Laura?" he inquired thickly. "You want more. You want it as much as I do."

As if to prove this contention, Thad lowered his head and captured her mouth with his. While the tip of his tongue darted along the tremulous outline of her lips to pry them apart, his hand swept over her body, tracing the curves from breast to belly to thigh in a long, delicious caress. He felt the involuntary shiver of excitement that rippled through her, and his own excitement grew.

Wrapping his arms around her, he turned her onto her side and moved his hips against hers so that she could feel his arousal. He rubbed his cheek against hers, so rough in his urgency that his beard scraped her skin, and buried his face in the hollow of her neck.

"God, how I need you," he groaned hoarsely. His body was tautly drawn, throbbing with the immediacy of his passion. "Let me love you, Laura."

"No, Thad. I can't! I'm sorry, but I just can't."

He heard the desperation in her voice, but it was not until he felt the sob that shook her that somehow he found the strength to lever himself away from her.

In one lithe movement he was on his feet, crossing to the porch railing. He leaned against the railing for support, his hands closing around it and knotting into fists, grasping it so tightly that his nails dug into the thick layers of paint that coated the wood. His breathing was ragged, and he gulped in deep drafts of the cool night air as he fought for control.

"I'm sorry," Laura repeated miserably, her voice almost inaudible.

"*You're* sorry!" Thad laughed harshly.

Ignoring his interruption, she continued more strongly. "It was wrong to ask you to come in tonight. I realize now that it was a mistake. It was selfish of me to lead you on—"

Thad swiveled around and gave her a scoffing glance. "I don't believe you were leading me on. I think you intended to go through with it."

"Believe what you want if it makes you feel better."

"It doesn't."

Laura closed her eyes to conceal the mist of tears that had formed there. "Well, then," she began diffidently, "I don't know what to say—"

This hesitant beginning was enough to snap Thad's tightly leashed temper. He slammed his fist into the railing so forcefully that he felt the impact of the blow all the way to the base of his skull.

Laura leaped to her feet and was at his side in an instant. "Your hand!" she cried. She reached out to touch Thad, but he pulled sharply away from her.

"Forget my hand," he muttered. "I don't want your concern any more than I wanted your gratitude. And don't ask me what I do want! After what almost happened between us, you damn well know the answer to that one."

"You want me," Laura said quietly. "You want us to be lovers."

"Very good!" Thad cheered abrasively. Then, glaring at her, he growled, "Dammit, Laura! At least tell me why you changed your mind in the middle of things."

"I'm not sure I know why," she murmured, lying without compunction.

"Was it something I did? Something I said?"

"No, Thad. Honestly. It had nothing to do with you."

"Now *that* takes the cake!" Thad's expression was incredulous. "Of *course*, it had something to do with me. Considering the circumstances, I'd say it has quite a lot to do with me."

"Not necessarily," she contradicted him coolly. "The same thing would have happened no matter who I'd been with."

"Would it?" Thad smiled sardonically. "Are you trying to tell me you get your kicks turning men on, then short-circuiting them at the last minute?"

Laura's face felt as if it were on fire, but she rose to the challenge in Thad's tawny eyes. Her own stalwart smoky-blue gaze never wavered as she said, "You know perfectly well that's not what I meant."

"Well, what did you mean then?"

"I—uh—it's a personal matter."

"Do you think I don't know that?" Thad asked evenly. "You have to trust someone, Laura, so why not trust me? Maybe we haven't known each other very long, but I've already learned a helluva lot about you. I know you don't like anchovies on your pizza or sugar in your coffee. I know that you bite your fingernails when you're anxious. I know that you enjoy bluegrass and jazz. You admire Barbara Jordan and Georgia O'Keefe and Dolly Parton, and although you're not basically the outdoor type, you've been a good sport about going canoeing and hiking. Probably that's because you're still embarrassed about the age difference between us, and you'd prefer that it didn't become public knowledge that we're seeing each other. And that's a funny inconsistency, because in so many ways you're not at all conventional."

Thad paused for a few moments, as if he were considering what he should say next. A ghost of a smile touched the corners of his mouth, and his voice was soft, soothing, oddly mesmerizing, as he went on.

"This is going to sound immodest, but so be it. I've felt the way you tremble when I touch you, Laura. I've seen the way your pulse quickens when I look at you."

His eyes relinquished their hold on hers to stray over her face and settle on the warm, pulsing hollows at the base of her throat. He had lulled her into complacency with trivialities, but now he was probing more deeply, peeling away the layers of the uncaring facade with which she disguised the truth.

Relentlessly Thad continued. "I'm aware that you're attracted to me—more attracted than you care to admit. And that scares the hell out of you because you need to feel in control."

Laura tried to turn away from him. She wanted to avoid hearing his analysis of her character, but he prevented her, holding onto her with his hands on her shoulders, forcing her to listen to him, forcing her to confront herself.

"You're a very private person, and I realize that you regard my intrusion into your affairs as a nuisance, but I don't take it personally." Thad smiled cryptically. "Since you sleep in a single bed, I presume that the last thing you want is a man in your life."

He was approaching the heart of the matter, and Laura broke in stiffly, "You're not overeager to give up your freedom either. Is that why you bother with me? Are you so positive that I won't pressure you for marriage?"

"The truth hurts, doesn't it, love?" Thad's voice was silky with confidence, but his eyes were shuttered and unfathomable as he said, "I think you know why I 'bother' with you."

For a moment, Laura was dumbfounded. Then comprehension dawned and she replied shortly, "Oh, yes. I'd forgotten about Bristol's Law."

"That's right." Thad nodded. "I still believe in it, you see."

His hands were outspread at the small of her back and his arms were crushing her to the implacable hardness of his body, but Laura didn't struggle to break his hold on her. *I will not give him the satisfaction of knowing how he affects me*, she vowed silently.

Aloud, she said, "There's one glaring flaw in your theory, Thad. By your own admission we met just after you'd returned from a month in the wilderness. Did you ever stop to consider that after being out of circulation for that length of time, your judgment could have been impaired? Most any woman you'd happened to meet would have looked awfully good to you."

"Granted." Thad smiled drolly. "But I'd actually gotten home the night before Kit's party, Laura. You weren't the first woman I saw. By the time we met, I wasn't exactly suffering from sexual deprivation."

Laura had known all along that Thad was an experienced lover. Everything about him virtually shrieked

70

that he'd forgotten more about women than most men ever learned. But at his disclosure that he'd spent the night before their meeting with another woman, a painful stab of emotion that felt suspiciously like jealousy ripped through her. Part of her wanted to stay in Thad's arms. Part of her wanted to beg him for reassurance that she was the only woman who meant anything to him. But another part wanted to strike out at Thad, to hurt him as he had hurt her.

Somehow she wriggled free of his hold on her. He did not try to stop her when she moved away, but she had managed to take only a few shaky steps when her knees gave way, and she collapsed into the glider.

"Laura . . ." Thad said her name huskily, as if he had deciphered the emotional turbulence in the stormy blue of her eyes. "I know you think I'm insensitive—"

"No. I don't think that."

He sat in the chair opposite her, so close that his knees brushed hers.

"Then why not tell me what the trouble is," he prompted. "If it doesn't serve any other purpose, at least talking about it might help you to define your own feelings."

Laura hesitated, but only for an instant. "Perhaps you're right, Thad," she mused. "Perhaps I should tell you why I don't want to get involved—not with you, not with anyone. I've tried playing hard to get, and I've tried playing easy to get, and nothing I've done seems to make any difference, so maybe it's time to play it straight. If I did that, you might understand how hopeless it is to go on seeing me. Maybe I owe you that much—"

"You owe me *nothing,* Laura! It's yourself you should be honest with."

"Please, Thad, if you insist upon hearing my long sad story, spare me the clichés." She tried to smile at him, but her eyes were wintry. "You've already guessed a good part of it."

71

Thad nodded. "You had an unhappy love affair."

"That's right, except that it wasn't really an affair. Brian and I were engaged to be married, but we were never really intimate."

"What caused the break-up? Was he unfaithful?"

"No. Not physically, at any rate. You might say that we broke up because of philosophical differences."

Frowning skeptically, Thad leaned toward her and took her hands in his.

"Laura, if two people love each other, they don't let matters of principle come between them."

"Oh, yes, Thad. Sometimes they do. Sometimes they can't help it. Sometimes things happen to people. Events catch up with them and take over their lives, and they're forced to take a stand. And if the people they love don't agree with them, it can lead to a lot of bitterness. Too much bitterness."

"And something like this happened to you and Brian?"

"Yes." Laura drew in a deep, steadying breath. "I became a . . . a statistic." Although her hands were encompassed in Thad's warm grasp, her fingers felt icy. In a low, tormented voice she said, "I was sexually assaulted."

Thad went pale beneath his tan. "You were *what*?"

"I was raped."

"My God, Laura! I had no idea—"

Thad's grip on her hands tightened so convulsively that her fingers grew bloodlessly numb. She watched him closely, searching for signs that he was repelled by her or embarrassed for her, but she saw only shock and concern.

"Please, forgive me for prying." He spoke in a horrified whisper. "If you'd rather not talk about it—"

"No. I've told you this much, so you might as well know the rest." Laura lifted her chin proudly. "Anyway, as it turned out, being assaulted was just the beginning of the nightmare. In a way the aftermath was even more traumatic."

"You pressed charges?"

"That's right, and it was as if *I* were the one on trial. It was all very textbook. The man—who assaulted me— was an old family friend. He was well-known and widely respected, and the burden of proof fell upon me. My father—"

Laura faltered momentarily. Just mentioning her father was enough to revive the awful jumble of emotions she'd felt all those years ago. The outrage. The humiliation. The hurt and pain and guilt. She'd felt guilty because she had gone against her father's wishes; her father had made her feel guilty for having been a victim.

Squaring her shoulders with determination, she went on. "My father wanted me to keep it quiet. We lived in a small town, you see, and he was concerned about what the neighbors would think. Oh, he said he was concerned for me, but the truth was, he was ashamed. He didn't want anyone to know what had happened.

"He told me there'd be gossip. He said there'd be rumors and that my reputation would be ruined. He made it clear that if even *he* had doubts about my story, if even he believed that somehow I must be to blame and that I must have done *something* to encourage the man, everyone else would feel the same way. He warned me how it would be, but I felt morally bound to report the crime to the police. I mean—well, if I *hadn't* gone to the police and the man had ever attacked another girl, I'd have felt partly responsible."

"How old were you, Laura?" Thad inquired gently.

"Not quite eighteen."

"Yet you testified against him!" Thad exclaimed admiringly. "That was a very courageous thing to do."

"No, Thad. It wasn't brave at all. Mostly I wanted to retaliate. I was prepared to testify because I wanted him to be punished for what he'd done to me, but the case never came to trial. At the arraignment the man saw how

73

incriminating the physical evidence was, and when he realized that it wouldn't be my word against his, he committed suicide." Laura shook her head ruefully. "He left a note implicating me, and that was when things really got unpleasant."

"Your father believed the note," Thad surmised gruffly.

"I don't know. I'm not sure he believed it." Laura cleared her throat. "I'd prefer to think he didn't. My father was terribly old-fashioned and very proud, and I suppose what was most important to him was that everyone else seemed to believe it."

"Even Brian?"

"No, not Brian. We'd grown up together, and he knew me too well to believe I had invited the attack. He knew I was far too prudish to suddenly depart from the straight and narrow. He knew that in many ways I was my father's daughter. I guess, in the final analysis, he was a victim too."

"Of the old double standard."

"And of gossip," Laura added.

"He couldn't take the heat?"

"No, he couldn't," she replied woodenly. "Not when so many of his friends believed the worst about me. At first Brian challenged them, but after a while I think he began wondering if they might be telling the truth. We drifted apart. He called less and less often, and before I left town, I offered to give him back his ring, and he took it."

"Did you ever see him again?"

"Yes. Once. About a year later, he came to my apartment in Saint Paul and made a pass of his own."

Thad's grip on her hands tightened painfully, but Laura hardly noticed. She felt only a merciful numbness as she continued. "He'd been drinking, and things got rather difficult, but I finally managed to get through to him that I wasn't interested in sleeping with him. Before he left, I asked him why he'd done it, and he told me that my willingness to make the rape public was . . . not nice. He accused me of being an exhibitionist."

"So he abandoned you too," Thad cried angrily. "Lousy bastard! I'd like to punch his face for him."

"Please, Thad, don't," Laura pleaded. "You must understand that Brian was very young. He wasn't much older than I."

"Youth is no excuse," Thad retorted grimly. "Dammit, Laura. After what he did to you, how can you defend him? I wish I'd known you then. If I'd been there, you wouldn't have been so alone. I'd never have deserted you—"

Withdrawing one hand from Thad's grip, Laura laid it against his mouth, silencing him.

"I know you wouldn't have," she murmured. "I wish you'd been there too."

A sudden thought struck her, and she laughed shakily. When Thad raised a quizzical eyebrow, she added, without thinking of how it would sound, "It just occurred to me that you'd have been all of ten years old at the time."

For a few seconds Thad's mouth went taut with anger. Then his expression softened, and he framed her face between his hands.

"Laura, the point is that I'm not ten years old now. And you're not eighteen."

His arms went around her, and she swayed into them weakly. She buried her face against his shoulder, welcoming his solidness, his warmth, needing his strength. He rocked her slightly to and fro, offering her comfort. His voice was gravelly with emotion as he said, "I'm sorry as hell you had to go through all that, and I can appreciate why you've been cautious about committing your affections. But I'd say it's time you put the past behind you and tried again."

"You're right," she agreed in an anguished whisper. "But it's been so long, Thad. I'm not sure I can."

"Of course, you can," Thad said firmly.

He touched her cheek and caressed the side of her neck as if he sensed her need, as if he were trying to infuse her with his confidence. Weaving his fingers through her hair, he tugged at it gently, tipping her face toward his.

"The only question in my mind is, do you want to try again with me?"

"Oh, yes!" she cried. "Yes, I want to! But can't you see how much that frightens me? It would be so very easy to rely on you, Thad . . . to fall in love with you. . . ."

"Yes, Laura, I do see."

She had answered with a fervor that told him she was only just beginning to realize how much she wanted to trust him, and Thad's eyes crinkled at the corners as he grinned, lightening the mood between them.

He dropped a kiss on the tip of her nose and said, "Why else do you think I waited so long to try to make love to you?"

"Was it so obvious that I was afraid?"

"Uh-huh."

He leaned his forehead against hers and smiled into her eyes, melting her resistance and taking her breath away. She was so breathless, she hardly recognized her own voice when she asked, "Will you give me time?"

Thad chuckled. "In case you haven't noticed, sweetheart, *I* am a very patient man."

As if to illustrate how patient he could be, he kissed her eyelids, her cheek, the corners of her mouth. His mouth moved over hers lightly, barely grazing the softness of her lips, brushing from side to side with a sweet restraint. Her mouth was rosy and tingling with the promise of passion when he finally pulled away.

"M-maybe it would be wisest not to see each other for a while," Laura suggested tentatively. "That way I could decide—"

Thad shook his head. "I said I was patient, Laura, but it's not my nature to be passive. You wouldn't ask me to just stand aside and do nothing if you knew how much I care for you . . . how much I *want* you—"

"But I do know, Thad, and that's part of the problem. I can't think straight when I'm with you."

This grudging admission seemed to shatter Thad's control. His arms folded about her, hugging her close, and when she wrapped her own arms around his waist, she felt him trembling.

"Do I have any choice?" he murmured hoarsely.

"I wish you did."

"So do I." Thad pressed his cheek against her hair. "I also wish you weren't so blasted tempting!"

Reluctantly putting her away from him, he got to his feet. "It won't be easy, Laura, but if that's your best offer, I'll give you all the time you need." Smiling wryly, he added, "But I hope to God you won't need too much."

CHAPTER SEVEN

Unfortunately Monday was Labor Day, so the shop was closed. In the morning Laura picked the last of the raspberries and made preserves. That afternoon she caught up with some routine household chores and worked in her studio, but she couldn't settle down to any one task for any length of time.

If she had been preoccupied with Thad before, she was even more preoccupied with him now.

She reminded herself that she wouldn't have been with him today in any case. Thad was spending the afternoon and evening at his parents' home. He had asked her to come with him, but when he'd informed her that his parents were hosting the annual Bristol family reunion, she had declined.

Now, however, with a fine disdain for consistency, she wished she had agreed to go with him.

She found herself hoping that Thad would ignore her request that they not see each other until she had arrived at a decision as to whether they should see each other at all. She wished he would call. No matter what she was doing, she listened for the telephone, and more than once she very nearly yielded to the impulse to dial his number.

Laura knew she should try to think their relationship through coolly and clearly. She told herself that now, of all times, a logical plan of action was essential.

But how could she be logical when she was barely rational? How could she plan anything when she was constantly distracted by the memory of Thad's kisses? Of the way she'd felt when he'd touched her? How could she think when even Groucho missed Thad and was following her around like a lost soul?

The hours passed so slowly that the holiday seemed interminable, and on Tuesday, when the Gallery of Gifts was open for business again, she was grateful that a steady stream of customers kept her from thinking of Thad.

Nevertheless, during a lull in business late that afternoon, she looked up the number for Northwoods Canoe Outfitters, Inc., in the yellow pages.

Even if Laura had seriously intended to phone Thad, there was no need to look up his number. She had already committed it to memory. But seeing the quarter-page ad, reading through the list of services Thad's firm offered sportsmen, made her feel closer to him. And the worst of it was that once she'd found the ad, she was unable to tear herself away from it until the bell above the street door chimed a warning that someone had come into the store.

When Laura heard the bell, she closed the telephone directory and returned it to its shelf beneath the counter hastily, guiltily, as if she were hiding something sordid.

It was enough to make her wonder if she had taken leave of her senses.

That night she chewed her thumbnail to the quick, and when she saw what she had done, she began weeping.

She knew, of course, that the disreputable state of her nails was merely an excuse. It was her uncertainty about Thad that had reduced her to tears.

"What am I going to do, Groucho?" she sobbed disconsolately. "If I don't reach a decision s-soon, I'm not going to have any fingernails left, and I m-might not have any f-f-fingers!"

The cat looked so wise, staring at her so fixedly with his

enigmatic green gaze, that for one crazy moment, Laura half expected him to answer her.

"This is ridiculous!" she cried, and her echo chorused agreement through the empty rooms of the house.

Even Groucho seemed to agree with this evaluation. He jumped off her lap, arched his back, stalked disgustedly to the farthest corner of the bedroom, and began preening himself, smoothing the white ruff of fur at his neck that her tears had dampened.

"I'm talking to a cat," Laura whispered, as if someone might overhear the shameful admission. "I always swore that never, under any circumstances, would I talk to myself, and here I am, talking to a cat. And I'm getting maudlin too! *Anything* is better than that."

The instant she had said the words, Laura was convinced she had stumbled upon the truth, for the final sentence filled her with a sense of purpose.

After drying her tears on the hem of her nightgown, she got to her feet and ran to the dressing table, where she had left her handbag. Her heart sank when she opened the coin section of her billfold and saw that it was empty. She rummaged through the bag frantically and dumped the contents onto the dressing table before she found a dime that had sifted to the bottom of the purse.

She held the coin up, triumphantly displaying her find to the uninterested cat, before she flipped it into the air. She caught it one-handed, which seemed a good omen, and slapped it onto the back of her other hand.

"Heads, I call Thad tomorrow and tell him I want to go on seeing him," she proposed. Silently, fervently, she added, *And seeing him, and seeing him!* Chastened by the realization of how desperately she wanted to be with Thad, she concluded in a small voice, "Tails, I don't."

She glanced at Groucho, who was busy grooming his front paws. He didn't even look at her.

"Are you listening to me?" she inquired. "Is it a deal?"

Groucho's ears twitched to the upright position, so she knew that he'd heard her.

"It's a deal," she said firmly, then she laughed, pleased by the bargain she'd struck, and added, "One thing I like about talking with you, fella, is that you don't quibble over petty details."

She was stalling for time, and she knew it. Her heart was racing, thudding almost painfully against her breastbone. Slowly, carefully, she lifted her hand away from the coin, and when she peeked at the dime, her heart skipped a beat.

It was tails.

"No!" Laura cried. It *couldn't* be.

She looked at the dime again, and when she saw that her eyes hadn't deceived her, she wiped away one last tear with the back of her hand. With a defiant shake of her head she tossed the coin into the air again and said, "Groucho, my friend, make that the best two out of three."

For a time it seemed that nothing was destined to go right for her that evening. She had to go to the best seven out of ten before the law of averages went into effect, and things wound up the way she wanted them to.

That night she slept soundly, dreamlessly, and when she awoke clear-eyed and refreshed the next morning, cool reason seemed to prevail.

She still wanted to phone Thad. She still wanted desperately to see him. If Thad had wanted nothing more than sex from her, she would have phoned him. But she sensed that he wanted more than a temporary affair.

She'd got as far as she had by making plans and sticking to them, and it wasn't her style to gamble. The independent life might not always be a bed of roses, but it was the only way of life she knew. Until she'd met Thad, it had served her well. It had allowed her to survive. How could she have contemplated risking her entire future on the capricious flip of a coin?

It took every ounce of willpower she possessed, but Laura made it through the week without calling Thad.

The following Monday, Trina paid her a visit.

When she walked into the shop, Trina remarked casually, "I haven't spoken to you for a few days, so I thought I'd drop by and see how you're doing."

"I'm fine," Laura replied, "but how are you?"

"Hunky-dory."

Trina didn't look hunky-dory. Her smile was strained and mauve shadows ringed her eyes. She walked as if each step were an effort, and when she arrived at the deacon's bench beside the Franklin stove, she sank into it wearily.

Indicating the teakettle that had begun to whistle on the back of the stove, Laura inquired with some concern, "Would you like a cup of tea? I was just going to have some."

"That would be lovely, thanks," Trina replied weakly.

While Laura fetched another cup and prepared the tea Trina eased into a more comfortable position on the bench and rested her head in her hands. She took the cup Laura offered, squeezed a wedge of lemon into her tea, and inhaled the spicy fragrance of the brew gratefully, as if it might revive her lagging spirits.

"I just came from the obstetrician," she said, smiling wanly. "He tells me I should be through the worst of the morning sickness by now."

"But you're not," Laura surmised.

"No, and my doctor is kind of irritated with me. He says it's purely psychological—a bid for attention or something—and he informed me that women from primitive countries don't have any problem with morning sickness." With a wry grimace Trina concluded, "Somehow that's not very comforting when I'm spending so much time staring at my face in the commode."

"He'd probably change his tune if he'd ever been pregnant," said Laura.

"Oh, heavens!" Trina rolled her eyes prayerfully toward the ceiling. "Wouldn't I love to see that!"

"If there's anything I can do to help out, I hope you'll call on me. I mean, if you need someone to look after Kit or anything."

"That's sweet of you, Laura. Kit goes to preschool mornings, and we've made arrangements for him to stay with Aunt Dorothy on the afternoons when I can't keep up with him, but it never hurts to have a backup."

Trina smiled again, this time more brightly, and for a time neither of them spoke.

On the surface the scene in the shop was a companionable one. The pale September sun shone through the windows, striking gold highlights in Laura's hair and shimmering darkly on Trina's as the two women bent their heads over their teacups.

The flames leaped merrily in the fireplace, and the brass fittings on the stove glistened with the loving care Laura had given them. The glazes on the pottery in the store reflected the earthy autumn colors outdoors, and Groucho had curled up in a pool of sunlight on the floor next to Laura's feet for his afternoon nap.

Laura should have felt contented, but she didn't. She had never been uneasy with Trina before, but today she was. And while Laura fought to suppress the urge to ask about Thad, Trina tried to think of some diplomatic way of bringing his name into the conversation.

For several minutes the awkward silence was broken only by the rattle of china and the crackle of the fire.

Phil had counseled Trina not to interfere. He'd said, "Whatever happened, it's strictly between Thad and Laura. Your woman's intuition could be way off-target, and if Thad didn't intend for you to approach Laura, you're liable to alienate both of them by trying to plead his case."

Trina had to admit that Phil's advice made a lot of sense. The prudent thing to do would be to stay out of it. But if Phil's argument was sensible, that didn't necessarily mean that it was right. Her obstetrician's comments about morning sickness proved that.

And besides, she loved Thad. When she was a little girl, he'd been her idol, and in many ways he still was. Her affection for him outweighed both Phil's logic and her own misgivings. And although she had known Laura only a few months, she was very fond of her. She admired Laura, too, and she thought it was sad that Laura should be so alone.

When her cup was empty, Trina decided that in the light of all this, tactful or not, she had to say what she had come to say.

"I—uh—I saw Thad this morning," she began stiltedly.

"Did he send you here?" Laura hastily asked.

"No, he didn't." And he hadn't; not in so many words. "Thad told me you'd decided not to see him for a while. "But," Trina emphasized, "it was *my* idea to come here."

Was Laura disappointed by her reply? Trina wondered. Had she seen a flicker of regret in the other woman's clear blue-gray eyes, or was it only her imagination?

"Did Thad tell you why I need time to think about us?" Laura inquired.

"Not specifically, no. All he said was that you're not sure you want to be involved with him."

"Then what did you hope to accomplish by coming here?"

"Two things actually. I wanted to let you know that I'm available if you need someone to talk to—"

"I appreciate your concern," Laura inserted tartly.

The little confidence Trina had was badly shaken by Laura's astringent tone of voice. *Phil was right*, she thought. *All I've done is offend Laura.* But it was too late to change direction and too early for recriminations, and she went on tensely, "I also wanted to tell you that you're making a big mistake. Thad really cares for you, Laura."

"Does he? How can you be so certain of that?"

"Because he told me he does." When Laura confined her response to a skeptical shake of her head, Trina persisted. "*Really* he does. You've got to believe me. Thad and I are very close, so I'd know if he were putting me on. Anyway since he met you, he hasn't so much as *looked* at another woman."

"Don't worry," said Laura. "Eventually he will."

"If you won't see him anymore, naturally he will," Trina replied heatedly. "Sooner or later, he'll find someone else."

"And chances are it will be sooner!"

Trina's shoulders drooped dejectedly at this rejoinder. Setting her cup on the bench between them, she rose and stood looking down at Laura.

"I shouldn't have come here," she said. "I only hope you won't think that I did it out of idle curiosity or something like that. I'm not a snoop, and I'm sorry I've offended you, Laura, but I just had to do something or I couldn't have lived with myself."

She had turned to leave when Laura stopped her, saying contritely, "I'm the one who should apologize, Trina. I know you meant well, and I wish there were some way I could repay your kindness. I wish I could give you my word that I'll phone Thad the minute you've gone, but I can't."

"Don't you care for him at all?"

"Yes, Trina, I do. I care for him—more than I can say."

"Then why can't you call him, Laura? If you care for Thad, phoning him should be the easiest thing in the world."

"It isn't though," Laura said gently. "Not for me, at any

rate. You see, Trina, Thad's feelings aren't the issue. It's my feelings that frighten me. I don't know whether I can cope with a serious relationship, and I certainly don't want to fall in love. I've been there once, and it hurts too much."

"Well, of course, it does!" Trina was wide-eyed with astonishment. "My goodness, Laura. That's the sort of observation I'd expect from Kit!" An involuntary gurgle of laughter escaped her. Not only was she taken aback, she was also amused by Laura's confession. But when she realized that Laura did not share her amusement, she sobered.

"Forgive me!" she exclaimed. "I don't mean to sound condescending, but don't you think you're borrowing trouble? No one's asking you to make a lifetime commitment. All Thad wants is to see you occasionally. If he ever asks you to do anything you don't want to do, all you have to do is say no."

"God, Trina! You make it sound so easy. If only it were as simple as that."

"But it is simple, Laura. I know it is because I've been through the mill myself."

Laura found it hard to believe that pretty, placid Trina had ever known a moment's anxiety over anything, and when she was unable to repress a smile, the younger woman frowned at her so sternly that her fine, rounded features sharpened.

"It's true," Trina declared. "When Phil and I were first married, I was an awful worrywart. I used to tear myself to pieces if he was a few minutes late getting home from work. I'd imagine all sorts of horrible things—that he'd been in an accident, or that he was with one of his old girl friends, or that he didn't really want to be with me. I worried that someday he might get tired of me—stop loving me. But after six years we're still married, and he still loves me, so all my worrying was just wasted energy."

As she concluded her speech Trina searched Laura's face. She was discouraged by Laura's impassive expression, for it told her that Laura was unmoved by her arguments. In spite of this her voice rang with the certainty of her conviction as she delivered her parting salvo.

"Maybe I'm only twenty-four, but I know that all of life is a risk, Laura. If you give in to your fears, if you let them stop you from doing the things you really want to do, before long you won't even bother to get out of bed in the morning."

On that compelling note Trina left the shop, and that evening she told Phil, "You were right, honey. I shouldn't have interfered."

Phil tried to reassure her. "It will all turn out for the best," he said consolingly, but Trina would have been more comforted had she known that she was not the only visitor Laura had that afternoon.

And it was Laura's next visitor who inadvertently swung the balance in Thad's favor.

CHAPTER EIGHT

Laura had made every effort to avoid becoming the focus of speculation, but the population of Ely was slightly less than five thousand. In a town that small, gossip was a way of life. It was inevitable that some well-intentioned soul would inform Thad's mother that her only son was—heaven help him!—keeping company with an older woman.

Dorothy Bristol had not seen fit to dignify this information by commenting upon it, but that didn't mean she hadn't an adequate response. On the contrary in case anyone else should mention Thad's unfortunate entanglement, she planned to arm herself with firsthand knowledge of the woman in question. That way she would be prepared to refute the rumors.

Therefore, when she found herself in the neighborhood of Powell's Gallery of Gifts, Dorothy decided to reconnoiter the enemy and see for herself how great a threat Laura Powell posed, but she had no intention of driving Laura back into Thad's arms. Far from it.

Without ever having met Laura, Dorothy disliked her. Once she had seen Laura, however, Dorothy did not make the mistake of underestimating her.

Laura was not at all the bohemian type some of the gossips had predicted she would be, nor did she appear to be the "adventuress" others had described.

Of course, Dorothy took it for granted that Thad's taste

in women was as impeccable as his taste in everything else. That was as it should be. After all, he was her son, and she was the acknowledged arbiter of fashion in Ely.

Dorothy was not sure exactly what she had expected of Thad's latest inamorata, but when she walked into the Gallery of Gifts and saw the proprietor, she immediately recognized that the affair was much more serious than her informant had led her to believe. And when she'd had an opportunity to observe Laura, when she had taken note of the cool elegance that was part of Laura's public image, Dorothy wondered if the situation might be beyond redemption.

But Dorothy Bristol was not a woman who admitted defeat easily. Indeed, one reason she had managed to reach her present lofty position on the social ladder was that she refused to admit even the chance of failure, and in the end her doubts served only to magnify her determination.

While Laura finished gift-wrapping a parcel for Emily Carruthers, Dorothy watched her covertly, looking for the chink in the younger woman's armor.

Yes, she thought, Laura Powell was undeniably lovely. Not only that, she was soft-spoken, polite, and ladylike in the most fastidious sense of the word. She appeared to be serene and self-contained, yet at the same time there was a hint of vulnerability about her that Thad probably found irresistible.

No doubt she makes him feel terribly macho and protective, Dorothy told herself petulantly.

But where there was vulnerability, there had to be a weakness, and somehow she would find that weakness. And when she had found it . . . Well, perhaps she would use it against Laura, and perhaps she wouldn't. But it never did any harm to be prepared.

As for Laura, when Dorothy Bristol came into the shop, her first impression was that Dorothy was just another customer, but she recognized her mistake in less than a minute.

The stately titian-haired woman had sailed into the shop dramatically, as if she were making an entrance onstage, but once inside she remained unmoving by the street door. She nodded a greeting to Mrs. Carruthers and even offered a pleasantry or two, but her smile was as glacial as her frosty green eyes, and her unmistakable air of hauteur made it plain that she had summed up the store and its owner in a single glance and found neither of them worthy of her notice.

While Laura's neighbor paid her bill and bundled herself into her coat, the woman was conspicuously silent. In fact, it seemed to Laura that there was an almost sinister quality about her stillness.

It was not until the street door had closed behind Mrs. Carruthers that the woman approached the counter.

"I'm relieved to find your shop is quiet today," she announced. "It gives us some time alone. Not that it will take much time to conclude my business with you."

"Business?" Laura repeated. "I'm afraid I don't understand."

"You are Laura Powell, aren't you?"

Laura nodded.

"Then you're acquainted with my son."

"Your son?"

"Thaddeus Bristol."

"Yes," Laura said simply. "Thad and I are friends."

"Are you sure you're only friends?"

Dorothy Bristol's smile was a study in coyness, but she was glancing about the room, inventorying the contents of the shop, and she did not seem at all interested in hearing Laura's reply.

"I believe you've only recently opened this store."

"That's right. About five weeks ago," said Laura. She wanted to shiver when Dorothy's eyes met hers.

"You've obviously put a good deal of thought and effort into it, so I assume it's important to you, and I happen to be in a position to do you a good turn."

"Oh?" Laura remarked noncommittally. "How so?"

"All it would take to assure your success is a few well-placed words from me. If I were to sponsor you, the women of Ely would beat a path to your door. You have my guarantee on that."

I'll just bet I do, thought Laura. But if Dorothy Bristol could guarantee the success of the Gallery of Gifts, she could just as easily assure its failure.

Laura studied Dorothy stoically, hoping she might have misunderstood the implied threat in the older woman's words. She ignored the chilling sensation of impending doom that had beset her and drew herself to her full height, but she still had to look up to meet Dorothy's eyes.

"Naturally you'd expect me to do something to return the favor."

"Naturally." Dorothy inclined her head regally. "All you have to do is stop seeing Thad."

"Why should you object to my seeing him?"

A pained expression crossed Dorothy's features. "Must I spell it out?"

"Yes, I think you'd better," Laura answered smoothly.

"Very well then. Let's just say that I enjoy my position of leadership in Ely, and I'm honest enough to admit that it's a position many—if not most—women in this town would envy. The Bristol name carries a certain amount of prestige in this area, and any woman with a taste for social prominence would certainly recognize the value of a connection to the Bristol family."

"Then you're concerned that I'm more infatuated with the Bristol social set than with Thad?" Laura replied coolly.

"Exactly," said Dorothy. "You're certainly not the first, and I've become rather adept at recognizing the

91

signs, which is why I'm asking you to end your—shall we say, liaison?—with Thad."

"Do you honestly expect me to believe that's your only reason?"

"Now that I've met you, no; I don't suppose I do. But my reasons aren't important."

"They are to me," said Laura. "I've a right to know if you're accusing me of something more unsavory than social climbing."

"Try cradle robbing then. Try fortune hunting."

"You can't be serious!" Laura cried. Then she saw that Dorothy was serious, and she shook her head. Too dismayed to defend herself, she murmured, "I don't believe this is happening."

"Believe what you want, Laura, but end it," Dorothy replied without inflection.

"And if I don't?"

"In that case your business might go into a rather steep decline." Dorothy sighed. "Have I made my position clear?"

"You've made it very clear, Mrs. Bristol, but you seem to be laboring under a misconception. As you can see, I sell pottery, leather goods, candles, and other craft items, but my loyalty is *not* for sale, nor is my friendship."

An unbecoming flush rushed into Dorothy's face, mottling her fine complexion with an angry red.

"That's a pretty speech, my dear, but if I were you, I wouldn't be so rash. Not unless I were prepared to face the consequences, that is."

Laura's knees had gone watery, but her step was steady as she walked to the door of the shop. As she opened the door she said, "It isn't my policy to be rude to customers, but since you're obviously not a customer, I'd appreciate your leaving now, before either of us says anything more we'll regret."

The older woman regarded her narrowly. "Come, come now," she chided. "Don't be so hasty, my dear."

It required a monumental effort, but Laura managed to keep her voice low and even as she replied, "I'm not being hasty and I am not your 'dear' and I will not be intimidated, Mrs. Bristol. Do I make *my* position clear?"

"Perfectly!" Dorothy Bristol snapped. She stepped past Laura and through the door, but once outside, she paused. "It's really very sad," she said affably. "If we had met under other circumstances, we might have been friends. You're a woman I could respect, Laura."

"I could respect you as well, Mrs. Bristol," Laura replied evenly, "but I doubt that we'd have been friends, no matter how we'd met."

"Perhaps not," Dorothy allowed.

She turned away from Laura and prepared to leave, but as she walked toward her car, she got in one last disturbing threat.

"Don't pride yourself that you've won this little skirmish, and don't think that you've seen the last of me, Laura Powell, because I promise you, you haven't."

CHAPTER NINE

"I will not be intimidated!" For the next hour, whenever there were no customers in the shop, Laura repeated this sentence to herself again and again.

Dorothy Bristol might sound like a character from a soap opera, but the fact remained that her threats were disturbing.

Laura had known people of that ilk before. Manipulative people who enjoyed wielding power. Self-righteous people who had spread ugly lies about an eighteen-year-old girl, who had hounded and persecuted her, who had considered it their civic duty to drive her out of town.

Because of this experience, Laura knew that she had good cause to be frightened. But she was also angry.

This time, she vowed, she would not give in to her fears. She would not allow them to stop her pursuing what she really wanted.

And she wanted Thad.

That afternoon, Laura closed the shop a few minutes early so that she could freshen up, drive into town, and be at Thad's store before it closed at six.

Perhaps it was foolhardy to flout Dorothy's wishes. Perhaps it was the wrong thing to do. Or perhaps she was doing the right thing for all the wrong reasons.

What would Thad think when she told him about his mother's visit? Would he believe she'd simply *had* to see him again, or would he think seeing him was her way of showing disdain for his mother's warnings?

Should she tell him?

Laura pondered this last question while she locked the house, got into her car, and drove the few miles into Ely. But when she arrived at the big, barnlike building on Sheridan Street that housed Northwoods Canoe Outfitters, she had no satisfactory answer to it.

The main street of the town was oddly quiet now that the tourist season was officially over, and she drove around the block several times, mustering the courage to go inside. When she finally parked the car near the front entrance and walked into the retail outlet, it was almost six o'clock.

She had never been to Thad's store before, and she was impressed by its size and the variety of merchandise it offered. There were racks of durable outdoor clothing for men, women, and children. There were displays of sporting goods: everything from fishing and hunting gear to backpacks and camping equipment to skis and snowshoes. There were books and cameras and souvenirs. There was even a dogsled.

Laura had stopped for a closer look at the bulletin board, with its array of brochures, snapshots, and complimentary letters from satisfied customers, when the man behind the cash register asked, "Can I help you find something?"

"No, thank you," she stalled. "I'm just browsing."

"Let me know if you change your mind." Glancing at the wall clock, the clerk added politely, "We close in ten minutes."

"Thanks," said Laura. "I know you do."

Aware that the clerk was watching her curiously, she wandered into the next room and was astonished to find herself in what was apparently a reception area.

This must be where Thad met with prospective clients

to advise them and help plan their canoe trips, Laura thought as she surveyed the room. It was furnished simply, not unlike a hunting lodge, with comfortably rustic sofas and chairs, sheepskin rugs on the floor, and framed aerial photographs of the dozens of lakes that composed the Boundary Waters National Park on the walls.

At one end of the room there was a massive stone fireplace flanked by mounted game fish and hunting trophies, and at the opposite end, another set of doors stood open, inviting Laura to explore further.

She intended doing just that, but she had just stepped through the doors and seen that this area was the firm's warehouse when she heard the low rumble of men's voices coming from some distant corner of the building.

The overhead doors that led to the alley were open, allowing a dusty swath of sunlight to filter through, but other than this the warehouse was dimly lighted, and she paused for a moment to get her bearings.

She was surrounded by rows of neatly stacked canoes. They reached higher than her head, and she couldn't see where the men were, but the occasional snatches of conversation she overheard enabled her to identify one of the voices as Thad's.

Following the sound of the voices, she walked from aisle to aisle, past floor-to-ceiling metal shelves containing paddles and tents and lifejackets, but the men, Laura noticed, were moving also. Their voices were receding rather than growing louder. Finally she came to a vast open area near the garage doors, and when she heard an engine being started, she realized that the men must have gone outside.

Was Thad preparing to leave? At this thought Laura's steps quickened until she was almost running, the high heels of her shoes clicking sharply against the cement floor of the warehouse. She rushed into the alley and saw that Thad was leaning against the driver's door of a van, talking to the sandy-haired youth behind the wheel.

"Whatever happens, don't let Behrendt talk you into stopping off for a drink," Thad was saying. "If you do, you may not make it back from Fall Lake till spring."

"You can count on me, Thad," the youth replied soberly.

Thad grinned. "I know I can, Jeff," he teased. "Particularly since you have a date with Angela this evening."

Even through the window of the van, Laura could see the brick-red flush that was creeping up the back of Jeff's neck. "I-I wanted to th-thank you for letting me use the van tonight," he stammered.

"Consider it a fringe benefit," said Thad. "You've done a great job for us since you started last June, so you've earned something extra."

"Okay, boss."

Thad backed away from the van, and the youth released the hand brake and shifted into first gear, but before he drove away, he asked, "Is there anything else I need to do besides finishing the paperwork on the Behrendt party and locking up?"

"You might show 'em where the washrooms are in case they want to shower," Thad replied. "Other than that, though, they should be pretty well set."

"Okay," said Jeff. "I think I've got it all straight."

"And no stops at bars on the way back," Thad repeated.

"Got you!" Jeff said with a laugh. "See you tomorrow."

"You'd better," Thad returned, feigning sternness.

Jeff responded with a smile and began revving the motor. With a spurt of gravel and a cloud of dust, the van leaped forward, gathering speed until Jeff braked it to a stop at the end of the alley.

Thad watched after Jeff until he had turned the corner onto Central Avenue, and only when the van had disappeared did he turn toward the warehouse. Laura was standing motionless in the shadow of the roof overhang near the garage doors, and he had taken several steps before he saw her.

His eyes brightened and his gaze swept over her, roving hungrily from the top of her honey-blond head to the tips of the dainty toes peeking through the straps of her sandals, lingering on the muted burgundy fabric of her dress, which clung lovingly to the curve of her breasts and floated about her legs as she walked toward him.

"Laura."

Thad spoke her name softly, caressingly. He held his hands out to her, palms up, silently urging her to run into his arms. It was all she could do to resist his appeal, but when she reached him she contented herself with slipping her hands into his.

"You don't seem at all surprised to see me," she murmured huskily.

"No, I'm not surprised," Thad affirmed. "I knew it was only a matter of time before you'd give in, but I can't begin to tell you how pleased I am that you came here today."

The fiery gleam in his eyes and the tender way he looked at her confirmed that he was delighted to see her. He raised her hands to his mouth, pressed a slow kiss into each palm, then lifted her hands to his shoulders.

Laura automatically wound her arms around his neck, and as his arms encircled her waist, she whispered breathlessly, "You certainly know how to make a woman feel welcome."

"I try my best to please."

Thad held her close and began scattering fervent little kisses across her eyelids, her cheeks, her temples. He nuzzled her earlobe and rubbed his cheek against hers, evoking delicious tingling sensations that rippled outward from every point of contact with him. The ripples spread inward, too, in an erotic chain-reaction that touched the innermost core of her being and kindled tantalizing flickers of desire.

Suddenly weak-kneed, Laura leaned pliantly against him, and he touched her hair, the nape of her neck, caressing her as if he never wanted to stop. His touch was seductive, yet at the same time it was as if the pleasure he derived from the texture of her hair and the silky warmth of her skin, from the simple act of molding his hands to the ripe curves of her hips and waist and breast was an end in itself.

"God, you feel good," he growled. "Have you any idea how much I've missed you?"

"I missed you too, Thad." Her voice was barely audible, and she reluctantly loosened her hold on his shoulders and took a step away from him. She studied his face, looking for the slightest trace of evidence that he had suffered as she had during the past week.

The night they'd met he'd told her that she had the face of a Renaissance angel. At the time she had accused him of exaggerating. But today, when she'd freshened her make-up, she'd noticed the new fragility of her cheekbones. She'd seen that after little more than a week without Thad, her delicate coloring had faded to an ivory pallor, and she'd decided that she looked so wraithlike, his compliment was not far from wrong after all.

But unlike her, Thad seemed to have survived the week very well. In fact, he practically oozed vitality.

Did he care for her at all? Laura wondered. Didn't it matter to him that she had stayed away from him for so long? Perhaps, Laura mused, he'd had company to keep him from getting lonely.

She bit her lower lip in order to keep from crying out at the anguish these thoughts caused. Then, making light of her turbulent emotions, she forced herself to smile, but she was only half joking when she complained, "You're looking disgustingly healthy."

Thad laughed. "Did you expect to find me in a drunken stupor, crying into my beer and calling out for you?"

"Nothing so dramatic as that, but I had thought you might look a bit haggard. It's rather daunting to think you weren't at all worried that I might decide not to see you again."

Daunting as it was, given Thad's knowledge of her, given his self-assurance, if she'd thought about it at all, she might have predicted his unshakable calm. Not for a moment would he have questioned the outcome of their trial separation.

"Would you rather I'd pretended to be surprised?" he asked. His tawny eyes danced wickedly, daring her to be honest.

"No," she answered truthfully.

Inside she was trembling. Thad's question had stripped away another of her defenses. She felt naked and exposed, and she suddenly realized that she would have to tell him about Dorothy's visit. Neither could she continue turning a blind eye to the seriousness of the commitment she was making.

Oddly enough, having admitted this much, she felt unburdened, as if a great weight had been lifted from her. Her smile was radiant as she said, "I'm glad you didn't pretend, Thad."

"That's good," Thad replied gruffly. "It's not that I take you for granted or anything like that, Laura. It's just that there have already been too many pretenses between us."

"And most of them have been mine," she acknowledged ruefully. "I'll try to be more open with you, Thad, but I can't give you any guarantees. I . . . it's difficult."

"I know it is, love."

Smiling at her encouragingly, Thad draped one arm about her shoulders, and they started walking toward the building. Their steps matched perfectly, and Laura wondered if Thad had noticed how naturally her body fitted into the protective curve of his arm.

"So where do we go from here?" she inquired tremulously.

"To my place."

Thad had deliberately misinterpreted her question, and when she would have protested, he drawled, "You know as well as I do where our relationship is heading, Laura. Someday we'll be lovers."

He must have felt her shiver with anticipation because his arm tightened possessively about her shoulders.

"I realize how vulnerable that makes you feel," he said gently. "I know you'd feel safer if you had some sort of timetable showing when we'd enter each new level of intimacy and when we'd go on to the next one, and I'll do my damnedest not to rush you. You have my word I'll never do anything you're not ready for, Laura. But relationships can't be planned. They don't conform to schedules. Sometimes they get out of control.

"Besides," he added, grinning lazily down at her, "you rely too heavily on plans. You need to learn to relax and let things happen. So for tonight all I'll tell you is that we're going to drop your car off at your house, and then we're going to my place. We're going to have dinner together—"

"And then?" Laura asked anxiously.

Chuckling, Thad finished lightly, "Why, then I'll take you home!"

Laura postponed telling Thad about his mother's visit until after dinner. She had missed him more than she'd thought possible during the past week, and it was so marvelous being with him again, she didn't want to risk spoiling the evening.

Preparing the meal was a joint effort. They worked together so comfortably, it was as if they'd done it hundreds of times before. Both of them were in high spirits, and they bickered good-naturedly all the while.

101

Predictably enough, Thad cooked by instinct, sprinkling an experimental dash of various seasonings over the fresh trout before he put it in the oven, adding a variety of herbs to the oil and vinegar dressing. Laura, on the other hand, went by the book, carefully following tried and trusted recipes for the wild rice and Caesar salad that were her contributions to dinner.

With tongue-in-cheek gravity Thad scolded Laura for her lack of imagination, and she responded in kind, telling him that it was nothing short of sacrilege to put crushed dill on trout.

When dinner was ready, however, both of them agreed that the food was delicious.

Finally, when they had cleared the table and were finishing the last of the wine, Laura knew she couldn't put it off any longer. She tried to remain objective in the way she described Dorothy's threats. She emphasized that Dorothy apparently had nothing against her personally, and that her only objection was to Laura's involvement with Thad. Nevertheless, it was not a pretty story. It showed Thad's mother in a harsh, unflattering light, and Laura was astonished when Thad only laughed and apologized for his mother's behavior.

"How can you be so . . . so cavalier about it?" Laura demanded. "Don't you believe me?"

"Certainly I believe you," Thad replied brusquely.

"And you don't think I came to see you just to show your mother that I'm not afraid of her threats?"

"No, Laura. You said you'd have contacted me before much longer in any case, and I'm willing to take your word for it."

"But why?"

"Why not?" Thad returned crisply. "You've learned to trust me. You've demonstrated that by coming to my home for the first time. Is there any reason why I shouldn't return your trust?"

"No, of course, there isn't. It's just that I was so worried that you might think I had some other reason for coming to see you. I dreaded telling you about your mother."

"I'm very glad you did tell me, Laura."

As he spoke Thad reached across the table to hold her hand. His eyes reflected the amber glow of the candles and his smile made her pulse race wildly. In the same instant, as if they were reacting to the same invisible prompter, they got to their feet. Thad led her into the living room, and as he touched a match to the kindling in the fireplace, one corner of his mouth quirked into a wry grin.

"My mother has pulled stunts like this before," he said. "That's one reason Connie and Lila chose to settle down so far from Minnesota." He stared into the flames, waiting until the logs had begun to burn before he went on.

"I'll speak to her about it, of course, although I doubt that it's necessary. My mother is a law unto herself, so it's impossible to second-guess her, but I honestly don't think you need to lose any sleep over the fate of your business."

"Do you really think it will be all right?" asked Laura.

"Yes, I do, and I'll tell you why. My mother may or may not tell her friends to stay away from your shop. If she doesn't, that's okay, and even if she does carry out her threat, it will backfire. The ladies of the Thursday Afternoon Bridge Club will come to your place in droves to see what Dorothy Bristol's fuss is all about. You might be a nine days' wonder, but your sales will go right through the roof, and in a week or two it will all blow over. They'll have found someone new to gossip about."

Laura shuddered with distaste at the thought of being a nine days' wonder, and seeing this, Thad smiled at her reassuringly. He seated himself on the sofa, stretching his long legs out toward the fire, and patted the sofa cushion next to him.

"And now," he said softly, "that's enough about my mother. Come here, Laura."

She accepted his invitation without hesitation, and when he pulled her down beside him and into his arms, she didn't object. Even if she'd wanted to, she was incapable of resisting him. But she didn't want to resist. She wanted to be near Thad, to be in his arms, to inhale the clean masculine scent of his skin and the sweet aroma of woodsmoke that clung to his sweater.

She pressed closer to him, relaxing against his chest and rubbing her cheek against his shoulder, savoring the hard strength of his body, wishing that the two of them were not separated by layers of wool and Qiana.

Perhaps it was the influence of the wine or the romantic ballad playing softly on the stereo, but just being in Thad's house made her ecstatically happy.

The living room was decorated with a cheerfully eclectic blend of traditional and Scandinavian-modern pieces and a few antiques, and the predominating golds, browns, and creams of the room were especially mellow in the firelight. The room suited Thad and, secure in the shelter of his arms, Laura remained cozily where she was.

They sat that way for almost an hour. They spoke in whispers, and now and again they exchanged languorous glances and honeyed kisses. After one kiss Laura outlined Thad's mouth with her fingertips.

"I've wanted to do that ever since we met," she confessed.

Thad caught her hand in his and kissed the tips of her fingers. "Why didn't you?" he asked. "I must have made it plain that I wouldn't object to your touching me."

"You made it abundantly plain, but people don't just touch other people like that."

"The world might be a happier place if they did."

"Maybe it would," she agreed doubtfully. "But I'm not a trend-setter, and I guess I was afraid you'd take it as a come-on."

Thad smiled suggestively. "Is there anything else you'd like to touch?" he asked.

Just thinking of the parts of him she would like to caress made Laura feel as if she were blushing all over. Her eyes shied away from his as she murmured, "Yes, but I think I'll wait till later."

"Later," Thad repeated solemnly, as if it were some sort of pledge.

"*Later,*" she repeated emphatically, so that he wouldn't argue the point.

"You're not afraid anymore, are you, Laura?"

She raised her eyes to his and laid her free hand against his cheek, relishing the crispness of his beard, the firm line of his jaw, the supple warmth of his skin.

"No, Thad," she replied. "Not with you. I feel very safe with you."

"I'd advise you not to feel too safe," Thad said dryly. "You're pushing your luck as it is."

Laura had been tracing his ear, intrigued by its contours, but now she stopped.

"Is this one of those times you warned me about when things could get out of control?"

Thad shook his head incredulously. "Laura," he said with some bemusement, "did anyone ever tell you that you're delightfully, adorably naive?"

"Not so far," she answered pertly.

"Then let me be the first."

Thad laughed deep in his throat, but his eyes had darkened with desire. She couldn't bear their intensity. To avoid them she hid her face in the curve of his neck.

She had not intended the gesture to be provocative, but it must have been because Thad molded her to him so that he could feel the soft imprint of her breasts against his chest, and she felt the passionate surge of his arousal.

"Don't you know by now," he muttered almost unintelligibly, "that anytime we're alone together is one of 'those' times?"

When the meaning of what he'd said sank in, she stiffened, and his hold on her immediately slackened. Tilting her face toward his, he asked, "Does my answer scare you?"

"No," she replied feebly.

His lips were only a whisper away, and when they kissed, it was with the same exquisitely gentle insistence as before. His tongue played over her lips, parting them and invading the moist, silky recesses of her mouth. But when Laura responded, meeting his ardor with a desperate eroticism she hadn't known she possessed, Thad's kiss deepened. The pressure of his mouth upon hers rapidly changed from sweetly sensuous to frankly demanding.

The record on the turntable spun to a stop while they were kissing, and the heavy thudding of Thad's heart seemed deafening in the sudden stillness of the room. It was a long time before he ended the kiss, and when he did, she hastily qualified her answer.

"Well, maybe it is a little scary," she said in a hushed voice.

Thad's hands moved over her almost reverently: wooing her, courting her, erasing her fears, eroding her inhibitions, creating a need that only he could satisfy.

"Laura," he sighed, his breath mingling with hers. "I want you, Laura. Soon."

"I know you do, Thad. I want you too."

Excited by her honesty, he kissed her ear and touched the tip of his tongue to the sensitive little hollow behind it, and when he felt the fine tremor of desire that shook her, his own desire threatened to flare out of control. His voice was so thick with passion, he hardly recognized it as he said, "I have to go out of town next weekend."

Laura tensed as if she had foreseen what he would say next, but she waited for him to continue.

"One of our tourist cabins on Windigo Lake needs some maintenance work. I've been putting it off, but it's getting late in the season—"

"I understand," she broke in.

"Do you?" When she made no response, Thad said, "I'd like to show you Windigo Lake, Laura. It's on the old Gunflint Trail and it's very beautiful, especially in the fall. I think you'd enjoy going with me."

Laura was so still, she scarcely seemed to breathe. She remained in his arms, warm and soft, totally female and utterly desirable, yet he sensed a new remoteness about her and knew that part of her had withdrawn.

He touched a strand of hair that curled against her temple. He twined it around his fingers and it clung to his hand, silky and fragrant, gilded by the firelight.

Perhaps it was only an illusion, but all at once she looked ephemeral, unattainable.

Have I misjudged Laura's readiness? Thad wondered. *Have I overestimated my powers of persuasion?*

He'd known from the start that if he tried to force matters he could lose Laura. Perhaps his timing was way out of sync, but dammit, he had been patient, and not seeing her for the past week had made him realize that he could lose her by being *too* patient. And the most compelling argument of all was that he wanted her too much to wait any longer.

Normally Thad was not a fatalist, but now he told himself that the decision was out of his hands. It had been since the first time he'd seen Laura.

"I'll be driving up to the cabin Friday afternoon," he went on slowly. "Will you come with me, Laura?"

Laura raised her eyes to his. "Only a few hours ago you promised not to rush me, Thad."

"I know I did, but if you'll recall, I also said that emotions don't always conform to schedules."

107

"That doesn't mean you have to act on them. Emotions can be sublimated or suppressed—"

"Or ignored?"

Laura had already withdrawn emotionally, and now she withdrew physically. Sliding to the far corner of the couch, she kicked her shoes off, drew her knees up under her chin, and arranged the folds of her skirt about her legs with painstaking care.

"Is that what you're trying to do, Laura?" Thad persisted. "Are you trying to ignore the way you feel?"

She hugged her knees to her chest, curving her body into a tight, protective ball. "What if I am?"

"It could mean you feel something for me."

"You know I do, Thad," she replied huskily. "It's just that it's not easy to break the habits of a lifetime."

"A lifetime?" Thad repeated dubiously.

Laura nodded confirmation. "My parents raised me strictly by the book, and the book they used had endless regulations. My mother used to insist that I lay out my school clothes for the next day before I went to bed at night, and even before I started school, my father made this chart. . . ."

In talking about it, she envisioned the chart, with its stick-figure drawings of a four-year-old Laura bathing, brushing her teeth, saying her prayers, putting her toys away; there were squares to be checked off when these tasks were completed.

"My father tacked that one to my bedroom door, and when I learned to read, he made another chart to remind me of chores and homework. He Scotch-taped that one to one of the kitchen cabinets. His charts were the first thing I saw when I woke up in the morning and the last thing I saw at night. They were always the first thing I saw whenever I came into the house."

"And as you grew up he replaced the originals with new ones," Thad surmised.

"Yes," said Laura. "More complicated ones. And when I was a very good girl—"

"Don't tell me. I can guess." Thad was frowning. "I'll bet you got a gold star."

"Yes."

"But no hugs or kisses?"

"No. No hugs or kisses. My parents were never particularly demonstrative."

Thad shook his head sadly. "How long did this go on, Laura?"

"Till I was thirteen."

She averted her face and rested her forehead on her knees as she continued, telling Thad how, over the next two years, the gold-star days had become increasingly rare, until finally, at fifteen, she had torn down the hateful charts and thrown them away. By then she had known that she wanted more out of life than the quiet feeling of accomplishment her parents' lukewarm approval gave her. She had been openly defiant, but not to the extent that she hadn't had an explanation ready.

When her father asked about the charts, she'd planned to tell him that, despite their luster, the glittery gold stars were only tawdry imitations of real ones, and that she had let his regimentation blind her to that fact for too long.

As it turned out, she never had the opportunity to deliver her glib little speech because her father hadn't asked about the charts. Laura had never understood why he hadn't—until now.

Now she realized that while it had been comparatively easy to destroy the symbol of her parents' restrictions, because she had never directly confronted her father, she hadn't stopped living by his charts. Not entirely.

Much as she had resented his rules, she'd felt bound by them. And although her parents' way of life hadn't left much room for spontaneity, she had been willing to sacrifice spontaneity for structure, familiarity, safety . . . until she'd met Thad.

She couldn't bring herself to say this last part aloud, of course, and when she had finished speaking, Thad moved along the couch to sit close to her again. She wished that he would take her in his arms, but he only touched her hand and said, "I understand what you're trying to tell me, Laura."

She lifted her face and tried to smile at him. "I'm glad you understand, because I'm not at all sure I do."

"One thing you've told me is that, even when you were a teenager, you knew that there were alternatives to complying with your father's wishes, and that your parents' wants were very different than your own."

"Yes," she replied. "I did know that."

"What did you want then?"

"I wanted"—as if to illustrate her longings Laura spread her arms wide and tilted her head back—"I wanted to hitch my wagon to a real star! I wanted to live, really live, not just exist. I wanted tenderness and love and joy and passion—"

"Then here's your chance," Thad broke in eagerly. "Come with me this weekend, Laura."

Her arms fell limply to her sides. "Have you forgotten the gallery is open on Saturdays?"

"Trina could cover for you. I checked with her several weeks ago, and she said she'd be happy to look after the shop anytime you wanted to take off."

"I see," Laura replied evasively.

She was stunned by Thad's confidence in himself, by his certainty that she could let herself go and enjoy whatever developed in their relationship. She wished she had even a fraction of his assurance. She wished she could believe it was possible to break out of her shell, but at the moment the idea seemed awesome.

"Is this an ultimatum, Thad?" she asked quietly.

"It's an invitation, nothing more."

"What if I refuse?"

"I'll ask you again some other time." Before she could offer further objections, Thad rushed on. "I don't mean to pressure you, Laura, but I want you so badly. I think I'm falling in love with you."

"Do you think *that* doesn't pressure me?"

"I think it frightens you, and I wish I knew why. I used to think you were afraid of sex, but now I'm not so sure. After the way you've responded to me—"

"No," Laura broke in softly. "I'm not afraid of sex. Not with you, Thad."

Encouraged by this admission, Thad took her in his arms. "You know I'd never hurt you, Laura. I care for you far too much ever to hurt you."

Deeply moved, Laura put her arms around his waist and returned his embrace.

"I know you do," she murmured. "And I"—her breath caught in her throat—"I care for you, Thad."

"Do you trust me?"

"Yes. Yes, I do."

"Then I don't get it, Laura. What's holding you back? Is it that you're afraid of making a commitment?"

"Yes, that's it," she agreed quickly. Too quickly. Trying to divert him, she said, "Do I have to give you my answer tonight? Can I have some time to think about it?"

"I should have known you'd say that!" Thad groaned. Then he laughed relievedly because it had dawned on him that Laura hadn't given him a flat no, and this supported his belief that sooner or later they would be lovers. He hugged her close and kissed the top of her head.

"My lovely Laura," he whispered, "I told you I don't want to pressure you, and I meant it. Of course, you can have time."

CHAPTER TEN

At some point in the next few days Laura acknowledged that it was futile to fight against her longing for Thad. He had blazed his way across her horizon like a shooting star, sweeping her into his orbit and shining his light into the dark, lonely corners of her life. He exerted a dynamic gravitational force that she was powerless to resist. He dazzled her, yet for all his dangerous brilliance, the more she tried to talk herself out of accepting his invitation, the more she wanted to go away with him.

She would never know precisely when she became resigned to the inevitable, nor did she know why she decided to accompany Thad on his trip to Windigo Lake.

Perhaps it was because Thad was so sure that she would. Perhaps, like him, she had become convinced that their affair was predestined. Or perhaps it was simply because Trina proved to be such an able and willing accomplice.

Since the Gallery of Gifts had opened, Trina had spent so much time there with Laura that there was no need to teach her the relatively simple tasks of writing out sales slips and packaging whatever articles a customer purchased. And since Thad's cousin had at least a nodding acquaintance with most of the population of Ely, if a customer wanted to pay by check, she wouldn't have to ask for identification as often as Laura did.

Neither did it help that Thad had to make an unexpected trip to International Falls to deal with a personnel problem that had cropped up in that town's branch of his sporting goods store. He left town Tuesday morning, and by the time he phoned that night, Laura had admitted to herself how essential he was to her.

She didn't have a photograph of Thad, but she had made a sketch of him, and after he called, she propped the drawing against the lamp on her nightstand. She fell asleep looking at her sketch of Thad's face, and when she woke on Wednesday morning, she knew she was in love with him.

When Trina had pleaded Thad's cause, she'd told Laura that if Thad asked anything of her she preferred not to grant, all she had to do was say no. At the time, Laura had known it would not be easy to refuse him. What she hadn't reckoned with was that it would be impossible.

Common sense told her that drifting into sexual intimacy with Thad would leave her completely defenseless, but it seemed that her misgivings were no longer relevant.

Nevertheless, she discussed her uncertainties with Thad when he called on Wednesday night. He'd shown surprising compassion when she'd told him about her childhood troubles on Monday evening, but she sensed that now he would make light of her doubts. She thought he would probably try to reassure her with nonsensical remarks about Bristol's Law, and as it turned out, she was right.

"You're borrowing trouble, Laura," Thad said dismissively. "We could argue about this till doomsday, but the bottom line is that you want to go away with me this weekend. You know you do. So why not bite the bullet and accept my invitation?"

"You're constantly saying I know all sorts of things," Laura hedged. "What I'd really like to know is where you get your information."

Adopting a lilting brogue, Thad answered evasively, "Ah, now, mavourneen, that would be tellin'."

"That's the general idea," Laura parried tartly.

"Well then, darlin', let's just say that I could tell by the gleam in your bonny eyes and the pricklin' in my thumbs that you've worked yourself into a sorry state with all your worryin', and the reason you're so worried is because you want me as much as I want you." Dropping the accent, Thad concluded, "Now, you tell me . . . am I wrong?"

Try as she might, Laura could not make herself issue a denial. The words trembled on the tip of her tongue, but she found that she couldn't lie to Thad—not about her feelings for him—and when she remained silent, he asked, "Why fight it, love? Remember Bristol's Law? What we feel for each other is bigger and stronger than both of us, and the only possible way to win is through surrender." After a significant pause he added in a deep, seductive growl, "*Unconditional* surrender."

With that, Thad hung up, leaving her to stare at the telephone with frustration. The phrase *unconditional surrender* echoed and reechoed through her mind, and she was shocked at how appealing it was.

As Laura replaced the receiver in its cradle, Groucho rubbed against her ankles. She knelt down to pet him, and he arched his back and purred at her consolingly.

"I love him so much, Groucho," Laura murmured. "And I do want him."

The cat blinked one green eye as if he understood and was winking at her.

"I'm going to go away with him this weekend," she said calmly. "I don't know whether it's the end of the beginning or the beginning of the end, but no matter what happens afterward, at least I'll have that much to remember."

She rose and wandered into her bedroom with Groucho scampering after her. She sat on the edge of the bed, studying the drawing of Thad's face, and when the cat leaped onto the mattress beside her, she spoke conversationally.

"Do you think it's possible to squeeze a whole lifetime of loving into a single weekend?"

Groucho meowed and shook himself.

"You're absolutely right," said Laura. "I haven't had much practice. But oh, Groucho, I love him so!"

The cat curled up on her pillow and gazed at her steadily. It seemed that he had no arguments that outweighed her love for Thad. And neither did she.

Although she followed her bedtime ritual of checking the locks and turning off the lights, Laura didn't expect to sleep that night. She did, however, and on Thursday afternoon when Trina came into the gallery, Laura was busy at work in the studio, humming as she removed the last tray of porcelain Christmas ornaments from the kiln.

"These are adorable!" Trina exclaimed, surveying the rows of tiny, perfectly modeled elves and sugarplum fairies, unicorns and prancing reindeer. "They should sell like hotcakes."

"They did turn out rather well," Laura allowed cheerfully.

Trina did a double take and remarked, "You're certainly in a good mood today."

"Yes, I am."

"I'm glad you are," said Trina, "because I've done something you probably won't like very much."

"What's that?"

Before Trina could answer, the bell above the street door rang. Trina started, whirled around, and peeked into the shop.

"Oh, Lord," she groaned. "She's early."

"Who's early?" asked Laura, smiling blithely.

"Aunt Dorothy," Trina whispered.

"Thad's mother?" Laura's smile faded. In an impassioned undertone she demanded, "What's she doing here?"

"I invited her to come for tea—in your behalf naturally," Trina hurriedly replied. "I'd planned to explain it all before she got here, but I got hung up at home, and now she's early and—Please, Laura, just play along with whatever I say. Trust me!"

"It seems I have no alternative," Laura muttered ruefully.

For the next half hour she complied with Trina's request and played along with her, although at times she was hard pressed to keep a straight face.

While she washed up and ran a comb through her hair, Trina prepared tea. She even produced a batch of butter cookies that she must have baked especially for the occasion.

When Laura finally came into the shop, she found Trina and Dorothy chatting in front of the Franklin stove. After Laura and Dorothy had exchanged stilted but polite hellos, Trina picked up the thread of her conversation with her aunt.

"The gallery's business has slacked off a bit," said Trina.

Looking terribly grande dame, Dorothy arched one eyebrow. With blatant insincerity she remarked, "What a shame."

"Yes, isn't it?" Trina replied. "But you understand that sales haven't fallen off any more than Laura expected they would now that summer's over."

"I'm relieved to hear that," Dorothy said dryly.

"Somehow I knew you would be, Aunt Dorothy," Trina remarked sweetly. "Anyway Laura came up with this fabulous idea for enticing new customers into the shop and keeping the interest of her regulars."

"Really?" Dorothy glanced sharply at Laura. "What is your idea?"

Laura took a sip of tea and helped herself to a cookie before she replied, "Why don't we let Trina answer that question. She's doing such a beautiful job of explaining this—uh—this project of mine."

Trina smiled broadly, her eyes dancing with mischief. "Thank you, Laura. I appreciate your confidence in me." Turning to her aunt, she continued. "Laura thought that she'd try a whole new approach to retailing by having a sort of open house every afternoon between three and four o'clock. She plans to serve refreshments—simple things like tea or coffee and cookies, maybe more elaborate pastries on very special occasions. What's your opinion, Aunt Dorothy? Do you think it would be worthwhile to advertise afternoon teas at the Gallery of Gifts? To really promote them?"

"It sounds feasible to me." Shrugging negligently, Dorothy took a bite of cookie. Her forehead creased in a frown, and she studied the cookie as if she were still pondering Trina's question. At last she replaced the cookie on her saucer and took a sip of tea. "Actually," she went on judiciously, "the idea of holding afternoon teas is quite a good one."

"Then you approve?" Trina cried. She sounded elated, but she looked as if she were mystified by her aunt's reaction. "I'm so pleased," she finished lamely.

"However," Dorothy amended, "there is one problem." She touched the cookie with a fingertip, moving it about on the saucer as if she found it repellent. "These," she proclaimed regally, "are the worst cookies I've ever tasted. If your plan is to succeed, Laura, you'll need some assistance with the baking."

Her curiosity aroused, Laura would have sampled her own cookie, but Dorothy stopped her, saying, "I wouldn't if I were you. Take my word for it, it tastes as if someone substituted lard for the butter that the recipe calls for."

117

Trina choked on her tea, and Dorothy patted her on the back while Laura watched, fascinated.

"We'll excuse you now, dear," said Dorothy when Trina's coughing fit had ended. "You must have any number of things to do at home."

"But Aunt Dorothy—"

"I'll see you soon," Dorothy interjected, dismissing her niece.

Red-faced, Trina kissed her aunt's cheek, made her farewells to Laura, and left the shop; for several minutes after she had gone, Laura and Dorothy did not speak to each other. Laura was puzzling over Trina's decidedly odd behavior—baffled by it, wondering what she had hoped to gain with her deception—and Dorothy seemed equally lost in her own thoughts.

At last Laura shook herself out of her introspection and, remembering she had a guest, offered Dorothy more tea. She refilled her own cup as well, and when she had replaced the teapot on its tray, she saw that Dorothy was watching her above the rim of her cup.

"I presume this whole charade was Trina's idea," Dorothy remarked amiably.

"It was," Laura acceded. "Obviously when she asked you to come here today, she hoped that we would establish a truce. Thad must have told her that you and I had had a falling out, but I haven't the foggiest notion why she pulled the stunt with the cookies. Could it have been an accident?"

"No," Dorothy replied. "Trina's too good a cook to make such an error unintentionally. She deliberately used lard instead of butter, you can be sure of that."

"But why would she do that? What did she hope to accomplish by making me look like a klutz?"

"Apparently my niece thought that if I could be made to believe you were totally inept in some area, it would engage my sympathies."

118

"If that was her purpose, why did she have to choose cooking?" Laura smiled wistfully and shook her head. "Heaven knows I'm no pastry chef, but I wouldn't mistake lard for butter any more than Trina would, and there are lots of things I'd like to be able to do well that I'm not particularly skilled at."

"For instance?" Dorothy queried.

"Gardening, for one. You'll notice that I don't have any houseplants."

"Now that you mention it, yes."

"Well, that's because I tried everything before I finally learned that, much as I wish I had a green thumb, I just don't."

Dorothy nodded thoughtfully.

"I'm a nail biter too," said Laura, "whenever I get nervous—which is much too often, as you can see," she said with a laugh.

"You? Nervous? I find that hard to believe," Dorothy said thoughtfully. "My husband would tell you that I've always trusted my instincts and that I attach a great deal of weight to first impressions. As a matter of fact, Ira would say that I give them too much importance, but that's neither here nor there. The point is, the first time I saw you, you struck me as the type who never has to get nervous—the type to whom everything comes easily . . . *too* easily."

Laura was astonished, not because she didn't try to project exactly that impression of self-assurance, but because her performance had fooled someone as knowledgeable as Dorothy.

"So when you threatened to tell your friends to stay away from the gallery—"

"I hoped you'd choose the course of least resistance," said Dorothy. "But it wasn't my social position I was protecting."

"It was Thad," said Laura.

119

"You're right again." Dorothy smiled with real warmth. "You see, Laura, it's been my experience that when everything comes to a person effortlessly, they tend to react to obstacles in one of two ways. Either they'll give up at the first sign of opposition, or they'll bulldoze their way through almost anything to achieve their goal."

"And when I refused to stop seeing Thad—" Laura prompted.

"I thought you were one of the latter," Dorothy finished. "I also thought you were an opportunist. I was convinced that you saw a golden opportunity in my son, and that you'd stop at nothing to get him. And you were so cool—so clearly in control. I've always been suspicious of people who are that controlled."

As she got to her feet and drew her mink jacket about her shoulders, the older woman declared, "That's about all the baring of my soul I can take in one sitting, except for one thing. I'm still not convinced that I was wrong about you, Laura, but I'm beginning to hope that I was."

"I hope I was wrong too, Mrs. Bristol," said Laura as she accompanied Dorothy to the door of the shop. "You once said that if we'd met under different circumstances, we might have been friends—"

"And you told me you doubted we'd have been friends no matter how we'd met." With her hand on the doorknob Dorothy turned to look at Laura. "Are you saying you think we might be friends after all?"

By no means was this a plea. There was nothing at all apologetic in Dorothy's demeanor. On the contrary Laura had never seen her look more regal. But at the same time she also seemed more approachable.

"Perhaps," Laura answered doubtfully, her face pensive. But when Dorothy offered an encouraging smile, she said more firmly, "Yes, Mrs. Bristol, I do think we might be friends."

CHAPTER ELEVEN

Shortly after Dorothy left, Trina telephoned the gallery to ask how Laura and her aunt had got along after she had been summarily dismissed.

"Better than we did before," was Laura's ambiguous reply.

"That's not saying very much."

"No, it isn't," said Laura.

A long silence ensued while Trina mulled over Laura's saccharine but uncommunicative responses. At last she said, "You're angry with me, aren't you?"

"How did you guess?" Laura answered crossly.

Trina sighed. "I can't say I blame you, Laura. Obviously my plan to engage Aunt Dorothy's sympathies backfired, but I hope you'll try to bear in mind that my intentions were good."

"You know what they say about good intentions," Laura pointed out evenly. Her voice rose heatedly as she said, "From now on, Trina, if you feel the need to smooth a pathway to hell, I wish you'd grease your own skids and leave mine alone!"

"I will, Laura. You have my solemn oath that I will never interfere again," Trina promised contritely. "But please, tell me one thing. Was it really all that bad?"

Somewhat mollified, Laura replied, "Not really. In an odd sort of way, it was entertaining. It was also a bit embarrassing for both of us, but your aunt and I talked for a few minutes after you left, and that cleared the air. I think we understand each other better now. Given time, we might even become friends."

"Oh, I hope so, Laura," Trina said fervently.

"So do I," Laura agreed.

She realized she had crossed her fingers while she wished for a more amicable relationship with Dorothy, and she silently chided herself for indulging in superstition. But, she acknowledged, childish though it was, the indulgence underscored how anxious she was for Thad's mother to like and accept her.

Before Trina said good-bye, she stated her intention of working in the gallery the next morning so that Laura would have time to pack for the weekend and take care of miscellaneous last-minute errands.

"I've already packed," Laura demurred. "And, Trina, it's only a weekend trip. What sort of errands would I have?"

"Well, I thought you might want to have your hair done or do some shopping."

"Shopping? For what?"

"Carroll's is having a sale," Trina answered enthusiastically. "They have perfectly gorgeous lingerie, and I thought if you needed nightgowns or negligees or anything like that—"

"You're about as subtle as a sledgehammer," Laura cut in, "and you're interfering again."

"Am I?" Trina's voice was shrill with amazement. She sounded so innocent, Laura couldn't help laughing.

"You know very well that you are," she said lightheartedly. "And you must also know that you're incorrigible, so I won't bother telling you that. But after seeing Dorothy in action, at least now I know where you and Thad got your streak of stubbornness."

"We're not at all stubborn. We're merely determined," Trina said with a laugh, defending Thad and herself, and

122

on that friendly note, she and Laura ended their conversation.

Laura's lighthearted mood was even more marked the following morning.

For the past week the weather had been seasonably crisp and clear—Thad called it "football weather"—but Friday dawned warm and balmy, a perfect Indian summer's day. The scent of burning leaves perfumed the air, and a slight haziness muted the autumnal blue of the sky. The glare of the sun was diffused by the haze, so that it washed over the landscape, soft as melted butter, turning the tarnished-copper leaves on the maple trees in Laura's front yard to flame.

Trina arrived at the gallery bright and early, as soon as she had delivered Kit to his preschool, which enabled Laura to spend the morning installing a harvest display in the front windows of the shop.

It was almost noon before she was satisfied with the arrangement of cornstalks and scarecrows, fat orange pumpkins and a few of the jaunty earthenware jack-o'-lanterns she had made in honor of Halloween.

"They'll sell like hotcakes," Trina predicted when she saw the jack-o'-lanterns.

Laura laughed merrily. "That's a lovely compliment, Trina, but you say that about everything I make."

"Can I help it if I admire your work?"

"And I'm glad you admire it," said Laura. "It's just that I wonder what you'd say if I made some ceramic hotcakes. Maybe I could make whole stacks of them and they could be used as bookends."

"I'd have to see them first," Trina countered, reproachfully tossing her head. "But just you wait, Laura Powell. You'll see how right I am about the jack-o'-lanterns. I might even buy one myself."

Not only did Trina decide to do that, but by two o'clock

123

she had sold three more of them, and for the next hour she gloated over her salesmanship, repeatedly reminding Laura of the accuracy of her judgment.

"Now that you've learned how infallible I am," she teased, "perhaps you'd care to reconsider about going to the sale at Carroll's. Are you sure you don't need a nightgown or two?"

"*Yes,* I'm sure," Laura insisted.

But when Thad arrived a few minutes after three, she wondered if it would have been wise to heed Trina's advice.

Perhaps she had also chosen wrongly when she'd packed her suitcase and when she'd got dressed that morning. Since the cabin was miles from the nearest town, she had assumed that the most casual clothes were called for. With that in mind she was wearing a denim wraparound skirt and a bandanna-print blouse, but Thad's attire was more formal.

He wore fawn slacks, a suede jacket, and an open-collared shirt in a tawny amber-brown that matched his eyes; he was, she thought, more attractive than any one man had a right to be.

Laura's uncertainty faded, however, when Thad caught her in his arms and kissed her hello.

"This has been the longest week of my life," he whispered, and when Laura nodded agreement, she saw that her own eagerness to be alone with him was mirrored in his smile.

"When did you get back?" she asked.

"About half an hour ago." Thad's grin broadened. "I dropped by my place to pick up some clean clothes and check in with the store, but I didn't even stop to change."

And that, thought Laura, explained why he wasn't dressed more casually.

"Are you ready to leave?" he asked.

"Are you kidding!" Trina exclaimed. "She's been ready since sunup."

Thad looked at Laura quizzically. "Is she putting me on?"

"No, she isn't," Laura confessed. Turning to Trina, she said, "Are you sure you'll be all right on your own?"

"Don't worry about the gallery," Trina answered. "Everything's under control."

"Maybe I should leave a phone number—"

"There's no telephone at the cabin," Thad broke in. "It has all the other conveniences, but no telephone. That's part of its charm."

"Laura," said Trina, "will you just get out of here! You have my word that everything will be fine."

"Well . . ." Laura began hesitantly.

"Come on, love." With his hand at the small of her back, Thad propelled her toward the door. "Let's collect your suitcase and be on our way."

She felt the impatience in his touch, saw the urgency in his eyes, and her momentary uncertainty vanished.

"All right," she agreed, laughing, and as Thad hurried her toward the kitchen she called a hasty good-bye to Trina.

Her suitcase and handbag were ready and waiting by the kitchen door, and she could have sworn her feet hardly touched the ground as Thad rushed her to his pickup.

Once they were in the truck, he took her in his arms. They kissed again, and this time his kiss was deeper and more satisfying than the one he'd given her in Trina's presence. Laura wanted to stay in his arms forever, and when Thad moved away from her and started the engine, it was apparent that he was as reluctant to end their embrace as she was.

"The sooner we get going, the sooner we'll be at the cabin," he remarked gruffly.

Unsure of her voice, Laura merely nodded.

They talked very little during the ninety-minute drive to Windigo Lake. She inquired about Thad's week, and he told her his work had gone well. He felt sure that he had solved the personnel problem at the International Falls store. He complimented her on the new window displays at the gallery, and she was taken aback that he'd noticed.

"Given the proper incentive, I'm a very observant fellow," he said lightly. "You should know by now that I notice everything about you, Laura."

They reached the shore of Lake Superior and turned north, following Highway 61. They drove through the town of Little Marais, past Caribou Falls and the Temperance River, and stopped at a general store in Lutsen to purchase fresh meat and produce for the weekend. When they began the last leg of their trip, Laura told Thad about Trina's attempt to negotiate a truce between his mother and her. They were still laughing over the ill-fated butter cookies when Thad pulled into the narrow county road that led to Windigo Lake.

Laura was enchanted by the cabin. Small and quaintly rustic, built of dark-stained cedar logs, it was nestled in a birch grove on the lakeshore. The living room was a smaller version of the reception area in Thad's Ely store, right down to the native-stone fireplace that filled one wall. The only discernible difference was that this room had windows that offered spectacular views of the woods and the lake.

As they stowed away the groceries Thad explained, "All of our cabins are similar to this one. Some are larger —built to accommodate six or eight instead of four—but the living room is our trademark, so all of them are virtually identical."

Laura glanced through the archway into the living room. From her vantage point in the kitchen she could see the hall leading from the far end of the living room, but there were only two doors opening off the hall.

"You said this cabin sleeps four?"

"That's right," said Thad. "The sofa makes into a double bed. Come along and I'll show you the bedroom and bath."

She followed after him slowly as he completed the tour of the cabin. The bathroom was compact, and the bedroom not much larger than the bath. The wide double bed with which it was furnished occupied most of the floor space.

The sight of the bed, the thought of sharing it with Thad, revived Laura's misgivings. Tonight, she told herself, they would sleep in that bed together, and with this reminder the bed no longer looked so wide.

But it wasn't the idea of sleeping with Thad that disturbed her. She had told him she wasn't afraid of being intimate with him, and that was true. Sex was easy, and loving Thad was easy too. In fact, it was impossible not to love him.

What was hard was believing that he loved her. What was frightening was thinking of what might happen if he did love her.

For a few fleeting moments Laura's doubts threatened to chase away her lightheartedness. Then Thad touched her shoulder. He smiled at her, and something inside her seemed to melt and yearn for him. Her heart skipped with happiness, and her carefree mood prevailed.

Acting on an impulse, she hugged him and cried, "It's a wonderful cabin, Thad, and we're going to have a wonderful weekend."

"Yes, we are," he said quietly, and she was buoyed by his confidence as they returned to the living room.

While Thad laid a fire in the fireplace, Laura sauntered about the room, exclaiming over the view and admiring the wood carvings on the mantel.

"Everything appears to be in tip-top condition," she

127

observed. "What kind of maintenance work do you have to do?"

"This and that," Thad replied. "A section of the roof needs to be reshingled, and this cabin isn't used in the winter, so the utilities have to be switched off and the water pipes drained. There's also a broken window in the bedroom that I should replace."

Laura's smile became a bit strained when Thad mentioned the bedroom, but she resolved not to dwell on what the evening would bring. More than anything else, she wanted to relax and let whatever happened between them *happen*. She even dared to hope she would enjoy making love with Thad. Surely loving him as she did, wanting him so desperately, she should be able to respond.

Her nagging doubts calmed, she went into the kitchen and began preparing the clam sauce for the linguine they'd planned for dinner.

She concentrated on the tasks at hand and tried to forget about the past. She refused to worry about tomorrow or fret about tonight. She vowed to live for the moment, but as the afternoon waned and twilight fell she became more and more uneasy.

By the time dinner was over and they had cleared away their few dishes, Thad had sensed her nervousness.

"There's nothing to be uptight about, love," he reassured her. "I'm not going to pounce on you without warning or anything like that."

"I know you're not," Laura replied timorously. But when they went into the living room, she sat stiffly on the very edge of the couch with her hands clasped in her lap, staring into the fire.

"Relax, Laura," said Thad. "Nothing's going to happen unless you want it to."

But I want something to happen, she thought. *I want* everything *to happen.* She couldn't seem to say this aloud, but she managed to produce a smile.

128

"Why don't I see if I can find some dance music on the radio," said Thad. "Would you like to dance?"

She nodded stiffly, and Thad crossed to the radio and fiddled with the dials. At first it seemed that he would find only static, but eventually he tuned in an instrumental arrangement of a sultry, hauntingly evocative torch song. Laura couldn't identify the orchestra, but the breathy wail of the saxophones was as torrid as a tropic wind.

Thad turned toward her, snapping his fingers and moving his shoulders in time to the music.

"How's that?" he inquired.

"Fine, I suppose," Laura answered tentatively. In her agitation she babbled on. "With all those saxophones it sounds like a theme from an old detective movie. Do you remember them? They almost always had one scene where a blonde who looks like a contestant from a Miss Sexpot Pageant slithers into the detective's office and says something terribly suggestive—"

"As a matter of fact," said Thad, "I'm not sure I do remember. Refresh my memory."

Laura faltered momentarily, thinking that she had dated herself. Then she recalled that she had seen the detective thrillers only on TV and she said, "Well, she'd probably begin by making some corny reference to her well-endowed figure. Then she'd explain that she had no money, but she'd find some way to pay his fee if he'd take her case, and she'd end up by flattering him and giving him a come-on. Maybe she'd say something like, "A little bird told me you're a guy who enjoys living dangerously."

Grinning, Thad picked up the narrative. "And our fearless gumshoe would reply, 'The only little birds I know are stool pigeons, but I could go the limit with a gorgeous broad like you, sweetheart.'"

Thad flipped the wall switch, turning off the table lamps so that the room was bathed in the flickering glow of the fire.

"How about you, Laura?" he asked softly. "Are you ready to live dangerously?"

Was he joking? Laura wondered. His face was ruddy in the firelight, but it was too dark to read the expression in his eyes. Even so, when he held his arms out to her, she went into them willingly.

They started dancing, and initially she felt awkward. When she felt his body against hers, her nervousness increased. She followed his lead clumsily until he pressed her forehead into the curve of his shoulder and began massaging the back of her neck.

"It's all right, love," Thad whispered.

The touch of his hand was soothing, quieting, and she was completely disarmed by his gentleness. Gradually her tension drained away, leaving her soft and pliant in his arms, and she found herself moving with him automatically to the slow cadence of the dance.

The firelight projected their shadows onto the walls and ceiling of the room, and for a time she watched them through half-open eyes, entranced by the graceful movements of the shadow pair. Then Thad wound both arms around her waist, and she swayed closer to him. He tipped her head back and studied her face while his fingertips traced her eyebrows, her temples, her earlobes, the delicate hollows at the base of her throat; when he laid his cheek against hers, her body flowed into his.

Thad began pressing little biting kisses along the side of her neck and the shadow pair blended into one figure, but Laura was no longer watching. She closed her eyes and entered a dreamlike state as his mouth slid across her cheek. His lips found hers, and he kissed her tenderly at first; then again, more deeply; then a third time with a fierce ardor that told her how much he wanted her; and she responded unrestrainedly to the hot open-mouthed urgency of his kiss.

His hands skimmed over her lightly, tantalizing her,

arousing her, searing her through her clothes, caressing her back, her shoulders, the sides of her breasts, and she returned his caresses, luxuriating in the rugged strength of his body.

She worked at his shirt buttons, her fingers shaking with eagerness, and his hands clutched at her hips, fitting her softness to his hard masculinity, letting her feel his arousal. She rubbed her cheek against his chest, then repeated the caress with her mouth. She trailed a feverish line of kisses over his smooth, warm skin, and when she touched her lips to his hard male nipples, his passion grew until his body was as tautly drawn as a bowstring, and she experienced a rush of pride that she could excite him so.

By now Thad had dropped any pretense of dancing, but the radio played on, wrapping them in an invisible web of music, and when he unbuttoned her blouse and slipped it off her shoulders, it seemed an integral part of their love dance. It seemed to her there was was a graceful choreography about their gestures as slowly, garment by garment, they removed the rest of their clothing. And when they were naked, Thad caught her in his arms and crushed her close against him, holding her so tightly that she felt as if his body were being indelibly imprinted upon hers.

Laura almost cried out at her deprivation when Thad's mouth left hers, and though his hands stopped caressing her momentarily, he lifted her in his arms and carried her to the sofa. He set her on her feet, letting her body slide down against the proud, hard length of his, and as he sank back on the couch he drew her between his thighs and held her so that she was standing in front of him.

His passion-darkened gaze strayed over her with excruciating slowness, as if he wanted to memorize the way the firelight honeyed her skin; as if he wanted always to remember every line, every curve, every mysterious hollow of her body. At last his eyes sought hers and, reaching up, he ran the backs of his fingers over one flushed cheek.

131

His hands were a bit rough with impatience as they coasted downward over her shoulders to cup her breasts.

"You are so beautiful, love," he whispered raggedly. "Do you see what you do to me?"

Laura could not answer, and she couldn't bear the small distance between them. She had to touch him, and when she cradled his head in her hands, his arms closed about her and pulled her nearer. She wove her fingers through his hair, delighting in its springy texture. She touched his shoulders and ran her hands over his back again and again in light repetitive caresses while his hands played over her intimately, tenderly, and his lips explored the satiny slope of her breast.

A husky cry of pleasure escaped her as his mouth fastened around the nipple. His tongue swirled over it with exquisite slowness; outlining the rosy blush of the areola; working sweetly at the tip, teasing it, coaxing it into a tight bud, tugging at it until it was impossibly swollen.

"I love you, Thad," she breathed, "and, oh darling, I want you so!"

Her voice was barely audible, but Thad must have heard her because his hold on her tightened and his mouth moved lower, blazing a line of kisses along her rib cage and across her belly. He paused to draw moist designs about her navel with the tip of his tongue, and when she trembled with anticipation, he groaned and pulled her down so that she was seated across his thighs.

Again his mouth claimed hers and they kissed deeply, hungrily, caressing each other, pleasuring each other. He fondled the velvety petals of flesh between her thighs, touching her and touching her and touching her until she was giddy and her senses reeled with wanting him.

Sensing her readiness, Thad tumbled her off his lap so that she was lying beneath him, and when she opened her eyes and saw his face poised above her own, when she felt his hardness pressing against her, demanding entry, hot and throbbing with urgency, a faint twinge of alarm shot through her.

But Thad felt her tense. He saw the shadow of fear in her eyes, and he took her face between his hands and kissed her again. His tongue twined with hers playfully, sampling the sweetest recesses of her mouth, thrusting and darting with gentle insistence until, overwhelmed by his passion, she arched her hips to receive him.

When Thad felt her eagerness, he very nearly lost control. He yearned to plunge into her, but he was afraid he might hurt her and he didn't want to frighten her with the violence of his need. He penetrated her slowly, almost languorously, so that their bodies seemed to melt together, and Laura knew only that one minute she was empty and aching for him, and the next she was filled.

She gave herself over to instinct, lifting her hips provocatively, responding to his slightest movement, and suddenly she was caught up in a dizzying maelstrom of desire, swept into a spiral of delight that seemed timeless and endless, a spiral that was bounded by the sensations Thad evoked with his bold caresses, a spiral that was measured by pulsebeats and whispered love words and the electrifying clash of naked flesh with naked flesh.

The tempo of their movements quickened, then quickened again explosively, and Laura abandoned herself to the wild, primitive rhythm of their lovemaking.

She felt the fluid pulsations that signaled release, yet when the moment of release came, it took her by surprise. Her rapture erupted in fiery starbursts behind her closed eyelids, and she was stunned by its brilliance, awed by its splendor, shaken by its intensity. The earth seemed to stand still, to send her spinning off into oblivion, and when she cried out to Thad to hold her, he wrapped his arms and legs around her and held her painfully, wonderfully close. He rained soft kisses on her mouth and smoothed the damp wisps of hair away from her face, gentling her as the spinning stopped and she floated down to earth.

"I love you, Laura," he whispered.

Her eyelids fluttered open, and when she saw his face so close to hers, she felt as if she might burst with joy.

"I love you," he repeated hoarsely, "more than I can say."

"I love you, my darling," she murmured, "and I thank you for not giving up on me."

Thad frowned. "Now, why would I do a damn-fool thing like that? You have to know how much I've wanted to make love to you, especially after I told you about my theory. . . ."

"Bristol's Law?" Laura supplied, smiling.

Thad nodded agreement. He was so close, they rubbed noses.

"Then it wasn't a line?"

"No way!" he cried indignantly. "When I told you about Bristol's Law, I meant every word, and now I'm convinced that my theory is correct. I mean, what just happened between us . . ." Pausing, he shook his head with wonderment. "All I know is that it must be very rare. I've never experienced anything quite like it."

Laura smiled again, this time incredulously, which prompted Thad to erase the smile with a hot, marauding kiss, punishing her sweetly for teasing him.

"Stop taking me so damn literally and be serious," he growled. His usual coolness seemed to have deserted him as he continued. "You'll probably take this the wrong way too—or maybe you'll understand me perfectly and still think I'm being foolish, but—well, making love to you was—It was—Oh, hell! It was physical, sure. And it was sexual. I wouldn't deny that if I could! But there was something else, Laura. Something . . . spiritual. . . ."

"I know, darling. I felt it too." Laura averted her eyes

as she confided, "Bristol's Law frightened me, Thad. I didn't think I could live up to your expectations—"

"But you did, love, and then some!" Thad shouted exultantly. His voice dropped an octave as he said, "I always knew that if you gave me half a chance, I could make you respond to me, but I never dreamed that you'd be so passionate."

"Neither did I," Laura admitted shyly. When she raised her eyes and looked at him, she seemed to see him through a romantic haze. "Being with you was beautiful, Thad. It was—"

Thad silenced her with a kiss. His lips brushed hers as he murmured, "Why are you using the past tense, Laura? The night is young—and so are we—and I intend to make the most of our weekend together."

He moved against her in a lithe, suggestive caress that told her more eloquently than words that he wanted to make love to her again. His body was hot and hard and possessive against hers, and this time her response was immediate and unequivocal.

"My God," she gasped. "You really are amazing!"

"You inspire me," Thad replied seductively. "But please, love, save your applause for later."

"Applause?" Laura laughed breathlessly. "You deserve a standing ovation!"

"I'll settle for an encore," Thad whispered thickly.

After this, Laura let her body speak for her, and they came together in a joyous surge of passion that consumed them utterly and left them spent and devastated.

Afterward they clung to each other, too fulfilled to speak, too contented to move.

The music played on, the fire burned down to glowing embers, and the room grew chilly. Thad left her long enough to turn the radio off and find a blanket, but neither of them thought to fold out the sofa bed.

He spread the blanket over her and lay down beside her

on the couch. Then he took her in his arms and they made love again, this time with a tender sensuality that stirred her very soul. Laura wept at the beauty of it, and sometime after midnight, still clinging together, they drifted into sleep.

CHAPTER TWELVE

When Laura was in high school, she had taken the required sex education courses. She'd read a few magazine articles on the subject and she'd listened avidly whenever her classmates discussed it in the locker room, but after the traumatic assault upon her, she had lost her adolescent curiosity about sex.

Now she wished she were more knowledgeable, for she found that none of those early sources had prepared her for this moment. Not one of them had offered any practical advice about what you were supposed to say or how you were supposed to behave when you saw your lover for the first time after you'd made love.

When she saw Thad coming toward her along the lakeshore the next morning, she was amazed that this was the first thought that popped into her head. Surely she should have been concerned with something profound, and this seemed so prosaic.

But then all of her reactions—or rather the presence of some reactions and the absence of others—both last night and this morning, had been something of a revelation to Laura.

The ease with which Thad had infiltrated the barrier of her misgivings had been the first surprise, and her relative lack of inhibition had been the second. That these had been due to the intensity of her response to Thad was the third.

When she had awakened before dawn this morning, her first concern had been simply that she did not wish to disturb Thad's sleep. For several minutes she had lain close beside him, studying his face.

Perhaps it was an illusion created by the dusky light in the room, or perhaps it was only that in repose his boyish grin was gone, but she had thought he looked unnaturally solemn. He'd also seemed oddly vulnerable.

She'd wanted to stay with him, to watch over him while he was sleeping, but at the same time she'd needed to be alone for a while. Finally she had crept quietly away from the sofa.

As she was showering and getting dressed, she realized that she felt no regret, no guilt—only a healthy feeling of wholeness. By some strange paradox, the act of giving her body to Thad had made her feel complete.

The frosty morning had beckoned her. Everything was so glistening and clean, the world had seemed brand-new, and she had sneaked out of the cabin and arrived at the lakeshore in time to say good-bye to the morning star and hello to the sunrise.

At first the eastern horizon had been tinted rose and peach and gold. Then, as the sun moved higher, the sky turned a soft turquoise-blue, and a breeze sprang up and cleared away the last of the mist that had blanketed the surface of the lake.

In the next hour the breeze became more brisk. It gusted over the indigo water, trimming it with lacy, white-capped waves, and whipped Laura's hair about her face as she watched Thad's approach. When he reached her side, he smiled and brushed back a honey-gold strand of hair that clung to her cheek.

"Why didn't you wake me?" he asked.

Despite his smile he still looked uncharacteristically solemn, and since Laura had no wish to hurt his feelings, she answered with a half-truth.

138

"You were sleeping so peacefully, I didn't have the heart to wake you up."

"You wanted to be alone," Thad surmised.

Astonished that he should have guessed this, she summoned up a rather feeble smile and nodded.

Chuckling at her confusion, Thad wound one arm about her shoulders. "Don't be afraid to admit it, love. Sometimes I need privacy too."

"Then you understand?" she asked hopefully.

"Of course, I do."

"And you're not offended?"

"Nope."

To show her how unoffended he was, Thad gave her a reassuring squeeze and kissed her lightly on the forehead. Sighing with relief, Laura slipped an arm about his waist, and they started walking along the shore.

"Where did you get that sweater?" asked Thad.

Laura glanced down at the garment. It was a soft black cashmere—and it was much too large for her—but it was warm and comfortable, and she had brought nothing suitable of her own to wear on such a frosty morning.

"I found it in the closet," she replied.

"I thought it looked familiar," Thad drawled laconically.

The delicate flush in Laura's cheeks deepened. That she wore Thad's sweater next to her skin seemed a terribly intimate thing to do, like an overt acknowledgment of his stamp of possession on her. Had he assumed that was why she'd worn it?

"Don't feel bad," he said smoothly. "For some reason I never liked that sweater, but with you in it, it could grow on me."

His eyes wandered over her body, deliberately lingering on the fullness of her breasts. An instant later a gust of wind molded the sweater to her so that the contours of her

139

breasts were plainly outlined, and beneath Thad's admiring gaze her nipples tingled and grew saucily erect.

"Oh, yes," Thad murmured huskily. "That sweater is definitely very sexy on you."

Her unbidden excitement fed his own. The burgeoning swell of her nipples invited him to touch them. His arm about her shoulders tightened convulsively, hauling her close to his side, while his free hand tunneled under the soft cashmere of the sweater to find even softer skin. Then, with tantalizing slowness, his hand inched its way up to her breasts.

Intoxicated by the irresistible glide of his fingers, Laura leaned against him weakly as he caressed her, and for a time he simply held her.

Then Thad's face worked with some indefinable emotion. He opened his mouth as if to speak, and suddenly she couldn't bear the ecstasy of his caresses, the tenderness in his eyes. Somehow things had got out of control. She had become a wanton, a stranger to herself. With every passing moment she was being drawn into a deeper involvement with him, and she was frightened by where their intimacy might end.

She freed herself, swinging abruptly away from him, taking him by surprise with the unexpectedness of her movement. For a matter of seconds she confronted Thad silently, but when he started to speak once again, she panicked.

Whirling around, Laura started running, retracing their path through the trees along the shore.

"Race you to the cabin," she called, laughing brittlely. "I'm starving!"

Her heart was pounding wildly even before she'd started running away from Thad. By the time she had climbed the hill to the cabin, her breasts were heaving and her heart felt as if it would burst, but it was not until she had dashed inside that she recognized that her haste had been unnecessary.

Thad hadn't followed her. He had remained on the beach, and from the occasional glimpse of him she was able to catch, he appeared to be skipping stones across the water.

Although she had instinctively wanted to escape him, she was dismayed that he hadn't tried to stop her. In fact, his lack of concern was maddening.

Why hadn't he come after her? she wondered. Had she tried his affection too far with her evasions? Had his patience finally snapped? *Dear God,* Laura thought, *if I were to lose him, I would never forgive myself.*

She was shaking so badly, the simple chore of preparing breakfast seemed impossible. Besides, she wasn't really hungry.

Had Thad known that? He seemed to know everything else about her, so he must have known her plea of hunger was just another in her long list of excuses.

Thinking it might help her regain her composure, Laura heated some water and made a cup of coffee for herself. She carried the mug of coffee into the living room and stood at the windows, watching for Thad's return as she drank it.

The next half hour was the longest she had ever known. She was nervously sipping her second cup of coffee when Thad finally came loping up the hill and entered the cabin. He saw her standing by the windows and stopped just inside the door.

Smiling mirthlessly, he said, "What was that little performance on the beach all about, Laura? Was it your inimitable way of saying that I can get just so close to you and no closer?"

Laura shook her head helplessly. How could she tell Thad that she was frightened by the depth of her love for him?

141

Recognizing that she was not going to answer him, Thad tried to reason with her.

"Listen," he said evenly, "I know you need your space. There's nothing wrong with that, and there's nothing unique about it. Everyone does. Lord knows, I do. But last night I felt closer to you than I've ever felt to anyone. . . ."

"I felt the same way, Thad," she broke in softly.

"Okay. I can accept that," Thad said soberly. "What bothers me, though, is that there seems to be an irreconcilable divergence between what each of us needs from the other."

His eyes were opaque and unwavering as they held hers, and he was so very solemn. Unable to withstand his scrutiny, Laura turned away from him and stared blindly out the window.

"What do you mean?" she asked distantly.

"Just that where you're concerned, my needs seem to be insatiable. I've tried to play it cool because I'm aware of how uneasy that makes you, but to be perfectly honest I'm not sure how much longer I can handle it. The closer I get to you, the closer I want to be. The more I have of you, the more I want you."

Hearing Thad say these things was heaven—and it was hell! His admission robbed her of the will to resist. It threw her off-balance, stealing her equilibrium so that she swayed on her feet.

She closed her eyes and pressed her forehead against the coolness of the windowpane. She was unaware that Thad was standing close behind her until he removed the coffee mug from her nerveless fingers. He set the mug on the windowsill, and in the next moment his arms went around her waist, embracing her from behind.

He rubbed his bearded chin against her temple, and her knees went rubbery with desire. She leaned into the protective curve of his body, grateful for his support.

142

"Till now I've never given a damn if the woman I made love to was still in bed with me when I woke up the next morning," he went on gruffly. "But things are different with you, Laura. Not only do I want to make love to you, I want you to sleep beside me. I want to wake up holding you in my arms."

His hands moved over her in a slow, cherishing caress, molding themselves to the sweet roundness of her breasts and waist and thighs. Then his arms pulled her hard against him and his hands spread across her stomach, fitting her hips to his.

"Can you feel how much I want you?" he demanded.

Weak with wanting him, Laura nodded.

"Do you want me?"

"Oh, Thad, I ache with wanting you."

She spoke in an anguished whisper, and before the sound of her voice had completely died away, he had spun her around, and his mouth intercepted hers. They kissed hungrily, with an almost primal eroticism, and it was a long time before either of them recalled that they had never got around to eating breakfast.

CHAPTER THIRTEEN

Thad kissed Laura awake on Sunday morning. When she opened her eyes, the first thing she saw was his face.

It was chilly in the cabin. The tip of her nose felt as if it were frozen, and she slipped her arms around Thad and burrowed her nose into the side of his neck, luxuriating in the warmth he was radiating.

Grumbling that Laura's nose was so cold, she must be healthy, Thad shifted position slightly, giving her a bit more space in the cramped confines of the sofa.

Still half asleep, she mumbled, "Trina was wrong."

"About what?" Thad prompted.

"She thought I'd need a whole trousseau of nightgowns, but I haven't had the chance to wear even one." Laura paused to stifle a yawn. Her eyes drifted shut as she murmured, "So far we haven't actually been to bed."

Thad threw his head back and laughed heartily. He was still chuckling when he said, "Maybe next time we'll use the bedroom."

Her eyes flew open. "Will there be a next time?"

"Yes," said Thad, his voice deep with promise. "Oh, yes." Smiling, he added, "But tell me, do you usually wear a nightgown?"

Laura nodded. "What about you?"

"Never wear 'em," Thad declared, and when she gave his hair a punishing tug, he chuckled.

144

"Smart aleck," Laura chided. "You know what I mean."

Grinning, Thad replied, "Usually I sleep in the raw."

"Somehow I knew you'd say that." Another question occurred to her, and she touched the slant of his eyebrows, the bridge of his nose, the angle of his jaw as she asked, "How long have you been watching me?"

"Not long enough," Thad whispered.

She kissed him on the mouth, thanking him for his courtly reply, and for a time they lay quietly, their heads close together on the pillow.

Laura was almost asleep when Thad began caressing her. Carefully, ceremoniously, as if he were unveiling a priceless work of art, he folded back the blanket. She blushed as his gaze left her face to wander over her pert pink-tipped breasts, but when he shaped her breasts in his hands and claimed each nipple with a moist lingering kiss, she sighed his name and held him closer to her.

Thad grinned at her abandonment. Then, with a suddenness that took her breath away, he sobered and said, "Marry me, Laura."

Disconcerted, Laura stammered, "Y-you're just full of surprises this morning, but if that was supposed to be a joke, it wasn't very funny."

"But I'm serious," Thad insisted. "As a matter of fact, I've never been *more* serious."

Staggered and oddly disoriented, Laura merely stared at him.

"If you want me to ask you properly I will," said Thad.

Laura's eyes were round with astonishment as he vaulted out of bed and dropped to one knee. Holding one of her hands in both of his, he said, "Laura Powell, will you do me the honor of becoming my wife?"

The color drained from Laura's face. This was the moment she'd longed for. It was the moment she'd dreaded. She wanted to laugh with the joy of it. She wanted to weep with regret because in all good conscience there was no way she could accept Thad's proposal of marriage.

"Aren't you going to answer me?" Thad prodded, but she only turned her face away and drew the blanket up to her chin. "I'll admit, since I'm buck-naked, my proposal is less than dignified," he went on hesitantly. "Probably I should have waited for a more opportune moment, but I love you, Laura, more than I can say, and I do want you to marry me."

"There's nothing wrong with your timing," she said huskily. "You know I love you, Thad, and I'm happy being with you. Why can't we just go on as we are?"

"Because an occasional night or weekend together isn't enough, Laura. Not for me. I want more of you than that."

Laura blinked, forcing back the tears that had welled up in her eyes.

"You've paid me a very great compliment, and I wish—"

"Think about it," Thad cut in brusquely, sensing that she was searching for a tactful way to refuse him. "I'll ask you again some other time—when I'm dressed."

Before she could say anything else, he got to his feet and began collecting his clothing, which was strewn about the room. "Christ, but it's cold in here!" he complained, and on that disgruntled note he strode toward the bathroom.

By the time he had showered and dressed, Thad seemed to have recovered his aplomb. Apparently he had forgiven her for her less than diplomatic response to his proposal. The truth was, he seemed to have forgotten the incident.

He treated Laura so casually, she began to wonder if he had been joking after all. But just when she had convinced herself she had only imagined his sincerity, she caught him studying her with a brooding intensity that told her he had been sincere.

Despite the awkward beginning to the morning and the

new constraint between them, Sunday turned out to be a pleasant day, perhaps because both Laura and Thad exerted themselves to make it so.

After breakfast Thad finished the last of the repairs to the cabin while Laura tidied the kitchen and packed her suitcase, and in the afternoon they went for a walk in the woods.

The day was cloudy, and the raw northwesterly wind carried a threat of rain, but they tramped for miles through golden showers of birch leaves and scarcely noticed the leaden sky. It was nearly dark before they returned to the cabin. They arrived at the front door just as a flock of Canada geese circled overhead in a lazy *V* and finally landed on the lake for the night.

Thad went inside to collect their luggage, and while he loaded it in the pickup and locked the cabin, Laura paused for one last look at the lake.

In the blue-gray light of the gathering dusk the water shimmered like pewter, and the pale yellow-green of the tamaracks on the far shore seemed alien and surreal against the lowering sky.

Thad opened the passenger door, and as Laura climbed into the pickup she glanced toward the cabin. She kept her eyes fixed on it, watching the last faint wisp of smoke that curled from the chimney, while Thad walked round to the driver's side and got behind the wheel.

Neither of them spoke as Thad started the engine and drove away. They hadn't talked much all afternoon, but Thad must have been as sorry as she was to see their time together end because when they reached the highway, instead of turning south, he began driving north.

They drove into Grand Marais and stopped for dinner at the Harbor Inn before they headed for Ely, which caused them to arrive very late at Laura's house.

At some time during dinner, their conversation had dwindled to nothing. Thad hadn't spoken half a dozen words to her on the long drive home, and he parked the truck near the kitchen door and helped her out of the cab, still without speaking.

He seemed remote, detached, cool; as if the intimacies they'd shared had never been. He carried her suitcase inside, and as she followed him into the kitchen, Laura wondered how she could tell Thad, how she could adequately express how much she loved him and how wonderful the weekend had been.

She couldn't bear to say good night to him and watch him walk out the door, yet she knew she must. Ely was only a village; they had to be discreet.

Groucho was nowhere in sight, but according to the note Trina had left on the refrigerator door, he was in fine fettle.

"He's miffed because you left him alone for the weekend, so he's spending the night at my house," Trina's note explained. "Boy is he spoiled!" In a postscript Trina reported that she'd had no problems with the shop. "*It was fun,*" she'd written, and had underlined this part of the message.

"So everything's in order," Thad commented tonelessly when Laura had read the note to him.

"Yes," she replied.

Except that she was despairing because he had turned to leave without kissing her good-bye. He hadn't even left, and already she was sick with wanting him. Her chin quivered and she bit her lip and swallowed hard, trying to dislodge the lump of tears that had gathered in her throat.

"Will I see you tomorrow?" she asked.

"Sure you will." Thad turned to look at her, but his face was as expressionless as his voice. "Tomorrow's going to be another first for us."

Her heart leaped into her throat. "In what respect?"

"Tomorrow we're going *out* for dinner," he declared firmly.

148

Laura nodded relievedly. She knew better than to argue with Thad when he used that stubborn tone, and while discretion was called for, since they were already the subject of gossip, there was no need for secrecy.

"All right, Thad," she replied. "Whatever you say."

Apparently her answer amused Thad. He grinned and winked at her.

"Hang on to that thought, my lovely Laura," he drawled, "and we'll do just fine."

CHAPTER FOURTEEN

The following night Thad took Laura to a supper club on the outskirts of Ely. He knew quite a few of the other patrons, and he introduced her to several acquaintances. They were obviously curious about her, but not extraordinarily so. In fact, Thad's friends seemed congenial and nonjudgmental, but Laura was ill at ease, and the evening was not a success.

As soon as they'd finished dinner, she pleaded weariness, and Thad drove her home. She didn't invite him into the house, and he didn't ask to come inside with her. He simply walked her to the door, gave her a chaste kiss on the forehead, and turned to leave.

"Wait a minute!" she protested.

Dissatisfied with his restrained good night, she threw her arms around his neck and kissed him soundly on the mouth. She put all the heat and passion she possessed into her kiss, but Thad did not respond. When she teased the corners of his mouth with the tip of her tongue, his mouth softened for a moment, but aside from that his lips remained cool and unresponsive against her own. At last Laura gave up.

"This is absurd," she muttered.

"I agree," said Thad.

Chagrined, she stepped away from him. "Can't two consenting adult even kiss in this town?"

"I thought you liked Ely," said Thad.

"I do like Ely! I absolutely adore the town. It's just that I'm so frustrated—"

"You're not alone," said Thad.

Near tears with disappointment she asked, "Then why won't you kiss me?"

"Why won't you marry me?" Thad shot back.

Laura stared at him incredulously. "Are you saying you won't kiss me ever again unless I accept your proposal?"

"Not the way I'd like to kiss you," said Thad. "Not the way you'd like me to kiss you. And *not* in Ely."

"But that's . . . it's emotional blackmail!"

"Yep."

At Thad's laconic agreement, Laura's disappointment gave way to outrage, and she glared at him accusingly.

"How can you be so mean? So petty?" she demanded. "It's horrid to withhold love in order to punish someone."

"That's true, but you leave me no choice, Laura. It's the only leverage I have, and I intend to use it."

"I'll be damned if I'll take the blame for this, Thad Bristol! You're the one who's the villain of this little melodrama."

"I'm sorry you feel that way, Laura." Although he'd expressed sympathy for her feelings, she could have sworn Thad was trying not to laugh. "Maybe it would help you keep things in perspective if you look at it this way," he went on calmly. "I'm not actually withholding my love. I'll tell you I love you. I'll put it in a letter. I'll take out an ad in the paper if you want me to—"

"But you won't kiss me."

"No," said Thad. "So you see, Laura, it's really sex I'm withholding."

"Of all the self-serving—"

Unable to come up with a word odious enough to describe his sophistry, Laura decided to try a different tactic.

"Thad, darling," she purred, smiling at him sweetly. "How long do you think you'll be able to hold out on me?"

151

"As long as it takes, Laura my love," he declared.

From Laura's point of view, the battle lines were drawn. Immune to her appeal, Thad said good night and left. He blew her a kiss before he drove away, and that cool, platonic farewell set the tone of their meetings for the next few days.

When they were together Thad was friendly, considerate, and unfailingly cheerful, while she acted the charmer, the seductress, the wanton. By the end of the week, when nothing she had done had had any visible effect on Thad, Laura was desperate. She had become an ill-tempered grouch even before Friday's mail brought an invitation from Thad's mother. The engraved lettering on the heavy cream-colored vellum read:

> *Mr. and Mrs. Ira W. Bristol request the pleasure of your company on the occasion of their thirty-fifth wedding anniversary.*

The hours of the open house, the date, which was a week from the coming Sunday, the senior Bristols' address, and the obligatory R.S.V.P. completed the invitation. And across the bottom, in a bold imperious hand, Dorothy had scrawled, *I expect you to stay for dinner.*

When Laura finished reading the invitation, she placed it on the counter so that Trina could see the note Dorothy had written.

"You're going to accept, aren't you?" Trina asked hopefully.

"Do I have a choice?" Laura replied, absently tapping one corner of the card against the countertop. "Thad told me his mother wanted to make amends for some of the things she said about me and for threatening me, but this is more of a command than an olive branch."

"I know it looks that way," Trina conceded. "But believe me, Laura, that's as close as Aunt Dorothy ever comes to apologizing to *anyone.*"

"Will it be a big party?" Laura inquired.

"Early in the afternoon it will be. To quote my aunt, 'Everybody who's anybody will be there.' But she's asked only family and close friends to stay on for dinner."

"I suppose I should be honored then," Laura said with some asperity.

"Yes, you should," Trina returned evenly. When Laura cast a perplexed look at her, she hastily explained, "Oh, not because of Aunt Dorothy's peace offering. She's the nearest thing I have to a mother, and I love her dearly, but I don't have any delusions about her. I know that she's a bit of a snob, and she can be pretentious as all get-out. But you always know exactly where you stand with her, and once she's in your corner, she can be incredibly loyal. She's also married to Uncle Ira, and he's got to be the kindest, sweetest man who ever lived. I swear his middle initial stands for *Wonderful* because that's the word that best describes him."

Laura nodded thoughtfully. After her first encounter with Thad's mother, she had wondered how a woman as hostile as Dorothy could have raised two people as charming and well-adjusted as Thad and Trina, and Trina's capsule description of Ira Bristol supplied the answer to that question.

Furthermore it was logical that Dorothy would be an entirely different person where her family was concerned. Both Trina and Thad had acknowledged that she was a meddler. They both knew how combative she could be with outsiders, but they were also genuinely fond of her.

Everyone has his faults, Laura reasoned philosophically. It just so happened that she'd seen Dorothy at her worst. But Dorothy had been almost pleasant when she'd come to the gallery for tea, so maybe she should give

Thad's mother a chance to redeem herself. Maybe she owed it to Thad. *Maybe,* she thought, *I owe it to myself.*

And besides, she really wanted to meet Thad's father.

Aloud Laura said, "I think I'll accept Mrs. Bristol's invitation."

"Really, Laura?" Trina exclaimed delightedly. "That's just super!"

The next week and a half passed quickly. Now that the summer was over, the canoe-outfitting segment of Thad's business had closed till the following June, which meant that he had more free time. Laura saw him every evening, and while her resistance to him seemed to crumble a bit more with each meeting, she was determined to win their battle of wills.

Once again she resolved to let events take their course, to enjoy whatever happened between them, and she found herself having a surprisingly good time.

They had dinner at the Embers and at Cranberry's café and at Paul Bunyan's Sawmill Tavern in Hibbing. They went to pep rallies and football games at the high school, and when the local team won, they celebrated the victory at the postgame dance with what seemed like the entire population of Ely.

To Laura, who was discovering how much fun she'd been missing in the last fifteen years, it seemed that every day brought some new cause for celebration.

One evening she and Thad went out with Trina and Phil, and that night was the most entertaining Laura had ever known. Trina was positively blooming, Phil was his easygoing self, and Thad was even more high-spirited than usual.

They started the evening at Dee's Bar and progressed from polkaing and discoing to slow dancing at Vertin's Pub. By midnight Laura's sides ached from laughing at Thad's antics, but less than an hour later Trina and Phil had gone home and Thad's mood had swung from the ridiculous to the romantic.

At regular intervals throughout the last part of the evening, Thad told Laura how much he enjoyed dancing with her. At first she took him seriously and she was flattered by the compliment. Then she realized that what he liked best about dancing with her was that it gave him an excuse to hold her in his arms. At least, from the way he took advantage of the opportunity, that was how it appeared to her. And that was even more flattering. And tantalizing. And exciting. And frightening.

She had vowed that she would beat Thad at his game of holdout, but she wanted him so badly, she was tempted to give in.

It was getting harder and harder to say good night to Thad at the front door, and that night was the most difficult of all. Somehow Laura found the strength to watch him leave without offering to pay any forfeit he demanded if only he would kiss her properly, but after he'd left, she wondered how she'd managed to do it, and she knew that her resolve was weakening.

If she insisted upon keeping her eyes fixed on some distant, dazzling star, how could she be certain that her feet were planted firmly on the ground?

CHAPTER FIFTEEN

On the day of the anniversary party Laura devoted more care than she usually did to her appearance. Trina might be positive that the invitation to the party was Dorothy's way of making amends, but Laura was not convinced. She was afraid that Dorothy might have a few more tricks up her sleeve, and she intended to be prepared for the worst.

The afternoon was clear, but it was cold and blustery, and she dressed accordingly in a long-sleeved frock of heather-blue matte jersey. The dress was a few years old, but its classic simplicity hadn't gone out of style. It had a deep, square neckline that displayed the enticingly creamy skin of her throat and bosom, but she'd always felt comfortable in it, and that it made her eyes look bluer than they were added to her confidence.

To soften her appearance she pinned her hair loosely on top of her head, allowing a few errant tendrils to curl around her temples and the nape of her neck. Her only other adornment was a white jade pendant that nestled in the hollow between her breasts.

When Thad arrived to pick her up, the glow of admiration she saw in his eyes told her that her efforts to look her best had not been wasted, and by the time they turned into the driveway of his parents' house she was eager to join the party.

The number of cars parked along the horseshoe drive

dampened her spirits a little, and when the house came into view, she was taken aback.

She had known Thad's parents were socially prominent —Dorothy had accused her of being a fortune hunter— but she hadn't realized how very wealthy the Bristols must be until she saw the resplendent white Georgian mansion they called home.

Even so, she walked unhesitatingly at Thad's side as he ushered her across the veranda and through the wide front doors. Once they were inside, however, an elderly, gray-uniformed maid hurried forward to greet them, and Laura dropped behind Thad. Even he seemed startled when the maid bobbed a curtsy.

"For Pete's sake, Mattie!" he exclaimed. "Why are you wearing a uniform? And what's with the bowing and scraping routine? Are you auditioning for a play?"

"Aw, go on with you," Mattie replied fondly. "I'm just doin' as I've been ordered."

Thad scowled. "I suppose this was my mother's idea."

"It was," Mattie agreed. "Dorothy's really puttin' on the dog today."

"Well, you've no cause to put it on with me," Thad returned grimly. "My God, Mattie! With your arthritis you shouldn't be on your feet all afternoon."

"That was my reaction too," Mattie said, snorting derisively, "but when I said as much to your mother, she informed me that it was her nickel, and if she ordered me to stand on my *head* for half the day, I could either do it or be handed my walking papers."

"I'll speak to her—" Thad began.

"Don't you bother," Mattie interrupted. "Your father already did that little thing. He told your mother if she fired me, he'd only hire me back at double my salary, so I guess you could say I'm doin' this to keep Dorothy from feeling she's lost face. I've been with her for more years than I can count, but I wouldn't want her to feel she has no authority over me. Now," Mattie smiled warmly at Thad as she took their wraps, "is this your young lady that I've heard so much about?"

Thad grinned, but he didn't argue over Mattie's calling Laura "his" young lady.

"That's right, Mattie," he said. "This is Laura Powell."

"I'm pleased to meet you, miss," said Mattie. "I've heard a lot of nice things about you."

Was Mattie being facetious? No, Laura decided. She appeared to be sincere and, warmed by her friendliness, Laura replied softly, "Thank you, Mattie. I'm happy to meet you too."

It was just as well that Mattie expected no further comment from her, because Laura was speechless with surprise when she saw that Thad was wearing a dinner jacket beneath his car coat. He was stunningly attractive in formal attire, and she thought that he fitted quite naturally into the opulence of his parents' home. She might feel swallowed up by the grand dimensions of the foyer, but in some inexplicable way, these same surroundings made Thad seem even larger than he was.

He exchanged a few more pleasantries with Mattie before he excused himself and tugged at Laura's hand, urging her to follow after him as he led her past the broad, branching staircase with its gracefully curving balustrade, and through the elegant drawing room.

There were a few older couples in that part of the house. Thad smiled and waved at several of them, but he didn't stop to speak to them or to introduce Laura. Instead, he continued through the drawing room to another hallway, and along it toward the sounds of revelry coming from the back of the house.

The moment they entered the game room, a flamboyantly pretty redhead in a hot-pink jumpsuit left the circle of people she'd been chatting with and rushed toward Thad.

Suddenly Laura felt drab and underdressed. Comfortable as it was, she regretted she'd elected to wear her old blue matte jersey.

The blow to her self-confidence was bad enough, but when the young woman reached them, she jostled Laura aside, flung her arms around Thad's neck, and kissed him on the lips. Thoroughly. Lingeringly.

Initially Thad seemed stiff and uncooperative, but that phase passed all too quickly. Even when the woman's hold on him relaxed, he didn't pull away from her. The kiss went on and on, and when he finally raised his head, his mouth was smeared with her lipstick.

As she dabbed at his mouth with the handkerchief she'd removed from his breast pocket, the redhead flashed him a thousand-watt smile that showed deep dimples in her cheeks and an abundance of small pearly teeth.

"You naughty teddy bear," she cooed, hugging his arm to her breasts. "You haven't called me for such a long time! I should be terribly angry with you, but it's lovely to see you all the same."

Laura saw that Thad was grinning foolishly, but she couldn't really make out his response. By then the young woman was towing him away and Laura chose not to tag along.

Thad seemed to have forgotten about her anyway, and she wondered, rather sourly, whether he appreciated the redhead's calling him teddy bear half as much as he'd enjoyed her kiss. He might not have instigated the embrace, but once he'd got involved, he'd been an extremely willing and inventive participant. He'd been so willing, so inventive, Laura couldn't even permit herself the luxury of snatching the younger woman's auburn hair out by its brown roots.

She hoped she appeared detached as she stood quietly to one side, surveying the throng of party guests as if finding a familiar face was a matter of life-and-death importance.

For the next few minutes Laura studiously avoided looking at Thad. She caught a glimpse of Mrs. Carruthers's carefully marcelled blue-white hair, and she recognized several people who were regular customers at the Gallery of Gifts. She registered that most of the guests in the game room were a generation younger than Thad's parents, but she didn't see Trina and Phil among them. Neither did she see Dorothy, so at least she had something to be grateful for.

Was the redhead the ace Thad's mother had up her sleeve? Laura wondered. Had the two women planned the whole amorous greeting to make Laura feel like an interloper?

Whether they'd planned it or not, that was exactly how she did feel, and the feeling intensified when at last she risked another glance at Thad and saw that he still hadn't disengaged his arm from the young woman's clasp.

From the moment she had seen Thad on the patio at the Gundersons' house, Laura had been aware of his attractiveness to women. She had seen other women flirt with him, and it hadn't bothered her at all, but the way the redhead was clinging to Thad's arm—fluttering her lashes and smiling at him—made Laura feel sick with jealousy. She was about to succumb to the temptation to intervene when a tall teenage girl tapped her on the shoulder.

"I see good old reliable Stacey is doing her thing," the newcomer observed.

"So it would seem," Laura agreed. "And what's even more outrageous is that Thad is enjoying it."

"That's true," said the girl. "But you can't really blame him for being flattered by Stacey's attention."

"Oh, can't I?"

"Of course, you can't. Not as long as it stops there. And

160

most definitely it will," the girl went on knowledgeably. "All Stacey's ever gotten from Thad—and all she'll probably ever get from him—was a quick fling. As a general rule, men prefer women who are hard to get for everyone but themselves—and no one in his right mind would ever accuse Stacey of being hard to get."

"No," Laura fumed. "Not any more than they'd accuse her of being subtle."

"You can say that again!"

The teenager laughed, and Laura turned to look at her more closely. After a single glance at the girl's dark hair and tawny eyes, she knew that this was Thad's younger sister.

"You must be Angela," she said.

The girl nodded. "That's right. And you're Laura. I've been anxious to meet you."

"Anxious? That's an odd way of putting it."

"Maybe it's odd, but it's true," Angela insisted. "You see, I've heard a lot of conflicting reports about you."

"Such as?"

"Well, my mother—"

"I know what your mother says about me," Laura interrupted. "She thinks I'm a cradle-robbing gold digger."

"Not anymore," said Angela. "Thad told us he's having a rough time persuading you to marry him, and that threw Mom for a loop. Now she doesn't know what to think. And Trina admires you immensely. She's the world's most dedicated hausfrau, yet she admits she envies your independence. She also thinks you're very lonely. . . ."

"Angela, I'm not sure I want to hear all this."

"Why not? Is Trina right?"

Perhaps because Angela was so open, Laura was more amused than offended by the girl's prying. "Probably," she replied, "but loneliness is the price one pays for independence, and I enjoy being independent. I'm not any

161

lonelier than most people, and I'm not morbid about it either."

"That's what Thad says. He also says he hasn't had a moment's peace since he met you, and that if you don't marry him soon, he'd going to go out of his mind—"

"Hold it!" Laura broke in. "I'd rather not hear what Thad says about me."

The teenager was not convinced, and it showed.

"Oh, all right," said Laura. "I'm dying to hear it, but I haven't sunk to the level of spying on him. At least not yet."

Angela smiled indulgently. "I wasn't going to betray any confidences, Laura."

"I never thought you were—not intentionally at any rate. It's just that your brother is entitled to a certain amount of privacy, and I'd rather not discuss this anymore."

"Okay. That's cool. But would you answer one question for me?"

"If I can."

In a conspiratorial whisper Angela asked, "Are you going to marry my brother?"

Laura shook her head. "I wish I could, Angela, but I can't."

"Why not? I can tell from the way you look at Thad that you're in love with him."

"I do love Thad, but marriage is out of the question. It wouldn't be fair to either of us."

Angela's expression sharpened. "Do you think you're being fair to Thad by not marrying him? He's crazy about you, you know."

For a full minute, too startled to reply, Laura stared at the teenager. Then, as if to refute Angela's argument, she glanced at Thad and Stacey, but now she saw them from a new perspective.

Stacey was still clinging like a limpet to Thad's arm. She

was still chattering and flirting with him, and Thad was still smiling at her, but now Laura saw that he was merely being polite to the younger woman. She saw the boredom behind his smile. She saw that he was shuffling his feet as if he were poised to make his escape at the first opportunity, and when Thad's gaze locked with hers, she read the appeal in his eyes.

He raised his eyes toward the ceiling and closed them briefly, pantomiming that he was finding it difficult to stay awake. Behind Stacey's back he beckoned to Laura to join them, sending increasingly frantic signals that Laura could not misinterpret.

Everything about Thad's stance communicated how much he wanted to make his getaway, and Laura knew that her assistance would be more than welcome. In fact, he managed to look so unhappy that Laura very nearly went to his rescue. But an instant later she recalled the way Thad had returned Stacey's kiss, and she decided not to help him after all.

Bored as he was by Stacey's small talk, a few minutes of tedium was the least he deserved for having enjoyed her kiss. And, Laura reminded herself, he definitely had enjoyed it. She had not imagined that.

After a last languishing glance at Thad, Laura tore her gaze away from his. Turning to Angela, she said, "That's three questions, and I agreed to answer only one."

"I didn't really expect an answer," Angela replied briskly. "It's just that lately Thad's been as miserable and cross as an old bear, and I wanted to give you something to think about."

"You've certainly done that," said Laura.

And she had. With her questions Angela had made Laura realize how shabbily she'd been treating Thad. Although she might not be able to define love, one thing it most assuredly was *not* was competition. Yet for the past two weeks she had reduced their love to a childish, selfish game that neither of them could win.

Angela had also demonstrated another way she resembled Thad.

"It's uncanny," Laura murmured. "In some ways you're very like your brother."

Angela frowned perturbedly. "Is that a tactful way of saying I'm too persistent?"

"Actually *obstinate* was the word I had in mind."

The teenager's frown was replaced by a sunny smile. "I guess I'll have to plead guilty to that charge. Jeff is always telling me how stubborn I am."

"Is Jeff your boyfriend?"

Angela nodded shyly. "He's not here just now, but he's coming for dinner later. I'll introduce you."

"I'd like that," Laura said softly. At the mention of Jeff's name Angela's sophistication had disappeared, and she seemed touchingly young. "I think I may have seen Jeff the other day at Thad's store," Laura added.

"You could have," Angela said eagerly. "He's been working there part-time."

"Is he tall and sandy-haired? Built like a linebacker?"

"That's Jeff! He's a tackle on the high school team. You should have seen the pass he intercepted Friday night."

"Thad and I went to the game, so I did see it, Angela."

"Did you?" Angela exclaimed. "Wasn't Jeff beautiful!"

"He was very impressive," Laura agreed enthusiastically. "How long have you been dating?"

"We've been going steady for almost two months now," Angela said with a dreamy sigh.

Smiling at the teenager, Laura said, "Tell me all about him."

Angela didn't need a second invitation. From the way her eyes lighted up, it was easy to see that Jeff Quinlan was her favorite topic of conversation. She happily obliged Laura, but she did more than that. She showed Laura around the house and introduced her to Connie and Lila and to quite a few of the other guests, and when Jeff arrived, she introduced Laura to him as well.

Just before dinner was announced, Thad freed himself from Stacey's clutches, but it was only temporary; when he tried to approach Laura, Angela promptly hustled Laura off to her room to meet her Siamese cat, Mousie Tongue, whose name, Angela proudly pointed out, was a play on Mao Tse-tung.

If Angela hadn't been so guilelessly friendly, Laura might have thought the teenager was another of Dorothy Bristol's secret weapons.

CHAPTER SIXTEEN

There were two tables at dinner. Thad sat next to Stacey at his mother's table, while Laura sat at Ira's. Angela was not available to explain away Thad's attentiveness to Stacey, and Laura found herself growing jealous all over again.

She thought she wouldn't enjoy the meal, but she did. She was completely charmed by tall, silver-haired Ira, and her dinner partner was a pleasant man in his late forties named Richard Gunther. Since he was an art teacher at Vermilion Community College, he and Laura had a lot in common.

They still hadn't run out of things to talk about when dinner was over, and after the way Thad had virtually abandoned her, Richard's display of interest was a balm for her wounded ego.

When dessert had been served and the appropriate toasts had been made, Richard held Laura's chair, offered her his arm, and escorted her away from the table like the perfect gentleman he was.

Earlier in the day, after her conversation with Angela, Laura had regretted the deceptions she'd been practicing with Thad, but at some time during the course of the meal, jealousy had supplanted remorse. She intended to spend the rest of the evening with Richard, but Thad had other plans.

Richard and she had joined the general exodus of guests

from the dining room and were walking along the hall toward the library, where coffee and liqueurs were to be served, when Thad broke away from Stacey and caught up with them. He muttered what was apparently an apology to Richard, and without further preliminaries, grabbed Laura's arm and shanghaied her, marching her into the drawing room and through the French doors to the terrace.

"W-what in the world do you think you're doing?" Laura sputtered angrily, stammering a bit because her teeth had started chattering the second they'd stepped out of the house into the icy night air.

"Do you realize we haven't had a moment alone all day?" Thad demanded.

Laura was fully aware of that, but she wasn't about to admit it to Thad. Uncertain how to reply, she complained, "It's cold out here."

"You can have my jacket."

When Thad took off his dinner jacket and draped it around her shoulders, she wrapped it snugly about herself and huddled into it, grateful for its warmth, but the chivalrous gesture was ruined by the way Thad was glaring at her.

"You didn't answer my question," he snapped.

"I know I didn't."

"Why?"

She glared back at him. "You implied you wanted to be with me, but you have a funny way of showing it."

"What's that supposed to mean?"

"Just that you appeared to be enjoying Stacey's company."

"Enjoying it! Couldn't you see that I was doing my damnedest to get away from her?"

"What I saw, teddy bear, was that you were smiling at Stacey and kissing her. At the dinner table it looked as if you were whispering sweet nothings in her ear, but maybe you were simply saying adieu."

Thad's expression brightened. "You're jealous!" he exclaimed softly.

"Me? Jealous? Don't be silly."

Infuriated by Thad's smug accusation, Laura presented her back to him and started walking toward the house, but she had put a pitifully small distance between them when the uneven surface of the flagstones caused her to stumble. She twisted her ankle and would have fallen if Thad hadn't been close enough to catch her.

As he scooped Laura up in his arms and carried her toward a bench, he said gruffly, "You're jealous, Laura. Admit it."

"I'll admit nothing of the kind," she countered stiffly. "And I'd appreciate it if you'd put me down."

It required all of her concentration not to go limp and yielding in his arms, and she knew that if he didn't put her down she would be lost. She would confess to anything and deny him nothing. But, not unpredictably, Thad paid no attention to her demand. He only grinned sardonically and kept on walking.

Out of desperation Laura tried a rational approach. "I'm capable of walking," she said. "Please put me down."

"I want to check your ankle first. You might have sprained it."

"I didn't. It doesn't hurt at all, and I only twisted it a little."

"We'll soon see about that."

Carefully Thad deposited her on the wrought-iron bench. Dropping to his knees in front of her, he began manipulating her right foot. His hands were strong and sure, and although his attitude was impersonal, her skin tingled wherever he touched her. When his fingers closed around her ankle, Laura shivered and drew the lapels of his dinner jacket higher around her throat.

Thad looked at her obliquely. "Are you still cold?" he asked.

"No. I'm quite warm, thank you."

The moment the words were out, it occurred to Laura that she should have lied. She glanced hastily at Thad and relaxed a bit when she saw that his face was impassive. He didn't appear to have guessed that her shiver had been elicited by the sheer pleasure of his touch.

As he bent his head over her ankle, he asked, "What did you think of my kid sister?"

"Angela's hardly a kid," Laura replied. "I enjoyed meeting her. She's very bright, very personable, and very much in love with Jeff Quinlan."

"Puppy love," Thad qualified impatiently.

Exasperated by his lack of sympathy, Laura asked, "How can you *say* that?"

"Because it's true," Thad said curtly. "Angela's only sixteen."

"Granted, she's young, but even so, you can't dismiss her feelings so lightly. She cares for Jeff deeply, and age doesn't matter—"

Belatedly Laura realized the import of what she was saying. She choked back the rest of her sentiments, and Thad grinned triumphantly.

"Ah-hah!" he laughed. "I knew that eventually you'd see that for yourself."

Laura was nonplussed by his rapid turnabout. "Why, you fraud!" she cried irately. "You were pretending! You— You're—"

"Don't bother saying it. I know how you feel." Thad bent over her ankle again, and there was a moment of silence before he asked, "How did you and Richard hit it off?"

"Very well," Laura replied guardedly, watching Thad's face, gauging his reaction. When she saw none, she added, "I like him."

"That's what I thought." Scowling, Thad slipped her shoe off. "Can you move your toes?" he asked.

Laura responded by wriggling her toes strenuously, demonstrating how well she could move them. She had to struggle to keep a straight face as she inquired, "Is there any reason why I shouldn't like Richard?"

"No."

Thad's expression revealed nothing, but his hold on her ankle had tightened. With his free hand he began probing the area around her instep. When Laura giggled, he frowned at her repressively.

As sternly as if she had committed some major offense, he instructed, "You can stop wiggling your toes now."

"I c-can't help it," she replied shakily. "You're tickling me."

"Sorry." Thad's frown deepened, and his grip on her ankle became very nearly punishing. "You realize, don't you, that Richard is old enough to be your father."

"Correction," Laura contradicted him evenly. "He's old enough to be *your* father, but since he's only forty-seven, he'd have had to be terribly precocious to be mine."

"Mmmph," Thad grumbled. He shoved her shoe onto her foot with unnecessary roughness and announced, "There's absolutely nothing wrong with your ankle."

He'd delivered his diagnosis as if he were angered by it, and Laura could no longer contain her amusement. When her laughter rang out, Thad straightened abruptly and stood with his hands on his hips glowering down at her, but this only made her laugh all the more.

"What's so damn funny?" Thad growled.

By now Laura was laughing too hard to reply. She shook her head and helplessly waved one hand in the air, as if she might pluck the answer to his question out of the darkness, and Thad stared at her as if she had taken leave of her senses.

"Either you have a warped sense of humor, or you're

hysterical," he observed harshly. Pivoting on his heel, he stalked toward the house.

Striving for control, Laura gasped, "I'm s-sorry, Thad. Honestly I am, and I really hate to have to tell you this, but it was the *left* ankle I twisted."

Thad stopped in midstride and swung around to face her. His usually graceful movements were jerky and disjointed, and his voice was raspy with fury as he shouted, "And you let me go through that whole rigmarole with your right ankle! Did making a fool of me give you so much pleasure?"

Laura shrugged her shoulders. "From where I was sitting, it looked as if you managed that without any help from me."

"Why you little—" Thad's hands clenched into fists. "I made an ass of myself, and you enjoyed watching me do it!"

He muttered an oath and started toward her, and when Laura saw how menacing he looked, she sprang to her feet. A twinge of pain in her left ankle caused her to wince, but as she circled to the far side of the bench, she quickly forgot about the pain.

"C-can't you take a joke?" she ventured, but Thad didn't answer and he didn't laugh. He just kept walking toward her. Before her courage entirely deserted her, she stammered, "Now, w-wait a minute, Thad Bristol—"

"I have waited, Laura. Can you deny that I've been patient with you?"

Suddenly dry-mouthed, she shook her head.

"Of course you can't," said Thad. "I've been extremely forbearing, and look what it's gotten me."

He'd spoken slowly, monitoring his words as closely as he monitored her efforts to elude him. He had almost reached the bench now, and Laura held out one arm to fend him off and shifted uncertainly from side to side, wondering whether it would be wiser to make a break for the house or to run in the opposite direction.

Playing for time to decide, she asked, "W-what has it gotten you?"

"Egg on my face, that's what!"

Laura very nearly giggled again when she heard Thad's somber reply, but somehow she contrived not to.

Thad must be joking, she thought. Then she saw that his mouth had thinned to a determined line, and she wondered if he might be serious after all. She studied his face, trying to decipher his expression, and for a time they confronted each other silently.

Thad remained perfectly motionless, and so did she. Then, as she watched, spellbound by him, he leaned toward her, bringing his face close to hers, staring intently at her all the while. He appeared to be completely serious, but Laura heard the levity in his voice as he inquired, "What do you have to say about that?"

"I—uh—" Her voice was wobbly, and she paused to moisten her lips and compose herself before she offered meekly, "To tell you the truth, I'm very fond of eggs."

The way Thad's lips twitched told her that he was suppressing a smile, and she dissolved into laughter.

Seeing his chance, Thad made a lunge for her. He was cat-quick, but in the instant before he'd made his move, his eyes had flashed a fiery warning, and this allowed Laura to elude him.

She ran from the terrace with Thad close behind, and although she was trying only halfheartedly to escape him, he seemed content to follow her lead as she crisscrossed the lawn. Even when she knew that he was holding back, some perverse imp of mischief seemed to spur her on. She kept on running, darting through the shrubbery and dodging around trees until her injured ankle gave way and sent her sprawling onto a pile of leaves.

Thad was at her side instantly, bending over her, holding out his hands to help her to her feet.

"Are you all right?" he asked anxiously.

Laura rolled onto her back and smiled at him. The moon was only a faint silver crescent, but the outdoor lighting on the grounds permitted her to see the concern in his eyes.

She was winded, and her breath came in great, ragged gasps. She had a cramp in her side and occasionally her ankle throbbed with pain, but never had she felt more alive, more exhilarated.

"Never felt better," she answered. She nestled deeper into the pile of leaves and inhaled their rich, earthy odor. "If yellow had a fragrance," she murmured, "it would smell like autumn."

She was unaware she'd given voice to the thought until Thad grinned at the whimsical remark.

She extended her hands to him, but instead of rising when he took them, she pulled him off-balance so that he toppled down beside her. For a moment he remained where he'd landed, then he rolled onto his side. Propping his head with one hand, he looked at her searchingly.

"What's gotten into you, Laura? I thought I'd seen every facet of your personality in the past few weeks, but I've never seen you this way before."

Laura brushed back a lock of hair that had fallen over his forehead. "What way?" she asked.

"I'm not sure." Thad's smile expressed his bemusement. "Playful. Teasing."

She lowered her eyelids slowly, fluttering her lashes and giving him a sexy, sidelong glance.

"Now you're flirting with me!" he exclaimed.

"You're so very right," she admitted with a throaty murmur. "Don't you like it?"

"Oh, I like it! I like it a lot."

"Then I'd suggest you relax and enjoy it while it lasts."

Falling in with her bantering mood, Thad returned lightly, "That's easy for you to say. You're the one with the jacket."

To illustrate how cold it was, Thad exhaled, and his breath turned to vapor in the frosty air.

"I'll share," Laura offered.

Without waiting for his reply, she sat up and removed the coat, then lay back invitingly.

"In that case," said Thad as he slid one arm beneath her and arranged the jacket so that it covered both of them, "anything to please my lady."

The leaves rustled as Laura snuggled closer to Thad, resting her head on his shoulder. In response he wound his other arm around her. He drew her into the sheltering length of his body, and the sharp chill of the fallen leaves on which they were lying gradually subsided.

"Warm enough?" Thad inquired softly.

"Yes, thanks. How about you?"

Thad chuckled. "I've got you to keep me warm."

"So that's what you wanted when you brought me out here!"

"Among other things."

In retaliation for his teasing Laura ran her fingertips lightly down his side, trying to tickle him, but Thad counterattacked. He captured her wrist and pressed her hand to the solid warmth of his chest, and suddenly neither of them was laughing.

"I needed to be alone with you, Laura," Thad said quietly.

"I needed it too," she confessed. "You were right, Thad. I was jealous of Stacey."

"But you aren't anymore."

"No. Not anymore."

"That's good." Thad's chest rose and fell as he sighed deeply, contentedly. "I was jealous, too, you know."

"Of Richard Gunther?"

Thad nodded.

"Great!" Laura cried delightedly. "I hoped you would be."

"Why, you little—"

"You said that before."

"So I did." Thad's hand released hers to travel lazily along her arm and over the slope of her shoulder, finally curving around the nape of her neck. He felt the wildly pounding pulses at the base of her throat and smiled. Then with mock sternness he declared, "This time, young lady, you'll have to pay the penalty."

"Which is?" she whispered.

He hooked his forefinger under her chin and tipped her face toward his, and when she saw the tenderness in his eyes, her heart seemed to somersault into her throat.

"This," Thad murmured. "Only this."

His lips barely brushed the corner of her mouth, but Laura was breathless with anticipation even before he kissed her. He traced the tremulous outline of her lips, moving his own mouth sensuously from side to side, and when her lips parted, silently pleading with him to kiss her properly, his mouth settled over hers hungrily, absorbing the cry of pleasure that escaped her.

Seduced by Thad's sweet assault on her mouth, Laura held him tightly in her arms and gave herself over to sensation. But she no longer heard the rustling of the leaves beneath them or the night wind sighing through the trees. She heard only the thunderous racing of Thad's heart. And she didn't feel the inert hardness of the ground beneath her body. She felt only the demanding hardness of Thad's body, the roughness of his beard, his soft invasion of her mouth, the hot glide of his hands as he caressed her.

They kissed again, and while their lips clung, desirous and urgent, Thad lowered the zipper at the back of her dress and impatiently pushed the cloth aside. As if he were desperate for the feel of her, his hands were seeking and finding, fondling the satiny curve of a shoulder, the supple ripeness of a breast, the tightly budded velvet of a nipple.

Laura felt herself melting beneath the incendiary passion of his touch. She could not get close enough to him. She fumbled at his shirttail and finally tugged it free of the waistband of his slacks. She slipped her arms beneath the fabric and arched her hips to his. His arms wrapped around her. He turned her onto her back so that she was lying beneath him. They were twined together, crushed together in a volatile fusion of desire, but even that was not close enough.

"Laura," he groaned against her lips. "God, how I want you. All I can think about is you. I dream of making love to you. It's driving me crazy—"

"Then love me, Thad!" She moved against him, unconsciously mimicking the rhythms of love, and when his hold on her slackened, she murmured breathlessly, "Please, my darling. I need you."

Despite her entreaty Thad released her. Slowly, reluctantly, but with an air of finality, he put a small distance between them and braced himself on one elbow so that he was half reclining. His breath came in tormented gasps as he fought for control.

"It wouldn't work," he said hoarsely. "I want to make love to you more than I've ever wanted anything, but it just wouldn't work."

"Why wouldn't it?" she cried.

"Because when it was over, we'd be at the same old impasse."

"We don't have to be. I know we'd have to be discreet, but we could be together sometimes, Thad. We could even go away for weekends now and then."

"There'd be gossip," said Thad.

"I don't care."

"Maybe now you don't, but you might care later."

"I wouldn't!" Laura sat up and tucked her legs beneath her. "I'm not ashamed of loving you, Thad, and as long as we're not hurting anyone by loving each other, I don't care what people say. Let them gossip all they want. I won't mind if I can be with you. I'd do anything—"

"Would you marry me?"

There was a long silence while Laura tried to muster enough willpower to decline Thad's proposal. After a while he got to his knees beside her and draped his dinner jacket about her shoulders. She hadn't even noticed she was trembling, but he had, and tears stung the backs of her eyes at this sign of his concern. She had to clear her throat before she answered.

"I don't understand why you insist on marriage—" she began weakly.

"You still don't get it, do you?" Thad broke in. "These last two weeks I've fought to keep my hands off you. I've been holding my feelings in check, trying my damnedest to demonstrate that it's not just sex I want from you, and you've seen it as some kind of game."

"I know I have," Laura admitted. "Something Angela said made me realize how unfair I've been, and I'm sorry for that."

"Are you?" Thad inquired bitterly.

This time Laura did not reply, but he saw the contrition in her face and knew that she was sorry. That she was prepared to risk public censure to be with him gave him hope.

He fingered the white jade cabochon that lay between the gentle swell of her breasts, nervously sliding it along its fine gold chain, as he tried to think of a new way to reason with her.

"We need to talk this thing out," he said at last. "We need to settle it once and for all."

Laura nodded.

"Then let's get out of here."

He got to his feet and began dusting leaves and bits of grass from his clothing, tucking in his shirttail, preparing to return to the house, and Laura followed suit.

She walked sedately by his side, favoring her injured ankle as they crossed the lawn, but Thad's fast-rising confidence put a spring in his step.

They had reached the terrace and were nearing the French doors before either of them realized that another couple had wandered outdoors. The couple were standing close together in the shadow of the house, camouflaged by the darkness. If they hadn't separated, Laura wouldn't have seen them at all, but when the woman moved away from the man, she recognized the pair as as Thad's parents.

"Hello, you two," Thad called. "I see you finally decided to have a private celebration."

"That's right, Son," Ira responded genially. He offered Laura a shy, lopsided grin that closely resembled Thad's. She saw a twinkle in his eyes as he observed, "And *I* see that we aren't the only ones who felt a private celebration was in order."

Chuckling, Thad replied, "Well, Dad, you know what they say about great minds thinking alike."

He chose that moment to remove a bit of dried leaf that was tangled in Laura's hair. He seemed to want his parents to believe that they'd been making love, and Laura's heightened color underscored his comment. She would have been even more self-conscious if it hadn't been apparent that Dorothy was every bit as embarrassed as she.

Seeing this, Thad's father pulled his wife close to his side and teased, "Why are you blushing, dear heart? Thad's seen us kiss before."

"I know he has," Dorothy hissed, "but Miss Powell is a stranger."

"Call her Laura, Mom," Thad instructed calmly. "She

won't be a stranger for long. If I have anything to say about it, she'll soon be one of the family."

Startled by her son's announcement, Dorothy looked at Laura. Her eyes narrowed as she took in the younger woman's flushed, disheveled appearance, but in spite of this, Laura detected conciliation in the rather shaky smile Dorothy gave her. And when Dorothy spoke, it became evident that she no longer questioned Laura's motives.

"Laura," she said warmly, "if what my son says is true, I want you to know that I'd be proud to have you for a daughter-in-law."

"And I'd be delighted," said Ira.

"Then it's unanimous," said Thad. "And since it is, we'll leave the two of you alone." Saluting his mother and father, he added rakishly, "As you were."

He had hurried Laura into the drawing room before she found her voice.

"Unanimous?" she said dazedly. "How can it be unanimous when my vote wasn't even considered? You deliberately gave your parents the impression that we're contemplating marriage, and you know very well that I can't marry you. Why did you tell them that I'm going to be one of the family?"

"Why not tell them, Laura?" Thad drawled. "With a little bit of lobbying on my part I think you'll change your mind."

When Laura only stared up at him, too stunned to challenge his statement, he hauled her into his arms. He planted a kiss on her forehead and another on the tip of her nose before he guided her away from the party.

179

CHAPTER SEVENTEEN

A forlorn and hungry-looking Groucho was keeping vigil by his food dish. He let out a distinctly plaintive yowl when T .d turned on the light, but after one look at Thad's ferocious scowl, the cat stopped in midyowl and made a beeline for the bedroom.

The drive to Laura's house had been marked by Thad's insistence upon marriage and Laura's pleas for time, and now, as they stood in the kitchen, Thad's face was frighteningly grim. His mouth was set in an implacable line, and Laura would have run after the cat if Thad hadn't positioned himself to block her retreat.

"No," he muttered angrily. As if she had argued the point, he repeated, "No, dammit! We sure as hell can't go on like this, and you've had all the time you need to think it over. I'm not leaving here until you've told me you'll marry me."

"Then you'll have a long wait," Laura cried defiantly, "because I can't marry you."

She saw the spasm of pain that crossed Thad's features and in the next instant he had caught her upper arms in a punishing grip and dragged her close to him. He glared at her as if he wanted to hurt her as she had wounded him and, seeking to propitiate his fury, Laura said gently, "I'm sorry, Thad. I wish I could give you the answer you want, but I can't marry you."

Thad's grip on her hardened, and she winced.

"Please, Thad, you're hurting me!" she cried. Her voice broke on the words, and her eyes were dark with indecision. Thad shook his head as if to clear it. His grip on her arms loosened a bit, but he didn't release her.

"Tell me why," he snapped. "Give me an explanation."

"You're younger than me—"

"Only chronologically," Thad countered harshly. "Not in experience. Not in any way that matters. And we've already established that age isn't important."

"Even so, I'm thirty-three. That's a long time to be single. Maybe I'm too set in my ways to change. Maybe I don't *want* to change."

"Who the hell is asking you to change? I love you the way you are. I want you the way you are. For the past few weeks we've seen each other almost every day, in all kinds of circumstances, and it seems to me we're pretty damn compatible."

"A few weeks aren't a lifetime," Laura objected doggedly. "I'm used to living alone, and nothing you've said alters the fact that I'm not accustomed to being responsible to or for anyone but myself. And I'm contented that way!"

"Sure you are," Thad replied abrasively. "That's why you have Groucho."

"At least when I go out at night, Groucho doesn't demand to know where I'm going or when I'll be home."

Thad smiled ironically. "Maybe that's your idea of contentment, but it sounds mighty lonely to me."

Laura was stymied and determined not to let Thad see it. She lifted her chin proudly as she told herself that Thad was right, dammit—and even worse, he knew it! She saw the new confidence in his eyes. She felt it in his touch.

"In that case," she ventured, "I don't know what I can say to convince you—"

"Why not try the truth?" Thad suggested silkily. "So far all you've come up with is a replay of a lot of old issues that we've already resolved. The day we met I realized that you were afraid of me. I didn't know why, but when I left here that night I knew that you were a bundle of defenses and that I'd have to break them down to get to you. But now you've trotted all of 'em past me—your looks, your independence and reserve, the way you gloss over your feelings with a lot of plans. You've run the age thing into the ground, and you've tried coolness and remoteness and independence and denial and I don't know what-all, but now it's honesty time, Laura, and I won't settle for anything less than the truth."

Appalled that Thad should have seen through her, Laura averted her face. "It's the commitment—" she began.

"Hogwash!" Thad interrupted abruptly. "You had to come to grips with that problem before you agreed to go away with me that weekend. You know it, and I know it, so who do you think you're kidding?"

Laura shook her head and kept her eyes downcast. She had always known Thad was obstinate, but she had never appreciated how tenacious he could be until this moment. For every argument she advanced, he had ten of his own, and she was fast becoming desperate.

"The truth is, I don't know what to say," she admitted dully. "Except—please, Thad, don't do this to me. Can't you see that it's hopeless?"

"No." Thad shook his head emphatically. "I can't see that at all. Hell, Laura! You've even stopped biting your nails."

Involuntarily Laura glanced at her hands. When she saw the telltale half-moons of her fingernails, the fight drained out of her, and her shoulders drooped defeatedly.

Dear God! she thought. Thad actually did notice everything about her.

Thad slid his arms around her waist, and she leaned against him, too bewildered to maintain her cool facade.

"Look at me, Laura," he instructed quietly.

She was incapable of refusing, and when she looked at him, he smiled into her eyes and said, "Now tell me you don't want to marry me. Tell me you don't love me. If you can do that, I'll believe you. You have my word that I won't bother you anymore."

Laura stared at Thad, stunned by his demand, knowing that he had outmaneuvered her. Even as a last resort, she could not bring herself to lie to Thad. She couldn't tell him she didn't love him, and although she found the idea of marriage terrifying, she wanted to marry him.

"All right," she acknowledged numbly. "You win." She rested her head against his shoulder, too humiliated to confront him as she confessed, "The truth is, I'm afraid of failing."

"Failing?" Thad echoed perplexedly. "I don't understand, Laura."

"Think about it." She stole a glance at him and discovered that she could not drag her eyes away from his. "Oh, I do love you," she murmured brokenly, "and I've never wanted anything as much as I want to marry you. But I don't have a terrific track record with the people I love. Sooner or later I'd let you down, just as I let my father down. Just as I let Brian down. . . ."

"My God, Laura," Thad muttered. "I thought I'd considered everything, but it never even occurred to me you felt that way. How can you possibly believe you were at fault when it was the other way around?"

Laura was weeping openly now, not even trying to hide her tears. "Perhaps it was reciprocal," she sobbed, "but I was at least partially responsible."

"Tell me how," Thad said gruffly. "You didn't invite the assault. You didn't want to become the victim of ugly rumors. And you didn't expect anything of your father or Brian that they shouldn't have given you without your having to ask."

Thad's arms closed around her, folding her in a breathtaking embrace as he went on. "Please, love, don't do this. What happened to you was tragic, but the real tragedy would be to give up—to not even *try*. Say you'll marry me, Laura. Concentrate on us. Think about here and now, about this moment."

"Oh, Thad, I wish I could. You'll never know how much. But I couldn't bear disappointing you the way I disappointed my father. I couldn't bear losing you—not that way."

"Laura," Thad said quietly, "if you say no, we'll both lose. I can't promise you that we'll never disappoint each other, but I can promise I'll never stop loving you."

"How can you be sure?" she cried. "What if you're wrong?"

Thad smiled. Answering her question with one of his own, he inquired, "Have you ever known me to be wrong about us?"

"No," she answered tremulously. "No, I haven't."

"That's right," said Thad. "So why should I be wrong now? I've never felt more certain of anything in my life than I am about the fact that if you marry me, we can't miss! We have too much going for us."

He saw the conflicting emotions on her face, and his voice took on a playful, cajoling note as he said, "We have love—and great sex. Lots of common values—and great sex. All kinds of common interests—and great sex. We have our youth and our health and our work, and you've even brought my mother around—"

Laura attempted a watery smile, and Thad stopped to kiss away her tears.

"Don't forget great sex," she amended, completing the litany.

Thad grinned jubilantly, and Laura laughed outright because suddenly her fears seemed so unnecessary.

184

"Right on!" Thad cheered. "And on top of all that, we've got Bristol's Law on our side!"

His tawny eyes seemed incandescent with love for her, and Laura surrendered unconditionally. She stood on her tiptoes and lifted her mouth to his so that their lips met in a tender exchange of vows.

Now that the shouting was over, Groucho's curiosity was aroused by the protracted silence in the kitchen. He stalked out of the bedroom, and when he saw that Laura and Thad's altercation had ended peacefully and that they had nothing better to do than stand there in each other's arms, he plopped down beside his food dish and let out a particularly pitiful yowl.

"I'd better feed him," Laura murmured.

"Ignore that cat," Thad whispered against her mouth. "He's spoiled enough as it is, and besides, you've got a man who's starving for your love to worry about."

Although Groucho couldn't understand the words Thad had spoken, he sensed Thad's meaning well enough, and when Thad and Laura went into the bedroom, closing the door behind them and leaving him unfed and alone in the kitchen, the cat resorted to his longest, most sorrowful howl.

Inside the bedroom, Thad eyed Laura's chaste single bed dubiously and announced, "On second thought, there is one thing I'll ask you to change."

Laughing, Laura remarked, "My bed might not be king-size, but it's wider than the sofa at the cabin."

"And longer than a bread box," Thad finished dryly. Shrugging good-naturedly, he said, "But who am I to complain? When I'm with you, I'm very much in favor of togetherness, and by noon tomorrow it'll be all over town that I spent the night here. You'll be so compromised, you'll have to marry me."

"Is that a threat?" Laura teased.

"That, my love, is a promise!"

Thad's hands were busily dispensing with her clothing when an earsplitting screech from Groucho split the air and jarred them out of their preoccupation with one another. For a moment Thad only frowned. Then Groucho meowed again and he threw up his hands in mock surrender.

Thad's scowl was dark and forbidding as he started toward the door, but Laura's eyes were sparkling with amusement as she watched him leave the room.

Although she already knew the answer, she asked, "Where are you going?"

"To feed the damn cat!" Thad replied abrasively.

He'd sounded so outraged, Laura barely managed to suppress a giggle as she called, "While you're at it, why don't you tell Groucho about Bristol's Law?"

"I intend to," Thad growled. "Maybe then he'll show a little respect for his new master."

When Thad returned to the bedroom a few minutes later, Laura was standing beside the bed, wearing a lacy, delectably sheer nightgown. She looked so lovely, he could scarcely believe his good fortune, and he paused in the doorway to look at her.

"Was Groucho a respectful audience?" she inquired softly.

"He was purr-fect," Thad quipped. "Especially after I bribed him with a can of tuna."

"That's an awful pun," Laura complained mildly. "But I'm glad to see you're in a better mood."

"I'm easily pacified. All it takes is you and the night and a bed—of sorts—and no untimely interruptions." In a few long strides, Thad had crossed the room. His face was grave as he said, "I don't think I've made a believer out of Groucho, but I hope I've made one out of you."

"Oh, I'm a believer," Laura replied fervently. "I have all the faith in the world in Bristol's Law, and in you, my darling."

Before she'd finished, Thad had stretched out on the bed and was pulling her down with him.

"Stay with me forever, my love. Promise you'll marry me," he pleaded gently.

Thad's hands moved over her, settling her slight weight on top of him. They trembled with eagerness as he molded her close and explored the sweet curves of her body. His eyes were bright with passion, and she shivered with the excitement of his caresses.

Her desire for him consumed her, but her love for him sustained her, and she knew that loving him was the star she must follow and, oh, but it gave off a splendid light!

"Promise me, Laura. Say it!" Thad whispered fiercely.

"Yes, I'll sleep with you," Laura replied without hesitation. "I'll marry you and stay with you forever."

She would risk everything she possessed and build her future on the adoring smile he gave her. Her face was radiant, and her voice was husky with love for him as she cried, "Oh, yes, my darling. I promise."

Candlelight Ecstasy Romances™

Candlelight
Ecstasy Romances™

$1.95 each

At your local bookstore or use this handy coupon for ordering:

DELL BOOKS   B072C
P.O. BOX 1000. PINE BROOK. N.J. 07058-1000

Please send me the books I have checked above. I am enclosing $ _____ [please add 75c per copy to cover postage and handling]. Send check or money order—no cash or C.O.D.'s. Please allow up to 8 weeks for shipment.

Name _____

Address _____

City_____ State Zip _____

CANDLELIGHT **Ecstasy Supreme**

- [ ] 1 **TEMPESTUOUS EDEN**, Heather Graham 18646-3-37
- [ ] 2 **EMERALD FIRE**, Barbara Andrews 12301-1-10
- [ ] 3 **WARMED BY THE FIRE**, Donna Kimel Vitek 19379-6-12
- [ ] 4 **LOVERS AND PRETENDERS**, Prudence Martin 15013-2-12
- [ ] 5 **TENDERNESS AT TWILIGHT**, Megan Lane 18574-2-17
- [ ] 6 **TIME OF A WINTER LOVE**, Jo Calloway 18915-2-15
- [ ] 7 **WHISPER ON THE WIND**, Nell Kincaid 19519-5-13
- [ ] 8 **HANDLE WITH CARE**, Betty Jackson 13424-2-44
- [ ] 9 **NEVER LOOK BACK**, Donna Kimel Vitek 16279-3-43
- [ ] 10 **NIGHT, SEA, AND STARS**, Heather Graham 16384-6-29
- [ ] 11 **POLITICS OF PASSION**, Samantha Hughes 16991-7-16
- [ ] 12 **NO STRINGS ATTACHED**, Prudence Martin 16416-8-54

$2.50 each

At your local bookstore or use this handy coupon for ordering:

DELL BOOKS
P.O. BOX 1000. PINE BROOK. N.J. 07058-1000

B072D